Research in Service to Society

Research in Service to Society
The First Fifty Years of the
Institute for Research in Social Science
at the University of North Carolina

by Guy Benton Johnson
and Guion Griffis Johnson

The University of North Carolina Press   Chapel Hill

© 1980 The University of North Carolina Press
All rights reserved
Manufactured in the United States of America
ISBN 0-8078-1420-2
Library of Congress Catalog Card Number 79-21247

Library of Congress Cataloging in Publication Data

Johnson, Guy Benton, 1901–
    Research in service to society.

    Bibliography: p.
    Includes index.
    1. University of North Carolina at Chapel
Hill. Institute for Research in Social Science—
History. I. Johnson, Guion Griffis,
joint author. II. Title.
H67.C37J64   300'.7'152   79-21247
ISBN 0-8078-1420-2

Contents

Chapter 11

Foreword

When I read this book in manuscript form I enjoyed it very much. That may not much surprise anyone, for I serve as director of the Institute for Research in Social Science whose history is being recorded. Certainly it would not surprise the members of my staff who know my pride in the history of the Institute and know that every grant application I write begins with the statement: "Founded in 1924 by Howard W. Odum, the Institute for Research in Social Science is the oldest university-associated social research organization in the United States."

Yet in some ways it is surprising. The enthusiasm is neither personal nor egocentric. I personally played a very small role in the history of the first fifty years of the "oldest university-associated social research organization in the United States." Nor is it typical of American social research, or corporate business, or other bureaucratic organizations to be very much concerned with institutional history. Today is today, and yesterday's problems have little relevance to the present.

But if such an attitude is prevalent, as I think it is, it is sadly mistaken. The past does provide insight into the present, and no problem that I have faced and thought unique turns out to be without precedent in the history of the Institute. The Institute has been many things and different things at different times; its history in this sense parallels and reflects the history of American social science generally. It has endured attacks upon freedom of inquiry brought by powerful economic interests. It has survived the fiscal problems that reflected the economic depression of the 1930s. In the late 1940s and early 1950s the Institute became deeply involved in contract governmental research, some concealed behind security classification. It has reversed course and opted for pure academic, discipline-defined research. It has been the major beneficiary of the first National Science Foundation science development grant awarded in the social sciences, reflecting the shift in American social science to a new world of computers, data banks, and quantitative analysis. Its breadth of interest and diffusions of purpose in more recent days reflect the "knowledge revolution" in American life.

To many, however, the most interesting passages will be those concerned with the early years of the Institute. That is not, I believe, simple sentiment or nostalgia but reflects the ambiguity of meaning that modern Americans attach to the word "school." To most of us a school is a building, an edifice; only in museums does a "school" connote commonality of purpose. There was a time when a university was expected likewise to have a distinctiveness of outlook and to offer something different from its collegial institutions. That certainly was true of the North Carolina of the Odum days when a particular viewpoint on region was found pervasively and almost alone at one institution. That identity of person (Odum), institution (the Institute for Research in Social Science), and idea (region) will be for many the most intriguing aspect of the story that Guy and Guion Johnson tell. We can appreciate the breadth and variety a more modern form of academic structure provides yet regret the loss of the vitality with which a novel viewpoint was advanced, institutionalized, and propagated.

This and other parts of the Institute story the Johnsons have told with warmth and skill. I am deeply grateful to them for their efforts. Yet in all candor I must state that I could hardly expect anything else from two people who quietly entered their own history in the Institute's first year when Guy B. Johnson became Odum's first nominee for a research assistantship and his wife Guion Johnson became the first woman research assistant. Writing from such intimate personal knowledge, the authors can be expected to give their best. They do. We all profit.

Frank J. Munger

Preface

On June 30, 1924, the Institute for Research in Social Science was organized at the University of North Carolina. It was the first institute of its kind in the nation, and it was destined for a distinguished career. It stands today as an enduring monument to its founder, the late Howard W. Odum, a remarkable figure in twentieth-century social science. Odum left other legacies to the University, notably the Department of Sociology, the School of Social Work, and *Social Forces*, but the Institute was probably his favorite because it embodied his commitment to "cooperative research in the social sciences" and his firm belief in the role of research "in service to society."

In the spring of 1975 Elizabeth Fink, assistant director of the Institute, approached us with the proposal that we do something to commemorate its fiftieth anniversary—something like writing the history of the Institute's first fifty years. Having fully enjoyed the delights of retirement for several years, we were extremely loath to give up our freedom for even a short time. We were inclined to give Miss Fink a firm negative response, but we told her we would like to think about it. That was probably a mistake.

The more we thought about reasons for not getting involved in such a project, the more our consciences pushed us toward involvement. In the first place, we surmised that the Institute had tried and failed to get one or more young historians to undertake the task, and since the golden anniversary year of 1974 had already come and gone we felt that unless we accepted the assignment the occasion might continue to go unmarked. Secondly, we had both come to Chapel Hill in 1924 as research assistants in the newly organized Institute, had been "hooked" on Chapel Hill and the University, and had remained here ever since, so we felt that we were probably as well qualified as anyone to write about the Institute's career. Thirdly, it occurred to us that although we had been married for more than fifty years and had collaborated on just about everything under the sun, we had never written anything together. If we were ever going to remedy this deficiency, it was time to get going. And so in the end we acceded to Elizabeth Fink's request.

At first we thought in terms of a small booklet about the Institute, but we decided that this was an unsatisfactory way of dealing with so deserving a subject. As we explored the source materials—the minutes of the governing board, the annual reports of the directors, the personal papers of Howard W. Odum, Harry W. Chase, Eugene C. Branson, Louis R. Wilson, and others that have been preserved in the Southern Historical Collection in Wilson Library—we were gradually seduced into dealing with the Institute's history in some detail. We hoped at first that we could do the job in a year, but the more we did the more the project expanded, and in the end we devoted more than two years to the researching and writing of this volume. Since we are now several years beyond the Institute's fiftieth birthday, we have not held rigidly to the year 1974 as our cutoff date and in some instances have chosen to bring the narrative more nearly up to date.

This work has been for us not only a venture in the social history of an organization but in some measure a sentimental journey back through the corridors of time, for in recreating from the documentary sources the Institute's beginnings, struggles, and achievements, we have also renewed our personal remembrances of things past. If we have occasionally included ourselves in the cast of characters in this narrative, we have done so with the hope that certain personal experiences and observations will help to illuminate the early history of the Institute. If a certain amount of sentiment has occasionally overshadowed the obligation of objectivity, particularly in the first few chapters, so be it. We have even provided a hero, and that hero is Howard W. Odum. He launched the Institute, preserved it against reactionary social forces and the ravages of the Great Depression, and lived to see it become one of the foremost social science centers in the nation. We knew this man from the day we arrived in Chapel Hill in August 1924 until his death thirty years later, but not until we had explored the archives of the Institute and its founder did we come to appreciate fully the man's genius and versatility and, above all, the extent of his sacrifices.

We acknowledge with gratitude the assistance of several members of the Institute staff. We are especially indebted to Elizabeth Fink. She has provided us with the custody and use of the Institute's archives and other source materials, has tolerated numerous interruptions when we needed information that only she could give us, and has never once uttered the word "deadline." In addition, she has read all of our chapters with an eye for accuracy. Frank Munger, who became director in the Institute's fiftieth year, read the entire manuscript and helped to improve it in several places. Angell Beza, associate director, was particularly helpful on details of the development of the Social Science Statistical Laboratory and computer facilities. Norma Scofield, publications coordinator, has aided us in numerous ways. Members of the Institute secretarial staff have patiently typed and retyped our chapters. We are grateful to Jane Dry, Robin Ratliff, Vonda Hogan, Lou Anne Robinson, and especially to Bonita Samuels.

We are also indebted to the Institute for employing a special assistant, Ellen Curtin, to help with our project for several months. She assembled data from library sources, abstracted the minutes of the governing board, and located relevant materials in the Southern Historical Collection. Later she was again available briefly for assisting in the preparation of the bibliography, verifying footnotes, and other chores. On her own initiative she also read the entire manuscript and offered useful suggestions.

Many other people have helped us. During the first few months of our work we often discussed the old days in the Institute with our longtime colleague, friend, and next-door neighbor, Rupert B. Vance. But three days after our first chapter was completed he suffered a stroke and lived only a few more days. His death on August 25, 1975 was a deep personal loss and it cast a long shadow of gloom over our endeavors. We shall always wish that he had been able to comment on our manuscript with his special brand of wit and wisdom. We were also saddened by the loss of another good friend and pioneer member of the Institute staff, Harriet L. Herring, who died on December 18, 1976. She had been in frail health for the past few years, and it was our great loss that we were not able to have the benefit of her rich store of recollections.

We have benefited from conversations with our longtime friend and colleague, Katharine Jocher, who joined the Institute in the beginning and served for thirty-five years, first as office manager and research assistant, then as assistant director, and finally as associate director. In addition she has read the entire manuscript and made many valuable comments. Paul W. Wager, one of the pioneer group of research assistants in 1924, who lives in retirement in Chapel Hill, read several chapters and made useful suggestions.

All of the living former directors of the Institute have been generous in their cooperation. During the early stages of the work, Gordon W. Blackwell, who has recently retired as president of Furman University, gave us several hours of personal reminiscences at his home in Greenville, South Carolina, and later read the manuscript. Daniel O. Price, chairman of the Department of Sociology at the University of Texas, discussed the Institute with us at Austin in May 1977 and later read several chapters of the manuscript. James W. Prothro, professor of political science at the University of North Carolina at Chapel Hill, helped us on several occasions with his recollections and evaluations of the Institute and also read part of the manuscript. Richard L. Simpson, professor of sociology at the University, who served as acting director of the Institute in 1966–67, has also been helpful and has read portions of the manuscript.

Numerous members of the staff at the University of North Carolina have facilitated our work in various ways. Stuart S. Chapin, Jr., made available some of his personal files on the work of the Center for Urban and Regional Studies and read portions of the manuscript. Alan Keith-Lucas gave us some particulars on researches in institutional child care, Earl Baughman helped with information on certain psychological studies, and Norman L. Johnson loaned us some rare early reports of the Institute of Statistics. Harvey L. Smith, John Reed, John J. Honigmann, John Gulick, James L. Peacock, Julia Crane, Cecil Sheps, George B. Tindall, and John W. Thibaut have all read portions of the manuscript that pertained to their particular areas of research and have made useful suggestions. Philip P. Green, Jr., and Elmer R. Oettinger, of the Institute of Government, have also been helpful. Carolyn A. Wallace, head of the Southern Historical Collection at Wilson Library, facilitated our use of the papers of persons who were associated with the Institute in its early days, and Ophelia Andrew, administrative manager of the Department of Sociology, lent assistance from time to time with her extensive file of University catalogs.

The children of the Institute's founder have given us a number of valuable insights. Mary Frances Schinhan of Chapel Hill gave us some little-known facts about her father's life and read several chapters of the manuscript. Howard T. Odum, professor of environmental engineering at the University of Florida at Gainesville, offered valuable insights into his father's work in a conversation with us during a visit to Chapel Hill in 1976. Eugene P. Odum, Callaway Distinguished Professor of Ecology and director of the Institute of Ecology at the

University of Georgia at Athens, provided an analysis of his father's theory of regionalism that we have used in Chapter 6.

A word on our chapter arrangement for the guidance of our readers is appropriate. Our first four chapters comprise the "historical" section in that they trace the Institute's origin, its tribulations in an early environment that was sometimes hostile, and its structural, administrative, and financial problems over a period of fifty years. The next six chapters describe the researches of the Institute. They follow roughly the chronology of the dominant research interests, beginning with the early folk and race studies, progressing through the concentration on regionalism and southern problems, and ending with the great variety of behavioral science studies that have characterized the Institute's program for the last two decades. Finally we present an overview, by way of summary and evaluation of the work of the Institute during its first half-century.

During the course of our work we have often had occasion to recall the old anecdote about a young scholar who had read a book about alligators. When asked how he liked the book, he replied, "Oh, it was all right, but it told me more than I wanted to know about alligators." A related story also often came to mind. Two people were having their first close-up view of an alligator. One asked, "Who on earth could love a creature like that?" The other replied, "Only another alligator." We are quite aware that this work runs the risk implied in both of these anecdotes. We have probably told the general reader much more than he wants to know about the Institute, and it may well be that the only readers who will be interested in our particular alligator, the Institute for Research in Social Science, are confirmed research-minded alligators. Readers who are interested primarily in the story of the origin, administration, and financing of the Institute are advised to read the first four chapters, and those who are more interested in the research programs of the Institute are advised to concentrate on the remaining chapters. The complete alligator will, of course, want to read the whole thing.

Chapel Hill   Guy B. Johnson / Guion Griffis Johnson
August 1977

Research in Service to Society

CHAPTER I

The Beginning

The Institute for Research in Social Science was formally organized at the University of North Carolina on June 30, 1924. It began in a small way, in an environment that was sometimes hostile, gradually won recognition and respectability, survived the Great Depression, and eventually became a taken-for-granted force in the life of the University, the state, and the nation. The guiding genius and founding father of the Institute for Research in Social Science was the late Howard W. Odum, Kenan Professor of Sociology at the University of North Carolina from his appointment in 1920 until his retirement in 1954. Even when he arrived in Chapel Hill in the summer of 1920, with two Ph.D. degrees and a head full of dreams, he envisioned a scheme whereby research in the social sciences would point the way to a new era of progress for the state and the South.

The Founding Father: Howard W. Odum

Howard Washington Odum was born in 1884 in the little community of Bethlehem in Walton County, Georgia. His parents were farm people of modest means, and he knew that if he was going to realize his early ambition of entering the world of the intellectuals, he would have to make it largely through his own efforts. He had a restless mind and a strong body, and he was not afraid of work. His parents were able to help him a little with his education, but it was chiefly with hard physical work, stints of schoolteaching, and some borrowed money that he gave himself a remarkable education: an A.B. degree from Emory College in 1904, an M.A. degree from the University of Mississippi in 1906, and two doctoral degrees.

His earlier college training had all been in classics, but at "Ole Miss" one of his favorite professors was Thomas P. Bailey, author of *Race Orthodoxy in the South*, who had studied psychology under the renowned G. Stanley Hall at Clark University in Worcester, Massachusetts, and from there on Odum's interest was centered in the social sciences. Bailey helped him to get a fellowship to study under Hall. Odum's first Ph.D. was earned in psychology at Clark University in 1909. During four years as teacher and student in Mississippi, he had assembled an immense collection of Negro folk songs and observations on the social life of the southern Negro people. He used his collection of religious folk songs as the basis of his doctoral dissertation at Clark. The next year he went to Columbia University to study under the distinguished sociologist, Franklin H. Giddings. In one year he earned a second Ph.D. degree. His dissertation, again drawn from his voluminous field notes, was later published as his first book, *The Social and Mental Traits of the Negro*.

At Clark University Odum had fallen in love with a brilliant young woman, Anna Louise Kranz, who was also studying psychology. After the completion of his second doctorate and several months of work in a new job in Philadelphia, Odum felt that he was ready for the responsibilities of marriage. On December 24, 1910, he and Miss Kranz were married at her home in Tennessee. The contrast between the gentle and somewhat frail woman and the restless, dynamic man was striking, but Mrs. Odum never lacked the inner strength to cope with the problems of married life with such a man. They were a devoted pair. She bore three children, managed the household and social affairs with efficiency and charm, and gave her husband constant emotional and intellectual support. This fragile woman, who lay at death's door several times during the Odums' Chapel Hill sojourn, was to survive her husband by more than a decade.

After two years with the Philadelphia Bureau of Municipal Research, Odum went to the University of Georgia at Athens in 1912 to teach educational sociology. At Athens he met Eugene C. Branson, who was to have a strong influence on his career plans. In 1919 Odum moved to his alma mater, Emory, as professor of sociology and dean of liberal arts. He helped in the relocation of Emory from Oxford to Atlanta and in its transition to university status. He had high hopes at first of making Emory a great center for social science training but was soon frustrated and disillusioned, and when he was offered a post at the University of North Carolina he was happy to accept it. This was to be his last move. He came to Chapel Hill in the summer of 1920 and plunged immediately into a remarkable career of teaching, research, writing, administration, and public service.

He organized the School of Public Welfare in 1920 and served as its director. In the same year he organized the Department of Sociology and began his long service as its chairman. In 1922 he founded the *Journal of Social Forces* and was its editor until his retirement. In 1924 he founded the Institute for Research in Social Science and was its director until 1944. During his thirty-four years at Chapel Hill he wrote seventeen books of his own, edited or coauthored eleven others, and wrote nearly two hundred articles, chapters, and pamphlets. Along the way he found time to engage in many state, regional, and national public service activities. As if all of this were not enough, Odum also maintained a herd of pedigreed Jerseys that earned him the distinction of being one of only five breeders in the nation to develop a genetic type. No one at the University during this century has surpassed him in the variety and volume of his achievements.

What kind of man was Howard W. Odum? Perhaps the most obvious thing about him was his tremendous energy, both physical and mental. He was always moving, and he moved at a rapid pace. It was often said by his associates in Alumni Building that "if you see a pair of coattails disappearing around a corner, you know they belong to Dr. Odum." His imagination was ebullient, and his thoughts poured out in a torrent of written or spoken words. Many students had trouble with his lectures until they learned how to pay attention to his meaning rather than his words. His writing was often a bit chaotic, but at the same time poetic, and one colleague described his style as "a blend of Walt Whitman, Thomas Wolfe, and William Faulkner."[1] Odum liked to plan a new project, get it organized and running smoothly, and then turn it over to someone else. He wearied of routine matters, and he did not enjoy such petty details as presiding over meetings, presenting speakers, or writing the minutes of meetings. Often, after he had opened a meeting, he would make an inconspicuous exit, go to his office, write for an hour or more, and return to the meeting just in time to preside over its adjournment.

Odum had an intense devotion to the South and an abiding faith in its people. What the South needed, he thought, was not harsh criticism but understanding, wise leadership, and self-development. From his own roots he had an appreciation of why certain people joined the Ku Klux Klan, lynched Negroes, and did other unjust things. He often said, "But for the grace of God you or I might be doing these same things. Let us condemn their evil deeds, but still love the people. We need to change the system in the South so that people do not feel compelled to do bad things.'' His own parents were to him the epitome of ''the folk.'' To condemn *people* was to turn his back on his own ''folk,'' and this he would never do.

With all of his remarkable talents, Odum was basically a very shy person. He was not urbane or smooth, and he had little facility for the small talk of teas and parties. He was always the country boy from Georgia, with a certain distaste for what he considered to be the trivialities of social life.

He worked incessantly, as if every day was to be his last chance to get something done. There were probably few days in his whole life when he relaxed completely and did nothing ''useful.'' Often he would be working on several different books. At his office every minute that he could snatch between lectures or conferences would be devoted to one of his manuscripts. In the late afternoon he might go to his farm to check on his Jerseys. After dinner he would retire to the study in his home and work on another manuscript. When he felt the need of sleep, he sank into a large lounge chair and slept for an hour or two, and then he would go back to his writing. He used to say, ''I relax by changing from one manuscript to another.''

Odum claimed that he really enjoyed working at this pace. He said that like his father he was naturally endowed with a robust constitution and that he had scarcely been sick a day in his life. His father had died at the age of ninety-two. Odum retired at seventy in the summer of 1954, and he was looking forward to producing several more books, particularly an autobiography that he planned to call *The White Sands of Bethlehem*. But at the very moment of his retirement he suddenly began to look tired and ill, and on November 8, 1954, he was dead from a cancer of the pancreas. Most people said that he had simply worked himself to death. Those who knew him best wondered what *caused* the cancer, and they thought it was not overwork but frustration and disappointment at not having achieved still more. For years he had carried the scars of the misunderstanding of his motives by fellow southerners who thought he was a traitor to the South. In his early years at Chapel Hill he had endured the barbs of faculty and townspeople who did not know the difference between sociology and socialism. He had also been the center of controversies over the right of *Social Forces* to publish articles that might give offense to religious fundamentalists and the right of the Institute to do research on such delicate subjects as the textile industry or race relations. He was disappointed in the casual and uncooperative way in which some of his social science colleagues played their roles in the Institute, and he was frustrated and embarrassed by the eternal explaining, cajoling, and begging that he had to do to get money from the foundations. And perhaps, worst of all, he had seen his last big dream for the University—a school of public administration, planned in detail and with financial support by a foundation all but assured—go up in smoke because the president of the University failed to keep an appointment in New York at which he was to put the administration's stamp of approval on the new school.

Odum left many monuments to his genius for pioneering. Aside from his prolific writings, the most enduring of these are the Institute for Research in Social Science, *Social Forces*, the School of Social Work, and the Department of Sociology. In 1933 the American Council on Education's Committee on Graduate Instruction made a study in which it attempted to identify the departments in American universities that deserved a good rating in terms of being "adequately staffed and equipped." At the University of North Carolina eleven departments were listed: Botany, Chemistry, Classics, Education, English, History, Political Science, Psychology, Romance Languages, Sociology, and Zoology. Only one of these was given the special rating of "distinguished," and that was the Department of Sociology. Not bad for a department that was only thirteen years old! The department's good fortune was made possible to a considerable extent by the existence of the Institute, which enabled Odum to attract able professors as well as promising young graduate students, some of whom would stay on after receiving their doctorates. The other social science departments likewise profited from the energizing presence of the Institute.

Those Who Helped

Several people besides Odum played important roles in the founding of the Institute: Harry Woodburn Chase, Jesse Frederick Steiner, Louis Round Wilson, Beardsley Ruml, and Eugene Cunningham Branson. The relation of the first four to Odum and the Institute may be sketched briefly. The role of E. C. Branson requires some elaboration.

Harry W. Chase was a native of Massachusetts. After earning his A.B. and A.M. degrees at Dartmouth, he went to Clark University to study psychology under G. Stanley Hall. There he became the good friend of one of his fellow graduate students, Howard W. Odum. Like

Odum, Chase fell in love with a young woman who was also studying psychology. He and Lucetta Crum were married on December 26, 1910, just two days after Odum's marriage to Anna Louise Kranz. The two couples were to be lifelong friends. It could well be that some of Odum's devotion to the South rubbed off on Chase, for as soon as he had received his doctorate in 1910 Chase took a position as professor of psychology at the University of North Carolina. In 1918 he became dean of the College of Liberal Arts. Following the untimely death of President Edward Kidder Graham during the great influenza epidemic, Chase was elected chairman of the faculty in January 1919, and in June he was elected president of the University. His formal installation did not take place until April 28, 1920. Among those who attended the inauguration was his old friend Howard W. Odum, who was then dean of the School of Liberal Arts at Emory University near Atlanta. Odum had accepted an offer from Chase several months earlier and was preparing to move to the University of North Carolina. After returning to Atlanta, Odum wrote Chase: "I congratulate you and the University on the remarkable success of the inauguration exercises. It was a great occasion. Personally, it was worth a great deal more to me than I am able to estimate. When one has staked his future on the belief in a certain institution and its youthful President, it is most refreshing to find them measuring up even beyond former estimates."[2]

Two months later Odum would move to Chapel Hill because his friends Chase and Branson had paved the way. In Chase, Odum had a warm friend who played a vital role in supporting and facilitating his proposals. Chase's departure in 1930 to become president of the University of Illinois was a hard blow to Odum.

Jesse Steiner, a native of Ohio, was born in 1880. He had a doctorate from the University of Chicago, and he had considerable experience as teacher, missionary, author, and administrator. During World War I he became national director of the Bureau of Training for Home Service and later director of educational service for the American Red Cross. When Odum founded the Department of Sociology in 1920, he was already searching for someone who would strengthen the depth and respectability of the department. He was fortunate to be able to bring Steiner to Chapel Hill in 1921. Steiner and his family soon made many warm friends in Chapel Hill. He was scholarly, calm, a lucid lecturer, and a friendly adviser to his students. For several years these two men *were* the Department of Sociology. When Steiner moved to Tulane University in 1927, Odum again had a deep feeling of loss.

Louis R. Wilson, born in 1876 in North Carolina, was already an old-timer on the campus when Odum arrived. He was Kenan Professor of Library Administration and director of the University Extension Bureau, and he was soon to be director of the University of North Carolina Press. He was a helpful adviser in planning the organization of the Institute, and he became a member of its governing board. He and Odum had occasion to disagree at times but these minor differences subtracted little from Wilson's role as friend, supporter, and defender. In 1932, after thirty years of service at Chapel Hill, Wilson left to become dean of the University of Chicago's Graduate Library School. Retiring there at the age of sixty-five, he returned to Chapel Hill in 1942 and made a new career as elder statesman and historian of the University as well as member once more of the Institute's Board of Governors. On December 27, 1976, he celebrated his hundredth birthday, still vigorous and able to relate his vivid recollections of a fascinating career.

Beardsley Ruml, a native of Iowa and a resident of New York City, was director of the Laura Spelman Rockefeller Memorial. The directors of this philanthropic foundation, which was founded in 1919, were particularly interested in helping universities to strengthen their curricula and research in the social sciences. Odum had occasion to see Ruml several times in the early 1920s. Ruml was impressed by the dynamism and the great plans of the young sociologist, and in the spring of 1924 he submitted to the Memorial, with his stamp of approval, Odum's application for the three-year grant that would make possible the founding of the Institute. In a sense Ruml was the key to Odum's plan, because he was "the man who knew where the money was." The Laura Spelman Rockefeller Memorial was to be the financial mainstay of the Institute in its formative years.

The Godfather: Eugene C. Branson

Each of these four men played a part, but the intellectual godfather of the Institute was Eugene C. Branson. Branson was born in Morehead City, North Carolina, in 1861. After his education at Trinity College (now Duke University) and Peabody College for Teachers, he worked in public schools as principal or superintendent in Raleigh and Wilson, North Carolina, and Athens, Georgia. Later he was appointed professor of pedagogy at the Georgia State Normal School at Athens, and from 1900 to 1912 he was president of that school. In 1912 he gave up the presidency to become founder and head of the Normal School's Department of Rural Economics and Sociology. In this same year, Howard W. Odum came to the University of Georgia at Athens as an associate professor of educational sociology.

Probably Branson and Odum already knew each other, but it is certain that they now became good friends and mutual admirers. The twenty-eight-year-old Georgian, full of energy and vision, was in a hurry to improve his beloved South, and the fifty-two-year-old Branson had a rich background of ideas and efforts in the application of knowledge to the solution of social problems. Branson urged his students to go out and organize Georgia Clubs, patterned after one he had organized at Athens. His exhortation was: "Know your community, know your state, through study and discussion, and see what you can do to make things better." Another major concern of Branson's was the importance of developing professional training in the field of public welfare, so that this emerging profession in the South could be staffed with competent people trained in applied social science.

These ideas complemented and reinforced Odum's own ideas, while he in turn made a very favorable impression on the older man. In 1914 Branson returned to his native state, accepting a position as professor and chairman of the Department of Rural Economics and Sociology (later named Rural Social Economics) at the University of North Carolina. Right away he began a quiet campaign to have the University create a school of social science or a school of public welfare, and always at the back of his mind was the notion that Howard W. Odum would be a good man to head such a school.

In the fall of 1916 Branson prepared a lengthy memorandum proposing "A School of Public Welfare at the University of North Carolina" and presented it to President Edward K. Graham. Branson later wrote that Graham "at once authorized me to search the field for a dean to head up the school—a real person, in his significant phrase.'"[3] But the nation went to war in 1917, and there followed a period of feverish activity on the campus to help with the war effort. Organizing and accommodating a large contingent of the Student Army Training Corps (SATC), for example, was a great strain on the University's resources. In addition, President Graham assumed responsibility for supervising the installation of SATC units throughout the Southeast. On top of this came the deadly influenza epidemic, and Graham did not live to present Branson's proposal to the University's trustees. Furthermore, as Branson sadly related, "the plans with the accumulated data, reports, correspondence, and the like, were misplaced in the President's office during the subsequent calamities of influenza and the S.A.T.C."[4]

After Harry W. Chase became president in June 1919, Branson pursued the matter of the new school of public welfare and "a real person" to head it. Now things began to happen. Odum, who had moved to Emory University with ambitious plans for making it into a great academic center and probably becoming its next president, was finding it difficult to work with Bishop Warren A. Candler and the ultraconservative Methodist power structure that controlled the school. He was ready to move on, and Chase and Branson were ready to bring him to Chapel Hill. Sometime during the fall of 1919 arrangements were made, although there was no public announcement for some months, since Chase had to proceed cautiously and wisely in order to get the trustees to agree to establish a school of public welfare and a department of sociology.

In November 1919, while Branson and Odum were attending a conference in Chicago, they discussed Branson's lost proposal of 1916, and Branson promised to reconstruct the whole thing *de novo* and send it to Odum. When he sent the proposal on December 5, he wrote: "I have not yet recovered from the fervor of interest in your coming into the faculty here to head up this school and to get it going wisely and effectively."[5] On the same day, he received a letter from Odum expressing a reciprocal feeling: "I think the pair of us can furnish equal enthusiasm! Needless to say that I am counting heavy [sic] on you and shall hope to carry out the plan to which you have given so much thought and time."[6]

Branson much preferred the title "The School of Social Science" to "The School of Public Welfare" for the new school that Odum was to direct. He had even made so bold as to write his friend John Sprunt Hill, a well-to-do alumnus who was a trustee of the University, suggesting that he endow such a school:

> The John Sprunt Hill School of Social Science—how does that sound to you?
>
> I have come to believe that long years will elapse before we have such a school unless you fund it and endow it.
>
> After five years of patient, faithful work here I find every once in a while to my utter consternation that "social," "sociology," and "social science" are fatally linked to the North Carolina

mind with "socialism." We have not been wise as serpents, but we certainly have been gentle as doves. Nevertheless, one of our senators in Washington is recently credited with the remark, that "the less we have of social science at the University, the better, that they will look after that end of the job in Washington."[7]

Mr. Hill evidently expressed some misgivings of his own in his response, for Branson wrote him in December 1919:

> Thank you heartily for your good letter. I agree with you that "there is a considerable element of danger in a school of Social Sciences at the University if it should be in charge of a Dean who was foreign to the soil and imbued with socialistic ideas. . . ."
>
> Dr. Chase is really considering my report and will be presenting it in some form to the trustees in January. This along with other matters of critical import will call for wisdom on the part of the trustees, and I am hoping that you will certainly be present.[8]

Horace Williams, professor of philosophy, who was later dubbed "the gadfly of Chapel Hill," also had some words of caution as well as encouragement for Branson. In replying to Williams, Branson said:

> . . . I think you undoubtedly wise in your choice of terms for the proposed new school here. Public Welfare means more, in North Carolina at any rate, than Social Science. It will probably get us further along.
>
> Sociology, however, is a recognized academic term and is fairly well standardized in the curriculum of our colleges and universities.[9]

Ever the wise strategist, Branson conceded that the new school would have to be called the School of Public Welfare. And it is interesting that in his letters to Hill, Williams, and others he never divulged the fact that a dean had already been selected, although he had known for months that Odum had accepted President Chase's invitation to direct the new school.

Thus Branson had smoothed the way for Odum's new venture. With his courtly manner, his geniality, and his intellectual vigor, he had won the admiration of faculty and students; and with his county surveys, his North Carolina Club, his Rural Social Science Library, and his *News Letter*, which circulated factual materials about North Carolina to the public, he had greatly enhanced the University's image among the people of the state. Approaching his sixtieth birthday, he now encouraged the young man from Georgia to take the spotlight.

From Georgia to Chapel Hill

On January 27, 1920, Chase eloquently presented to the University's Board of Trustees his recommendation concerning the proposed curricula in public welfare and sociology.

> . . . It is clear that North Carolina is destined to an immense extension of her material resources; it is equally clear that, with all her great increases in material wealth, she can function effectively as a fine democracy only if she sets in the foreground of her thought the fundamental truth that human values are greater than material values; that man is more precious than the goods he creates. . . .
>
> . . . I recommend the establishment in the University of a Chair of Sociology, about which there should grow up a School of Public Welfare. . . . A knowledge of the fundamental laws of society, of what democracy really means and what its problems are, a spirit of social-mindedness which leads the individual to look beyond himself and to think of himself in relation to his community, these things are more and more requisite for good citizenship. The social sciences, including economics, history, government, and sociology in its various aspects, must receive a new and more intense emphasis in the higher education of the future.[10]

The Board of Trustees approved the recommendation, and a month later Odum was elected Kenan Professor of Sociology. Odum's usual rapid pace now became downright feverish. He knew that unless he could lay hands on additional funds he would be the one and only staff member for the new School of Public Welfare and the Department of Sociology. He visited Chapel Hill several times, and he went to New Orleans, to Philadelphia, and to New York, where he talked to the administrators of various foundations about his dream of a center for social science teaching and research at Chapel Hill. He also turned to the American Red Cross, since he had served during the war as director of the southern division of their Bureau of Home Service Camps and Cities. The Red Cross agreed to fund and staff a series of special summer institutes for social workers and Red Cross secretaries. Thus Odum was able to begin operations at Chapel Hill with something of a flourish during the summer session of 1920. The Red Cross continued its assistance to the new school by providing some staff members and twelve scholarships, and in January 1921, Dr. Jesse F. Steiner, who had been educational director for the American Red Cross, joined Odum's staff as a professor of social technology.

Indicative of Odum's tendency to "think big" was the fact that his first catalog presentation of the new Department of Sociology listed twenty-one courses to be taught by him and Steiner, while the first catalog announcement of the School of Public Welfare listed a similar number of courses to be taught by Odum, Steiner, Branson, Samuel H. Hobbs, Jr. (Branson's young understudy), and the Red Cross specialists. After listing his "Special Staff of Instruction" for the School of Public Welfare, Odum listed "Other University Professors," including professors of education, economics, history and government, psychology, library administration, dramatic literature, and music—a significant indication of his passion for bringing the social sciences together in an interdisciplinary enterprise.[11]

In the four years between Odum's arrival at Chapel Hill and the founding of the Institute for Research in Social Science, he became known for his dynamism, his devotion to his department, and his willingness to work eighteen hours a day. He kept his new academic enterprises going, he traveled a great deal to attend conferences or to make addresses, he organized summer institutes and special conferences at Chapel Hill, and he founded the *Journal of Social Forces* in 1922. He had little time for research, and he published very little during this period except for his editorial articles in the new journal and some bulletins for the Extension Division of the University, but he was consciously building toward the time when he and his colleagues could study the social problems of the state and the region.

A Grant for the Institute

Early in 1924 Odum learned that the Laura Spelman Rockefeller Memorial was planning to distribute millions of dollars to encourage the development of the social sciences. He began a campaign to interest Beardsley Ruml, director of the Memorial, in making a grant to the University of North Carolina for cooperative research in the social sciences. Finally he persuaded Ruml to visit the South, and the two men met in Charlotte during the spring. In the end Odum allayed Ruml's doubts as to the willingness of any southern university to enter areas of social research that might be controversial. Apparently he assured Ruml that he and his colleagues and the University administration would have the courage to search for the truth regardless of the social and political consequences. Ruml then told him that if he would draw up a strong proposal for cooperative research for presentation to the Memorial, there was a possibility that the Memorial would act favorably on it.[12]

Odum lost no time in laying this new opportunity before Chase and some of his colleagues. Chase invited Ruml to Chapel Hill, and he came in early May and spent several days. Chase, Odum, and Ruml worked out the details of a memorandum to be sent to the Memorial setting forth the plan for an institute for research in social science and requesting a grant of $97,500 over a period of three years.

President Chase, always the careful administrator, wanted to make sure that the University trustees were aware of these plans, since their favorable action would be required. On May 12 he sent the following letter to the sixteen members of the Executive Committee of the Board of Trustees:

> During the last few days Mr. Ruml, Director of the Laura Spelman Rockefeller Memorial . . . of New York has been in Chapel Hill. This [Memorial], which was founded in 1919, is somewhat similar in character to the General Education Board, except that the funds at its command are available in general for research in the social sciences instead of for general education purposes.
>
> Mr. Ruml is very much impressed by the field which is open here for investigation into the problems of Statewide and Southern significance, and especially by the work which is being done by such men as Branson, Carroll, and Odum. He sees very clearly the enlarged field of usefulness which such men as these would have for the welfare of the State in case they are given completely trained assistants for field investigations into such things as county and municipal

government and various economic problems of the State, and also funds for clerical assistance and for collection of material and publication of results. In fact, so highly does he think of the quality of the men who are at work in these fields here and the opportunity which lies open to the University to be of immense help to the State and the South in these fields of investigation that I have been encouraged by him to apply for a grant of thirty-five thousand dollars a year for a minimum of three years to help these men in working out problems which require a considerable amount of field study and an accumulation of, for example, statistical material, all of which is a laborious undertaking. He feels clearly that the University of North Carolina is in a strategic position among Southern institutions to make a real contribution in these fields.

As his Board meets on the twenty-eighth of May I am taking the opportunity of getting this matter before you in this way, as there will hardly be time to call another meeting of the Executive Committee. There are no strings tied to the proposition, other than at the end of the three year period the [Memorial] would want to check up on the work that had been done up to that time to see what attitude it would take toward continuing it. The University does not obligate itself in any way to take over the work, but the whole matter is left open for further consideration at the end of the three year period. The University would have full liberty in picking the assistants and determining the projects to be worked on. . . .

I do not of course want the members of the Committee, particularly in this informal way to bind themselves in advance to accept any gift which should be offered, but I do think that I should write you to say that with your permission I desire to lay a statement of our situation and of what could be accomplished along these lines with assistants before the [Memorial]. . . .[13]

On the same day that Chase sent this letter to the members of the Executive Committee, he sent the grant application to the Laura Spelman Rockefeller Memorial. The proposal set forth a plan for the organization and management of an institute for research in social science and the uses to which the grant of funds would be put. The institute would be managed by a board of governors, consisting of the president of the University as chairman ex officio, and professors from various social science departments and administrative posts, namely, E. C. Branson (Rural Social Economics), D. D. Carroll (dean of the School of Commerce), H. W. Odum (Sociology), A. M. Jordan (Education), J. G. de Roulhac Hamilton (History and Government), L. R. Wilson (Librarian), and Edwin Greenlaw (dean of the Graduate School). The primary use of the grant would be to provide research assistants to facilitate the researches that would be conducted by social science faculty members on problems relating to the state and to the region. There would be eight or nine of these assistants for the first year. To qualify for the position, an applicant would have to have had at least one year of graduate work. Each assistant would receive a salary of $1500 a year and would be allotted $500 for field expenses. The fund would also provide $7,500 for secretarial help, supplies, schedules, and the like; $6,000 for publication of research reports and for books, pamphlets, and similar research materials; and $3,000 for a secretary who would be in charge of the routine work of the central office.[14]

On June 16 Ruml notified Chase that the trustees for the Memorial had unanimously passed the following resolution: "that the sum of $32,500 a year for three years, beginning July 1, 1924, be and hereby is appropriated to the University of North Carolina to be used in the development of its research in the social sciences."[15] However, Ruml expressed to Chase some concern over the lengths to which Chase had gone in his letter to the Executive Committee in assuring the trustees that "the University does not obligate itself in any way to take over the work." He wanted Chase to bear in mind that the time might come when the University would have to find some other source of funds for the research program.

On July 8 Chase wrote to the Executive Committee again. He reported that all but two or three of the members had replied to his letter of May 12 and that all of the replies were favorable. He quoted the resolution from Ruml's letter of June 16 and again wished to assure the trustees "that the resolution includes no obligation on our part to take over the work at the expiration of this period, nor are any conditions made which would embarrass or hamper us in our use of the gift." He then outlined the organization and management of the new institute and the uses to which the grant would be put substantially in the same way that he had presented these items in the proposal to Ruml. "I may add," he wrote, "that the Memorial is not interested in maintaining faculty chairs, but rather in putting at the disposal of the men already in our faculty increased facilities to do their work. . . . It is rare that a gift is given with so few conditions."[16]

Formal action by the trustees in accepting the grant and approving the formation of the Institute for Research in Social Science would come later, but in the meantime there were things that had to be done. The grant was to become effective on July 1, and the fall term would begin in September, so that someone had to act rapidly on such matters as having some research assistants appointed in time for the opening of the fall quarter, hiring a secretary or manager for the Institute's office, finding space for the Institute, and setting up guidelines for the operation of the Institute. That someone was, of course, Howard W. Odum. Unfortunately, documentary evidence of his procedures for resolving these problems is scanty, but he obviously accomplished a great deal in a short time. With Chase's help be obtained space for the new Institute on the first floor of Saunders Hall, a building that already housed the Department of History and Government and the Department of Economics and Commerce. He spread the word about the Institute and its need for research assistants and an office manager among friends in other universities, urged the other members of the provisional board of governors to submit their nominations for research assistants, and initiated correspondence with several potential assistants whose names had come to his attention. When the Board of Governors of the Institute for Research in Social Science held its first meeting on June 30, 1924, only two definite nominations were presented, but by the time the University opened in September at least eight assistants and an office manager had been appointed and were ready for work.

The First Meeting of the Board of Governors

The first meeting of the Board of Governors was of such historic importance for the Institute that the minutes of the meeting are reproduced in full here.

The University Institute for Research in Social Science

First Meeting for Preliminary Organization

At the call of President H. W. Chase the first meeting of the governing board for the University Institute for Research in

the Social Sciences was held in the President's office at 4 o'clock
on June 30th, 1924. There were present, in addition to the
President, D. D. Carroll, J. G. de R. Hamilton, A. M. Jordan,
H. W. Odum, L. R. Wilson; S. H. Hobbs representing E. C.
Branson. Absent Edwin A. Greenlaw. Howard W. Odum was
asked to act as secretary of the meeting.

President Chase made a preliminary statement giving brief
details concerning the events which lead [sic] up to the calling
of a previous group and of the formation of this Institute for
Social Research. The action of the Laura Spelman Memorial
Fund [sic] in appropriating $32,500.00 for research in social
science a year for three years was reviewed. The importance
of making the Institute a distinctive contribution to University
efforts, aside from departmental work, was emphasized.

The President then submitted a memorandum outlining the
general plan of organization. The memorandum was discussed
in general and in detail and the resulting preliminary organization
plan was as follows:

1. There is organized at the University of North Carolina an
   Institute for Research in Social Science.
2. The purpose of this Institute is the cooperative study of
   problems in the general field of social science, arising out of
   State and regional conditions.
3. There shall be a governing board for this Institute, of
   which the President of the University will be ex officio
   Chairman, and the members of which shall be appointed by
   him from the faculty of the University. Members of the board
   will be chosen to represent interests and subjects rather than
   departments.
4. The initial governing board of the Institute shall consist of
   the following, in addition to the Chairman: E. C. Branson,
   D. D. Carroll, Edwin Greenlaw, J. G. DeR. Hamilton, A. M.
   Jordan, H. W. Odum, L. R. Wilson.
   There shall be a secretary to be appointed by the Chairman
   with the approval of the board.
   (The appointment of a secretary is delayed to such time as
   an outstanding person may be available and from the funds
   provided for the secretary an extra assistant in municipal
   information and research may be provided if suitable
   applicant can be found.)

5. Such research assistants as may be available in any year
    shall be appointed by the board with the view not to their
    assignment to given departments, but with the purpose in
    mind of carrying through definite research projects and
    utilizing the best trained available candidates. All such
    appointments shall be for the term of one year, but these
    may be extended by the board whenever the nature of the
    project and the ability of the assistant shall warrant.
    Members of the faculty may themselves undertake, with the
    approval of the board, for a specific period, the duties of
    such research assistant, providing the teaching duties of such
    faculty member can be cared for without expense to the
    University. (It is the sense of the board that research assistants
    are to be appointed for the twelve months, matters of
    vacations and summer adjustments to be made by those in
    charge of specific research projects.
    It is the sense of the board that all research assistants
    appointed must have had a graduate degree or the equivalent
    of one full year of research experience.
    It was agreed, however, that during the first year if suitable
    candidates were not available the stipend of $1500 might
    be divided into two assistantships and mature graduate
    students be appointed to begin research on specific
    problems.)
6. It [being] necessary, in advance of the appointment of the
    board, to lay down a schedule for research assistants for the
    first year in terms of projects in hand and available
    material and men, it is understood that the research assistants
    for the year 1924–25 shall be appointed as follows:
    (a) Research in rural county public affairs 3
        (To be appointed by Professor Branson)
    (b) Research in municipal government 2
        (Professor Hamilton to make nominations)
    (c) Research in industrial relations and economic problems 2
        (Mr. Rowland [sic] B. Eutsler, M.A., was appointed)
    (d) Research in child welfare 1
        (Professor Jordan to make nomination)
    (e) Research in specified social problems 1
        (Mr. Guy B. Johnson, M.A., University of Chicago, ap-
        pointed.)

7. The stipend for these research assistants shall not exceed
    fifteen hundred dollars a year, and their time shall be devoted
    to research provided that

    (a) a research assistant may, with the approval of the professor
        in charge of his research, teach during any year not more
        than one full course, on a subject in harmony with his
        research.

    (b) that research assistants shall carry such amount of graduate
        work as will not interfere with their research.

8. A sum not to exceed four thousand dollars a year shall be set
    apart for the field expenses of these assistants, the initial
    and subsequent apportionments to each project to be made by
    the board.

    (The exact method of apportioning field expenses is to be
    determined along with the acceptance of projects.)

9. A sum not to exceed seven thousand and five hundred dollars
    a year is to be set apart for clerical assistance, including
    stationery and supplies, the printing of schedules and
    such expenditures of like character as would otherwise
    become a burden on the maintenance funds of the University.
    The apportionment of this fund shall be made by the
    board. (It was the sense of the board that a central office
    should be established as soon as possible with a head office
    secretary who should begin clerical and secretarial work
    necessary for research projects. Around this central office
    will be built up added secretarial services which can be
    utilized as best needed with the total projects. The secretary
    of the meeting was instructed to look for a suitable office
    secretary and members of the board instructed to keep on the
    lookout for such person.)

10. The sum of six thousand dollars annually is set apart for the
    publication of the results of the research and for the purchase
    of library material for research projects, such expenditures to
    be approved by the board. (Details of the appropriation for
    publication and library material will be worked out in
    subsequent meetings and in connection with definite
    projects.)

11. Research projects to be carried out, material intended
    for publication, and such reports as the board may desire
    from time to time on the progress of such projects are

to be submitted to the board for its approval. Outlines
submitted shall be in suitable form for permanent record.
(Members of the Board were requested to prepare outlines
of research projects to be considered during the next
year with suggestions also for the following two years. A
form to insure uniformity of outlines is to be sent to
each member.

Publications of the Institute, while published regularly under
the University of North Carolina Press, are to have the special
sub-title bearing the imprint of the Institute for Research
in Social Science.)

12. (Suggested) Such research assistants shall be affiliated with
and registered in the Institute. How shall they register
for advanced degrees?

(Research assistants are to be primarily registered and
affiliated with the Institute and registered in the Graduate
School in accordance with details to be worked out in
subsequent meetings.

In general it was suggested that sub-committees on special
research projects be selected to work with research assistants.)

The board adjourned to meet again before the end of the first half of
the summer session.[17]

These minutes of the first meeting of the Board of Governors contain
intimations of certain problems that would plague the Institute from
time to time. For example, were research proposals to be originated
only by the faculty, or would the research assistants be allowed to
propose and pursue projects of their own choosing? Just how would a
research assistant on an Institute stipend differ from an ordinary graduate student on a University fellowship? How many courses could a
research assistant take without endangering his research position? And
was the Institute to have the sort of autonomy that could lead the Board
to suggest that "research assistants shall be affiliated with and registered in the Institute?"

The First Research Assistants

How had the new Institute laid hands on even two research assistants
as early as the meeting of June 30? One of these was Roland B.

Eutsler, who was already a graduate student at the University and had just completed his M.S. degree. Dean Carroll knew him and was glad to sponsor him for research in economic problems.

The other was a young Texan, Guy B. Johnson, who by a chain of fortunate circumstances had the honor of becoming Odum's first nominee for a research assistantship. After receiving his A.B. degree in sociology from Baylor University in 1921, Johnson went to the University of Chicago to study for a master's degree in 1921–22. There he made the acquaintance of an amiable young Georgian, Wiley B. Sanders, who had studied under Odum at Emory University and at Chapel Hill, and he shared a room with Sanders during the second half of the year. Sanders often spoke admiringly of Odum, and when he learned of Odum's plan of launching the *Journal of Social Forces* he urged Johnson to submit to Odum a paper based on his master's thesis. Later, after Johnson had gone to teach at Ohio Wesleyan University, he submitted the paper. Odum accepted it, and this article, "A Sociological Interpretation of the New Ku Klux Movement," which appeared in May 1923, became Johnson's first professional publication. The two men began a correspondence. Odum suggested another paper, and Johnson contributed "The Negro Migration and Its Consequences," which was published in March 1924.

In the fall of 1923 Johnson was married to Guion Griffis, whom he had known since freshman college days, and he took a position at Baylor College for Women where she was head of the Department of Journalism. Early in 1924 Odum and Johnson exchanged letters on the possibility of the Johnsons' coming to Chapel Hill for further graduate study. At first Odum could offer Guy Johnson a teaching fellowship at $500 and Guion Johnson some promotional chores for *Social Forces*, but he held out hope that something much better might develop. On April 7 he wrote Johnson: "If we should get this social science foundation under way, I am frank to believe that there would be no better place in the country. It takes time, however, and the coming of such folk as you will help us to work it out." Subsequent letters expressed Odum's increasing optimism, and finally, on June 18, he wrote, "This is just a note to confirm the letter of a few days ago saying that we should be able to offer you $1500 and a research assistantship instead of $500 and a teaching fellowship, and that we shall be able to provide Mrs. Johnson some clerical assistance."[18]

Early in the exchange of letters Johnson had told Odum that Mrs. Johnson, who had a professional degree in journalism, was just as interested as he was in doing further graduate work and that they would not want to leave their very attractive positions without some assurance that she too would have some kind of graduate stipend. Odum readily agreed, offering her at first the job of trying to improve the circulation of *Social Forces*, and later, after the Institute became a reality, a half-time research assistantship. This presented a delicate problem: she would not only be the first woman research assistant, but she was also the wife of another assistant. However, Odum took the challenge, and shortly before the opening of the fall term he secured her appointment by the Board of Governors as a research assistant whose project would be "The Press as a Social Force in North Carolina," under the direction of Gerald W. Johnson, professor of journalism. Thus the chain of circumstances that began with the chance event of Johnson and Sanders sharing a room at the University of Chicago led the young couple from Texas to decide to take a leave from their jobs and go to Chapel Hill for what they thought at the time would be two years of graduate work. Soon they were "hooked" on the University and the Institute. Guion Johnson would be affiliated with the Institute for ten years, and Guy Johnson would be affiliated, first as research assistant, then research associate, and then research professor until his retirement in 1969 as Kenan Professor of Sociology and Anthropology.

There were two more meetings of the Board of Governors before the opening of the fall term. Additional nominations for research assistantships were made and approved, so that shortly after classes began in September Odum could report the roster of assistants and projects as follows:[19]

>Roy E. Brown—(A.B., A.M., residence work completed, North Carolina)
>>"The Small Town in North Carolina"
>G. A. Duncan—(A.B., A.M., Trinity College, Dublin)
>>"A Study of Rural Adaptation of Industrial Mill Villages"
>Roland B. Eutsler—(B.S., M.S., North Carolina)
>>"A Study of Transportation in North Carolina"
>W. D. Glenn—(A.B., A.M., North Carolina)
>>"Effect of Work on Mental Growth in Rural and Mill Communities"
>Guion G. Johnson—(A.B., Baylor College; B.J., Missouri)
>>"The Press as a Social Force in North Carolina"

Guy B. Johnson—(A.B., Baylor; A.M., Chicago)
"Studies in Race Progress."
Orlando Stone—(A.B., Virginia; A.M. credits, North Carolina)
"Reading as a Southern Problem"
Brandon Trussell—(A.B., A.M., Texas)
"County Government in North Carolina"
Paul W. Wager—(B.S., Hobart; A.M., Haverford)
"County Government in North Carolina"

One assistant, G. A. Duncan, of Dublin, Ireland, was on an International Fellowship granted by the Laura Spelman Rockefeller Memorial. Beardsley Ruml directed him to Chapel Hill, and Odum was glad to affiliate him with the Institute. Two other names appeared in the list of appointments approved by the Board at its meeting of August 22, 1924: B. S. Hobart and Buxton Mydyette. Apparently these men either relinquished their positions or dropped out of school, since there is no subsequent record of any research activity by them.

During this period the Institute also made one of the most important appointments of its entire history: it chose Katharine Jocher as its executive secretary. At its meeting of July 25, the Board listened to Odum's summary of the applications for this position and instructed him to invite Miss Jocher to visit Chapel Hill and "look over the situation." The minutes of the August 22 meeting record that "The secretary [Odum] reported that Miss Katharine Jocher, previously nominated for office secretary, had accepted the position on her recent visit." With an A.B. from Goucher College and an A.M. from the University of Pennsylvania, and with experience in social work, administration and teaching, she was eminently qualified to manage the central office. She became Odum's "right hand," and she supervised the secretarial, business, and personnel aspects of the Institute with loyalty and dedication for thirty-five years. She also served the University as professor of sociology, and she was associated with *Social Forces*, first as managing editor and later as editor until her retirement in 1961. She has continued to live in Chapel Hill since her retirement.

At first the secretarial staff consisted of a half-time typist, the wife of a faculty member. When she discovered that she was to work under the direction of Katharine Jocher rather than Odum, she was unhappy. It was not "becoming," she felt, for the wife of a professor to be "taking orders" from another woman, and after a couple of months she resigned. In December 1924 she was succeeded by a full-time secretary, Ina Young. Miss Young had had special secretarial training and had done graduate work at Trinity College (soon to become Duke University). About the same time, Jessie Alverson, a young woman who had formerly worked as secretary for Guion Johnson in Texas, came to Chapel Hill and was employed as a full-time secretary by the Institute. Odum was fortunate in having the services of Minnie Queen, secretary of the Department of Sociology, who took care of much of his correspondence related to the Institute. Miss Queen later married John S. Bennett, who served the University for many years as Director of Operations.

The First of Its Kind

Odum often said that he believed the Institute for Research in Social Science to be the first of its kind. In this he was probably quite right. In 1934 Professor Wilson Gee of the University of Virginia, who had been a student of Branson's at Chapel Hill, published a study entitled *Social Science Research Organization in the United States*. Gee found dozens of university committees and councils that had such functions as finding financial support, allocating funds, and otherwise encouraging social science research, and he found quite a few bureaus and centers that were engaged in some specialized field of research, such as municipal government, child welfare, and international relations. Some of these existed prior to 1924. But there was no organization with an interdisciplinary governing board and a budget of its own that was doing cooperative social science research through the medium of salaried assistants directed by senior faculty members.

Evidently the pattern that Odum and Chase had worked out was worth repeating. Within a few years, the Laura Spelman Rockefeller Memorial itself had made grants for the organization of four similar centers: the Columbia University Council for Research in the Social Sciences (1925), the University of Virginia Institute for Research in Social Sciences (1926), the Stanford University Social Science Research Council (1927), and the University of Texas Bureau of Research in the Social Sciences (1927). No two were exactly alike—for example, Wilson Gee, founder and director of the University of Virginia's Institute, did not like the research assistant pattern that Odum had originated, and he always wanted it known that his funds went only to faculty members, with never a cent to graduate students—but all of them owed something to the pioneering of Howard W. Odum.

A Matter of Urgency

When the Johnsons arrived in Chapel Hill in late August 1924, they lived for a time at the Odums' home until their own quarters became available. During this time they got an intimate glimpse of Odum, the man. He was like a human dynamo, always active, constantly generating new ideas. Over and over in the evening discussions on his porch he would communicate this message: Here we have something unique, the first thing of its kind in the whole United States. We have this grant for three years, and if we haven't shown that we can do something big before the three years are up, that will be the end. What a challenge! But we can do it. We've all got to work hard, we've got to produce and publish, so that we can put this University and this Institute on the map. The University is behind us, and it is ready to go places. We have our chance, and if we don't make good, we will have nobody to blame but ourselves.

Later in the year, when Odum was preparing an editorial for *Social Forces*, "University Research and Training in the Social Sciences," he showed some of the newcomers the chart he had prepared to accompany the editorial. The chart, reproduced here on page 28, is eloquent testimony of the man's tendency to "think big" and to think far ahead of his time.[20]

Something of Odum's spirit of challenge and urgency was communicated to all of the young research assistants who soon gathered at the University of North Carolina. One happy circumstance was the physical arrangement that had been worked out for them. Instead of being split up among the quarters of their research directors, they were all situated in one large room in Saunders Hall that could accommodate ten or twelve desks—an arrangement that was later known as "the bull pen." Here they had daily contact with one another, and they were easily accessible to the secretary of the Institute and to Odum and other faculty members. They soon became a real team.

Thus, after much dreaming and hoping and with the normal amount of confusion and loose ends, the Institute for Research in Social Science became a reality and a promise in the fall of 1924. Its promise was to try to lead the way to a new state and a new South through social science research and interpretation.

UNIVERSITY OF NORTH CAROLINA

CO-OPER-ATING

STATE OR REGIONAL CENTER FOR SOCIAL
RESEARCH AND PROFESSIONAL TRAINING

CO-OPER-ATING

*University
Departments
Directing Research*

*University
Schools and
State Departments*

	RESEARCH AND STUDY	TRAINING AND TECHNIQUE	
HISTORY AND GOVERNMENT Municipal Government. . .	*INSTITUTE FOR RESEARCH IN SOCIAL SCIENCE*	*PROFESSIONAL PROGRAM AND OBJECTIVES*	**GRADUATE** Standards. . .
ECONOMICS Industry, Transportation, Labor, Finance. . .	RESEARCH PROGRAM AND GUIDANCE	PREVOCATIONAL INSTRUCTION	**EDUCATION** Teacher-Training. . .
EDUCATION Child Welfare, Vocational Guidance. . .		EDUCATIONAL LEADERSHIP	**COMMERCE** Business Training. . .
RURAL SOCIAL ECONOMICS County Government, Rural Problems. . .	ANALYSIS AND PUBLICATION OF RESULTS	COLLEGE AND UNIVERSITY TEACHING	**MEDICINE** Public Health. . .
SOCIOLOGY Community, Race, Industry, General Social Problems. . .	CONFERENCE OF SOUTHERN SOCIAL SCIENCE TEACHERS	CITY AND COUNTY GOVERNMENT	**LAW** Social Legislation. . . **ENGINEERING** Town Planning. . .
PSYCHOLOGY Child Welfare, Mental Tests. . .	SOUTHERN RECRUITING GROUP OF ONE HUNDRED	GENERAL PUBLIC ADMINISTRATION	**PUBLIC WELFARE** Social Work. . . **CHILD WELFARE STATION** Child Welfare. . .
JOURNALISM Social Attitudes and the Newspaper. . .	INDUSTRIAL CLEARING COMMITTEE	SOCIAL WORK SOCIAL ENGINEERING	**EXTENSION DIVISION** Institutes. . .
LAW Social Legislation, Municipal Corporations. . .	COLONY OR APARTMENT HOUSING PLAN	BUSINESS ADMINISTRATION	**CAROLINA PLAYMAKERS** Community Drama. . .
LIBRARY Reading Problems, Source Material. . .	FIELD VISITS TO SOUTHERN UNIVERSITIES	SOCIALIZED LAW	**BUREAU OF VOCATIONAL GUIDANCE** Orientation. . .
ENGLISH The Folk Life and Literature. . .		PUBLIC HEALTH	**STATE DEPARTMENT OF PUBLIC WELFARE** Field Work. . .
BUREAU OF EDUCATIONAL RESEARCH School Research. . .	A REGIONAL CENTER FOR INTERNESHIPS FROM WHICH RESEARCH SPECIALISTS, TEACHERS OF SOCIAL SCIENCE, SOCIAL WORKERS AND PUBLIC OFFICIALS MAY BE SUPPLIED CONSISTENTLY TO THE SOUTH.		**STATE DEPARTMENT OF HEALTH** Nursing Program. . .
JOURNAL OF SOCIAL FORCES Recruiting and Publication. . .			**STATE DEPARTMENT OF AGRICULTURE** Demonstration. . .
THE UNIVERSITY PRESS			**STATE DEPARTMENT OF EDUCATION** Practice Teaching. . .
			STATE ECONOMIC AND GEOLOGIC SURVEY Surveys. . .
			STATE HIGHWAY COMMISSION

CONTRIBUTIONS TO SOCIAL DISCOVERY AND
TECHNIQUE WITH PERMANENT EFFORTS TOWARD
LARGER INQUIRIES INTO SOCIAL PROGRESS AND SOCIAL VALUES

CHAPTER 2

The First Decade:
Struggle and Growth

When Howard W. Odum moved from Georgia to North Carolina in 1920, he was moving from a southern state that was racing toward industrialization to one that was just beginning to stir from a long period of stagnation. He was moving from a rapidly growing metropolitan area to a small village called Chapel Hill, the seat of an institution that was in the midst of its struggle to become a modern state university. To understand the climate of opinion in which Odum would try to realize his dreams for the South, and especially his hope for creating a social science research center, it is necessary to take a look at North Carolina and Chapel Hill in the 1920s.

North Carolina in the Twenties

At the close of the American Revolution, North Carolina was the third most populous state in the country, but geography had made it a state less favored than its neighbors and destined it to play a declining role in the competition for population and commerce. After the opening of the lower South and the West for American enterprise, North Carolina was drained of its surplus population and much of its wealth. In time it came to be called "the Rip van Winkle of the nation." Robert Strange, a North Carolina political leader in the late antebellum period, pointed to some of the causes of this backwardness in an address at Wilmington in 1850: "Our wide extent of territory, and sparseness of population, together with those geographical disadvantages which prevent that speedy interchange of sentiment between one portion and another of the people, enjoyed by other states, renders it necessarily very slow in collecting, and, therefore, in expressing, the public sentiment of the State."[1] North Carolina was a landlocked region with a preponderance of small farms, and consequently it was a poor state, said Strange, but he believed that this did not mean that her people were "deficient in moral, physical, and intellectual resources.'' The state needed more industry, he thought, and pointing to one of the few manufacturing enterprises at that time, he declared that the sight of a piece of tweed manufactured at the Rock Island Factory in Mecklenburg County was enough to make ''our North Carolina blood boil with ecstacy.''[2] There were indeed some signs—new cotton mills and railroad construction, for example—that North Carolina was on the move, but the Civil War brought industrialization to a halt. Reconstruction bred an era of despair, and another forty years or so were needed before ''Old Rip'' would wake up and move forward again.

One consequence of North Carolina's geography and history was an intense sectionalism.[3] The east, an area of plantation lands where slavery had been concentrated, was long the center of financial and political power. The Piedmont was predominantly an area of small slaveholdings, small independent farmers, and small industrial enterprises based on water power. The mountain area was isolated, sparsely settled by people who were individualistic and self-reliant. Each section had its own interests and values. Their differences were still strong when Odum came to Chapel Hill in 1920, and even today sectional rivalries in North Carolina politics and economic affairs have not disappeared.

North Carolinians were deeply religious, and most citizens were affiliated with a protestant religious denomination. The church was by far the most important community institution. Although religion was at times a divisive force, it was on balance a very cohesive factor because there was strong agreement on basic religious beliefs. Those beliefs were generally rigid and conservative, based on the complete acceptance of the Holy Scriptures as the literal word of God. To be called ''atheist'' was the worst epithet which could be hurled at an enemy. Howard Odum was to have that barb thrown at him many times.

In 1920, on any measure of economic, educational, and cultural well-being, North Carolina stood near the bottom of the forty-eight states. It was predominantly rural and agricultural, and the majority of its people were poor. Nearly 80 percent of the population lived in rural areas, and the largest city in the state, Charlotte, had only 45,000 residents. Sixty-four percent of the land area was in farms, compared to 50 percent for the nation and 62 percent for the South. Almost half of the population was engaged in agriculture, and the average farm contained less than fifty acres. In the cotton and tobacco areas, Negro farmers were typically sharecroppers on white-owned land, and they eked out a precarious existence. Statewide, 71 percent of all nonwhite farm operators were tenants, and nine-tenths of these were in the lowly sharecropper category.[4]

Per capita income in the state in the late 1920s was only $394, as compared with $424 for the South and $703 for the nation.[5] Almost three-fourths of all employed workers were men. The few white women who were employed in industry were mostly in textile and tobacco factories, where they sometimes worked as long as fourteen hours a day for ten to fifteen cents an hour. As for black women, a few found factory employment in the least desirable jobs in tobacco, but nine-tenths of nonfarm black women could expect no employment except in domestic service, where wages were the lowest of all. The rigid race-caste system confined Negro workers, male and female, to the bottom of the economic ladder.

The school system reflected the general poverty in the state. Rural schools of one or two rooms were still common in 1920, and many areas had no high school facilities. Illiteracy was high—8 percent among whites and 25 percent among nonwhites. The statewide average of 13 percent was two points higher than the rate for the South and over twice as high as the national rate of 6 percent.[6]

The industrial growth that would transform the state in the ensuing fifty years was in the making, but wages, hours, and working conditions were substandard, sometimes inhuman. Industrial leaders were typically conservative men with a deep religious orientation who saw themselves as benevolent providers of work, food, and shelter for laborers who might otherwise starve. They sincerely believed that labor unions were godless organizations that were a menace to them and to the welfare of their workers.

But the picture was not entirely dismal. North Carolina in 1920 was beginning to stir, beginning to think of itself as a "progressive" state. Its leaders were talking about the importance of better schools, better roads, more industry, and social welfare "reforms." When Odum arrived in 1920, he would see the promising signs of change: new schools, new factories, the beginnings of a system of paved highways, and especially an intellectual ferment at the University of North Carolina.[7]

The University Community

The growing spirit of progress in North Carolina owed much of its stimulus to educational leaders. At the turn of the century, Edwin A. Alderman, president of the University, and Charles D. McIver, president of the State Normal and Industrial Institute for Women, at Greensboro, both of whom were eloquent orators, had visited every corner of the state, speaking on "the spirit of the New South" and the importance of education in building a brighter future for North Carolina. Edward Kidder Graham, who was president of the University from 1915 to 1918, continued the effort to enlarge the role of the University in the state.[8] The people became aware of their university as they had never been before, and they were proud of it. Graham's successor was the dynamic and liberal-minded young Harry W. Chase, Odum's friend and fellow student at Clark University. Odum was now convinced that the University of North Carolina was the place on which he wanted to stake his future.

Chapel Hill must have appeared to Odum in 1920 as a mere "wide place in the road." It was rich in the natural beauty of its great oaks, poplars, and elms, its abundant dogwoods and redbuds, and its lovely old buildings and stone walls, but it lacked many of the amenities of comfortable living. In 1920 it had no paved streets or sidewalks, and it could not boast one first-rate hotel, restaurant, grocery, or clothing store. Telephone service was haphazard; street lighting was poor. Some families still had their own wells and outhouses, some were converting stables and carriage houses into garages or apartments, and at least one professor still kept poultry, a horse, and a cow on his premises. The professors—the aristocracy of the village—lived on East Franklin Street and its environs. Here many of the houses were old and in need of paint, but vine-covered porches and plentiful shrubbery bestowed an air of quiet gentility. When Howard Odum bought a tract of land and built a house on Pittsboro Road only half a mile south of the campus, it was whispered about that he had moved to "the wrong side of the tracks."[9] For entertainment there was one small movie theater and an occasional concert at the University. Social life was intense but somewhat limited. There were quite a few avid bridge players, and dinners, teas, and receptions were frequent affairs. "Dining out" was virtually unknown in the village, for there was no suitable place to go and there would not be until the Carolina Inn was built in 1924, the year of the Institute's birth.

Chapel Hill in 1920 was indeed a village—small, isolated, provincial and easy-going, a place where everyone knew everyone else and where the fine art of gossip was the most reliable way of spreading the news. But soon several changes put an end to Chapel Hill's isolation. In 1921 the road to Durham, twelve miles to the northeast, was paved. It was a narrow strip of concrete that came up East Franklin Street and ended in the middle of the village. Now one could drive the thirty-seven miles to Raleigh or the sixty miles to Greensboro on paved roads by first going through Durham. Later, when the "short cuts" were paved, these distances became reduced to twenty-nine miles and fifty miles respectively. In 1923 Louis Graves started the *Chapel Hill Weekly*, a newspaper that would soon gain renown as a unique Chapel Hill institution. When the Carolina Inn opened in December 1924, it provided gracious and modern accommodations that quickly became a favorite stopping place for alumni, guests of the University, and tourists. After these changes—the highway, the newspaper, and the Carolina Inn—the village would never be the same again.

As for the University, it too was small and provincial. In 1920 it had fewer than two thousand students and a faculty of about one hundred. The academic strength of the University lay mostly in such old-line departments as mathematics, chemistry, zoology, geology, classics, English, and philosophy. In the social sciences, the Department of History and Government was achieving some repute. The Department of Economics was in its infancy, and the Department of Sociology was just being organized. In the University community there were factions and cleavages which, while not virulent, were often quite evident: between classicists and modernists, old-timers and newcomers, natives and outsiders, faculty and townspeople, and especially between the old established departments and young upstarts like Odum's Department of Sociology and his School of Public Welfare. Many on the faculty shared the popular conception of sociology as a meddling, reformist, "socialistic" discipline.

Odum's task was further complicated by the circumstances under which he began his work at Chapel Hill. As was mentioned in chapter 1, he began during the summer of 1920 with a series of special institutes for social workers and Red Cross secretaries under the sponsorship of the American Red Cross. This brought to the campus a group of young women, some of whom had served in the Red Cross during World War I.[10] They were not accustomed to the quiet and conventional ways of the village. They soon became bored and resorted to behavior that was considered "unladylike"—laughing, singing, and playing leapfrog over the fireplugs on Franklin Street. It was said that some of them even smoked cigarettes in public! Soon the "welfare girls" were being called "Odum's hell-fire girls," a label that hung on for years. Odum found it difficult to break through these popular notions and to explain to faculty colleagues exactly what he was trying to do. Some of his colleagues never became reconciled to his presence, and for many years they made him the butt of jokes and sarcastic comments in their classrooms. Odum's strategy was to ignore those who misunderstood him and to go ahead with his work with the help of those who did understand him—men like President Chase, E. C. Branson, and L. R. Wilson. In the end Odum prevailed, but in the beginning the going was rough. He often referred to his embarrassments and setbacks as his "sufferings." To his close associates he would sometimes say, "You have to expect to do some suffering in this kind of job, but it is good for you. It makes you show what kind of stuff you are made of."

In the summer of 1924 when Guy and Guion Johnson were preparing to set out from Texas for North Carolina to join the new Institute for Research in Social Science, their ardor was dampened by the comments of a visitor, Joseph K. Hart, who had come to lecture at Baylor College for Women. Hart, who was nationally known as an editor of *Survey*, had recently visited Chapel Hill. On learning of the Johnsons' plans, he said: "I think you'll be unhappy in Chapel Hill. It is a dusty, sleepy little town, and the University is small. The University runs the town because it owns the public utilities and the laundry. Everyone knows everyone else in the village, and there is a lot of gossip. As for this man Odum, he's not going to last long. He stays up all night writing and then goes to give lectures the next morning with practically no sleep. He has too many projects going at the same time. No man can endure this kind of strain, and I'm convinced that Odum will soon develop permanent fatigue."[11] During their first weeks in Chapel Hill, the Johnsons often had occasion to wonder whether Hart might not have been right. It would be quite a while before they were convinced that Chapel Hill was "the Southern part of heaven" and that they could work with a man who set the kind of pace that Odum did.

Delicate Areas: Religion, Labor, and Race

It was into this setting, in the state and the University community, that the Institute was born in 1924. The state's conservative attitudes, especially in the areas of religion, labor, and race, were potential hazards to the Institute's program of objective research on social problems. A few examples of conflicts arising in these delicate areas will help to make clear the social and intellectual climate in which the Institute functioned in its early years.

The attacks on Odum's new journal, *Social Forces*, which are described in the next section, were indicative of the widespread resistance to any ideas that challenged the conservative religious beliefs held by people throughout the state. One aspect of this resistance was the campaign that was mounted in a number of states during the 1920s to prevent the teaching of the theory of evolution in the schools. During the Institute's first year Tennessee passed a law prohibiting such teaching in the public schools, and fundamentalists in North Carolina almost succeeded in their efforts to have a similar law enacted. It was only after hundreds of opponents of Representative D. Scott Poole's bill jammed the House of the General Assembly at the crucial session on February 17, 1925, that the antievolution measure was defeated. President Chase had stirred opposition to the bill in a dramatic appeal for intellectual freedom.

A few months later the notorious Scopes trial made Tennessee the laughingstock of the nation. Scopes was convicted for teaching the theory of evolution, and North Carolina conservatives resolved to try again. Representative Poole introduced a bill in the next General Assembly (1927) that would have made it unlawful to teach "any doctrine or theory of evolution, which contradicts or denies the divine origin of man or the universe, as taught in the Holy Bible." After a lengthy hearing, the bill was soundly defeated in committee, thus ending the hopes of the antievolutionists.[13] However, the basic conservative climate continued as a part of the intellectual environment in which the Institute and the University had to function.

In the area of labor and industrial relations, which became one of the important early concerns of the Institute, the situation was also delicate. Industrial leaders were so accustomed to running their domains in a paternalistic and authoritarian fashion that they reacted negatively to any suggestion that there might be problems of wages, child labor, and working conditions which ought to be studied. Any criticism of the status quo was promptly branded as "socialistic" and the work of "outside agitators." The Institute's first ventures into research in the textile and tobacco industries had unpleasant consequences for the Institute and for the University. These episodes are described in chapter 7.

As for race relations, which was probably the most delicate subject of all, the negative attitudes that prevailed were not called forth in full force immediately. Odum's plan of concentrating race studies on Negro folk songs and folk narratives in the Institute's early program was a fortunate one, since there was a long-standing tradition of popular interest in such studies. In other words, these studies were more or less "safe." From the beginning, however, there were minor incidents on the racial front. When Odum and Guy Johnson first began to correspond with some of the Negro leaders in the state, they sometimes had to reassure a secretary at the Institute that it was quite all right to address such people as "Mr." or "Mrs." when typing letters and envelopes. When they brought Negro visitors to speak to their classes, they were criticized by the more conservative faculty members. In 1927 James Weldon Johnson, the distinguished Negro poet and journalist, was invited by the student-sponsored Institute of Human Relations to speak at the University, and Odum was asked to introduce him. When he addressed the speaker as "Mr. Johnson," he was mortified to see a member of the Institute's Board of Governors get up and stalk out of Memorial Hall.[14] The next day he was still more embarrassed to discover that one of the Institute's research assistants had joined with a group of irate students who wanted to run James Weldon Johnson out of town.[15] Fortunately the group did not muster enough support to carry out their plan.

It was not until the early 1930s, when Odum and Guy Johnson began to move their researches more directly into the area of race relations, that strong resentment was aroused. Both men then began to receive letters of complaint, some of which were anonymous and threatening, and the president of the University also began to receive protests concerning the "subversive" racial ideas being promoted by the Institute and the Department of Sociology.

Fortunately, these complaints remained manageable, as few of them reached the stage of public awareness, but an incident occurred in November 1931 that caused prolonged turmoil. Johnson had learned that the young black poet, Langston Hughes, was making a tour of the South, and, in keeping with his practice of inviting Negro guests to speak to his class on the Negro, he invited Hughes to visit the campus and make several talks. Hughes accepted, and Johnson raised a modest honorarium for him from faculty colleagues. Hughes spent a busy day at the University addressing Johnson's sociology class, an English class, the Carolina Playmakers, and a large evening audience in Gerrard Hall. His listeners were delighted with his poems and his witty observations on his recent trip to Europe, and his visit was regarded as a constructive event on the campus.

A few days later the picture was entirely different. In Chapel Hill at the time, a small literary periodical with leftish leanings, called *Contempo*, was being published by two young men, Milton Abernethy and Anthony Butitta, who had formerly been students at the University. They had obtained from Langston Hughes two brief and undistinguished pieces for publication in *Contempo*—one was an irreverent little poem about Christ and the other a sarcastic comment on Alabama's then notorious Scottsboro case—and they published these pieces on the day of Hughes's arrival, taking care to spread free copies about the campus and to alert the press to Hughes's visit and his contributions to *Contempo*. In a few days the state was in turmoil. The general impression was that Hughes had read blasphemous poems and insulted white womanhood in his talks at the University and that the offending pieces had been published in a student newspaper with the full knowledge and consent of the University administration. Letters, telegrams, petitions, and delegations poured into the president's office, demanding explanations, apologies, and the firing of whoever was responsible for bringing Hughes to the campus. Johnson went to Frank P. Graham, who had become president in 1930, and said: "I started all of this trouble by asking Hughes to come and speak. I didn't consult you or Dean House, so the administration knew nothing about it. I am the one who should take the blame." Graham replied, "No, you must stay out of the line of fire. If you are identified, you would be vulnerable, because they could hound you personally until you reach the point of thinking that you should resign in order to restore peace to the University. As president, I can take the fire better than you can. My answer to all of the complaints is simply that the University must stand up for academic freedom and that I take full responsibility for allowing Hughes to appear on the campus."

The affair raged for months, then subsided but revived intermittently for several years. In 1941, ten years after the event, President Graham received a blistering communication from a group of ministers in South

Carolina who had just learned of the Hughes episode! His answer was the same as it had been in 1931. Because of Graham's courage in handling it, the affair did no visible damage to the Institute or its staff members, but it was a vivid reminder of the delicate milieu in which the Institute operated in those days.[16]

Social Forces under Attack

In November 1922, two years after arriving in Chapel Hill, Odum published the first issue of his social science periodical, the *Journal of Social Forces*. He usually called it "the Journal," but three years later the name was simplified to *Social Forces*. It was soon to be the object of bitter attacks and it occasionally suffered from financial anemia, but it eventually became one of the "big three" sociological journals of the world.

Odum had visualized the *Journal of Social Forces* not only as a medium for promoting his new School of Public Welfare and later his research center, but also as a voice that would shake the South out of its lethargy, arouse and solidify the liberals, and lead the way to what H. L. Mencken called a "war of liberation" against southern backwardness. Odum set forth the purpose of the *Journal* in an editorial in the first issue. Its "primary objective" was "to build well for North Carolina, and to become a Southern medium of study and expression," but also it was intended to appeal to national and international audiences: each issue would contain something for a variety of readers, and experts in the field of the social sciences would analyze new data on social issues, present new perspectives on old issues, suggest ways of solving some of society's most persistent problems, and thereby give the average citizen new insights on how to approach solutions. Odum fervently hoped that the journal would soon be recognized as an important new publication and would help build the prestige of the University and of his School of Public Welfare and lay the groundwork for a research institute. Above all, Odum required that contributors to the journal be objective in their presentation of data and write without bias so that all, scientists and laymen alike, might be able to interpret "the actual facts," recognize the problems, and come to some common agreement on needs and solutions.[17]

In the second issue of the *Journal*, Odum addressed the subject of the "unequal places and the unequal folk . . . in our Southern states and throughout our American life.'' The fault was not with society, but ''with the inability or the lack of disposition to have government and community services conform to facts and to keep pace with inevitable progress.'' He listed some of the forces in southern society that were retarding ''inevitable progress,'' and singled out the Ku Klux Klan. He promised a study of the Klan and said the study would show that the objectives of the Klan are ''un-American, un-democratic, and un-Christian.'' He found the unequal places to be ''in the treatment of crime and criminals; of poverty, dependence and ignorance; in isolated rural areas and in congested city populations; in race groups and foreign elements being added to the nation; in race groups already in the population; and it is true wherever there is not an approximating balance between agriculture and commerce, capital and labor, big business and community life, local and central governments, the people and leaders, extremes and means.''[18] By inference, the unequal people were those who were the victims of the unequal places in which they found themselves: the mill workers, the tenant farmers, the illiterate, the slum dwellers, prisoners who had been given unequal sentences, racial minorities.

The editorials pleased his supporters, including H. L. Mencken, who frequently praised the *Journal* in the *American Mercury*, the *Baltimore Evening Sun*, and his syndicated columns.[19] This was a time, however, when many prominent southerners were members of the Klan—politicians, religious leaders, and a few college presidents, and even a judge who was later to become a justice of the United States Supreme Court. It was a time when the nation thought that the Grandfather Clauses and *Plessy* v. *Ferguson* had forever settled the Negro problem, when poverty was thought to be the direct result of laziness, the death penalty a wholesome deterrent to crime, and low wages the necessary concomitant of southern economic progress. These powerful social forces would not for long submit to such frontal attacks without striking back.

Odum's vigorous editorials in the *Journal* continued and became even more direct with the May 1924 issue when Gerald W. Johnson's ''Critical Attitudes North and South'' launched a series of essays on southern problems that led H. L. Mencken to declare the *Journal of Social Forces* ''the most comprehensive and interesting publication of its kind, by long odds, in the whole United States.''[20] While he conceded that the *Journal* looked like a government publication on the outside, ''inside it is full of dynamite.''

The *Journal* was full of dynamite, both for Odum and for the University of North Carolina, despite the enthusiastic acceptance it was receiving from northern intellectuals. David Clark, managing editor of the *Southern Textile Bulletin* of Charlotte, exploded the first stick. In an editorial called "Dangerous Tendencies" in the issue of December 20, 1923, he attacked the University of North Carolina for permitting the *Journal of Social Forces* to be published there and condemned the *Journal* for listing Homer Folks, Owen R. Lovejoy, and Grace Abbott as contributors. Lovejoy, president of the American Association of Social Workers, had been listed as a contributing editor since the first issue but his only contribution had been a short article proposing that the Association's conference be held every three years instead of annually. Neither Abbott nor Folks had ever been included in the list of contributing editors, and Abbott's contribution to the journal's pages had been a brief news announcement of the place of meeting of the 1924 National Conference of Social Work. Folks had made no contribution of any sort, but he had contributed an innocuous essay on family welfare agencies to *Public Welfare in the United States*, a volume recently edited by Odum for the American Academy of Political and Social Science, which was advertised in the November 1923 issue of the *Journal*. Clark denounced Folks and Lovejoy as "parasites who have for years been professional agitators" and Abbott as "a tricky and underhand manipulator of statistics." It probably had taken Clark a year to discover that such an academic periodical as the *Journal* was being published at the University and that Lovejoy was a contributing editor. It is likely that his real concern was not so much that the *Journal* was being published but that Lovejoy, whom he claimed to have heard speak in Boston denouncing child labor in North Carolina, was being honored as an editor of a North Carolina publication. The University, wrote Clark, "was never intended as a breeding place for socialism and communism."

This was the beginning of many more blasts that David Clark and his brother, John, a textile manufacturer, were to direct at Odum, the Institute, the University, and Frank P. Graham, president of the University. The brothers worked also to enlist other textile manufacturers, their friends, and trustees of the University to be alert to "professors and instructors" who "turn aside from their duties as teachers . . . and seek to develop fads and fancies" that might prove to be of "great injury to our State."[21]

A second attack from Charlotte on Odum and the *Journal* followed a little more than a year later. A committee of ministers from the Presbyterian Ministerial Association issued "An Open Letter to the President and Board of Trustees of the University of North Carolina" and simultaneously released it to the press. They protested two leading articles in the January 1924 issue of the *Journal*, the first a detailed listing by Franklin H. Giddings, a professor of sociology at Columbia University who had been Odum's research director while Odum was a student there, of the techniques for discovering societal facts; the second was an essay in the field of intellectual history by Harry Elmer Barnes, professor of history at Smith College. To the average layman, the two essays were dull and academic, but to the ministers they were "a serious offense against the faith, feelings and life work of the Christian people of North Carolina."[22] The upheaval that ensued throughout the state subsided after two years, but never quite died down for decades thereafter. The fears expressed by Professor Branson in 1921 in a letter to President Chase concerning the growth of an "ominous" attitude toward the University as "a godless institution that offers a purely pagan culture" now seemed to be fully justified.[23]

A year after the Presbyterian Ministerial Association of Charlotte had complained of Giddings and Barnes, they again appointed a committee, this time to address a formal complaint to the president and the Board of Trustees of the University protesting an article by Harry Elmer Barnes, and another by Luther L. Bernard, a well-known social theorist who was later to join the Department of Sociology at the University. The letter specifically objected to Bernard's view that gods were mythological human creations, but it aimed its chief criticism at Barnes, who denied the divine origins of revelation and of conscience and called for the replacement of moral beliefs by a scientific system in which the clergy would have no part.[24] The previous controversy had alerted the press and denominational leaders, but they had taken little part in the first protest because the charges were difficult to substantiate after a reading of the offending articles. The new protest, however, could be easily documented, and denominational periodicals as well as newspapers joined in calling the articles a "slur at the church and its agencies."[25]

As requests poured in for copies of the issue containing the objectionable articles, Odum admitted to one inquirer that parts of Barnes's essay were "in bad taste." He did not back down, however, and even sent one of the Institute's research assistants to Burlington, the home of one of the most threatening ministers, William P. McCorkle, to put five or six copies in a local bookstore if such a store could be found, and if not, to leave them in any store that would consent to handle them.[26] He steadfastly refused to censor the reviews that Barnes and Frank H. Hankins, coeditors of the *Journal*'s book review section, submitted for publication, but he did at one time during the heat of the controversy ask Hankins if he could change one part of a review that might cause offense. He chided Barnes about his and Hankins's "being regular artists at seeing how much trouble you can get us into, when it may not be necessary."[27] Odum courageously carried through with the commitment to Bernard to publish the two remaining essays in the series, although the first essay had helped to raise the storm and had led to a demand for censorship of the *Journal* and even threatened University appropriations. He also published the provocative reviews that Barnes and Hankins submitted for the May 1925 issue of the *Journal*, and he himself wrote a ringing editorial on intolerance in the South. He had, however, in defense of the University written a letter of apology to Governor Angus W. McLean, assuming full responsibility for the offending articles, and he had sent copies of the letter to prominent legislators.[28]

One of the results of this controversy with religious fundamentalists was that Odum gave up his dream of making the *Journal* an instrument for enlarging the horizons of the average citizen. Thereafter the *Journal* was to speak chiefly to the social scientist, and it became increasingly a prestigious sociological periodical with both a national and an international audience.

The attacks on Odum and the *Journal of Social Forces* came just as Odum was getting the Institute for Research in Social Science under way. Although he never intended the journal to be primarily a medium for the Institute, it was nevertheless a convenient means of presenting research data on southern social and economic problems, and the Institute staff, especially in the early days, assisted with editorial chores. When the first research assistants arrived from Texas in August 1924, Odum put them to work the next day reading copy for the *Journal* and mapping out a promotional plan for circulation.

Although *Social Forces* received no direct cash subsidy from the University, it was published by the University of North Carolina Press.[29] The publication of *Social Forces* and subsidies from the Institute for the publication of staff research gave the University Press funds and prestige that contributed greatly toward its becoming one of the foremost university publishing houses in the nation.[30] At its first meeting, the Board of Governors of the Institute appropriated $6,000 to the University Press for the publication of Institute research. This interlocking relationship between *Social Forces*, the Institute, and the University Press grew out of Odum's promotional abilities harnessed to his intense drive to build prestige for the University, enhance his own intellectual standing, and at the same time relieve North Carolina and the South from the caustic criticism of "outsiders." He believed that the Institute would become the region's own self-critic, that through scientific study "the actual facts" could be presented accurately by those who knew and loved the state and the South best.

A Role for the Institute

The attacks on Odum and *Social Forces* led members of the Board of Governors to the conclusion that these criticisms should be countered before the Institute itself came under fire. The Institute, they thought, should demonstrate a sincere desire to explore sympathetically the gaps in the development of the state that Branson's Department of Rural Social Economics had been publicizing for years through its *News Letter*, a clipsheet that was being sent without cost to several thousand North Carolina leaders. The *News Letter* had won favorable comment from the state press, and the social welfare news it contained was frequently reprinted in local newspapers.[31]

An Institute board meeting on May 20, 1925, devoted most of the time to a discussion that Odum initiated by raising the question, "What are the major problems through which the Institute may function and demonstrate the University at work as a State University in an American commonwealth?" Odum presented a list of "the major problems of North Carolina and the South" that the Institute might explore:

Social Attitudes
Social-Industrial Relationships
Leadership
Taxation and Finance
Government
Country and Village Life Problems
Social and Economic Waste
Legislation and Public Welfare
Race
Economic and Social Organization

After a lengthy discussion, Gerald W. Johnson, professor of Journalism, suggested "the need to interpret these problems to the University's constituency in terms they could understand." Professor Branson thought that a listing of the information and services requested of the University by citizens of the state would show how deeply involved the University was in serving North Carolina. Mrs. Floyd Edmister, already a part-time employee in the library of the Department of Rural Social Economics, was employed to tabulate requests over a six-month period. Later she reported the number to be 16,000, and the Board suggested that these findings be published in the *News Letter* and that the social science departments thereafter keep tabs on requests for information.[32]

All of the ten major problems listed by Odum were explored during the first decade of the Institute's existence. The only serious attacks on the Institute from conservative forces came as a result of a proposed project on the sixth item, Social-Industrial Relationships, and they served to remind Odum of the hazards facing the Institute. These episodes will be discussed in chapter 7. On the whole, however, the Institute was carving out a constructive role for itself and was making more friends than enemies.

Introducing the Institute to the South

Even before the Institute had been formally set up, Odum had laid plans to introduce it to North Carolina and the South through a regional conference on the social sciences in southern universities. At his suggestion, the annual meeting of the North Carolina Conference for Social Service in the spring of 1924 had appointed a committee to make a survey of social science curricula in southern universities. In Odum's plan the report of this committee was to serve as the focus of discussion at his south-wide conference. In addition, the research assistants in the Institute would describe their various projects. Thus Odum hoped to advertise the existence of the Institute to the South and at the same time demonstrate to Beardsley Ruml, director of the Laura Spelman Rockefeller Memorial, that the Institute was moving vigorously in its researches and that it had the support of southern leaders. Odum asked his old friend, T. J. Woofter, dean of the School of Education at the University of Georgia, to preside over the conference.

The conference was held in April 1925. Those attending made an impressive list: the governor of Mississippi, the president and a former president of the University of South Carolina, the president of the University of North Carolina, who welcomed the conference to Chapel Hill, and deans from the state universities of Alabama, Florida, Georgia, Virginia, from North Carolina State College, and from such private institutions as Emory, Vanderbilt, and Birmingham-Southern College. The morning session was devoted to reports of the Social Science Study Committee. In the afternoon session, six research assistants in the Institute presented their projects. Odum asked Marion R. Trabue, of the Department of Education at the University, to preside over this session. The presentations reviewed the least controversial topics being explored by the Institute, and included papers on economic development in North Carolina, child welfare, county government, rural adaptation of mill villages, and rural social work, and one described by a newspaper reporter as "an especially clever paper telling about the part North Carolina newspapers have played in social change." It was an important occasion, well reported in the *Raleigh News and Observer*, but scarcely mentioned elsewhere.[33]

The plan and execution of the conference was typical of Odum's low-key approach. He did the planning and most of the implementation, but remained in the background when the time came to present the "show." His bringing William Allen White, editor of the *Emporia* (Kansas) *Gazette*, as the evening speaker for the conference was also typical of his attempt to broaden the thinking of the research staff, the University community, and citizens at large. In the years he was director of the Institute, and after 1944 its consultant and staff member, he brought many distinguished speakers to Chapel Hill and set up numerous conferences to challenge the University faculty and student body.

Growth of Staff and Research Activity

Despite attacks from the outside and the failure of some of the first research assistants to perform as Odum had hoped, the Institute continued to grow. During the first year Odum had looked about for promising young scholars who wanted to explore the problem areas he had outlined to the Board of Governors as the major ones in North Carolina and the South. One of these problems was industrialization in North Carolina. He wanted to uncover "the actual facts" and perhaps be able to put in proper perspective some of the accusations that were being made against the South by northern liberals. Frank Tannenbaum, a northern economist and journalist, had written a book in 1924 called *Darker Phases of the South* that had shocked the region with its highly critical reports of social ills. One of his chapters had previously appeared in *Century*, and the *Southern Textile Bulletin* declared that it had "greatly incensed the cotton manufacturers of North Carolina." True to form, the *Bulletin* blamed the University. "That article," it said, "was conceived if not actually written at Chapel Hill."[34]

Odum hoped the Institute could carry on scientific research that would either refute or confirm Tannenbaum's findings, and he had discovered a competent person to assume the responsibility. She was Harriet L. Herring, a native of Kinston, North Carolina who had a master's degree from Radcliffe College, and who had been employed for several years as personnel director of Carolina Woolen and Cotton Mills. Herring had actually been one of the first staff members Odum had sought to employ, but she did not agree to come to the Institute until July 1925. When she did arrive she fulfilled Odum's highest expectation. She remained in the Institute until her retirement in 1965 as professor of sociology and research professor in the Institute.

Jennings J. Rhyne, a Commonwealth Fellow in the Department of Sociology, had already been working on mill villages in North Carolina under the direction of Professor Jesse F. Steiner in the Department of Sociology and Professor Walter J. Matherly in the Department of Economics. In 1925 Rhyne was appointed a research assistant, and five years later the University Press published his doctoral dissertation, *Some Southern Cotton Mill Workers and Their Villages*, which will be discussed in more detail in chapter 7. Rhyne went on to become chairman of the Department of Sociology at the University of Oklahoma.

The second year of the Institute also saw the arrival of two mature research assistants from Massachusetts: Edward J. Woodhouse of Smith College, at one time mayor of Northampton, whose field of interest was research in city government, and Lee M. Brooks, who gave up a successful business to do graduate work in sociology and research in criminology. The following year, Woodhouse was appointed to an acting professorship in the Department of History and Government to "carry on the work of municipal research and information" through that department and through the University's Extension Division. He became one of the most popular professors in the University and remained in Chapel Hill until his retirement. Brooks also remained in the University, and when he retired he was chairman of the Department of Sociology and Anthropology.

Three other research assistants who went on to distinguished careers were added to the Institute staff in 1925: Arthur F. Raper in sociology, and Fletcher M. Green and William S. Jenkins in history and government. Raper's research project for the Institute concerned farm tenancy, an issue thought by some to be the most crucial problem facing the South. After receiving his doctorate, he became research director for the Commission on Interracial Cooperation in Atlanta and produced the monumental study *The Tragedy of Lynching*. He later followed Will W. Alexander, director of the Interracial Commission, to the Farm Security Administration in Washington and produced five important monographs on farm tenancy.[35] Fletcher Green's project at the Institute was a study of changes in South Atlantic state constitutions from 1776 to 1860. He continued research in southern history, and after several years as professor of history at Emory University he returned to Chapel Hill and stayed until his retirement as Kenan Professor and chairman of the Department of History and a senior staff member of the Institute. Jenkins's research was an analysis of pro-slavery thought in the South, the first exhaustive study of its kind in the field of intellectual history. He too remained in the University, as a professor of political science, and undertook the collection and microfilming of constitutional documents relating to state, national, and international governments until his retirement in 1967.

The following year, 1926, Rupert B. Vance, a native of Arkansas with a master's degree from Vanderbilt University, arrived for graduate work in sociology, and remained as research assistant, associate professor, and later Kenan Professor of Sociology. He cheerfully accepted for his doctoral dissertation a subject that Odum had sought from the beginning to persuade some research assistant to undertake, "Human Factors in Cotton Culture." His first book bore this title and was published by the University Press in 1929. Three years later his award-winning *Human Geography of the South* appeared. He soon became Odum's friend, confidant, and adviser. During his long career with the Institute he earned international renown for his researches in sociology and demography, an achievement that was all the more remarkable in that he was paralyzed by polio when he was four years old. He retired in 1969 and died at Chapel Hill in August 1975.

In the meantime, Branson, with the assistance of his associate S. H. Hobbs, Jr., and Brandon Trussell, one of the original research assistants, had been exploring the intricacies of county government. In a memorandum that Branson submitted in September 1924, he outlined the projects he hoped to undertake. He wanted "county court house studies made on the ground—two counties per year, if possible, by each Field Research Assistant." In the "light of all the facts," he wanted the research assistants to propose improvements in county government, even suggest bills for this purpose to be submitted to the General Assembly. One of his postulates was that "the conditions that overly tempt human nature in county officials must be reduced to a minimum by guidance and oversight on [the] part of state officials and county managers."[36]

Paul W. Wager, who had been in the first group of research assistants, soon joined in Branson's work, and in 1926 Odum announced to the Board of Governors that "the results of this study in detailed reports on county finances and organization have been furnishing material for the recommendations of the special commission on county government appointed by the Governor."[37] Twenty field surveys of North Carolina counties, "representing an enormous amount of travel and work under difficulties," had also been completed. Wager's doctoral dissertation, completed in 1927, was published by the University Press in 1928 under the title *County Government in North Carolina*. He remained in the University until his retirement in 1964 as professor of political science.

In addition to Wager, three others from the original group of Institute assistants were appointed research associates after the completion of their doctorates: Guy and Guion Johnson in 1927, and Katharine Jocher in 1929. Guy Johnson began research and field work on the legend of John Henry, and Guion Johnson pursued her study of the social history of antebellum North Carolina. Both would soon be engaged in the St. Helena Island project, as described below. Katharine Jocher assisted in the management of the Institute and studied methods of research in social science.

The first grant to the Institute expired in 1927, and in preparation for a request for an extension Odum drafted a summary of the work accomplished. President Chase sent the grant request to the Laura Spelman Rockefeller Memorial, outlining seven areas of research that the Institute would undertake: local government, southern history, mapping North Carolina's social resources and waste, studies of the

Negro, studies of the social institutions that would include social and child welfare, studies of crime and justice, and a three-pronged study in the field of economics—taxation, industry, and cooperatives.[38] On March 30, 1927, Chase reported having received a telegram from Ruml announcing an appropriation of $240,000 to be distributed over a five-year period.[39]

In a moving memorandum to the Board of Governors on April 24, 1927, Odum spelled out his thinking on how the new funds should be used. As he saw it, the Institute had three main "opportunities": to focus more effectively on the North Carolina community; to promote "the social science program at the University of North Carolina, maintaining the University's wholesome leadership in the state and in the region, and contributing, so far as we may, to the very promising outlook of the social sciences in the South"; and finally, to devise a "more effective internal organization of the Institute."[40] The opportunity to focus more effectively on North Carolina was an objective "in accord with the Institute's first purpose, namely to demonstrate how a state university, well equipped and holding the good will of its constituency, might discover new truths within its domain and make them usable to the people. . . . If now we can integrate and coordinate our efforts, it will be possible to have the Institute take its rightful place in the esteem of the state as a logical product of the University's rich heritage and ideals." These were the same goals he had outlined in the first issue of the *Journal of Social Forces*. He had not given up. Mindful of the turbulence during the first three years, Odum added, "If, in addition to such an integrated program, we can chart our course with fair diplomacy, we shall better be able to understand certain criticisms which must inevitably arise because of misunderstanding."[41]

The St. Helena Island Project

At the same meeting of the Board of Governors in April 1927, Odum recommended that Thomas Jackson Woofter, Jr., the only child of his old friend and benefactor, the dean of the School of Education at the University of Georgia, be appointed a research associate. The Board accepted the recommendation. From this appointment arose a situation that was personally distressing to Odum and threatening to the Institute but that later added to the Institute's prestige.

During the summer preceding his move to Chapel Hill, Woofter undertook some research for the International Missionary Council in preparation for the Council's conference in Jerusalem. While on his way to New York for a planning meeting on this conference, he was arrested at Danville, Virginia, and charged with drunken driving. Whether he was completely at fault or was the victim of an overzealous policeman was not clear, but he was rushed to a police court where he was convicted, fined, and sentenced to thirty days in jail.[42] Through the efforts of Odum and others, Woofter's sentence was suspended and he was allowed to go on his way to New York. Newspapers, however, picked up the incident, and there was consternation in New York, where the International Missionary Council had an office and where Thomas Jesse Jones, educational secretary of the Phelps-Stokes Fund, was participating in planning the Jerusalem Conference, in Chapel Hill, where Woofter was soon to join the Institute staff, and in Atlanta, where he had recently been employed with the Commission on Inter-racial Cooperation.[43] In Chapel Hill at least one member of the Institute's Board of Governors declared that he would never consent to Woofter's coming to the University.[44]

To relieve the tension and convert a catastrophe into an asset, Woofter's three most influential friends—Odum of Chapel Hill, Thomas Jesse Jones of New York, and Will W. Alexander of Atlanta—met in Greensboro, North Carolina, to seek a solution to the situation.[45] The day following the meeting, Odum wrote to Alexander, "We had one of the most satisfactory conferences yesterday I ever attended, and my only point is to make out of the accident an asset, and we must not let anything cripple us in our plan to turn it into the biggest possible solution."[46] A few days earlier he had written to Beardsley Ruml of the Laura Spelman Rockefeller Memorial, who had only recently informed Odum that a second grant for the Institute had been approved, and with whom Odum was still negotiating for additional funds for the School of Public Welfare: "Here are clippings which are self-explanatory. Of course, the story is exaggerated, and it is one of those Greek types of punishment, but it is another in our series of difficulties, of which I hope you will have a sympathetic understanding."[47] The plan that Woofter's friends worked out was that he should come at once to Chapel Hill, live with the Odums until his wife, Ethel, arrived in July to set up a temporary residence in an apartment near the campus, and bring his distinguished parents for a visit to meet and be entertained by friendly faculty members.[48] In the meantime, Woofter's three mentors determined to search for a project that would take him from Chapel Hill for a year or so.

It was probably Thomas Jesse Jones who suggested a study of the Negroes of St. Helena Island, South Carolina, because of his special interest in Penn School, a private school which had served the island people since Civil War days.[49] St. Helena Island was one of the sea islands lying off the coast of South Carolina. It was separated from Ladies Island by a tidal creek, and Ladies Island was separated from Port Royal Island and the county seat of Beaufort by Port Royal Sound. Prior to the Civil War, when the area was renowned for its prosperous sea-island cotton plantations, the island had a population of over 7,000 slaves, the so-called Gullah Negroes, and a few hundred whites. In 1861 when Union forces took the Port Royal area in a surprise attack— the Confederates had fully expected them to attack either Charleston to the north or Savannah to the south—the white planters fled in haste, leaving homes, lands, and slaves to the occupying troops. The Union commanders now had on their hands thousands of blacks who were neither slaves nor free but, for the time being, merely "contrabands of war." A massive effort was launched to deal with this situation. The federal government confiscated the plantations and sold the land in small tracts to the Negroes. Hundreds of missionary-minded whites came down from the North to supervise the schools which were being set up by the government and to help in other ways in the transition of the blacks from slavery to freedom.

This enterprise became known as the Port Royal Experiment, because its purpose was to demonstrate to President Lincoln and to the world that the freedman was educable and capable of becoming a full-fledged citizen. As Guion Johnson was to point out later, Port Royal was a testing ground for the coming era of Emancipation and Reconstruction. On St. Helena Island thirty schools were organized. One of these, supervised by two young women from Pennsylvania, Miss Laura Towne and Miss Ellen Murray, who arrived in 1862, came to be known as Penn School. It attracted the attention of northern philanthropists, outlived the other schools, and became an independent secondary school that offered the islanders their only chance of getting a good basic education at the high-school level. In 1905 the founders were succeeded by Miss Rossa Cooley and Miss Grace House. In the 1920s Thomas Jesse Jones had visited Penn School several times and had become the devoted friend of Miss Cooley and Miss House.

In 1927 the island had about 5,000 inhabitants. Ninety-nine per cent of them were blacks who still farmed their little one-acre to five-acre tracts and eked out a sort of peasant existence. On St. Helena and other sea islands the Negroes, with their distinctive Gullah dialect and folk culture, had been isolated from the mainstream of American culture for sixty years or more. Now, in 1927, the completion of a bridge across Port Royal Sound from Beaufort to Ladies Island signaled the end of their isolation and the almost certain disruption of their way of life. Here was a rare opportunity indeed to study a "cultural isolate," an opportunity that should be grasped at once. Odum turned to the Social Science Research Council with an urgent request for a grant to support the study of the Negroes of St. Helena Island, with Woofter as director of the project. Soon Odum had the money in hand.

In reporting to the Board of Governors on the proposed study, Odum outlined it as "a project of the Social Science Research Council and to be the joint effort of Yale University Institute, The Southern Interracial Commission, The Phelps Stokes Foundation, The University of North Carolina Institute, and Clemson College."[50] The share of the Institute at North Carolina would be the assignment of several research associates—Guy and Guion Johnson, Roy M. Brown, and perhaps others—for "short time special investigations" of possibly two months duration. To emphasize the significance of the study, Odum added, "This is one of the most important projects yet presented."

By January 1928 the project was under way. The field work required more than six months, and the writing kept the principal workers busy for an additional year. The Johnsons were the only staff members to remain with Woofter on the island through the entirety of the field work, but others came and went—Roy M. Brown and Clarence Heer from the Institute at Chapel Hill; Clyde V. Kiser, a former graduate student at Chapel Hill who was now working for his doctorate under Frank A. Ross at Columbia University; William Muskovits, a young physical anthropologist working under the direction of Ernest A. Hooten of Harvard; Joseph Peterson, a psychology professor from Peabody College; and an assortment of scholars who made brief visits to the island. At the conclusion of the study, the Institute published two books of findings, one on folk culture by Guy Johnson and another on the social history of the sea island area by Guion Johnson, while commercial publishers brought out Woofter's summary volume and Clyde Kiser's migration study.[51] The reports were highly praised and they stimulated research that is continuing to this day. The "accident" had been turned into "the biggest possible solution."

Further Expansion of Staff and Research

In 1926 Odum had proposed that the Institute adopt a policy of naming staff members who already had obtained their doctorates either as research associates or research professors, according to their academic rank, in an effort to attract senior social scientists who would add prestige to the Institute and the University.[52] President Chase had requested a yearly grant of $80,000 from the Laura Spelman Rockefeller Memorial to enable the Institute to employ three research professors, five research associates, and fifteen research assistants. When the grant amounted to less than half that requested, to be spread over a five-year period, the Board nevertheless determined to carry through with a part of the plan. One of the first actions was to appoint Professor Ernest R. Groves of Boston University, specialist in the family, as a research professor in social science. Groves joined the staff in September 1927 and served until his retirement in 1945. In 1928, after a year devoted to the St. Helena Island project, T. J. Woofter, Jr., became a research professor in sociology and remained until 1935, when he resigned to take a position with the federal government in Washington. Also in 1928 Clarence Heer, who had a background of research in public administration and finance, was appointed research associate and associate professor of economics. By the second year of the new grant (1928–29) the Institute had two research professors, seven research associates, and eight research assistants. The staff continued at about this level to the end of the first decade.

In 1930, at the end of his own first ten years at the University, Odum wrote a memorandum, "Ten Years' Progress in the Social Sciences at the University of North Carolina," which he presented to the Board of Governors. With justifiable pride he could declare, "The University is in far better position to conserve and extend its leadership than it was at the beginning of the decade." The University, he said, had led a number of campaigns for liberalism and had gained prestige by doing so. Because of the Institute, the University of North Carolina now by far exceeded other southern universities in the increase of research and in the number of courses of study offered in the social sciences. The

program as originally mapped out had been followed with fidelity, and
he added that "a reasonable continuation of this program seems at the
present time to be of fundamental importance to the present stage of
cultural development in the South."[53]

Odum further summarized the achievements of the Institute at a
conference of representatives of university councils and institutes for
social science research held at Lake George, New York, in 1934. The
Institute at the University of North Carolina, he told the conference,
"is attempting to 'liquidate' the work of its first ten-year period with a
view to ascertaining the best form and procedure for its next period of
development." He listed "the studies and materials of the Institute"
under four main categories, and gave the number of research reports
available either in manuscript or as published volumes as follows:[54]

Economic and industrial studies	29
History and regional culture studies	26
The Negro and folk-regional backgrounds	40
Social problems and social policy	67

Projects were selected, said Odum, with a view to the available personnel, the time required for research, and the finances available. The
projects related to state and regional issues, and "priority was given to
those which would have generic value in both the practical results and
the possible methodology which might be evolved." The research staff
represented most of the social science disciplines except psychology,
which in the early years of the Institute "had been focusing upon the
more specialized physical-scientific character of that discipline." By
the end of the Institute's first decade, according to Odum's tabulation,
nearly sixty assistants and faculty members had been involved in its
research program for periods varying from one to ten years. Seventeen
of these came from the Department of Economics, fourteen from Sociology, seven from History and Government, seven from Education,
seven from Rural Social Economics, four from the School of Law, and
one or two from the Department of English in connection with folk
studies.[55]

It had been a productive decade for the Institute. A tabulation made
from a list of publications shows that staff members published 48
books and 142 papers during the decade. Odum's own contribution far
exceeded that of any other staff member, for he turned out published
works at an almost frantic speed. He kept up his practice of spending a
ten-hour day at his office on the campus and of continuing writing in

his study at home far into the night. Students who rented an up-stairs room over the study often commented that they could hear him pounding away at his typewriter any time of the night they awakened. In the first ten years that the Institute functioned, Odum wrote seven books, coauthored four, and edited two others. He also wrote a pamphlet entitled *Public Welfare and the Community, As It Relates to the North Carolina Plan of Public Welfare*, which appeared as an issue of the *University Extension Bulletin* for study by the State Federation of Women's Clubs; this was his personal effort at interpreting the work of the Institute and the University to its constituents within the state. All this would not have been possible, he often reminded the Board of Governors, had not the University excused him from a full teaching load because of his direction of the Institute, and had he not been granted a leave of absence for a year to do research and writing.

The Institute ended its first decade in the midst of the Great Depression, which bore heavily on the University as a tax-supported institution and was a threat to the Institute's continued existence. To Odum, this was merely one more challenge in the series of obstacles that had confronted him. His struggle to save the Institute from financial starvation is recounted in chapter 4. The Institute's first decade was a time of trial and error, of misunderstandings and controversies, and of financial uncertainty as well, but it was also a decade of growth and solid achievement.

During its first few years the Institute had a structure that was simple and informal. Although Odum was its actual director, he did not own that title, and he was content at first to be known merely as secretary of the Board of Governors. Time and experience, however, showed the need for what Odum called "more effective internal organization." The Institute was to undergo important changes in structure, function, and management in the years ahead.

CHAPTER 3

Organization and Administration

While the basic organization of the Institute has persisted through the first fifty years, it has undergone some inevitable changes. The structure has become more complex, the functions more varied. The governing body has changed its character over the years, and the role of the director of the Institute is somewhat different from what it was when Howard W. Odum assumed the task in 1924. Positions and responsibilities have changed drastically. This chapter describes the major changes in the structure and administration of the Institute in terms of personnel, problems, and policies.

The original plan of organization, as developed by Odum, Branson, and Chase in 1924, was described in detail in chapter 1. The gist of that plan may be restated as follows:

1. The purpose of the Institute was "the cooperative study of problems in the general field of social science, arising out of State and regional conditions."

2. A governing board was to be appointed by the president of the University from among faculty members, and these members were to represent "interests and subjects rather than departments."

3. Research assistants were to be appointed by the board "with the view not of their assignment to given departments, but with the purpose in mind of carrying through definite research projects." It was required that assistants already have a graduate degree or one full year of research experience. Appointments would be for one year, subject to renewal, and assistants would receive a stipend of up to $1500 a year. They might teach one course a year with the approval of their supervising professors, and they might take "such amount of graduate work as will not interfere with their research." Research assistants were to be "primarily registered and affiliated with the Institute and registered in the Graduate School."

4. Funds were set aside for field expenses and for clerical assistance.
5. Provision was made for a central office, with "a head office secretary."
6. Board members were to "prepare outlines of research projects" for future consideration.
7. Institute publications were to be handled in a cooperative arrangement with the University of North Carolina Press.

The Governing Board

The original Board of Governors of the Institute as was mentioned in chapter 1 was composed of seven members and Harry W. Chase, president of the University, as ex officio member and chairman. Since the size of the membership was flexible, new members being nominated by the Board and appointed by the president, it was easy to add to the Board from time to time. Gradually the membership was augmented from the disciplines already represented, such as history and economics, and from other disciplines, such as journalism and law. In 1934, following the reorganization of the state institutions at Raleigh, Greensboro, and Chapel Hill during the administration of Governor O. Max Gardner to form the "Greater University," Odum felt that it was an auspicious time to add members from the sister institutions. Accordingly, R. Y. Winters, director of the Agricultural Experiment Station at North Carolina State College in Raleigh, and Miss Margaret M. Edwards, head of the Department of Home Economics at the North Carolina College for Women at Greensboro, were appointed to the Board.[1]

Thus the Board of Governors grew gradually, and when Gordon W. Blackwell succeeded Odum as director in January 1944, it was almost twice its original size. Apparently Blackwell felt a need for a still larger and more representative governing board, but the details of how he achieved this aim are not available. Unfortunately, following the recorded minutes of a meeting of the Board on June 14, 1945, there is a gap in the Institute's archives for two and a half years. The next official document now available is headed "Minutes of the Meeting of the Advisory Board of the Institute for Research in Social Science, December 9, 1947." Nineteen persons were present. Chancellor Robert B. House presided. He greeted "the reconstituted Board" and spoke of "the need for such a Board to meet the growing and expanding scope of the Institute," after which he turned the meeting over to Blackwell. The director "explained further the importance of making the Board representative in order to include all groups with whom the Institute has had cooperative relationships."[2]

This is the only record of the new "Advisory Board." Whether the title had been bestowed deliberately or inadvertently is not known, but the next meeting, June 1, 1948, is recorded under the old name, "Board of Governors." The list of twenty-three members of the Advisory Board of 1947 and the list of twenty-four members of the Board of Governors of 1948–49 are almost identical, showing that these two bodies were one and the same. The Board of Governors would last quite a bit longer. Nevertheless, Blackwell had achieved a better representation of interests on the Board, for in addition to the traditional departments there were now representatives from the Department of Geography, the Department of Mathematical Statistics, the School of Public Health, the Institute of Government, the Inter-American Institute, the Bureau of Industrial Relations, the Communications Center, the University Extension Division, and others.

Blackwell had also seen the need for a committee smaller than the Board of Governors that could meet more frequently "to handle details and emergencies." In 1948 the chancellor appointed a committee to study the desirability of setting up an executive committee, and at the Board meeting on June 1, 1948, the chancellor's committee reported favorably on the idea and presented a detailed proposal for the functions of the Board and of the proposed executive committee. The Board, with its twenty or more members drawn from various departments, divisions, and bureaus, was well suited to deliberation and determination of policies, said the committee's report, but it was unwieldy for routine administration. Therefore the policy-making and the administrative functions should be separated and an executive committee created to act as agent of the Board. The Board would hold an annual meeting in May and other meetings on call of the chairman.

With minor editorial changes, the report was approved. The functions of the Board of Governors were stated as follows:

1. To determine and define general policies having to do with research activity in the social sciences within which the Institute is to operate.
2. To approve nominations of members of the professional staff

of the Institute, upon recommendation of the Executive Committee, the final appointment to be made by the Chancellor.

3. To receive and approve annual and biennial budgets of the Institute. To consider any matter pertaining to the general welfare of the Institute.[3]

The Executive Committee would have five elected members, from five different fields or disciplines, and the director of the Institute would be a member ex officio and serve as chairman. Elected members would be chosen from the membership of the Board and would serve five-year staggered terms. Professional staff of the Institute would not be eligible for membership on the Executive Committee. The functions of the committee would be as follows:

1. The Executive Committee shall be charged with the duty of seeing that the policies of the Board of Governors are carried out; it shall act for the Board between meetings in accordance with instructions of the Board.
2. With the assistance of the Director, the Executive Committee shall prepare and submit annual and biennial budgets to the Board of Governors. These budgets shall in turn and on approval be submitted to the Chancellor.
3. The Executive Committee shall approve requests for financial assistance from foundations or other possible donors involving amounts of $5,000.00 or more; it shall approve all projects of contract research.
4. The Executive Committee shall approve the allocation of funds for publication.
5. It shall review quarterly the expenditures of the Institute.
6. It shall approve plans for social science seminars sponsored by the Institute.
7. It shall approve nominations of persons recommended for the professional staff on a permanent basis.
8. It shall discharge any other duties assigned to it by the Board of Governors.[4]

At this same meeting, June 1, 1948, the Board selected the first members of the new Executive Committee: Harold Hotelling (Department of Mathematical Statistics), A. R. Newsome (History), C. B. Robson (Political Science), L. R. Wilson (Library Science), and H. D.

Wolf (Economics). Thus began the first major change in the administrative structure of the Institute. In his annual report for 1948–49, Blackwell praised the work of the Executive Committee. "This Committee," he wrote, "has devoted long hours to discussion of problems of the Institute and ways of increasing its effectiveness. The Committee's deliberations have proved of definite value in strengthening the Institute."

In 1952 Blackwell revived the idea of having an advisory board, saying that such a "committee of citizens" might function to advise on "(1) kinds of social science research which would help meet needs of the State; (2) interpretation of the Institute's program to the people of the State and how the committee itself might serve as a medium of such interpretation."[5] In May 1953, he mentioned the matter again to the Board of Governors.[6] The records for 1953 and 1954 are incomplete, and it is not known whether there was any negative action by the Board, but at any rate the subject seems to have been dropped. However, in 1952 Blackwell did establish on his own initiative an internal committee for staff planning, composed of seven members and chaired by N. J. Demerath, to help him in coordinating and planning the future research programs of the Institute. It is probable that he found this committee to be more helpful than the "committee of citizens" that he had envisioned, although its basic functions were different. The Staff Planning Committee made a number of constructive suggestions over the next several years. Among these were the establishment of *Research Previews*, a mimeographed organ that gave staff members a chance to make brief tentative reports on their researches, and the initiation of the Institute's Monographs and Working Papers series.[7]

In 1957 Daniel Price succeeded Blackwell as director. Like his predecessor, Price was concerned with the machinery of administration. In 1960 he had extensive discussions with Chancellor House, the Executive Committee, and colleagues on the need for a reorganization that among other things would aim at "clarifying channels of authority and responsibility."[8] Details of the new plan were presented to the Board of Governors on October 5, 1961. According to the plan, the existing Board, composed of twenty-five members who were deans, chairmen, or directors of various components of the University, would be replaced by an Administrative Board composed in the same manner but only half as large. The old Executive Committee and the Staff Planning Committee would be replaced by a seven-member Advisory Committee, whose members would not necessarily be members of the

Administrative Board but would be representative of ongoing research interests. The plan called for the appointment of members of the Administrative Board on recommendation of the director and approval of the chancellor, and appointment of members of the Advisory Committee by the director. The Board of Governors had some reservations about this latter proposal, since it seemed to give the director "unmitigated power" of appointment, so it was amended to allow the director to appoint members of the Advisory Committee with the approval of the Administrative Board. The plan was then adopted. The Board of Governors, which had served as the Institute's governing body for thirty-seven years, had voted itself out of existence.[9]

Since the founding of the Institute the presiding officer at meetings of the Board of Governors had been a member of the University administration—President Harry W. Chase, President Frank P. Graham, or Chancellor Robert B. House. The director or some other member presided only when the president or chancellor was not present. This arrangement made for a very close communication between the Institute and the University administration. With the adoption of the new plan in 1961, the director of the Institute not only presided over the Advisory Committee, as he had previously presided over the Executive Committee, but he now became chairman and presiding officer of the Administrative Board. Although the names of the chancellor, the provost, and the dean of the Graduate School are still carried on the roster of the Board as ex officio members, an inspection of the minutes of Board meetings over the past several years indicates that they rarely attend the meetings. The growth of the University and the proliferation of structures like the Institute have made direct participation by high University officials impracticable. In addition, the chancellor of the University has indicated that his policy is not to attend meetings of administrative boards whose actions he may later be called on to review.

The frequency of meetings and the attendance record of members are rough indicators of the participation of members in the governance of the Institute. The original Board of Governors in 1924 was composed of eight members, including President Chase as chairman. It was augmented by one member late in 1924 and three during 1925. In its first three years the Board met eighteen times. The ratio of actual attendance to maximum potential attendance was 80 percent.[10] After the Board was doubled in size, it usually met only once a year, and a random sampling of attendance shows a score of only 56 percent; but the smaller Executive Committee of the Board met on the average four times a year, with an excellent attendance record of 92 percent. The present Administrative Board has met once a year except when some special business such as the selection of a new director has called for more frequent meetings. The attendance record of its elected members is 80 percent, but attendance by the University officers who are ex officio members of the Board has dropped to nearly zero in recent years. The Advisory Committee, which was discontinued after a few years, met two or three times a year during its existence and had an attendance ratio of about 85 percent.

In summary, the trends in governing the Institute seem to be as follows: (1) The governing body evolved from the original small board to a large board of twenty-five or more members, then to a dual system of small bodies, the Administrative Board and the Advisory Committee, in which the policy-making and the routine operating functions were for the most part separate, and finally to the Administrative Board alone, thus coming full circle back to the original plan for a small governing board. (2) The role of the director in policy-making and administration has been enlarged. (3) The direct participation of University officials in the governance of the Institute has diminished.

The Directors

Interestingly enough, there was no provision in the original plan of organization for a director or chief administrative officer of any kind. It was simply understood that Odum, the man who had done the most to bring the Institute into being, was the man who would direct the enterprise. At the first meeting of the Board of Governors he was asked to act as "secretary of the meetings," and for several years thereafter he was often referred to in the minutes by such phrases as "the Secretary reported" or "the Secretary recommended," in a context that indicated he was the head man.

Finally, at a Board meeting on May 22, 1927, the position of director of the Institute was created and Odum was elected director. His duties were spelled out as follows:

1. All recommendations for appointments to the Institute staff shall be made through him, and it shall be his duty to notify persons elected by the Board of their appointments.

2. All research assistants employed by the Institute shall report to him from time to time as he and the Institute may agree.
3. All courses approved for research assistants by their directors of research shall be reported to him, and he shall keep a record of them and of the students' work in them.
4. He may recommend to the Board the dismissal of any research assistant for incapacity or neglect of duty.
5. He shall approve the expenditure of all funds allotted to the Institute, such expenditures to be in accordance with the general budget approved by the Board.
6. He shall carry out such regulations for the general conduct of the affairs of the Institute as are passed by the Board.[11]

Thus Odum's status was defined and legitimated. As far as can be ascertained, this document remains the Institute's basic statement of the duties of the director, although several of the items soon became obsolete.

Odum was not particularly fond of administrative work, but in an enterprise like the Institute there had to be a head man, and he gladly accepted the responsibility. He knew that there was no one else who could match his understanding of what the Institute was all about. He preferred to manage with a minimum of bureaucratic machinery, and in general he was impatient with boards and committees, but he recognized the vital importance to the infant Institute of having on its Board of Governors a supportive president and some of the strongest men of the University faculty. He often went to great lengths to prepare detailed agenda, progress reports, and proposals for consideration by the Board, and he was very skilled in getting the Board to see the wisdom of decisions and actions that he had already taken in behalf of the Institute. In so far as Odum had a philosophy of administration, it might be summarized in this fashion:

1. Administration is best when it is not felt too heavily. Set up a good framework, make the rules clear, and then give the staff a chance to function without undue interference.
2. Don't run to the president or the dean to ask permission to do something that you can risk going ahead with. They might feel that they have to say no, and this could set a precedent that could stifle some good ideas for years to come.
3. Be quick to reward signs of productivity, imagination, and

loyalty with praise or promotion or some other manner of approval.
4. Be quick, too, to detect the nonproducers, the troublemakers, and try to ease them out as gracefully and painlessly as possible.

Three years after the founding of the Institute Odum was able to move the Institute and the Department of Sociology from the cramped quarters in Saunders Hall to Alumni Building. At first the building was shared with the Department of Philosophy, the Department of Journalism, the University Press, and the School of Social Work, but eventually the first three of these moved to other quarters, and the Institute enjoyed the luxury of relatively spacious quarters for the first time. Successive remodelings of the building increased its usefulness. The third floor provided space for the central office, for the research assistants, and for some of the research associates; and the fourth floor, which had been an unfinished storage attic, yielded five or six offices, a lounge, a kitchenette, two restrooms, and an auditorium that could accommodate about 150 people. The high-vaulted auditorium with its ample wall spaces was a perfect place for exhibits. Gradually the walls were covered with maps, charts, and photographs portraying the results of researches on state and region, while shelves along two sides of the room held a collection of books and more than fifty journals, which came as exchanges with *Social Forces*—the beginnings of what was to become an extensive library for the Institute. This room soon became one of the most attractive meeting rooms on the campus. The whole arrangement in Alumni Building facilitated the work of the staff and helped to build a solid esprit de corps in the Institute.

This favorable situation enabled Odum to promote more effectively another of his ideas: to bring in as visitors and speakers as many distinguished social scientists as possible and give the staff a chance to hear them and interact with them. Odum's wide contacts in academic circles and his connections with eminent foundations like the Laura Spelman Rockefeller Memorial gave him an inside track on the plans of many scholars. If a distinguished Austrian political scientist, or German economist, or British anthropologist was planning to visit America, he knew about it, and often he was able to get that person to spend a day or two in Chapel Hill, with little or no expense to the Institute. Thus a constant stream of visiting scholars, some of them foreign but many more of them home-grown, came to visit the Institute.

The Great Depression confronted the Institute with a financial crisis that threatened its very existence. State revenues declined to the point that the salaries of University faculty, along with all other state employees, were reduced by one-third. Odum was able to shield the Institute from drastic salary reductions because most of its support came from foundation grants and gifts rather than state funds, but support from foundations was dwindling and its future was uncertain. The Institute's annual budget, which had ranged between $60,000 and $70,000 during the late 1920s, dropped to $45,000 in 1932 and a few years later was less than $35,000. Odum became so discouraged with the outlook for the Institute that he decided that what was needed was a complete change in its structure and in its relation to the University.

At the meeting of the Board of Governors on January 20, 1932, Odum presented a plan whereby the Institute would be transformed into "a Southern Regional Research Institute, with an independent dual board composed of faculty of the University of North Carolina, members of the Board of Trustees of the University, and others from other regions." The Institute would still be quartered at the University, but the University would have a limited responsibility, and the new autonomous Institute "could then receive monies from any number of different foundations or individuals." The Board approved the proposal "as a basis for study and planning," but took no action for more than two years. Finally a long dinner meeting on May 15, 1934, was devoted to Odum's proposal. By this time he had developed five possibilities for resolving the problems of the Institute. His lengthy presentation may be summarized as follows:

1. Enlarge the Institute into a southeastern regional research institute, with a board on which University of North Carolina members would predominate, or alternatively a board on which no institution had a majority of members.
2. The Institute might focus on North Carolina, devoting the resources of the Greater University, recently formed by the "consolidation" of the institutions at Raleigh, Greensboro, and Chapel Hill, to intensive research and planning to meet the pressing problems of the state.
3. A combination of 1 and 2, but hinging on working out a plan for extensive cooperation and coordination between the Greater University and Duke University.
4. The Institute might become a sort of service agency, like the Brookings Institution in Washington.
5. The Institute might simply be dissolved.

The Board did not even wish to consider the fourth and fifth alternatives, but was rather taken by the third, and it authorized further exploration. Actually the Greater University and Duke University already had a joint committee on cultural relations at work, and Odum was a member of the committee. Eventually a certain amount of cooperation between Duke and Chapel Hill was achieved, especially in the area of library use, but after all, these were separate institutions, one private and one public, and there was no realistic way in which they could arrive at the sort of cooperation in social science research that Odum had dreamed about. Thus the Institute's problems continued, but they were not fatal. Support from foundations, though inadequate, did continue, the Depression gradually subsided, and the Institute survived.

Odum served as director until January 1, 1944. He had seen the Institute through its turbulent infancy, through the Great Depression, and through most of the war years. He had helped to recruit a group of bright and aspiring young research assistants and senior staff, and he had seen the fruits of an ambitious program of research in the burgeoning volume of the Institute's publications on race, folk culture, regionalism, industry, taxation, county government, penology, public welfare, and other subjects. The Institute was "on the map" now, and it would endure. Odum was ready to step aside as director, and he had chosen his successor. On September 22, 1943, he recommended to the Board of Governors the election of Gordon W. Blackwell to succeed him as director. He spoke at length on Blackwell's training and experience and his connection with the University, and the Board unanimously approved Blackwell. Blackwell began his duties on January 1, 1944, and on January 16 Odum presented him to the Board. The meeting then became an informal "love feast" during which members of the Board expressed their appreciation for what Odum had meant to the Institute. When the secretary, Katharine Jocher, was given an opportunity to speak, she praised "Dr. Odum's unusual talent for choosing and developing personnel," and stated that she "had never felt or seen in the Institute any discrimination on the basis of sex."[12]

Gordon Blackwell was born in South Carolina in 1911. After earning his A.B. degree from Furman University at Greenville, South Carolina, in 1932, he came to the University of North Carolina. He served as a research assistant in the Institute in 1932–33 and received his A.M. degree in 1933. He then spent several years with two of the New Deal agencies, doing research first for the North Carolina Emergency Relief Administration and later for the Works Progress Administration. In

1936 he went to Harvard, where he received a second master's degree in 1937, and began work toward a doctorate in sociology. From 1937 to 1941 he was head of the Department of Sociology at Furman. During this period he not only served on the staff of the Greenville County Council for Community Development, but completed his course work and dissertation at Harvard and received the Ph.D. degree in 1940. Odum had been impressed by Blackwell's qualities from the beginning of their acquaintance, and in 1941 Odum brought him back to Chapel Hill as associate professor of sociology and research associate in the Institute. In January of the following year Odum "loaned" him to the Commission on Teacher Education of the American Council on Education to make a field study of thirteen institutions and write up the results in a volume entitled *Toward Community Understanding*. In April 1942, as a contribution of the University to the war effort, Odum approved a leave for Blackwell to serve in Washington as chief of the Training Section of Civilian War Services in the Office of Civilian Defense. Thus Blackwell returned to the University to become director of the Institute with a background of administration, teaching, research, and writing, and with considerable experience in the application of knowledge to problems of community organization and human relations.

Blackwell had personal qualities that admirably suited him for the role of administrator. He was scholarly, but communicated in language that could always be understood. He was calm in manner and had an easy-going grace in personal relations. He worked quietly and productively. It was often said of him that he was a "well organized person." From his work experiences and his training at Harvard he had developed an abiding interest in organizational patterns and how organizations might be structured in ways that would best serve their goals. He liked to involve his colleagues in the Institute in discussion of issues and in decision-making, and he believed in the importance of rotating the membership of boards and staffs in order to encourage new ideas and to prevent the onset of vested interests.

Several immediate changes were evidence of the new director's concern for thoroughness in record keeping and for keeping his staff informed of administrative activities. The minutes of the Board meetings were now prepared in more detail, often reaching nine or ten pages in length, and abstracts of important actions taken by the Board were circulated to the senior staff. Likewise, frequent memoranda were addressed to the staff to transmit information or to seek advice.

"Strengthening the Institute" was a passion with Blackwell. His numerous plans and actions cannot be detailed here, but the following summary will suffice to indicate some of his main contributions.

(1) He initiated a plan for Institute staff luncheons. The large lounge room in Alumni Building was fitted with folding chairs and tables, and some minor equipment was added to the kitchenette. On Mondays at noon there was a simple luncheon that had been brought in by staff members or assistants who took turns in doing the chores. After a brief period for eating, a research assistant or a senior staff member would speak, usually on his current research. Occasionally a distinguished visitor was asked to speak, and the president or chancellor sometimes attended. There was often animated discussion, and people from the various social sciences on both senior and junior staff levels who might ordinarily have no occasion to know one another now became well acquainted. Reporting on the luncheons during one year, Blackwell said that there had been twenty-eight meetings and that "attendance averaged between 50 to 55, with a high of 70."[13] The esprit de corps of the Institute staff was never higher than during these luncheon affairs of the 1950s.

(2) He succeeded to some extent in arranging turnover or rotation of personnel on the Institute's senior staff. He felt that some members who were not particularly active in research and did not need the Institute's usual benefits of clerical service and the like might well be terminated as Institute affiliates so that their places could be filled by persons who were attached to one of the ongoing sponsored research projects. In discussions with the Board of Governors it was agreed that every staff member would be asked to "apply" for affiliation each year, setting forth his research program and its needs, and be subject to possible termination by the Executive Committee, with due consideration, however, for certain old-timers who had long enjoyed a presumption of tenure as staff members. This plan had no drastic effects, but it did lead to an occasional vacancy, usually on a voluntary basis. Actually, a more fruitful device from the standpoint of achieving more staff rotation was a plan approved by the Board of Governors in 1945, namely, short-term or temporary appointments of promising young scholars as research associates. Blackwell also proposed shorter terms and rotation on the Board of Governors, but the Board responded that the composition of this body, based as it was on the headship of departments, schools, and divisions of the University, was such that

the normal changes in official personnel would make for an adequate turnover on the Board.

(3) Following a pattern that Odum had set, Blackwell enlarged the Institute's reputation as a place where there was a steady stream of visiting scholars, lecturers, seminars, and conferences. In his annual report for 1948–49, for example, he stated that among the many visitors had been twenty who gave lectures or led seminars. Among these were such names as Gordon Allport of Harvard, Wendell C. Bennett of Yale, A. N. J. Den Hollander of Amsterdam, Robert MacIver of Columbia University, Lewis Mumford of New York, and Audrey Richards of the London School of Economics. In 1950 the Institute, in cooperation with the social science departments, initiated a series of lecture-seminars on the theme "Toward a Unified Science of Man." The six seminars that were held during the course of the year 1950–51 were led by Pendleton Herring, Ralph Linton, Frank Knight, Talcott Parsons, Louis Gottschalk, and John von Neumann—a formidable array of talent indeed![14]

(4) He set up the Staff Planning Committee, composed of seven senior staff members, which surveyed the research activities and plans of members of the Institute and periodically brought to him recommendations on the future research plans of the Institute.

(5) He steered the Institute through a period when patterns of foundation grants were changing, and when the rising importance of contract or sponsored research confronted the Institute with new problems, such as an unwanted dependence on federal contract funds and the difficulty of obtaining sufficient general funds to finance the central office and the work of staff members who were not engaged in sponsored research.

(6) He broadened the scope of the Institute's interests by affiliating able scholars in such fields as city planning, public health, and social psychology, and he encouraged multidisciplinary research projects whenever possible.

Blackwell served as director for nearly fourteen years. In his final annual report he included a section entitled "A Look Back and Ahead," in which he evaluated the role of the Institute in the University:

> The present director leaves the Institute in good shape
> financially and securely functioning within the administrative
> framework of the University.
> Over the years the Institute has helped give recognition to the

University in the social sciences; has brought able men and women to the faculty and has helped make Chapel Hill attractive enough to keep the vast majority of them; has facilitated the research of faculty members and the graduate education of scores of social science students; has developed the areas of regionalism and studies of the South and of North Carolina; and more recently has helped place the University in the forefront of developments in the behavioral sciences, often using the state and region as laboratory areas for research.

During the past 14 years (since January 1, 1944) outside funds from grants have come to the Institute in the amount of approximately $1,242,626, and contractual arrangements for research have provided $1,234,171, a total of $2,476,797. The senior staff has been expanded and broadened from a few in sociology to become much more representative of the social sciences and related areas. More flexibility in staff membership has been achieved.[15]

Blackwell's talents inevitably brought him to the attention of other institutions that were looking for able leadership, and in February 1957, he was appointed chancellor of the Woman's College of the University at Greensboro. He took up his duties there in July and served until 1960, when he became president of Florida State University. In 1965 he returned to his alma mater, Furman University, as president, and served there until his retirement in 1976. In all of these positions he was distinguished for his dedication and administrative ability.

The search for a successor to Blackwell was thorough. During March and April 1957, the Executive Committee held seven meetings devoted in whole or in part to defining qualifications, soliciting nominations, and screening the nominees, who included two local faculty members and several outsiders. On April 12, the committee voted to submit to the Board of Governors the names of the two faculty members and four outside persons. On April 15 the Board met. A motion to limit the slate that would be sent to the chancellor to the two local faculty members was defeated, 5 to 2, and the Board then voted to submit these two names plus four from outside the University who were thought to be suitable but who needed some further screening. Shortly afterward the chancellor appointed Daniel O. Price, professor of sociology in the University, as director of the Institute.

Price was a native of Florida and received his early education there. He earned the B.S. degree at Florida Southern College in 1939, after which he taught high school for a year. He then entered the University of North Carolina, where he received his M.A. degree in 1942, serving meanwhile as an instructor in the Department of Sociology and a research assistant in the Institute. He specialized in statistics, and his chief mentor was Margaret Jarman Hagood, a research associate in the Institute. After receiving his Ph.D. from the University in 1948, he became a research associate in the Institute and an associate professor of sociology, advancing to the rank of research professor in 1951. He became known as one of the most promising young statisticians in the nation, and he held visiting posts at Harvard in 1950 and at the Massachusetts Institute of Technology in 1957. Hagood and Price laid the groundwork for the Institute's statistical laboratory, and they collaborated in 1952 on a revision of Hagood's highly successful book, *Statistics for Sociologists*, which was originally published in 1941. Because of his training in mathematics and statistics, as well as sociology, and his friendly personality, Price was well qualified to fill the post of director of the Institute.

Very soon after he took over as director, Price began to formulate some thoughts on the long-range problems and prospects of the Institute. At the Executive Committee meeting of November 16, 1957, he presented a rough draft of a memorandum, "Long Range Plans for the Institute for Research in Social Science," which was discussed at the meeting of the Board of Governors five days later and was revised for submission to the dean of the faculty. The memorandum reviewed the functions of the Institute, but its main theme was the insufficiency of state funding for the Institute and the importance of increasing the state funds in proportion to the expected heavy increase in student enrollment. Some excerpts follow.

> Major functions of the Institute are: (1) to encourage and stimulate research in the social sciences at the University of North Carolina and to map out a coordinated and integrated research program; (2) to serve as a center for discovering and developing personnel in social science research; (3) to serve as a center for cooperation with other agencies toward the development and testing of procedures for making social science research of more functional value.
>
> The only faculty members on the payroll of the Institute . . .

are the Director, the Associate Director, and one nearly full time research person. . . .

. . . With the exception of the three faculty members on the Institute payroll, all other senior staff members of the Institute are paid by the departments of which they are members. . . . At the present time there are 37 faculty members affiliated with the Institute, and it is contemplated that such affiliation will increase at least as rapidly as the faculty of the University increases.

. . . At the present time, the Institute has 8 research assistantships on state funds as well as 2 research fellows, 6 social science and mental health trainees, 22 research assistants, and 4 special assistants on grants and contract funds. . . .

. . . The present research assistantships are at $1,800. This figure is barely competitive, and it will be necessary shortly to increase graduate assistantships to $2,000 and upward. Before the student population of the University doubles, graduate assistantships will doubtless have to pay $2,400–$3,000 a year in order to maintain the quality of graduate students we need.

. . . It is not contemplated that state funds should meet the entire secretarial needs of the Institute, but it is felt that increased support in this area is needed as the research program of the Institute grows with the University. . . .

The trend has been for the large scale cooperative projects to increase over the past ten years. We expect this trend to continue, and, therefore, the Institute will need additional space. . . .

. . . It is recommended that one of the new buildings which should be included in the University's development plans be a social science research center, housing the Institute for Research in Social Science, the Department of Sociology and Anthropology, and perhaps the Department of Political Science, with the balance of the space in the building allocated on a temporary basis to specific research projects. . . .

The growing difficulty of obtaining unrestricted funds from foundations indicates that the state will have to increase its support of the Institute's research program if its services are to be held at their present level even without any extension of staff. . . .

One way of meeting these needs from state funds would be for the University to establish a policy whereby a percentage of indirect costs, which accrue to the University from all federal contracts, would revert to the department, division, school, or research agency responsible for the project, to be applied toward administration and other research projects not specially financed. . . .

In the most recent year for which figures are available, fiscal 1957, the state funds budget for the Institute . . . was a little over $56,000. . . . In contrast to this . . . the Institute, during fiscal 1957, spent more than $260,000 from other funds. This money came from grants, contracts, and other sources of research support. In other words . . . for every dollar invested in the Institute by the state, the Institute brought an additional five dollars into the University. . . . It seems reasonable to ask for additional support for an agency where, in the past, such support has paid off at a five to one ratio, and where a ratio of this sort is likely to continue in the future.[16]

There would be no quick solution to the problems that Price described, but the young director was forcefully putting the plight of the Institute before the University administration. His vision of a new social science building was fulfilled in some measure several years later when Hamilton Hall became the home of the departments of History, Political Science, and Sociology.

In interpreting the role of the Institute, Price on several occasions observed that the Institute was primarily a facilitator rather than an initiator of research. For example, in his annual report for 1962–63, he said, "Research is not initiated by the Institute as an organization but by the faculty researchers who are its members, so there is a diversity both in research problems and in the means of investigation." Likewise, in the annual report for 1965–66, he stated, "Research projects are usually initiated by the faculty who compose the Institute's membership rather than by the Institute itself." While this conception of the Institute's role deviated somewhat from the way it was conceived in an earlier era, it was probably an accurate statement of the current situation, in which contract research had come to dominate the Institute's program.

Price's administration was marked by other developments, among which the following are noteworthy.

(1) As the University grew in size, so did the Institute. Price reported that in 1960–61 the number of graduate assistants appointed to the junior staff had reached a new high—fifty-seven. Also he con-

tinued the pattern of augmenting the senior staff by using Institute funds to make initial appointments of research associates.[17] Faculty affiliation with the Institute increased, and in 1965–66 the number reached forty-four members, elected from eleven different departments of the University.[18]

(2) The Institute's annual budgets exceeded $400,000 in the earlier years of Price's tenure. Support from foundations continued strong and government contract projects grew in volume. In 1960–61, for example, government contracts amounted to $174,000, foundation and other private grants accounted for $178,000, and other sources of funds brought the total budget for the year to $455,000.[19] Later, because of the completion of several large projects, the annual budgets dropped to a lower figure.

(3) Since Price himself was an expert statistician, he had a special interest in improving the Institute's statistical capabilities. Three IBM data processing machines were added to the Social Science Statistical Laboratory in January 1960, and Price reported later that the machines had been used at least 3,500 hours during 1960–61.[20] In 1964 Angell G. Beza was made a full-time supervisor of the laboratory. The Triangle Universities Computation Center (TUCC) in the nearby Research Triangle had acquired some advanced facilities, and in 1966 Price stated that "within a year it is hoped that a computer input-output terminal can be installed in the Lab to provide direct access to TUCC."[21]

From June 1963 to September 1964, Price was on leave as a fellow at the Center for Advanced Study in the Behavioral Sciences at Palo Alto, California. In October 1963, the assistant director, Ruth Searles, resigned, and Katharine Jocher came out of retirement to fill the position until Searles's successor could be found. The Administrative Board offered the position to Elizabeth M. Fink, who accepted and took over as assistant director on July 1, 1964. In November 1965, Price, who had resisted a number of attractive offers from other institutions, gave notice that he was resigning as director of the Institute, effective May 31, 1966, to take a professorship in the Department of Sociology at the University of Texas. Since the process of finding a new director would take considerable time, the Administration Board asked Richard L. Simpson, a professor of sociology, to serve as acting director. Simpson, already taxed with duties of researcher, professor, and book review editor for *Social Forces*, accepted this responsibility with characteristic unselfishness and ably directed the affairs of the

Institute during 1966–67. But in October 1966, at the beginning of his tenure, Simpson made it clear to the Administrative Board that he was not a candidate for the directorship and that he would like to be relieved of his duties by the end of the academic year.[22]

Shortly before Price's decision to resign, the University administration had decided to reexamine the various research organizations and institutes within the University with a view to improving their functioning and coordination. The Administrative Board discussed the Institute's role at some length at its meeting of November 11, 1965, and decided that "this is an appropriate time for the re-examination of the Institute and for determining its basic direction in the years ahead." A week later Vice-Chancellor Everett Palmatier appointed the Ad Hoc Committee to Study the Functions of the Institute for Research in Social Science and gave it the responsibility for making recommendations for the future of the Institute. The committee was composed of James W. Prothro (Department of Political Science), chairman; John Cassel (School of Public Health); F. Stuart Chapin, Jr. (City and Regional Planning); Arnold Nash (Religion); and Richard L. Simpson (Sociology).

This committee submitted its report on October 18, 1966.[23] Its recommendations were accepted by the Administrative Board with only minor changes and were transmitted to the University administration in December. Most of the fifteen recommendations were the familiar ones having to do with the need for more state funds, more assistantships at better stipends, better opportunities for visiting research professors and associates, the development of a data center, the improvement of computer facilities, and the like. Several, however, touched on important aspects of the structure and role of the Institute. One of these stated the unanimous opinion of the committee that the Institute should not attempt to recruit a staff independent of social science departments and schools. In other words, the Institute should retain its basic structure and should not go the way of the Michigan or Chicago models of self-contained research centers. Another recommendation called for a continuing emphasis on interdisciplinary research. Most significant, however, was the theme running through the whole series of recommendations: the Institute should take the lead in *initiating* research programs, and particularly large-scale interdisciplinary programs. As research funds had become more plentiful in recent years, various individuals were finding it relatively easy to obtain funds for their studies, and the report remarked that "the role of the Institute in initiating research and securing outside financing has been diminished relative to the total amount of social science research in the University.'' The new director would be the key to implementing these changes, and the University was urged to offer ''whatever is necessary to attract a Director of the highest vigor and imagination.''[24]

A search committee was appointed, with Amos Hawley, professor of sociology, as chairman, to bring in nominations for director, and this committee completed its work during the summer of 1967. On August 1 the chancellor appointed James W. Prothro, the man who was the chief author of the report of the committee that had studied the functions of the Institute, as the new director.

Prothro, a native of Louisiana, took his undergraduate degree at North Texas State College in 1943. He earned his M.A. degree at Louisiana State University in 1948, another M.A. at Princeton in 1949, and the Ph.D. at Princeton in 1952. After this he joined the Department of Political Science at Florida State University. In 1960–61 he came to Chapel Hill as a visiting professor of political science and collaborated with Donald Matthews on a study of Negro political participation. During the year he was offered a permanent appointment as professor of political science at the University. He accepted, and he has remained at the University. The first director of the Institute who was not from the Department of Sociology, he possessed a splendid record of research and publication in the field of politics.

As director, Prothro strove to implement his ideas concerning interdisciplinary research programs and the Institute's role in initiating research. Two grants that the Institute received during his first year were helpful toward these ends. The National Science Foundation gave the University a Center of Excellence grant, a substantial portion of which went to the Institute. This was to be used for the improvement of computer facilities and related services and for the proposed Southeastern Regional Survey, which was to be very much an interdisciplinary project. Another grant, $300,000 from the Ford Foundation, was for the purpose of studying national elections through statewide electoral analyses. While the personnel involved were largely political scientists, this study also had its interdisciplinary aspects. These projects are discussed in later chapters.

During his first year as director, Prothro took steps toward the improvement of computer facilities and services as a way of meeting the rapidly increasing needs of the Institute's staff members. In the next few years his efforts brought the Institute to a high point in its potential for processing data. A new position, director of research services, was created, and Angell Beza became the first to assume its duties. Thus Prothro moved toward two of his major goals, more interdisciplinary research and improved computer facilities. He also had a third goal, the initiation of research programs, very much in mind when he stated in his first annual report that the Institute "plans in the future to intensify its efforts to generate sizeable research projects which in most cases will cut across departmental lines."[25]

Like all of his predecessors, Prothro had his worries concerning the financial health of the Institute. In March 1970, as the three-year grant from the National Science Foundation that had made possible the expansion of the Institute's program was drawing to a close, he told the Administrative Board that unless the University gradually assumed financial responsibility for the program the Institute would soon face serious financial problems.[26] The perennial problem of overhead funds was also brought before the Board again.[27] These financial worries were not resolved, but fortunately they were alleviated somewhat by additional foundation grants. Even more encouraging was that in the early 1970s the General Assembly began to make substantial increases in the amount of money appropriated for the Institute's operating budget.[28] This was due in large part to Prothro's persistent efforts.

In October 1970, the Institute was able to move from Alumni Building, where it had been housed for nearly forty-five years, into its long-awaited new quarters. Manning Hall, former home of the School of Law, had been renovated and was to be shared by the Institute and the School of Library Science. On the ground floor, and in several rooms in the Library Science area above, the Institute had nearly ten thousand square feet of floor space and was able for the first time in its life to bring together in compact, attractive, and comfortable quarters its administrative, clerical, statistical, and other major activities. Even so, the need for still more space soon became apparent. In March 1971, Prothro reported to the Administrative Board that "the new quarters are proving quite satisfactory, but . . . space is already becoming tight."[29] He had hoped that the new social science building then under construction, one wing of which was within thirty-five feet of Manning Hall, could somehow have a passage connecting it with Manning, but this turned out to be an impossibility.

One of the most interesting features of Prothro's administration was the enormous increase in the Institute's senior staff membership. For years the number of faculty affiliated with the Institute had stood at about fifty, representing eight or ten social science or closely related disciplines. Soon after Prothro became director he developed a statement concerning the Institute, its functions, its structure, and its services, and circulated it widely among the University faculty. "Membership in the Institute," he wrote, "is open to any UNC faculty member who is performing social science research, whether or not his project is funded." Any faculty member whose application was accompanied by a letter from his chairman or dean approving his application and agreeing to give him a reduced teaching load would be considered for a one-year appointment. The statement went on to enumerate seven services provided by the Institute, including research development, data analysis, and computational facilities.[30] This "advertisement," which was circulated yearly, plus the growing reputation of the Institute's computer facilities, led to a remarkable growth in staff membership, as indicated in Table 1.

Table 1. Growth of Staff Membership

Year	Staff Members	Departments, Schools, etc.
1966–67	46	10
1967–68	64	13
1968–69	69	13
1969–70	90	16
1970–71	95	16
1971–72	116	19
1972–73	128	20

While Prothro made some progress toward his goal of seeing the Institute seize the initiative in "generating sizeable research projects," his most important contribution was that he brought the Institute's data bank and computer facilities to the point that they ranked among the best in American universities. In his last annual report (1972–73) he recounted in considerable detail the operation of the Social Science Statistical Laboratory and the expansion of the Social Science Data Library.[31] The laboratory had placed "an increased emphasis on training in computer usage and its relation to sound research." Arrangements had been made with the University's Computation Center for "high priority of execution of jobs emanating from the Laboratory's terminal," and the "turnaround" on such jobs was often less than ten minutes. As for the Social Science Data Library, it had carried on seven major projects, including implementation of the DATA-TEXT system, the production of library reference material, and the building of a data base from the 1970 Census of Population and Housing. The Data Library had also acquired a system that gave it easy access by computer to a great network of data banks. The age of the computer had indeed arrived, and the Institute was in a privileged position to take advantage of that development. Further details of the work of the Statistical Laboratory and the Data Library are presented in chapter 9.

In November 1972, Prothro notified Chancellor Ferebee Taylor that he would like to be relieved of his duties as director as of August 1, 1973, so that he could return full time to his post of professor of political science. A search committee of eight members was appointed, with John D. Martz of the Department of Political Science as chairman. This committee reported to the Administrative Board in May 1973, and shortly afterward the chancellor appointed Frank J. Munger, professor of political science at the University, as director of the Institute, effective September 1.

Munger received his B.S. degree from Northwestern University and the degrees of M.P.A. and Ph.D. from Harvard. He taught at Syracuse University from 1955 to 1970, at the University of Florida at Gainesville from 1970 to 1971, and was appointed professor of political science at the University of North Carolina in 1971. His research interests were extensive: public policy concerning water resources, education and urban affairs; comparative state politics; and Irish politics and government.[32] His first connection with the Institute was in April 1968, when he was among a group of state election analysts who were brought to Chapel Hill to assist the Institute in designing its Comparative State Elections Project. As the Institute entered its fiftieth year, Munger took up his duties as director. He shared Prothro's concern for improving the Institute's data bank and data processing capabilities, and he continued to move in that direction. He also enlarged the senior staff, and at the end of the Institute's fiftieth year, the membership stood at 150 from 21 different units of the University.[33]

The Assistant Directors

The unsung heroes—more precisely, the unsung heroines—in the task of administering the affairs of the Institute are those who have occupied the position of assistant director. As managers of the intricate details of the daily operations of the Institute, they have played an indispensable role in the whole enterprise. The Institute has had three assistant directors: Katharine Jocher, 1929–59 and 1963–64; Ruth Searles, 1959–63; and Elizabeth M. Fink, 1964 to the present.

As pointed out earlier, the original plan of organization for the Institute, which was adopted on June 20, 1924, made no provision for the office of director. There was likewise no mention of the office of assistant director, but there was provision for "a head office secretary." This was the position to which Katharine Jocher was appointed in August 1924. Initially her duties involved supervision of the two clerical employees, office supplies and research materials, travel schedules and expenses of the research assistants, and the periodic activity reports that were required of the assistants, as well as handling the accounting of the Institute funds and helping with the editing and management of *Social Forces*. In addition to these central office duties, she was pursuing graduate work toward her doctorate in sociology, performing research, and lecturing in the School of Public Welfare and the Department of Sociology. After receiving her Ph.D. degree in 1929, she was designated assistant director and research associate in the Institute and made associate professor of sociology.

In time Miss Jocher's responsibilities became even larger. Since the late 1920s her name had frequently appeared in the minutes of meetings of the Board of Governors as among those present, and occasionally she had been asked to report or comment on some item of business, but in 1936 she was made secretary of the Board, and from that time until her retirement she was responsible for taking the minutes of meetings and distributing them to Board members. As the Institute grew in size and complexity, the demands of the central office increased rapidly. Eventually the central office required four or five secretaries, a bookkeeper, an office manager, and an editorial assistant. Miss Jocher handled these administrative affairs as well as her academic duties with wisdom and good humor.

In September 1957, the Executive Committee of the Board of Governors voted unanimously "that Miss Jocher be designated Associate

Director instead of Assistant Director of the Institute since her responsibilities and services together with her rank as professor in the Department of Sociology and Anthropology are more in line with this title.''[34]
Two years later she retired. She had served with three directors—
Odum, Blackwell, and Price—and her period of service, thirty-five
years, is by far the longest of any person who has served the Institute
in an administrative capacity. In his annual report for 1958–59, Price
paid tribute to Katharine Jocher:

> Dr. Jocher has been with the Institute since its establishment 35
> years ago and in addition to giving invaluable assistance to three
> directors has provided continuity to the Institute's program.
> She has contributed more than any other person to the success
> of the Institute as a research-facilitating agency of the University.
> We view her retirement with deep regret for she is one
> of the people to whom a compulsory retirement age is unfair. She
> is physically well, mentally alert, and an active and valuable
> member of the University community.[35]

Miss Jocher's successor was Ruth Searles, who took up her duties
on September 1, 1959. Miss Searles, who was nearing completion of
her doctoral program in sociology at the University of Michigan, had
been a teaching fellow in sociology and assistant study director at the
Survey Research Center at the University of Michigan. Before that,
she had worked with the Detroit Area Study.

After she had evaluated the process of administering the central
office of the Institute, Miss Searles decided upon a reorganization
of several procedures. Before 1960 the Institute had done the book-
keeping for all of its research projects. She decided that most of this
work should be handled in the University Accounting Office. Special
programs that had their own budgets and were housed in various places
on the campus could thus handle their business matters directly with
the University. The secretarial operations of the central office were
also reorganized. Miss Searles reported to the Executive Committee on
February 7, 1961 that ''an attempt is being made to shorten the lines of
communication by having secretaries directly responsible to members
of the senior staff and by enlarging the job of the office manager to
include more managerial and planning responsibility.'' In the director's
annual report for 1960–61, Price indicated that the new policies were
working well. A reduced staff, he said, was actually turning out more

work, and he added that "the secretarial staff has also contributed substantially with a growing ability to relieve the research staff of certain administrative tasks."[36]

Even so, Miss Searles, whose main interest lay in research rather than administration, found that she was not able to devote as much time to research as she had anticipated, and in October 1963 she resigned as assistant director. After serving for a year as executive secretary of the Governor's Commission on the Status of Women, she went to the University of Cincinnati and later to the University of Toledo. Katharine Jocher returned to serve as associate director of the Institute until another assistant director could be found.

The position of assistant director was offered to Elizabeth M. Fink, and she took up her duties on July 1, 1964. Miss Fink held an M.A. degree in sociology from the University of North Carolina. Before studying at the University she had been in charge of public relations at Georgia State College in Valdosta. Since 1954 she had been administrative assistant to Ellen Black Winston, Commissioner of Public Welfare for the State of North Carolina. As the Institute completed its fiftieth year, Miss Fink, in addition to assisting the director in the general management of the Institute, was supervising a central office staff that consisted of an administrative assistant, a publications coordinator, an editorial assistant, a secretary, and two typists.

On July 1, 1971, the title "Associate Director" was revived when Prothro appointed Angell Beza to that position. Beza, who had served as director of research services for several years, had come to the University as a student in 1957 and had devoted his talents to the development of the Institute's Statistical Laboratory. His appointment as associate director of the Institute was in recognition of the vastly increased importance of the data-processing side of the Institute's work.

The Senior Staff

The original plan of organization for the Institute contained no mention of what later came to be called the senior staff, that is, persons in the various ranks of the University faculty who were affiliated with the Institute. Indeed, the whole plan of the Institute in 1924 was so much oriented around the idea of the graduate student research assistant that it referred to "professors" or "faculty" only casually. The main reference was in the following language: "Members of the faculty may themselves undertake, with the approval of the board, for a specific period, the duties of such research assistant, providing the teaching duties of such faculty member can be cared for without expense to the University.''[37] This curious provision was a far cry from the structure that later developed, but it did contain an idea that soon became the *sine qua non* of appointment to the senior staff: arrangement with one's academic department for a reduction in teaching load.

In May 1926, Odum presented to the Board of Governors some proposals for expanding the Institute personnel, with the hope that the University would be able to obtain a substantial increase in state funding in its next budget. The proposals called for an increase in the number of research assistants and the creation of two new categories, research associates and research professors. The Board approved his plan. The new positions were described as follows:

> *Research Associates.* It is proposed to request in the next budget appropriations for several research associates. The research associate would rank in general in salary and status from the assistant professor to the associate professor, and, in addition to making researches in his own problem, would assist directors of research problems and give concrete direction to research assistants.

> *Research Professors.* It is expected that the policy of the Institute will be to provide ultimately for research professors in the several fields of social research, the policy being to let the salary range from the present University schedule to one a little higher.[38]

The original three-year grant from the Laura Spelman Rockefeller Memorial was due to expire in 1927, and in anticipation of this Odum drafted, for President Chase's use, the letter requesting renewal of the grant. This letter, which went to Beardsley Ruml in early February 1927, included a request for $24,000 a year for ''five research professors or associates.''[39] On March 30, 1927, the Board held a special meeting to hear Chase announce that the Memorial had approved a grant of $240,000 over a five-year period. It then proceeded at once to recommend to the president the appointment of Ernest R. Groves as research professor at a salary of $5,000 a year and T. J. Woofter, Jr., as research associate at $4,000 a year. These men joined the staff in September 1927. Guy B. Johnson, who had completed his doctorate in 1927, also was given an appointment as research associate and associate professor of sociology. Guion G. Johnson, who had completed her doctorate in history, was named research associate on a half-time basis with the rank of associate professor but without teaching responsibilities. In the following year Rupert B. Vance, who had completed his doctorate in sociology, was appointed research associate and associate professor of sociology; Roy M. Brown of the School of Public Welfare was made research associate; and Clarence Heer was brought to the University as research associate and associate professor of economics. In 1929 Katharine Jocher completed her doctorate in sociology and was named assistant director and research associate in the Institute. Thus Odum's plan was speedily implemented, and the chief beneficiary other than the Institute was the young Department of Sociology, which was badly in need of new personnel, particularly with the departure of Jesse F. Steiner in 1927.

The salaries of the persons named above were paid in whole or in part by the Institute. Obviously the Institute, with its rather modest budget, could not continue to add research professors and research associates and pay them from its own funds. Gradually the pattern in the arrangement of appointments, salaries, and affiliation changed. Salary obligations were shifted to the senior staff members' academic departments as soon as possible, and the Institute's role in initiating appointments declined. Eventually faculty members who already held appointments in the social science departments and who had strong research interests would be elected to membership in the Institute if they could arrange some reduction in their teaching load. Thus the membership could grow without salary expense to the Institute, and the Institute's salary budget could be devoted primarily to the research assistants, the secretarial staff, and administration. The senior staff member could expect clerical help from the Institute, and often could be assigned a research assistant.

The senior staff grew, but quite slowly. When Gordon W. Blackwell succeeded Odum as director in 1944, the senior staff numbered about fifteen, and in the Institute's twenty-fifth year, 1949, it had reached only twenty-one. Furthermore, the early pattern of dominance by the Department of Sociology still existed, and Blackwell keenly felt the need to enlarge and diversify the senior staff. In 1945 he obtained the approval of the Board of Governors for a proposal for making initial short-term or temporary appointments to the senior staff, with the understanding that when the term was over the appointee would either be taken over by his academic department or his appointment terminated. In the years that followed, a number of capable persons were brought in under this arrangement and were taken over by various departments in the University, among them being John Gulick and John Honigmann in the Department of Anthropology, Alexander Heard and James Prothro in the Department of Political Science, and Shirley Weiss in the Department of City and Regional Planning.

Blackwell also moved to reorganize the membership structure to provide for rotation on the staff by requiring all members to apply annually for reappointment and to submit statements concerning their proposed researches that would be subject to administrative review. The Board of Governors eventually approved his plan on May 19, 1955, after several revisions, but it was noted that "staff rotation and the approval of projects on a competitive basis may be moving away from the IRSS basic organization and policy as formulated over the years."[40] The plan had no drastic effects, but it did lead to an occasional vacancy, and it seems to have resulted in a more equitable allocation of research assistants to the newer members of the senior staff.

In 1955 Blackwell circulated to all members of the faculty a memorandum containing information about the services that the Institute could offer to researchers and procedures for applying for financial support. This move, plus the opportunities presented by the upsurge of contract research in the postwar period, made it possible for Blackwell to achieve a substantial enlargement in numbers and diversity of the senior staff. When he resigned in 1957 after fourteen years as director, he was able to report with some feeling of pride:[41]

> An objective of the Director during the past 14 years has been to extend further the assistance of the Institute into the several social sciences and related fields. As indication of success achieved in this effort, the 45 members of the senior staff for 1956–57 were distributed among the following disciplines:

Anthropology	3	Political Science	4
City Planning	2	Psychiatry	1
Economics	4	Psychology	6
Engineering	1	Recreation	1
Geography	1	Social Work	1
History	1	Sociology	14
Journalism	1	Statistics	2

There were now fourteen disciplines represented in the senior staff. This was progress indeed, yet the fact remained that sociologists still made up nearly a third of the staff members.

The Institute's requirement of reduced teaching loads for its senior members was a source of tension between the Institute and the University. Following the approval of his proposed changes in the membership structure of the Institute, Blackwell wrote to the dean of the College of Arts and Sciences, J. Carlyle Sitterson, to inform him of certain developments in the Institute and to transmit to him a statement on administrative structure and policies. In a letter to Blackwell on October 24, 1955, Sitterson wrote that he particularly liked the new policy statement relative to rotation and tenure of the senior staff, but he also took occasion to discuss the matter of reduced teaching loads. After expressing his satisfaction at learning that several recent appointments to the Institute had been made on the basis of no reduction in teaching loads, he continued:

> No one would deny the real difficulties a person faces in trying to carry on active research with a full teaching load. At the same time, as you well know, the College of Arts and Sciences is facing increasing difficulty with its present limited personnel in fulfilling its obligations for undergraduate teaching. I am wondering whether it would be possible when new staff appointments are made to the Institute carrying any reduction of teaching load . . . [to require] persons already on the Institute staff with reduced loads to resume full teaching loads. By using some such rotation plan it would seem possible to maintain teaching commitments without crippling the work of the Institute. . . .
>
> I realize that certain commitments of tenure in the Institute have been made by the University, but should we not be especially cautious in making such commitments in the future? I refer specifically, of course, to commitments to individuals for a reduced teaching load for an indefinite period of time.[42]

For another decade the matter of reduced teaching load was an important factor when new Institute appointments were being negotiated, but in more recent years the general trend toward reduction of teaching load in the University has made it virtually irrelevant. However, during the forty years or more in which the Institute maintained a firm policy on reduced teaching load, the University made an immense "invisible" contribution to the Institute by absorbing much of the financial burden of that policy.

While the continuing dominance of sociologists in the composition of the senior staff and thereby in the research program of the Institute did not lead to overt conflict in the governing body, it was a source of tension between the Department of Sociology and the other disciplines. In 1963 Daniel O. Price took occasion in his annual report to comment at length on this matter. "By circumstances of history and location," he said, "the Institute has had an especially close association with the Department of Sociology and Anthropology. A large share of the Institute's funds have been used for assisting research in that department." He then presented tabulations showing that 18, or 43 percent, of the 42 senior staff members during the year were on the faculty of the Department of Sociology and Anthropology and that expenditures for research assistance and for research projects under way were likewise heavily biased in favor of the department.[43] His comments weighed both sides of the issue.

> The data presented above are the consequences of a variety of factors. One qualification for faculty membership in the Institute is a reduced teaching load; the small number of senior staff from some departments may reflect the scarcity of reduced teaching loads there. A motivation for requesting Institute membership is the belief that it symbolizes and/or will produce or provide certain good things; to the extent that persons do not perceive either symbolic or material benefits from membership, there is little reason to seek it. The reciprocal of this is that, from the perspective of the Institute's office, faculty members who neither request nor inquire about Institute membership and assistance presumably are not interested in or do not want it. . . .
>
> From one point of view, the close association between the Institute and the Department of Sociology and Anthropology is mutually beneficial. From another, it can be seen as inhibiting the appropriate development of each. . . . It seems obvious . . . that if the Institute for Research in Social Science is to properly serve social science research at the University of North Carolina, it must orient its activities to a broader range of interests.[44]

Price's analysis was perceptive. The reluctance of some departments to grant reduced teaching loads and the lack of interest among many faculty members in requesting Institute membership were indeed factors that favored the continuation of dominance by the Department of Sociology. While the dominance was real, it was not ill-intentioned or conspiratorial. And it would soon be ended.

As was mentioned earlier in this chapter, James W. Prothro was eminently successful in his efforts to enlarge the membership of the senior staff. In 1966–67 the membership was 46 from 10 departments. From Prothro's first year as director, the staff grew from 64 members from 13 departments or other units in the University to 128 from 20 different units in his final year, 1972–73. By 1973 the roster included faculty members from the School of Business Administration, the Carolina Population Center, the Center for Alcohol Studies, the Center for Urban and Regional Studies, the School of Medicine, and the Department of Religion. But what had happened to the distribution of members among the various units is even more significant. The trends in membership from the areas most heavily represented in the Institute are indicated in Table 2, which is based on information contained in the annual reports for the years indicated in the column headings.

Table 2. Distribution of Staff Membership by Departments

Department	Year					
	1967–68	1968–69	1969–70	1970–71	1971–72	1972–73
Sociology	14	16	15	14	12	12
Political Science	9	11	11	14	16	17
Planning	9	10	17	11	9	8
Psychology	9	5	7	7	10	10
Anthropology	7	9	10	9	9	7
Public Health	3	4	7	9	11	16
All Others	13	14	23	31	49	58
Total	64	69	90	95	116	128

Obviously a more equitable distribution of membership had finally been achieved. By 1969–70 the Department of Sociology was being equalled or surpassed by one or more other disciplines. It had actually shown a slight numerical decline in membership, while Political Science and some of the other disciplines showed an upward trend, and Sociology's share in the total membership dropped from 22 percent in 1967–68 to 9 percent in 1972–73. The same trends continued in the Institute's fiftieth year under its new director, Frank J. Munger. In 1973–74 the senior staff numbered at least 150 from 21 disciplines. Of these, 14 percent belonged to the Department of Political Science and 10 percent to the Department of Sociology.

In the first fifty years of the Institute, then, the senior staff had grown from a zero starting point to more than 150 members. It had also reached a remarkable amount of diversification, as the disciplines represented by its members grew far beyond the bounds of the traditional social science departments. These changes were accompanied by a process of decentralizing many of the research activities carried on by the Institute's members, while the Institute's role in relation to its greatly expanded staff became more than ever before that of a facilitating and servicing agency.

The Research Assistants

One of the few specific provisions for personnel in the original plan was for research assistants. They were, in fact, to be the backbone of the Institute in Odum's plan. They were to be graduate students with the master's degree or its equivalent, they were to devote most of their time to research, and they were to receive as much as $1,500 a year—a handsome stipend in 1924. Their exact relation to the research interests of the faculty and the extent of their autonomy was a matter that was not clearly spelled out in Odum's plan. In February 1925, Beardsley Ruml, of the Laura Spelman Rockefeller Memorial, sought clarification from Odum on this point, because he did not relish the idea of seeing the Memorial's grant being used to provide ordinary fellowships for graduate students. On February 16 Odum responded, and in the course of his letter he referred to "our list of applications for assistantships and the type of research which they wish to carry on." Odum's use of "they" in this connection bothered Ruml. In his reply on February 17, he quoted Odum's words and then went on as follows:

> Now presumably these people are research assistants, they are going to assist someone, and the thing that I was interested to know is: what are the projects which your own Faculty group have in hand or in mind for which they want assistants. I should suppose that before making any decisions as to what men would be selected as assistants, you would have secured rather definite statements from your own Faculty groups as to the projects in which they wish to engage. Unless the assistantships are looked on from this point of view there is some danger that they will become merely another name for fellowships.[45]

In his reply to Ruml on February 19, Odum tried to defend his idea of the research assistant's role:

> . . . I am glad to have this chance to elaborate a little further on my letter. As you will see when the complete list comes to you, we look upon these assistants from three viewpoints: their own ability and training, their special aptitude and preference for certain research topics in which they are qualified, and the degree to which these fit in with the ability and inclination of the men we actually have on hand to direct these studies. . . .
>
> Mr. Duncan is the type of man which I interpreted your statement to mean you might possibly turn our way; that is, he is a man very much interested in some of the same subjects that we think are paramount and in which we are prepared to assist. Mr. Duncan this year is in every sense of the word both a research assistant and a fellow, from our viewpoint; and as such is a very valuable acquisition to us. If, on the other hand, his subject were simply an abstract one which he could get somewhere else as well, and which did not fit in with any of our departmental direction, he might conceivably not be an asset.[46]

The fact was that it was very difficult to make a formal distinction between the ordinary graduate fellow and the research assistant. Both were students, and the research assistant was often preparing a doctoral dissertation in the same way as the graduate fellow, and sometimes with less supervision. Odum was running the risk of creating a group of pampered graduate fellows; however, his vision was better than his explanation of the rationale for the research assistants. The whole arrangement turned out to be a happy balance between the personal interests of the assistants and the interests of the Institute. Most of the assistants became involved in the idea of research on "state and regional conditions" and they developed a sense of pride and loyalty to the Institute. In the early years and for years to come, they were the solid foundation for the Institute's research achievements. The very ambiguity that had been built into their status paid handsome dividends in the end.

There were problems, however, in defining the status and role of the assistants. Such matters as how they were to register, how many courses they could take, how much vacation they should have, their stipends, and the like, were frequently before the Board of Governors during the first few years. Gradually most of these matters were resolved. Assistants, for example, were graduate students, and it was decided that they must indeed register with the Graduate School, although they would be considered members of the research staff of the Institute. The terms "senior staff" and "junior staff" arose to distinguish between the assistants and the professorial members of the research staff. Also research assistantships were divided into categories so as to provide for the "junior assistant," that is, one who would spend about half as much time on research as the regular research assistant would.

During the Institute's second year there was an episode that raised, and answered, a question of policy: could someone other than a research assistant's supervising professor requisition the assistant's services in his own behalf? A former Chapel Hillian, a distinguished judge and member of a family long connected with the University, had retired from the bench and returned to Chapel Hill to take courses and to begin some historical research. Being aware of the Institute and having some acquaintance with Odum, he went to the director and asked if he could have the services of a research assistant in history for a while. Odum was taken by surprise, and not wishing to offend his visitor, he told him that he should approach Guion Johnson, who was a research assistant in history. When the judge explained to Mrs. Johnson what he wanted her to do, she politely told him that her schedule of research and graduate study was extremely heavy and that she could not turn aside from this work to help him unless her supervisor, Professor R. D. W. Connor, directed her to do so. The judge was quite disappointed that the Institute was not able to offer him immediate assistance, but both Connor and Odum assured Mrs. Johnson that her stand was correct and that the Institute was indeed not intended to be an agency that could service the research needs of outsiders.

Not all of the research assistants lived up to the expectations of the Institute, and as director, Odum was the person who was most aware of flaws and failures. He had brought various problems before the Board of Governors, and the Board had dealt with them on a piecemeal basis. In February 1927, he asked the Board to rule that an assistant who devoted the third term to full-time work on his courses and dissertation should be reduced to the status of junior assistant, with reduction in pay.[47] He was quite annoyed by the Board's refusal to go along with his proposal. However, the Board did go on record "unqualifiedly for defining more clearly the duties of research assistants in the future." At the meeting of the Board on April 24, Odum could not be present, but he submitted a memorandum in which he set forth some of the opportunities and problems facing the Institute. He cited the need for "more effective internal organization" and attributed most of the problems to "the loose organization of the past three years, due largely to the need for considerable experimentation." He then listed eighteen "apparent mistakes" relative to the research assistants. A review of the thirty assistants who had served in the Institute revealed "a very great deal of successful work," he said, but there had been failures also. It was not a matter of assigning blame but simply of avoiding mistakes in the future. Some of the mistakes involved downright abuse of their privileges by the assistants themselves, as indicated by the following excerpts from Odum's list:

> A junior assistantship was awarded to an adventuring student to compare labor organizations north and south. The opportunity was turned frankly into propaganda, and the assistant steadfastly refused to give the Institute results of [his] study.

> At least three of the research assistants have devoted full time to the getting of a degree.

> One research assistant registered for undergraduate Spanish, French, and English, thus technically devoting full time to undergraduate work in no way related to the social sciences.

> Two research assistants were on the regular staff of the correspondence school receiving pay for correcting papers, while the Institute paid several hundred dollars to have the results of the research done by one of these assistants corrected.

Other instances in Odum's list of mistakes reflected directly on the professors whose duty it was to supervise their assistants. For example:

> One or more of the research assistants had gone through the entire year without any sort of adequate direction.

> A number of research assistants have been appointed who did not have the background to do the practical job to which they were assigned.

> In several cases appointments have been made by individual professors making commitments not known to the central office.[48]

It is only fair to add that in all likelihood Odum's list of mistakes involved a small number of the thirty assistants and that the multiple sins of certain individuals were listed separately for dramatic effect. He wanted the Board to see the need for more effective internal organization. His memorandum proposed a scale of stipends based on the amount of time an assistant spent on courses as against research. These ranged from $750 for an assistant who wanted to take six courses a year (in the quarter system then in use a full courseload was three each quarter or a total of nine for the academic year) up to $2,000 for a qualified person who was willing to take no courses and devote full time to research. Differential vacation times were also clearly specified. The Board approved these proposals at the April 24 meeting. More importantly, the members apparently did some serious thinking about the need for tightening the whole structure of the Institute, for as pointed out earlier, at their next meeting, May 22, 1927, they created the office of director, appointed Odum to fill it, and spelled out his responsibilities.[49] Thus the problems related to the definition of the role of the research assistants led to the first real change in the organization of the Institute.

In 1928 Odum tabulated the number of research assistants during the period of 1924 to 1928 by the departmental affiliation of their directors, with the results shown in Table 3.[50] The distribution of assistants showed excellent balance among the major social science departments. The balance soon began to change, however, particularly with the launching of Odum's program of southern regional studies, and the Department of Sociology came to have a disproportionate share of the research assistants. This became a sensitive point with Odum, particularly when it was intimated from time to time that he was trying to "hog" the research-assistant appointments for Sociology. Actually, he would have liked nothing better than to maintain an even distribution of the appointments, but he could not accomplish that on his own initiative. The fact was that some of the professors in the other social science departments who were members of the Institute staff and of the Board of Governors had relatively little interest in the use of research assistants. Some preferred not to be bothered by them, and one wrote that "there is no possible way in which I can have my research done by others."[51]

Such balance as had been achieved in the early years was in part due to Odum's prodding his colleagues in other departments to nominate assistants and to supervise their work. But in time he wearied of this, and when in some years there was no nomination for new appointments in the departments of Economics, History, or Rural Social Economics, he felt that unless he took a hand, money and positions would go begging. With a stack of research proposals and applications from qualified graduate students at hand, he would simply submit additional applications to the Board, and the Board would usually approve them. Thus sociology came to have some measure of dominance among the research assistants, but it was not overwhelming, and in later years the rising influence of political science, social psychology, and other disciplines helped to restore balance to the distribution of assistants.

Table 3. Distribution of Research Assistants, by Departments, 1924–1928

Department	Number	Percent
Economics	8	21
Sociology	8	21
History and Government	7	18
Rural Social Economics	6	15
Education and Psychology	6	15
Law	2	5
Miscellaneous	2	5
Total	39	100

The number of research assistants remained rather low, in the range of 10 to 15, for the first twenty-five years of the Institute's existence. Foundation grants for the general budget of the Institute and modest state appropriations were the main sources for financial support of the assistants, and these sources remained rather small from the beginning, on through the Great Depression, and through World War II. After the war, however, a notable change took place. The number of assistants increased sharply, growing from 22 in 1949 to 62 in 1952 and holding in the range of 50 to 60 for the next ten years. This growth was related to a drastic change in the financial support of the Institute. The foundations had shifted from the pattern of general or unrestricted grants to a pattern of grants for specific research projects, and at the same time government agencies, such as the Office of Education, the Social Security Administration, the Department of Defense, and others, were open-handed with money for contract research projects. Thus in the postwar period the Institute was involved with a large number of sponsored or contract research projects, some of which were quite large in scope and were extended over a period of years, like the Savannah River Project, the Air Force Base Study, and the Soviet Industrial Studies. The need for research assistants grew accordingly, and their numbers reached new highs, with a more equitable distribution among the social sciences.

This same situation led to a differentiation in the status of the research assistants. As teams of assistants were attached to certain projects, sometimes living at the research sites, the need for organization and supervision became apparent. To meet this need Gordon Blackwell, the director from 1944 to 1957, designated as research fellows certain assistants who were quite advanced in their doctoral programs, and appointed as research supervisors several others who were still more experienced in research. His annual report for 1951–52, for example, listed 3 research supervisors, 16 research fellows, and 43 research assistants, a total of 62 junior staff members. As the need arose, Blackwell created other categories. The list of junior staff members for 1955–56, for example, included a technical assistant, a research analyst, and a bibliographer. Stipends, of course, were adjusted according to rank, and some of the assistants received $3,000 or more a year.

The number of research assistants remained fairly high throughout the 1950s and 1960s, varying generally from 35 to 50, and reaching a high of 57 in 1960–61. By 1970–71, parallel with the greatly increased senior staff membership that occurred during James Prothro's administration, there was a new high of 63. But by this time a curious thing had happened: the research assistants were becoming more and more difficult to identify. For forty-three years the Institute's annual reports had contained the names of the research assistants and the projects they were pursuing, but the annual report for 1967–68 was the last to do so. In that report the assistants were covered in these words: "The Institute provided stipends for nine graduate assistants from its State funds, to one from its trust funds, and to five from NSF funds. In addition, research grants of senior members provided assistantships to 23 other graduate students." In the 1972–73 annual report one sentence was devoted to the assistants: "Graduate assistantships were awarded to 8 students through IRSS State Funds and to 2 from Louis Harris Political Data Center Funds."

What had happened to the long-standing concept of the research assistant? The answer is relatively simple. For one thing, the whole orientation of the Institute had undergone a change. While the Institute had a few major research projects of its own, the majority of its greatly enlarged senior staff were people who were pursuing projects for which they had obtained funding on their own. It had become increasingly evident to the director that the logical and simple way to deal with the problem of selecting assistants was to turn it over to the various project directors; once this system went into effect, the central office would handle the accounting but would have no other responsibility for those research assistants. In addition, the Institute was becoming a service center for social science researchers throughout the University and was increasing its emphasis on technical skills in the handling of research data. Thus the dozen or so assistants whose names now appear in the annual reports of the director are usually persons who are attached to the Institute's Statistical Laboratory and the Social Science Data Library. There are probably as many graduate students rendering research assistance to senior staff members as there ever were, but their visibility is minimal now that their traditional ties with the central office of the Institute no longer exist.[52]

Growth of Professional Staff

The most striking administrative developments in the Institute in recent years have been the elaboration of functions of the central office and the growth of technical and professional staff. In the Institute's early years the administrative staff consisted of the director, the assistant director, and two or three stenographers or typists. Later such positions as editorial assistant, statistical laboratory assistant, keypunch operator, and bookkeeper were created, but as late as the early 1960s the number of positions rarely exceeded ten. It was not until the middle of the Institute's fifth decade, with the rapid expansion of computer facilities, that the headquarters staff underwent a remarkable growth in size and complexity. In 1964–65 the central staff was comprised of fourteen persons. Five years later the number had grown to twenty-five, and in 1973–74 it reached thirty-five. The thirty-five positions that comprised the Institute's central-office staff in its fiftieth year were divided between administration and technical services. Technical services claimed twenty-five positions, sixteen assigned to the Social Science Statistical Laboratory, and nine to the Social Science Data Library.

Publications

At the organizational meeting of the Institute in June 1924, provision was made for the publication of its researches by the University of North Carolina Press, and the sum of $6,000 was appropriated "for the publication of the results of the research and for the purchase of library material for research projects."[53] Within a year after the founding of the Institute, the University Press had published three books for the Institute: *Southern Pioneers in Social Interpretation*, edited by Odum; *The Negro and His Songs*, by Odum and Guy Johnson; and *Systems of Public Welfare*, by Odum and D. W. Willard. Thus began a long and useful relationship between the University Press and the Institute. The Press had neither the exclusive right nor the obligation to handle all publications sponsored by the Institute, and some authors made arrangements with other publishers, including commercial houses, but in the Institute's first fifteen years two-thirds of the seventy or more books produced under its sponsorship were published by the University Press.

The details of the financial arrangement with the Press varied from time to time, but the basic pattern was as follows: the Institute would remit to the Press the cost of manufacture of a book, and the Press would handle advertising, distribution, and so forth. Periodically the Press would return to the Institute a percentage of the money realized from sales, and this money would be used to replenish the Institute's revolving fund for publication. Some of the books sold well, and these helped to offset the losses on those that did not. There was a certain amount of sparring between Odum and the Press over the details of contractual arrangements. In December 1925, the Board of Governors approved an agreement that would return to the Institute 60 percent of the proceeds from a book after certain deductions by the Press.[54] In April 1927, the Board ratified a new agreement that gave the Institute 35 percent, but had a different way of calculating the deductions.[55] In October 1928, a third contract was approved, with further revision in the way of figuring the Institute's share and with the stipulation that "balances shall be rendered separately so that the deficit on one Institute book shall not offset the credit on another."[56]

Finally, Odum became annoyed by the time required by the Press to prepare manuscripts for printing and by the expense deducted for editorial work, so he negotiated still another contract, approved by the Board in November 1929, which authorized the publication of Institute studies "on the written approval of three readers." As Odum explained it, this would save a great deal of time and "enable the Institute to edit with its own staff rather than to pay out in cash the editing services to the Press."[57] In a memorandum to William T. Couch, assistant director of the Press, Odum had stated that the new procedure meant that "when a MS is approved by the Institute staff and three readers, it shall be carefully edited by Miss Jocher and delivered to the Press ready for publication without further responsibility, authorization, or emendation."[58] There would be still other revisions in the publishing arrangement with the University Press, as well as a continuing tension between the Press and the Institute, but the Press would remain for years an important outlet for Institute publications.

The passage of time, however, has brought about a striking change in research publication. During the Institute's first decade tbe staff members were responsible for 190 publications, of which 48, or 25 percent, were books, and of these books 65 percent were published by the University of North Carolina Press. In the fifth decade, the staff had approximately 1,600 publications, of which only 43, or 2.8 percent, were books. Only two of these books were published by the University Press: *Causal Inferences in Non-Experimental Research* (1964), by Hubert M. Blalock, and *Folk, Region, and Society: Selected Papers of Howard W. Odum* (1964), edited by Katharine Jocher, Guy B. Johnson, George L. Simpson, and Rupert B. Vance.[59] Thus, for some time now, the role of the Press in the Institute's publications has been minuscule. The figures cited probably reflect two important trends: the enormous increase in the cost of publishing books, and an increasing specialization and fragmentation in research projects and the way in which they are reported. At any rate, the overwhelming majority of research reports are now published in the form of periodical articles, chapters contributed to books, and brief special monographs.

While the Institute's responsibility for handling the publication of books resulting from the researches of its staff members has been virtually eliminated, it continues to have a responsibility for several other publications. The editorial supervision of these publications has long been the task of the assistant director and the staff of the central office. The first of these is the *University of North Carolina News Letter*. It was founded in 1914 by E. C. Branson, who assembled a great variety of factual data about North Carolina for its columns. It was circulated free of charge by the University to hundreds of editors, public officials, and interested citizens throughout the state. After the Institute was founded, it began to lend a helping hand with the *News Letter*, and after Branson's retirement and the eventual absorption of the Department of Rural Social Economics into the Department of Sociology, the Institute assumed a direct obligation for its publication. Various members of the Institute staff from the Department of Sociology have taken on the task of preparing the *News Letter*. Its issuance was at times in doubt, and in 1965 it lost its second-class mailing permit for a time because of irregular issuance; however, it was later revived and is now published regularly under the auspices of the Institute. It absorbed the Institute's *Research Previews* in 1976, as described below.

A second publication with a long-standing connection with the Institute is *Social Forces*. It was founded in 1922 by Howard W. Odum, who served as editor until his retirement in 1954, and after the Institute was organized in 1924 it came to be a joint responsibility of the Institute and the Department of Sociology. The journal came close to financial suffocation several times—Odum once mortgaged his house and his dairy herd and bailed it out with his personal funds—but it survived somehow. Katharine Jocher served as managing editor for many years and had responsibility for the details of evaluation of manuscripts, copy reading, proof reading, and correspondence. Toward the end of her service the Institute was able to employ an editorial secretary. Norma Scofield, who is presently publications coordinator for the Institute and managing editor of *Social Forces*, has brought remarkable talents and enthusiasm to her work. One of her achievements in recent years was the production of a fifty-year index of *Social Forces*. The following persons, all of whom have been members of the Institute staff and of the Department of Sociology, have served as editors or coeditors of the journal:

Howard W. Odum (1922–54)
Katharine Jocher (1927–61)
Gordon W. Blackwell (1955–56)

Rupert B. Vance (1957–69)
Guy B. Johnson (1961–69)
Richard L. Simpson (1969–72)
Everett K. Wilson (1972–the present).

Today *Social Forces* enjoys good financial health and an international reputation as a social science journal. It has a circulation of 5,000 and is mailed quarterly to fifty states and seventy foreign countries. It is generally ranked among the three most important American sociological journals, the other two being the *American Journal of Sociology*, which was founded at the University of Chicago in 1895, and the *American Sociological Review*, founded in 1938 as the official organ of the American Sociological Association. It also has the distinction of being the second oldest sociological journal in the world that has been published continuously under the same name. Its survival and success are due in some measure to the close relationship it has had with the Institute.

More pertinent to the Institute's own primary concern with research are the three in-house publications that it originated. The first of these, *Research Previews*, was begun in 1953, on the recommendation of Gordon Blackwell's Staff Planning Committee, as a mimeographed paperbound booklet. Its purpose was to give both senior and junior staff members a chance to make interim or tentative reports on their research projects, with the idea that such reports would stimulate discussion and contribute to the esprit de corps of the staff. *Research Previews* performed this function quite successfully over a period of twenty-one years and fifty-eight issues. Its circulation reached into many other institutions. In 1976 it merged with the *University of North Carolina News Letter* under the title of the *News Letter*, which now serves as a news and public relations medium for the Institute.

The other two publications are the Institute's Monographs and Working Papers series. The Monograph Series was initiated in 1957 with John J. Honigmann's *Three Pakistan Villages*, an ethnographic report. By 1974 about twenty monographs had been issued, the majority of which had grown out of studies in such focal areas as comparative urban studies, the sociology of health and the health professions, and the Comparative State Elections Project. In addition seven working papers in methodology had been published by the time of the Institute's fiftieth anniversary. The Monographs and Working Papers series have proved to be a useful service, and their publications have circulated nationally and internationally.

CHAPTER 4

Financing the Institute

The Institute was made possible in the beginning by the existence of that great American institution, the philanthropic foundation, and for nearly twenty-five years its life depended largely upon grants from foundations. The story of Institute financing in those years is largely the story of Howard W. Odum's dogged efforts to obtain grants or the renewal of grants from such foundations as the Laura Spelman Rockefeller Memorial, the Rockefeller Foundation, and the General Education Board. An integral part of the picture was his largely fruitless effort to persuade the University to put the Institute into its regular budget requests and his persistence in trying to convince the foundations that the University was matching their gifts to a reasonable degree. For him it was often a story of frustration, misunderstanding, and personal embarrassment.

Odum, the Foundations, and the University

The story of the grant from the Laura Spelman Rockefeller Memorial that made possible the founding of the Institute in 1924 was set forth in chapter 1. It will be recalled that President Chase, in a letter in which he informed the Executive Committee of the University Board of Trustees that he wished to approach the Memorial for a grant, had assured the members of the committee that "the University does not obligate itself in any way to take over the work." It will also be recalled that Beardsley Ruml, in his letter notifying Chase that the Memorial had appropriated $32,500 a year for three years for the development of research in the social sciences at the University, gently chided Chase for having given the executive committee such assurances, because the time might come when the University either had to support the research program or give it up.[1] This exchange clearly symbolized the conflict, which would prevail for a long time, between the foundation's point of view and the University administration's point of view. Odum was the man in the middle. On the one hand, he understood the theory behind foundation grants, that is, that they were for development of new programs and that the receiving institution should show its commitment to the new program by matching and eventually taking over its full support. On the other hand, he understood the delicate situation in which President Chase found himself: North Carolina was a relatively poor state, and since there were many urgent needs facing the University, a strong espousal of a legislative budgetary item for the Institute in a state that distrusted social science might endanger support for other programs. Odum's strategy was to try to convince the foundations that the University was really doing a good job matching their funds, while at the same time keeping pressure on the president to put the Institute into the regular budget of the University.

No sooner had the original grant been given, than Odum began worrying about 1927, the year when it would expire. In a lengthy memorandum for the meeting of the Board of Governors on December 2, 1925, he wrote:

> Some sort of preliminary summary and report of the first two
> years of the Institute's work should be made on December 1,
> 1926, in order that the University may consider its value
> as a University institution and in order that the Memorial may
> study the question of a new grant. This is important from the
> viewpoint of the University's appropriation as well as the
> Memorial's.[2]

The meeting was long and covered many items, and Odum's main concern was briefly mentioned by President Chase just before adjournment. Still pursuing the matter, Odum wrote in his agenda for the Board meeting of May 23, 1926, after proposing the creation of two new ranks, research associates and research professors, that

> The general consensus of opinions on these subjects is important
> now in order that the President may include in his budget for
> the next biennium certain funds for the Institute which in turn
> should be supplemented by a considerable increase from the
> Memorial, from other foundations or agencies, and from private
> grants for which the Institute may be [a] receiving station.[3]

The next meeting instructed Odum to "proceed with suggestions to the president for his next biennial budget." In September, Odum submitted a tentative budget that allocated $16,000 for the salaries of three research professors, $16,000 for five research associates, $20,000 for fifteen research assistants, $9,000 for secretarial expenses, $10,000 for field expenses and equipment, and $9,000 for the publication fund, for a total of $80,000. He suggested that the Laura Spelman Rockefeller Memorial's share should be $60,000 and the University's share should be $20,000. He added: "It would be understood, of course, that there was no reason why the University's salary of a professor of statistics or of social history or of anthropology might not count toward the University's $20,000; provided, of course, the major part of these professors' time was devoted to research."[4]

In February 1927, the Institute's Board of Governors approved Odum's budget suggestions and his draft of a letter to be used by the president in his appeal to the Memorial for renewal and increase of the grant for a five-year period. The letter proposed a budget of $80,000 a year. After listing ten subdivisions of the Institute's work, the letter undertook to explain what the University would be contributing:

> Although this is apparently going to be "economy" year with our
> state budget commission, and funds both for maintenance
> and buildings will be smaller than needed, the University
> proposes to make its supplementary contribution to the Institute
> liberal. The University's contribution will include four major
> items: approximately $20,000 of the $100,000 maintenance,
> through its present and added faculty members; commodious and
> completely equipped buildings for the Institute and Press,
> well adapted and specially provided for these purposes, the
> construction of which would cost more than $150,000 at the
> present time; the raising of a $50,000 supplementary fund to be
> used largely towards publication, library, and general assistance;
> and general overhead, cooperation with schools, divisions, and
> departments of the universities, and supplementary funds to be
> raised from other sources.[5]

On March 30, a special meeting of the Board of Governors was called to hear Chase read a telegram from Beardsley Ruml announcing that the Memorial had appropriated $240,000 to the Institute, to be available over a five-year period in decreasing amounts as follows: $60,000; $60,000; $50,000; $40,000; $30,000. Odum had hoped for more, but this would have to do. In a sense, of course, he was being faced with exactly what he had proposed in his budget suggestions to the president in September 1926, namely, a budget of $80,000, with

$60,000 to come from the Memorial and $20,000 from the University. The talk about what the University was contributing was fine, but what he needed was $20,000 in cash if the Institute was to function at the level he had outlined. The Board voted that "a special committee be appointed to rearrange the budget for the next year on the basis of the present appropriation."[6] Odum served on the committee and prepared the budget for 1927–28, which was adopted by the Board on April 13, 1927. It allocated $12,500 for three research professors, $5,500 for two research associates, $15,750 for research assistants, $10,000 for the central office, $4,650 for field expenses, $2,500 for equipment and supplies, and $9,100 for publication and books, for a total of $60,000.[7]

For the time being, things were not so bad. For the next two years, at least $60,000 a year from the Memorial grant was available. Furthermore, during 1927 private sources made several small grants amounting to $5,000. The Commission on Interracial Cooperation contributed $1,500 for crime studies, and the Social Science Research Council's grant of $16,000 for the study of St. Helena Island supplemented the Institute's regular budget by taking care of Woofter's salary for a year and the salaries of Guion and Guy Johnson for six months. Thus, in the end the 1927–28 budget was about $71,000, by far the biggest in the Institute's first five years.[8] In addition, Odum was planning a leave of absence for the academic year 1928–29 to work for President Hoover's Committee on Social Trends, and his salary money from the Institute became available for other uses. But the crunch would come later when the Memorial's grant tapered down to $40,000 and then to $30,000, unless Odum could find additional foundation support or persuade the University to assume a larger share of responsibility for the Institute. It did not help matters any that in January 1929, the University was notified that the Laura Spelman Rockefeller Memorial had been consolidated with the Rockefeller Foundation. The Foundation announced that it would honor all of the outstanding appropriations and pledges of the Memorial, but it regarded itself as "in no way committed to the renewal of appropriations or pledges in the future."[9]

Odum's problems were complicated by his also being director of the School of Public Welfare, which he had founded in 1920. The School had struggled along with minimal support from the University and had leaned heavily on the Department of Sociology for much of its basic teaching program. Odum had in mind a plan that called for finding a new director for the School, a man of national reputation who would not only assure the School's growth and security but could transform it into a broader-based school of public administration. Thus the Institute, the School of Public Welfare, the hoped-for school of public administration, the University, and the foundations were all part of Odum's plans and problems.

Odum was already acquainted with members of the staff of the Rockefeller Foundation, particularly Edmund E. Day and Miss Sydnor Walker, and during the summer of 1929 he visited the Rockefeller headquarters in New York and had several discussions with them concerning the financial needs of the School of Public Welfare. He had earlier proposed to President Chase that the University bring in a distinguished administrator and educator, Frank Bane, to head the School, and apparently he believed that the University had made a commitment to take care of Bane's salary, provided that other funds for the School's budget were forthcoming from the Rockefeller Foundation. His conversations in New York revealed that the Rockefeller Foundation staff had a quite different understanding. The University, they told Odum, had made no such commitment, and it seemed to be expecting the Foundation to take care of everything. As for Odum, why did he insist on trying to "cover the earth"—the Department of Sociology, the Institute, the School of Public Welfare, research and writing, and outside responsibilities of all sorts? Why couldn't he let go of the School of Public Welfare, let it sink or swim? And when was the University going to show that it valued the Institute highly enough to give it some real financial support? Odum returned to Chapel Hill quite chastened but resolved to hammer away at Chase on the importance of showing the Foundation that the University deserved its support.

Ironically, earlier in the summer, at a conference of social science research organizations at Hanover, New Hampshire, at which Edmund Day and Sydnor Walker were present, Odum had overstated things a bit when he said that the University was "contributing $10,000 to the Institute this year." Now, back in Chapel Hill about the first of September he found the following memorandum from Chase:

> The University appropriation to the Institute for Research in
> Social Science for the fiscal year 1929–30 will be the net
> maximum sum of $4,500 with no estimated revenue to be added.
> Distribution . . . , made by the University budget officer,
> indicates that the amount is appropriated as salaries.[10]

This was the first time the Institute had been included in the regular University budget, and the amount was disappointing. Odum's summer had been fatiguing and frustrating, and on September 4, 1929, he wrote to Chase, who was spending some time in Washington, a lengthy letter in which he used some rather blunt and forceful language. Some of the more relevant passages are excerpted here.

First of all, I wonder whether you could arrange to go up to New York and see Day, while you have a Washington base of operations.

Here is the situation, at least in part. My impression is that the Rockefeller people are very much in favor of cooperating with us, both in the research and in the School of Public Administration. There has been, however, one rather disastrous point in which we seem to be at a misunderstanding. Miss Walker had assumed all along that the university was offering Bain [sic] the position of director with the expectation then that the Rockefeller people would do all of the rest. This is a perfectly natural assumption and, as suggested, I believe they are prepared to give whatever budget Bain [sic] and you thought necessary.

My understanding is, however, that with the university making no contribution and no promise of future contributions and with the Institute obligations entirely in abeyance they would not know how to move at the present time. We had a number of conferences, in which Mr. Day and Mr. Ruml and Miss Walker were delightfully frank and followed their usual pleasantries of hammering me pretty well—all of which, of course, I did not mind and found helpful.

If I understand them correctly, they feel that their policy makes it imperative for the university to offer at least something, and they think that the university has done a number of other notable things . . . [but] that the university is in reality not committed to any special social science program. . . . I see no way out of the present situation except for you and Day to get together, and if he will be as critical of you as he was of me, I believe the two of you could get together.

One impression I gave may be for the present moment inaccurate. I said in a conference on university research institutes where Ruml and Miss Walker were present that we were contributing $10,000 to the Institute this year. I find your notation here saying that the only absolute appropriation yet made is $4,500. I still feel, that is, we are obligated to make up the $10,000. I have a few contributions which can go to the publication fund of the Institute. . . . If I go along to help President Hoover . . . you could appropriate a part of my salary. . . . This, together with some other items which I have in mind, would make up your $10,000, and so I believe that with your general approval then my statement was not inaccurate.

. . . At the present time we are, as I see it, at a comparative standstill and I have told Ruml and Day that I was through. Indeed, I believe that was their advice, the intimation being that my business was to go on and attend to my research and writing and quit trying to cover the world. However, you and I know that it is not quite so simple as that. I simply can't say I am through and stop, and I think too much of the School of Public Welfare to do it anyhow. . . . My own impression is that the more frankly you talk with [Day] and the more straight to the shoulder the better. I have a very high opinion of him and am, of course very fond of him, and one of the qualities which one likes in him is his frankness and directness; and all of them are more or less naive in understanding practical situations in university administration in the South.

. . . Taking the combination of the Hoover opportunity, the Institute, and the School, it would be hard to find more concrete challenges to do something worth while, and to me at least it seems unnecessary to be limited at the very time that we should go forward. Please tell this to the Honorables Day et al.[11]

In November Odum was still fretting over the misunderstanding with the Rockefeller Foundation during the preceding summer. On November 11 he wrote a rather plaintive, "chins up" letter to Sydnor Walker in which he reviewed the situation but assured her that "I am not urging this on you as a part of your responsibility, but merely taking advantage of your kindness in helping us face certain issues." He was not willing to give up the School of Public Welfare. He was convinced that "the University is not in a position to do any more for the School than it does now." He had decided to stay with it and do the best he could. He was glad, however, to report that the Institute's Board of Governors was enthusiastic and was set to move steadily forward, and he cheered himself with the thought that the Institute was, after all, "the University's first obligation to the Foundation." He held the letter for five days and added an "endorsement," one section of which reveals how distressed he felt:

> My explanation for getting the situation so far wrong this summer
> seems to be about as follows: Certainly you made it very
> clear to President Chase and me that the Foundation would have
> to have cooperation. In later discussions with Mr. Day, purely
> informal, we had seemed to agree that the University must put
> forth a great deal of effort and match the Institute obligation. The
> question was raised, however, as to whether or not the University
> could do anything now for the School. I made it very clear to
> Bane that we couldn't at the present time, and the rest was a
> combination of enthusiasm and lack of specific understanding.[12]

Odum kept up his pressure on Chase, and in June 1930, he urged Chase to lay before the University's trustees a proposal that would help the Institute survive:

> If the Board of Trustees would go on record as guaranteeing to
> provide $10,000 a year for ten years on condition that from
> private sources we would furnish $90,000 a year for ten years, it
> would go a long ways toward heartening the situation here.
> In other words, we propose to raise $9.00 for every one, and they
> are not obligated unless we raise that much.
>   . . . Frankly, if the Board of Trustees is not willing to put up
> $1.00 for every $9.00 to guarantee a ten-year endowment for
> the social sciences, including education, psychology, and law, as
> well as the usual social sciences it seems to me that their
> enthusiastic talk about maintaining a high standard for the
> University doesn't amount to much.[13]

Chase was in no position to do anything about this proposal. The Great Depression was closing in, the University faced budget reductions and salary cuts, and besides, Chase was resigning to become president of the University of Illinois. His successor was Frank P. Graham, professor of history. Graham was a humanitarian, a gifted orator, and effective in public relations, and he had some acquaintance with the Institute, having held the title of acting director the previous year during Odum's leave from the post; but like Chase, he was not overly anxious to do battle in behalf of state support for the Institute.

Odum was busy, trying to "educate" Graham, writing memoranda, talking with representatives of the Rockefeller Foundation, and making plans to preserve the Institute. Since 1930 was his tenth year at Chapel Hill, he took occasion to prepare a report entitled "Ten Years' Progress in the Social Sciences at the University of North Carolina," which he hoped would help convince the Foundation that the University was really matching their grants. He made tabulations showing the growth of staff in the social science departments since 1920, the expenditures for new buildings or remodeling old buildings for the social sciences, and the growth in departmental budgets between 1919–20 and 1929–30. This latter tabulation showed increases ranging from 155 percent for the Department of Rural Social Economics to 881 percent for the Department of Economics, and an average gain for the combined social sciences of 408 percent. In a section headed "Matching Foundation Moneys" he dealt especially with the Institute. "It seems entirely likely," he wrote, "that because of the outside moneys the University itself has been led to appropriate more than equal amounts, exclusively of what it would have contributed had there been no such obligation." Taking the period of the second grant from Memorial, from 1927 to 1930, as an example, he tabulated the portion of social science faculty salaries that could be considered as subsidizing Institute research, added some of the Institute's assets, such as receipts from the sale of publications, and came up with the conclusion that "the University will have, at the end of the fiscal year, June 30, 1931, made contributions aggregating more than the implied obligations of the grant." In a concluding section, "The Next Ten Years," he reiterated the idea that the University had valiantly met its obligations and was deserving of consideration for further support so that it could maintain its position of leadership in the South.[14]

Odum presented this report informally to the Board of Governors on December 10, 1930, and it was approved as a part of "the final report which is to be made the basis of an application for funds for a ten year period."[15] Odum knew already, of course, that the Rockefeller Foundation was not ready to endorse these ideas. On December 8, he had written his good friend Will W. Alexander, director of the Commission on Interracial Cooperation, about a proposed Institute study of lynching that was being held up because of the Institute's inability to make funds for the project available to the School of Law. "I need not add," he wrote, "that the Rockefeller Foundation is holding us literally to the problem of matching funds. . . . They still maintain that if the

University believed that research was as important as these other things we could also get money for that."[16]

Another document prepared by Odum in 1930 illustrates his habit of thinking ahead and thinking big. Entitled "Suggested Cooperative Plan for University of North Carolina, 1930–1940," it laid out a plan for financial support for the next ten years at the rate of $100,000 a year. The University was to provide $450,000, the foundations $550,000. The University could obtain its money in several ways: (1) $100,000, or $10,000 a year, from the regular appropriations allocated by the trustees; (2) $100,000, or $10,000 a year, from such sources as the Alumni Loyalty Fund; and (3) $250,000, or $25,000 a year, from private individuals or other philanthropic sources. This money would be spent for Institute salaries, field expenses, supplies, and publications; for salaries for teaching in the social sciences; and for the salary of "a Director of the new School of Public Administration and Citizenship."[17]

This document, plus several others, became part of Odum's package for appealing for foundation funds. In a letter to his good friend L. R. Wilson, who was a member of the Board, in September 1930, Odum mentioned as his "hardest task" that of "trying to get together an appeal which will bring us in the ten-year appropriation. . . . President Graham is back of it, and there is fair prospect that both Embree [President of the Rosenwald Fund] and Day will do their part."[18] In February 1931, the Board of Governors authorized Odum and Graham to approach the Rockefeller Foundation and the Carnegie Corporation for grants covering a ten-year period. Odum proceeded to lay his requests before the foundations, but again the negotiations were stalled by the old question of University participation.

In September 1931, Odum wrote a rather fretful letter to President Graham. He wanted Graham to invite Edmund Day of the Rockefeller Foundation to visit Chapel Hill. "Before he comes," wrote Odum, "there are some interests here which, it seems to me, we ought to get coordinated. I have the impression that the group of foundations in discussing us in their joint councils do not feel that we are united in what we want to do. This, I am sure, is not the case, but there are certain appearances which give logical grounds for this conclusion." He went on:

> 1. Their premise is that the Institute for Research in Social Science from their viewpoint being a fundamental and organic

part of the modern university, established here a number of years ago with the sanction of the University, holds a first obligation.

2. They feel that the University administration was committed to turn into this channel funds both from its own appropriation and from extra appeals before undertaking new obligations except those which were absolutely necessary from technical and local viewpoints.

Odum then listed "later undertakings which give the appearance of lack of unity" in social science programs: new institutes or bureaus in folk music, economic research, and educational research, and separate appeals for funds for these projects that were allowed by the University. One of Odum's most telling points was what he called "the continuous assumption on the part of the University that the Institute is one of sociological research rather than social [science] research." He agreed that these new programs were splendid, and emphasized that the problem was one of priorities. He concluded: "The [question] is whether the University really wants to take the other alternative, go back to the old plan of scattering its efforts among departments, or whether they really want an Institute as a major division of the Univerity activities. . . . This last policy will have to be settled this year unequivocally."[19]

For some months it was uncertain whether the Institute could expect anything from the foundations. Odum was informed by Edmund Day that the ten-year plan was out of the question. He withdrew that proposal and submitted a request "for a smaller amount covering a shorter period and for one which would not place too great a burden upon the University at the present time."[20] Now the most he could hope for was a modest grant over a period of five years. He continued his discussions with the Rockefeller Foundation staff, and at the meeting of the Board of Governors on January 30, 1932, he reported that he believed there was a favorable attitude on the part of the Foundation. But he made it plain that if a new appropriation was made to the Institute over a five-year period, it would be on a descending basis and it would be made on the assumption that "the University will take over the Institute at the end of the next period."[21]

In February 1932, Odum informed President Graham that the Rocke-feller Foundation was basing its consideration of a five-year renewal grant partly on the understanding that the University would appropriate

$5,000 to the proposed School of Public Administration, an amount that the Governor himself had recommended. Odum went on:

> . . . It seems to me that we are really obligated to go ahead and develop this School. . . . It is a difficult situation, but, as I understand it, the Rockefeller people are simply asking us whether we want the Institute and this sort of thing or whether we [would] rather have something else.
>
> They make the point, without passing judgment on what we ought or ought not to do, that in each instance the Institute is not put in the budget. If now we give this up, and we have already given up my Kenan salary, which was going to the Institute, this would indicate to me that there was to be no matching of funds. It seems to me that we have to make a choice here. If we choose in the negative, it means, of course, that automatically I am out of the picture. This is not a pleasant prospect for me to contemplate, but, as I see it, that would be the verdict of any group looking at the facts.[22]

A day later, Odum was writing to Graham again about these same matters. Apparently at some point Graham had cited the salary of Ernest R. Groves as an example of University support of the Institute, so Odum closed his letter with these words:

> Coming back to the Institute and what the University will give, I recall that Professor Groves' salary did not come as an appropriation to the Institute, but was worked out in view of the fact that Professor Bernard [has left], and, of course, we could not attempt to replace him. This was, however, a manipulation rather than a grant to the Institute. Sad as it may seem, it does look a little as if the Institute will have to go, doesn't it?[23]

These letters are indicative of Odum's exasperation. For several years he would have moments of such deep discouragement that he would talk in terms of the Institute's closing or of his own departure for some other university. He felt that Graham was doing nothing to help him with the foundations, while Graham, for his part, no doubt felt that Odum was too demanding and was something of an "empire builder."

The Institute was facing almost certain extinction after June 30, 1932, when the Memorial's final grant—now down to $30,000 for the year 1931–32—would expire. Fortunately the Rockefeller Foundation relented, and in April 1932, it informed the University that the Institute had been granted $30,000 a year for three years. The Foundation staff members were, after all, reluctant to see the Institute die. They had respect for what Odum and the Institute had achieved, they were aware of the devastating effect of the Great Depression on the University's finances, and they were willing to give the Institute a fighting chance. Sydnor Walker, of the Foundation staff, wrote a plaintive note to Odum: "Congratulations on the North Carolina grant! At least I suppose you are pleased, since it was as much as you could have hoped for."[24]

Odum appreciated the reprieve, but he was not happy over the financial outlook. The Depression was worsening. All University employees, including the Institute staff, had taken a 10 percent cut in salary, and further cuts were in the offing. Even the modest appropriation that Chase had obtained for the Institute was not a continuing budget item, and Odum knew that unless other income could be found the Institute's budget would only be about $35,000 a year for the next few years. However, Odum did win one important concession from the administration. At the meeting of the Institute's Board of Governors on January 20, 1932, he stated that the Institute staff lacked the security of other members of the university faculty, and that since Institute funds were available to meet the current Institute salary schedule, the staff should not have to face further salary cuts. President Graham agreed and gave his assurance that Institute salaries would not be cut further.[25]

The Institute ended its first decade with a budget of $35,600, a figure only slightly higher than its initial budget in 1924–25. During the ten years Odum had obtained foundation grants that totaled about $460,000. Small grants from other sources, plus the University's meager appropriation, brought the total funds available to the Institute to nearly $500,000.

Throughout the 1930s Odum maintained a killing pace of work. In 1930 he was president of the American Sociological Society, the first resident southerner to hold that office. He served as assistant director of research for President Hoover's Committee on Social Trends from 1929 to 1933, chief of the social science division of the Chicago Century of Progress Exposition in 1933, chairman of the North Carolina Emergency Relief Administration from 1933 to 1935, chairman of the North Carolina Civil Works Administration in 1933–34, member of the State Planning Board beginning in 1935, president of the North Carolina Conference for Social Service in 1936–37, and president of the Atlanta-based Commission on Interracial Cooperation, from 1937 to 1944. He was in demand as a speaker and consultant on regional problems, social planning, and social policy, and during the winter terms of 1936 and 1937 he served as visiting professor at the University of Illinois. In addition, he drew up detailed plans for a comprehensive council for southern regional development and sought funding for it. Later, when the war brought intense racial tensions and a plea from black leaders for the South to do something about racial inequality, he put this project aside and helped in founding what he considered the next best thing, the Southern Regional Council, which he served as president from 1944 to 1946. Still further, he was writing constantly, and during this period six of his major books were published. Concurrent with some of these activities, Odum had taken leave without pay from his University duties in January 1932, retaining only his post as director of the Institute, to direct the research for the Southern Regional Planning Study under the sponsorship of the Southern Regional Committee of the Social Science Research Council, which was chaired by Benjamin B. Kendrick, professor of history at the Woman's College of the University.

Odum was not eager to accept so many outside obligations, but when they involved remuneration that would enable him to go on leave for a while, he was willing to accept them in order to free his salary for other Institute personnel. There were times when he wondered whether his efforts were appreciated or were having the effects he had intended. In July 1933, for example, he took occasion to go into some financial matters in a letter to Benjamin B. Kendrick, with whom he had been working on the Southern Regional Planning Study:

> . . . During this last year neither the University nor the
> Institute has paid me one cent either for salary or expenses,
> although I have taught my regular seminars, and at President
> Graham's request have tried to work at home a good deal more,
> making a dozen or more addresses and contacts, heading up the
> Interracial Commission, and holding many conferences. Of
> course you understand this is as it ought to be, and I have
> enjoyed it immensely, but I sometimes feel, with the tremendous
> sacrifice that my family pays and with working nights and days
> and trying to give maximum effort to the things that we
> believe are important here at home and providing not only for my
> own salary for the last several years but for the salary of a

considerable group—I sometimes feel a little inclined to think that if it isn't wanted we will just have to move the whole thing to one or two of the institutions which do want it.

But, of course, you knowing me, I do not have any such feelings at all. This is all a part of the very hard and fascinating job, and we are going to do the job.[26]

This closing sentiment was virtually a trademark with Odum. After revealing how he was inclined to think, he would almost invariably deny that he really had any such discouraging thoughts!

The story of the Institute's finances for the second decade is much the same as in the first decade, but again the Institute survived. In March 1935, Odum prepared a memorandum for submission to the Rockefeller Foundation requesting a terminating grant over a five-year period.[27] President Graham supported the request with a letter assuring the Foundation of the University's financial backing of the Institute. In April the Foundation made a final grant as requested—$75,000—to be spent in decreasing amounts over five years, beginning with $25,000 in 1935–36 and ending with $5,000 in 1939–40.

Now that the Rockefeller Foundation would be bowing out of the picture in 1940, Odum felt free to approach other foundations. In 1937 the General Education Board gave the Institute $15,000 to help with the completion of studies on the topic "These Southern People," and Odum followed up with a proposal for a larger grant to support the Institute's efforts to establish a center for regional development and training. In his twelve-page proposal he took pains to show that the University was doing a good job of matching the previous grant from the Rockefeller Foundation by "taking over" members of the Institute staff. Furthermore, he said, "it is expected that the University will go further by the next biennium and appropriate $10,000 each year specifically 'earmarked' for social research and allocated directly to the Institute."[28] President Graham's covering letter to the General Education Board endorsed the proposal enthusiastically and committed the University to an obligation to "put in the next biennial budget an additional support of $10,000 annually."[29]

The appeal was successful. In April 1938, the General Education Board gave the Institute $87,000, to be spread over a period of five years. At the May 30 meeting of the Board of Governors, Odum presented a budget showing $22,000 of the new grant allocated for the first year. He told the Board that "The new grant . . . is proportioned upon a decreasing basis contingent upon President Graham's agreement to supplement the grant by making specific request from the Legislature for the Institute of $10,000 annually during the next biennium, with correspondingly increasing appropriations thereafter. This, together with a continuation of the University's policy of gradually taking over Institute personnel, will insure the permanency of the Institute as an integral part of the University.''[30] There is no indication in the available records to indicate the extent to which the University fulfilled Graham's commitment of $10,000, but apparently the Institute was able to obtain all of the $87,000 that had been granted conditionally by the General Education Board. Thus the Institute was assured of at least a modest amount of financing through the year 1942–43.

The quest for support from foundations had been complicated by changes and variations in the policies of the foundations themselves. The original grant in 1924 from the Laura Spelman Rockefeller Memorial had been given to the University ''to be used in the development of its research in the social sciences''—a broad enough policy that gave the University considerable freedom in the use of the funds. Two years later the Memorial decided to reduce its aid for ''miscellaneous research purposes'' and give attention primarily to ''institutional centers for social research,'' a shift that was something of a tribute to the promising programs being developed by the Institute and several other centers.[31] In 1935 the Rockefeller Foundation, which had absorbed the Memorial in 1929, announced a new policy: it was withdrawing from the support of ''general research in institutional centers'' and placing its main emphasis on ''the development of special fields of interest.''[32] And now, in 1938, Odum had to contend with the fact that his first grant from still another foundation, the General Education Board, was restricted to certain purposes, such as population study and a ten-county survey. As he explained to the Board of Governors, it was doubtful whether any of the money could be used for research assistants unless they were associated with one of the specified purposes.[33]

Odum was growing weary of the constant search for funds, but he continued for several more years. Occasional driblets of foundation money came in, such as a grant of $1,200 from the General Education Board in 1941 for ''the permanent Workshop on Regional Research and Education,'' and a Carnegie Corporation grant of $3,000 in 1942 for the purpose stated by Odum, ''to prepare scientific agenda for our summer work conference on the delineation of major regions and administrative districts in the United States basic to defense planning and post-war building of a strong nation."[34] He kept on "badgering" the University administration for support. In June 1943, for example, he wrote a long letter to R. B. House, dean of administration, laying before him the proposed budget for the Institute for 1943–44 and asking his help in persuading President Graham to move for an appropriation by the University. Odum pointed out the tremendous interest in regional research and planning that was being shown around the nation, the challenge for the University to continue its leadership into the postwar period, the financial sacrifices that he and others were making for the sake of the Institute, and the importance that even a small University grant would have in terms of leverage with the foundations. Once more he reiterated that it was the policy of the foundations to grant funds only to "those agencies already supported by the university."[35]

Finally, Odum had enough of the eternal quest for money for the Institute. At a meeting of the Board of Governors on September 22, 1943, he announced that he would like to retire as director at the end of the year and proposed that the Board elect Gordon W. Blackwell as his successor. He also asked for approval of three new projects for which foundation funds would be sought: (1) a cooperative planning study to improve social science teaching in order to meet the needs of returning war veterans, (2) a study of southern leadership, and (3) an inventory of southern resources. Odum himself planned to work on the second and third of these projects.[36] After twenty years of managing the Institute, he wanted to be relieved of one of his greatest burdens so that he could devote more of his time to research. Odum had practically given up hope for any further substantial help from the foundations, and before he resigned as director he concentrated his efforts on securing support from a variety of sources, both public and private, for a variety of projects that emphasized service to the state and the region. Finally his efforts to get more state funds were beginning to pay off, and his successors would reap the benefits.

As was mentioned earlier, in the first decade Odum had secured about $500,000 for the Institute. Annual budgets ranged from a low of $33,000 to a high of $71,000, showing an average of about $50,000. The second decade was a time of starvation for the Institute because of the prolonged economic depression. Grants from foundations amounted to less than $200,000, and other funds were hard to get.

However, with small private gifts for special purposes, research jobs for state agencies, modest University support, and salary releases by Odum and others when they received pay for outside work, the Institute managed to survive. Its annual budgets during this decade were in the range of $30,000 to $40,000. When Blackwell took over in 1944, the Institute was far from affluent, but it was not in any immediate danger of extinction.

An Era of Affluence

Several more years passed before the Institute pulled out of the financial doldrums, but at last the University was coming to the rescue. In his first report as director, Blackwell wrote:

> Along with the coming of age of university research in the social sciences has come the necessity for southern institutions to rely less upon national foundations for financial assistance and correspondingly more upon support from the State and from local constituents. This is as it should be. The foundations have been of inestimable value in giving organized social research a start in many southern institutions not excluding our own. The time has come when the stability of continued State support, so necessary for the long-range planning of a well balanced research program, is essential. In this respect our University administration and the General Assembly have made an admirable beginning. Their continued and increasing support of the Institute is anticipated.
>
> Of the Institute's total fiscal operations of approximately $43,000 in 1945, the University was the source for almost two-thirds of the funds. Foundations accounted for 23 percent, public agencies 5 percent, private agencies 2 percent, and other sources 4 percent.[37]

Apparently the University's share of Institute funds in 1945 amounted to about $28,000. Presumably this was the first time that University support had ever exceeded the foundations' contributions to the budget.

Over the next several years Blackwell was able to enlarge the role of public and private agencies in financing the Institute's operations by making sponsoring or contractual arrangements with numerous agencies. Among these were the State Planning Board, the Governor's

Emergency and Contingency Fund, the City Planning Commission of Hickory, the Federal Public Housing Administration, the Tennessee Valley Authority, the Southern Association of Science and Industry, the Atlanta School Board, the University of Alabama Bureau of Public Administration, and the Presbyterian Church in the South. There were also a few small grants for specific projects from the Rockefeller Foundation, the General Education Board, the Rosenwald Fund, the Gardner Foundation, and others. Unfortunately, detailed budgets for the mid-1940s are not available, so the annual totals are not known, but it seems safe to assume that they were modest.

The late 1940s saw the emergence of three significant trends that would dramatically change the financial status of the Institute. The first of these was the rise of contract research, especially federally supported projects, to a position of dominance in the Institute's program. In Blackwell's annual report for 1949, in a list of projects under way, which included several sponsored or contractual items, the first federally supported project appeared. This was a relatively small study called "The Radio Communications Project," and it was sponsored by the Office of Naval Research. In 1950 Blackwell listed ten projects with special financing. Two of these were contract projects with federal agencies: $70,000 from the United States Air Force for research on human factors in efficiency at air force bases, and $35,000 from the Veterans Administration for a study of the transfer of patients from a psychiatric hospital to the home community. These two projects accounted for $105,000 of the total of $225,000 expended on the ten projects.[38]

Commenting on the Institute's shift toward contract research, Blackwell told the Board of Governors in May 1951 that the Institute's trust funds and other unrestricted funds available for secretarial assistance, travel, supplies, communications, and the like, were becoming low and that there would be "difficulty of expanding or even maintaining the present varied staff" unless there were "a continuation of foundation support or increased funds from the State." He added: "In order to relieve the present and anticipated financial stringency, the Institute has entered into an expanding program of contract research."[39]

Contract research on a large scale was an innovation for the Institute, and as Blackwell was well aware, research for federal agencies could involve a certain amount of risk. For one thing, federal contracts might involve classified subjects, and Blackwell was reluctant to see the University engaging in such research in a time of peace. He proceeded

cautiously, and in his annual report for 1953–54 he offered his evaluation of the Institute's experience with contract research during the past
three years:

> Having little experience to go by and practically nothing by way
> of policy directives from the University administration, we
> have cautiously and, we think, successfully made our way into
> this area of contract research which is beset with so many
> dangers and pitfalls. For the most part, our experience with
> contract research has been satisfactory and at times it has left
> nothing to be desired. . . . However, changes in national politics
> lead to rapid changes in research climate in Federal agencies. No
> university or any part of it should become largely dependent upon
> contract research. This we have avoided so that, as all
> except two of our contracts have come to an end, no particular
> stress or dislocation in a program has been occasioned. In spite of
> limitations which are now much clearer to us, it seems probable
> that a few carefully developed contract projects should be
> undertaken from time to time in the future.[40]

Blackwell reported further the next year on the Institute's experience
with contract research. His analysis of contract projects over the past
five years, he said, indicated that "the University can and does benefit
from such research." He cited as benefits the expanded opportunities
for graduate students to gain research experience, the provisions of
stipends for those students, and the saving in faculty salaries from state
funds when faculty were paid by the contract funds. He went on to say
that

> relations between the Institute and the contracting agencies have
> generally been satisfactory. Questions of security concerning
> personnel, the handling of materials, and the content and
> distribution of reports have arisen in several instances. . . . In all
> except one project, however, the Institute has been able to
> reproduce and distribute the findings without limitation. In this
> project, 2 of 23 reports are still classified and had to be deleted.[41]

Thus the financial and academic benefits of contract research seemed
to outweigh the problems that attended it. One financial aspect of
contract research, however, became a source of controversy between
the Institute and the University. It had to do with the disposition of
overhead funds, a matter that will be discussed later in this chapter.

The growth in government contract studies had been rapid. By the end of 1951, in addition to the two government-financed projects previously cited, the Institute had entered into contracts with the Air Force for a series of studies of Soviet industrial capacities and a study of day-and-night populations of Soviet and American "target cities," and with the Public Health Service for studies of urbanization in connection with the building of the Savannah River atomic energy plant.[42] In succeeding years contracts with other federal agencies were arranged. Some of the federal agencies sponsored one or more short-term studies, while others sponsored multiple long-term studies. The series of Soviet studies, under Air Force sponsorship, for example, covered a period of eight years. For a period of about fifteen years government contracts were the primary source of Institute funds. While it is not possible to assemble accurate and comparable data for the whole period because of incomplete information and a change in reporting procedures beginning in fiscal 1963–64, it is possible to tabulate fairly accurately from the appropriate annual reports the total of federal contract funds received during twelve years of a thirteen-year period running from 1950–51 through 1962–63. The year for which data are missing is 1951–52. The figures are as follows:

United States Air Force	$828,000
United States Public Health Service	502,000
Office of Education	221,000
Office of Naval Research	173,000
Social Security Administration	90,000
Bureau of Public Roads	75,000
Veterans Administration	69,000
National Science Foundation	50,000
Housing and Home Finance Agency	50,000
The State Department	16,000
Total	$2,074,000

This tabulation understates the total amount received during the thirteen years because of the omission of the year 1951–52, but for the twelve years covered in the table the average annual receipts from federal sources was $173,000. Thus from this source alone the Institute was receiving from four to five times what it had from all sources during the starvation years of the Depression. This was affluence indeed!

The second trend that emerged during the late 1940s was the resumption of significant support for the Institute from foundations and other private sources. Blackwell had begun to have discussions with foundation officials soon after he assumed the directorship. He found that they had little interest in making unrestricted grants to the Institute for general research programs or for nonresearch operating expenses. In June 1948, he reported to the Board of Governors.

> An over-all program, to which many disciplines would contribute and which was submitted recently to several foundations, is no longer receptive to foundations who now function on the basis of contributing to the support of smaller concrete projects within a clearly defined frame of reference. An immediate task, therefore, is a breaking down of our larger program into specific areas of research.[43]

Blackwell spent six weeks in New York in the summer of 1948, during which he laid a new prospectus, with emphasis on specific projects, before several of the foundations. His efforts began to bear fruit. At the end of the year, the General Education Board made a grant of $20,000 for the purpose of updating Odum's *Southern Regions*, and in March 1949, the Carnegie Corporation gave $100,000 on a tapering five-year basis. This grant was especially welcome because it was not based on specific projects, but was for "interdisciplinary research in the social sciences through the Institute staff."[44] In the meantime the Rosenwald Fund, of Chicago, which was in process of liquidating its assets, had given the Institute $25,000 in unrestricted funds, a good portion of which was used to replenish the badly depleted revolving fund for publication. Most important of all was the fact that the recently organized Ford Foundation, which had carefully surveyed the academic scene before embarking upon its grant program, decided to support research and development in the behavioral sciences at the University. The first grant to the Institute from the Ford Foundation, for $100,000, was made in 1950. In 1953 a second grant of $50,000 was made for self-study of the behavioral sciences at the University, and in 1955 a third grant was made in the amount of $246,000 for use in specific areas of research. Ford Foundation grants would continue over the next twenty years and would constitute the Institute's chief source of funds from foundations.

In addition to large organizations like the Ford and Rockefeller foundations, a few smaller foundations and a variety of other private agencies made grants to the Institute. These funds were for the most part for specific researches, some of them being granted on a contractual arrangement with a specific donor. The following tabulation, assembled from annual reports and covering the same period as the preceding summary of government contracts, indicates the amounts contributed by foundations and other private sources:

Ford Foundation	$715,000
Rockefeller Foundation	215,000
Commonwealth Fund	86,000
Stern Family Fund	66,000
American Public Welfare Association	42,000
Carnegie Corporation	25,000
Russell Sage Foundation	24,000
General Education Board	20,000
Gardner Foundation	19,000
Southern Regional Education Board	10,000
Alcoholic Rehabilitation Program of N.C.	10,000
North Carolina State Nurses Association	9,900
Nationwide Insurance Companies	9,400
Life Insurance Companies of America	9,300
Aaron E. Norman Fund	5,000
Health Information Foundation	3,500
Viking Fund	3,000
Doris Duke Foundation	3,000
Miscellaneous	6,300
Total	$1,281,400

The total of $1,281,400 received during the twelve years represented in the tabulation amounted to an average of almost $107,000 in annual receipts from foundations and other private sources. Since funds received from federal contracts were added to this figure, the Institute could expect to spend an average of at least $280,000 a year.

The third trend of the late 1940s was the accelerating pace of state aid for the Institute. What Odum had advocated during his twenty years as director had finally become a reality: the Institute was in the University budget, and the amount was becoming respectable. As was noted earlier, in 1945 Blackwell had reported that state funds accounted for two-thirds—about $28,000—of a budget of $43,000. By 1950 this figure had grown to about $75,000, and while it would show annual variations—from $70,000 to $95,000—over the next fifteen years, the general trend was upward. A tabulation made from data that are available for ten years in the thirteen-year period used in the lists presented earlier shows a total of $776,000 of state funds expended by the Institute, or an average of $77,600 a year. While this amount was small in comparison with the amounts being brought in by federal contracts and foundation grants, it played its part in the Institute's rise in affluence, for now the three sources together could support an average annual budget of more than $350,000. And the $77,600 in state funds alone was larger than any annual budget that the Institute had seen in its first twenty-five years.

The uses to which the state funds were put are of special interest. The expenditures in two selected fiscal years are shown in Table 4.[45] Two items in the table are of particular interest. First, it can be seen that the amount expended from state funds for research assistants was on the rise and was becoming fairly generous. This figure was to rise still higher during the next ten years and would range from $16,000 to nearly $22,000. Second, the item called "teaching load adjustment" in the budgets calls attention to the fact that reduced teaching loads for senior staff members were being treated as University allotments to the Institute. Thus if a faculty member with a salary of $12,000 was giving one-third of his time to Institute research, $4,000 of his salary was considered to be a use of state funds for the Institute and was so indicated in the Institute budget. Ironically, this was precisely the procedure that Odum had tried in vain to use as a way of convincing the foundations that the University was really matching their grants.

Table 4. Expenditure of State Funds in Selected Years.

	1954–55	1957–58
Personnel Items		
Staff	$20,000	$22,500
Faculty salaries	10,000	11,500
Teaching load adjustment	39,000	40,000
Research assistants	4,400	14,400
Total	73,400	88,400
Non-Personnel Items	7,853	6,100
Total	$81,253	$94,500

During its era of affluence the Institute's annual budgets ranged from $233,000 to $500,000. For the period that has been used in the tabulations above, eight annual budgets that show federal, foundation, and state funds separately are available in the annual reports. These budgets are summarized in Table 5, with all figures rounded to the nearest thousand dollars. The category labeled "Other" includes expenditures from trust funds that the Institute was able to set aside from time to time and from such other sources as the revolving fund for publications. If the total expenditures shown for each source in the table are converted to percentages of the grand total, the results are as follows: federal contract funds accounted for 41 percent of all expenditures, foundations and other private sources for 34 percent, State funds for 20 percent, and other sources for 5 percent.

The Problem of Overhead Funds

As stated earlier, the question of the disposition of overhead funds became a matter of contention between the Institute and the University. Overhead funds were the funds that the University claimed from all contract projects in order to reimburse itself for providing facilities,

Table 5. Institute Budgets, by Source of Funds, 1954–55 to 1961–62.

Year	Source of Funds Expended				Total budget
	Federal contracts	Foundations and other private funds	State	Other	
1954–55	$74,000	$71,000	$81,000	$23,000	$249,000
1955–56	114,000	111,000	80,000	15,000	320,000
1956–57	124,000	121,000	80,000	17,000	342,000
1957–58	168,000	123,000	95,000	15,000	401,000
1958–59	218,000	201,000	71,000	11,000	501,000
1959–60	197,000	141,000	70,000	18,000	426,000
1960–61	174,000	178,000	72,000	31,000	455,000
1961–62	207,000	112,000	73,000	12,000	404,000
	$1,276,000	$1,058,000	$622,000	$142,000	$3,098,000

maintenance, and other indirect costs. The Institute's position was that when it was responsible for bringing a research contract to the University it should receive a share of the overhead funds that the University took from the contract grant. The administration's position was that an agency such as the Institute had no automatic claim on such funds and that it was financially and administratively sound for the University to take the overhead funds into its general account and to allocate money for the promotion of research from time to time throughout the University.

The question of the disposition of overhead funds arose early in the era of contract research. At a meeting of the Executive Committee on November 19, 1951, the director, Blackwell, presented a memorandum entitled "Policy Questions Concerning Sponsored Research." Among the topics in the memorandum was the matter of salary savings and indirect costs. Blackwell pointed out that in addition to recovering overhead costs, the University was saving on salaries when faculty members were taken over on contract funds. There was a lengthy discussion, and the members agreed that there was a need for finding some way of allocating some of the overhead funds to units involved in contract research.[46] In the following month there was a similar discussion in a meeting of the Board of Governors, and it was agreed that there should be some way of including the indirect expense item in the budgets of individual projects.[47]

In January 1952, the Executive Committee suggested that the director draft a letter to the chancellor urging the University to transfer to the Institute a portion of the overhead and salary savings resulting from Institute contract projects. On February 18 the Executive Committee held a special meeting to consider the budget for the biennium 1953–55 and Blackwell's draft of the letter to Chancellor House. The letter was approved and was sent under the signatures of members of the committee on February 20, along with the proposed budget and a memorandum on the status of contract projects. It asked for a moderate increase in University support for the Institute, and explained that this would not be a burden on the University "in view of the financial benefits accruing from contract research under the Institute." It was pointed out that Harvard and Cornell had a policy of allowing "every benefit possible to the department conducting contract research."[48] The administration approved a modest increase in state funds for the budget, but on the matter of splitting the overhead funds on some regular basis it would not yield.

The effort to secure a share of overhead funds continued at intervals for twenty years. A few highlights may be mentioned. In 1954 the Board of Governors once more voted to recommend to the chancellor a policy of returning "a reasonable proportion" of overhead receipts to the research unit involved. In his annual report for 1954–55, Blackwell made a tabular summary of contract research expenditures for the preceding five years. Total expenditures were $740,000. Overhead funds took $115,000, and "allocated salaries," that is, salary savings when faculty members were taken over on contract funds, amounted to $26,000.[49] The message was clear: here was a sum of more than $140,000 in which the Institute should be able to have a share—money that would help to ease the stress on its general operations funds, which were being depleted by the very fact that it was carrying a heavy load of contract research. The University was still not impressed by such arguments.

In 1960, during Daniel Price's administration, the Executive Committee discussed the problem again and agreed that "a clear statement of what this group thought the policy on indirect costs should be would help in maintaining consistent and firm pressure for modifications in the University's present policy."[50] Apparently Price despaired of any favorable modifications and decided to take his own direct action. He reasoned that at the very least the Institute was entitled to reimbursement for such items as secretarial services and services of the Statistical Laboratory when they were utilized by one of the contract projects. The date of the beginning of this practice cannot be determined precisely, since the minutes of all meetings for the years 1962 through 1964 are missing, but it came to an abrupt halt at the end of 1964. At a meeting of the Administrative Board in January 1965, Price reported that "the Accounting Department has firmly prohibited such practices, with the result that about the only remaining source of replenishment of trust funds is from sale of publications, a comparatively negligible amount."[51]

Discussions and negotiations on overhead funds continued. A University faculty committee headed by James Godfrey, professor of history, gave some attention to the problem. In 1969, when the committee reported to the Faculty Council, the Council unanimously resolved that overhead funds should be retained for research use at the University. At a meeting of the Administrative Board of the Institute in March 1971, the situation was reviewed, and the director, James Prothro, said that "no action has been taken by the Administration to accomplish this purpose." After extended discussion the Board agreed that "Mr. Prothro should pursue the possibility of systematic funding of some of the Institute's programs from overhead funds."[52] The Institute was still trying, but its efforts came to naught. There was to be no change of University policy on overhead, but there was some consolation for the Institute in the fact that state support of the Institute was substantially increased.

Recent Trends in Finance

By the mid-1960s the surge of federal government contracts that had been the main source of Institute funds for more than a decade had begun to subside. Soon the federal contract projects were a minor source of income. Unfortunately, the Institute's financial records for 1963–64 are not available, and for the succeeding six years the budgets as shown in the annual reports pertain only to the expenditure of state funds, so that it is not possible to cite exact figures for total expenditures during those years. It is clear, however, that for several years the Institute's financial status was a source of worry for its directors. But the period of relative deprivation did not last long. By 1969–70 the Institute's budget, as recorded in the annual report, was about $393,000. In 1970–71 it was $467,000; in 1971–72 it was $470,000; in 1972–73 it was $376,000; and in 1973–74, the Institute's fiftieth year, it was $459,000.[53]

This return to affluence reflects several important developments that have occurred in recent years concerning the sources of Institute funds. In the first place, support from foundations increased considerably. The Ford Foundation, after a lapse of several years, resumed its assistance to the Institute. In 1967–68 it made a grant of $300,000 for the State and National Elections Project, and two years later it supplemented this grant with another for $91,000. In addition there were smaller grants from other private foundations, such as the Guggenheim Foundation, the Rockefeller Foundation, the Russell Sage Foundation, the Richardson Foundation, the Business Foundations of North Carolina, the General Electric Company, and the Planned Parenthood Federation of America.

Secondly, federal sources continued to be an important part of the Institute's financial health. In 1967–68 the National Science Foundation, a federally financed agency, gave the University a Science

Development Grant of about $5 million, a substantial portion of which was allotted to the Institute for the data analysis center. In 1971–72 the Institute received from these funds a supplementary grant of $228,000, and in 1972–73 a further supplement of more than $70,000. Other federal agencies that assisted with smaller grants included the Office of Education, the Office of Naval Research, the Department of Housing and Urban Development, the National Institutes of Health, and the Environmental Protection Agency.

Except for the grants from the Ford Foundation and the National Science Foundation, most of the funds from private foundations and federal sources did not enter into the Institute's own operating budget. For the most part they represented grants received by individuals affiliated with the Institute who found the money for their projects and utilized some of the Institute's services, such as clerical or statistical assistance. Thus the third source of funding, that is, state appropriations through the University budget, was the crucial factor that determined the level and the continuity of the Institute's operational services when the foundation grants expired. This problem, which had plagued Odum in the early days, was still a cause of anxiety for Prothro near the close of the Institute's fifth decade in spite of the seeming affluence the Institute enjoyed. In 1969 Prothro told the Administrative Board that "the Institute will face a serious problem after next year if the University does not assume responsibility for funding those parts of the program presently underwritten by the NSF Science Development Grant."[54] The next year the story was the same, as Prothro reported: "A proposal is being made to NSF for additional funding for 1971–72 and 1972–73, but it may not be adequate to carry on the present services. The University's failure to assume gradually the financing of this operation, as originally expected, may create serious financial problems after the spend-out year."[55]

But the tide was running in favor of increased state funding for the Institute. In 1967–68, the state appropriation for the Institute had exceeded $100,000 for the first time. The amount increased steadily each year, and in the 1971–72 budget a special allocation of $33,000 for the Louis Harris Political Data Center, which had been developed by the distinguished University alumnus and had recently been brought to the University, raised the level of state funding for that year to $200,000. A similar amount of state support continued in 1972–73, but in 1973–74, the Institute's fiftieth year, the state appropriation was practically doubled. It amounted to $388,000, or 84 percent of the

Institute's budget of $459,000. Frank J. Munger, Prothro's successor, reported happily that "this increased appropriation has permitted the Institute to continue, at the same level, the services of the Statistical Laboratory and the Social Science Data Library. This appropriation represents the first significant increase in the state budget in many years."[56]

In its fiftieth year, then, the Institute had finally achieved the goal that every director had fervently hoped for—an adequate allocation of state funds. The new level of state funding has continued since the fiftieth year. With all of its basic services now funded by the University budget, the Institute enjoys financial security for the first time in its long life. As Munger put it in March 1977, "Fortunately, the chapter on finance has a happy ending."

CHAPTER 5

Folk, Race, and Culture Studies

The next six chapters undertake to describe the research programs of the Institute. This is a difficult task. The published books alone run into the hundreds, the articles and other brief publications run into the thousands, and the unpublished studies constitute a sizable portion of the total number of researches. Obviously it is not possible to cite all of the studies that have been made. Those mentioned in the next six chapters, then, represent a selection of the most significant researches conducted by staff members of the Institute during the past half-century. Most of the works cited are published, but a number of important unpublished studies are discussed. Many of the works of the junior staff members are included, and a few publications in which the Institute played only a secondary role are mentioned because of their significance. Many works are cited by title and date only, merely for the purpose of illustrating the variety and scope of the publications of staff members of the Institute.

The present chapter presents first the folk studies that figured prominently in the Institute's earliest researches, then studies of race and race problems, and finally the researches on culture and cultural change that have been pursued by the cultural anthropologists on the Institute staff.

Folk Studies

The opening sentences of Howard W. Odum's first published work were these:

> To know the soul of the people and to find the source from which
> flows the expression of thought is to comprehend in large measure
> the capabilities of the people. To explain the truest expression
> of the folk-mind and feeling is to reveal much of the inner
> consciousness of the race.[1]

He saw "the folk" and folk society as "natural," as "the universal constant in a world of historical variables" in contrast to modern state civilization, which he saw as artificial, concerned with power, organization, technical processes, and change. His interest in the folk was lifelong. Although much of his early writing was concerned with the Negro folk he was equally concerned with the ways of the white South, and he made some significant contributions to the general field of folk sociology.

Odum's *An American Epoch*, published in 1930, was his first effort at portraying the "folk-mind and feeling" that made the South what it was. In the same year his presidential address before the American Sociological Society, entitled "Folk and Regional Conflict as a Field of Sociological Study," was a forceful statement of the importance of understanding folk societies and the conflicts involved in their transition to modern state civilization. A footnote in this address is of special importance in explaining his rationale for studying folk songs:

> The criticism has been made that in *An American Epoch*, the chapters, "Folk Music Survivals of the White South" and "Hymns and Religious Songs" were included either for literary effect or because of their interest to the author, whereas the author's hypothesis is that these songs, their singing, and the resultant emotional conditioning are perhaps the most powerful single force responsible for much of the culture pattern of the region. The fact that analyses and interpretations are reserved for more formal scientific study or that the superficial student does not recognize the meaning of the data in no way affects the scientific validity of the materials.[2]

Years later Odum again manifested his interest in a general sociology of the folk in two books that appeared in 1947. One was *The Way of the South*, in which he continued his portraiture of southern society, and the other was a textbook, *Understanding Society*, in which such chapters as "Folk Culture and Folk Society," "The Nature of Civilization," and "The Technicways in Modern Society" set forth his theories concerning the nature and dynamics of folk society and culture. He was moving toward a definitive work on folk sociology, and in March 1953 he published a lengthy paper in *Social Forces* entitled "Folk Sociology as a Subject Field for the Historical Study of Total Human Society and the Empirical Study of Group Behavior," which was an exploratory preview of the book he planned to write. He retired the following year and died soon afterward, so that this paper, replete with definitions, concepts, and problems for research, remains his best statement on folk sociology. His concluding thought was that ''folk sociology, then, seeks not so much to become a new or different sociology but to focus, utilize, and integrate much of the best that general sociology may contribute to the dynamic science of human relations.''[3]

Several of the junior members of the Institute staff were inspired by Odum's example to undertake research in folk culture. In 1925 Elizabeth Lay Green was appointed to a junior research assistantship to study folk life in the Piedmont area of North Carolina. Her husband, Paul Green, a promising young playwright, collaborated, and in 1930 they completed a voluminous manuscript entitled ''Folk Beliefs and Practices in Central North Carolina.'' Among other studies that have remained unpublished were ''Folk Interpretations of Social Values as Found in Folk Songs and Ballads'' (1926), by Clyde Russell; ''A Preliminary Study of the Planter Aristocracy as a Folk Level of Life in the Old South'' (1941), by Melville F. Corbett; and ''Folk Medicine'' (1941), by Nell Hines.

It was the Negro folk of the South, however, who comprised the most available and the most fascinating field for folk studies. As was described earlier, the Institute's first publications were in the nature of a crash program on Negro folk songs by Howard W. Odum and Guy B. Johnson. The choice of this field of work was a deliberate one on Odum's part. He wanted something noncontroversial, with popular appeal, that could be done rather quickly. He wanted to see the Institute achieve something that would gain national attention early in its existence and thus help to perpetuate itself. Furthermore, Odum had an intense interest in the folk songs of the Negro because he felt that they offered the best insight into ''the folk soul'' of the common Negro. During his years in Georgia and Mississippi he had collected hundreds of folk songs, so there was no difficulty in laying hands on source materials. Within a few days after Johnson arrived at Chapel Hill in August 1924 to become Odum's research assistant, he and Odum were plowing through this collection and laying out plans for their first volume on Negro songs.

The Negro and His Songs, by Odum and Johnson, appeared during the summer of 1925. It contained the texts of over two hundred religious and secular songs, supplemented by interpretative and appreciative commentary. The authors did not pretend to have made any deep sociological analysis, and their thesis was very simple: that the folk songs of the Negro were invaluable sources for "portraiture" of the life of the folk Negro. The book was well received by reviewers, although several expressed disappointment that it contained no music for the songs.

Before the first book was out, Odum and Johnson were at work on another volume of Negro folk songs. Since Johnson had some training in music, Odum agreed to let him introduce some tunes into this second volume. Fortunately both words and music were easy to come by. As both men had occasion to travel, they frequently encountered convict chain gangs, migratory workers, and wandering guitar players. It was a simple matter to listen and get the songs down on paper. Many of the songs, however, were collected within a hundred yards of the Institute quarters on the campus of the University. In the mid-1920s, the University was entering into a period of construction of new buildings and renovation of the old original buildings. In that preautomation era large gangs of pick-and-shovel men and other hand laborers were needed, and black laborers from several Deep South states came to Chapel Hill to work. Many a student and professor listened, spellbound, as a group of diggers sang a work song, with picks whirling in unison on the upstroke and a mighty "hunh" of exhalation at the end of the downstroke. At twilight and dawn plaintive calls and "hollers" could be heard in the barracks area where the workmen lived, only a hundred yards across the Pittsboro highway from the residences of Odum and Johnson.

The second volume of folk songs, *Negro Workaday Songs*, was published in 1926. It presented more than 250 songs, emphasizing ballads, work songs, blues, and love songs, along with the tunes of some typical songs. This book was also well received and was generally considered to be more readable and more interesting than the previous book. Both books appeared at an opportune time, near the beginning of what came to be called "the Negro Renaissance" or "the New Negro Movement," which was manifested in a great upsurge of writing by and about Negroes.

One of the chapters in *Negro Workaday Songs* was devoted to John Henry, a legendary black steel driver who was said to have worked on the construction of the Big Bend Tunnel on the Chesapeake and Ohio Railroad in West Virginia in the 1870s. When a mechanical steam-powered device was brought in to drill the holes for blasting out the stone, John Henry, so the story went, challenged the steam drill. After hours of drilling, man against machine, John Henry won the contest, but then "he laid down his hammer and he died." Johnson was intrigued by the apparent wide diffusion of this legend among Negroes and by the variety of work songs and ballads about it that had sprung up, and with Odum's approval he began in 1926 a special study of John Henry. In June 1927, he went to the Big Bend area in West Virginia and searched through old newspapers, collected John Henry songs, and interviewed men who were young workmen during the building of the tunnel. Johnson became convinced that while the evidence was not overwhelming, he was justified in concluding that John Henry was a real man and that the legend had a strong factual basis.

Two years later *John Henry: Tracking Down a Negro Legend* was published. It narrated the search for the answer to the question whether John Henry was a man or a myth, and it contained the words and music of John Henry ballads and work songs that had been collected from many parts of the nation. The book helped to popularize the John Henry story, with its appealing theme of man against machine, and in later years poems, plays, musicals, ballets, and sculptures were created around the John Henry theme. One of Johnson's informants had said that he had heard that at the entrance to Big Bend Tunnel a big statue of John Henry had been carved out of solid rock. This was pure fantasy at the time, but today an immense sculpture of John Henry with his nine-pound hammer does indeed stand near the east portal of Big Bend Tunnel, and the John Henry Memorial Foundation, headquartered at Princeton, West Virginia, which seeks to preserve "the heritage and life history of minority groups in the Appalachian region" sponsors an annual John Henry Memorial Festival.

In 1928 the Institute had assumed the sponsorship of the study of the Negroes of St. Helena Island, South Carolina, as described in a previous chapter. This study resulted in 1930 in three publications by members of the Institute that related to the life of the Negro peasantry of St. Helena Island: T. J. Woofter's *Black Yeomanry*, Guion Johnson's *Social History of the Sea Islands*, and Guy Johnson's *Folk Culture on St. Helena Island*. The third book was most directly concerned with the folk culture, as it dealt with the folk songs, the Gullah dialect, and folk tales of the island people.

It had often been said that these people were culturally the closest to Africa of any group in the United States, and Johnson fully expected to find on St. Helena a heavy survival of West African patterns in the folk culture. Instead, he was much more impressed by the survivals of obsolete English words, pronunciations and idioms, and of early American white spiritual songs. As for the dialect, he concluded that although there were a few African words still in use and a strong survival of African intonations, the basic structure, grammar, phonology, and vocabulary were derived from dialect patterns of early colonial English. Likewise, regarding the spirituals for which St. Helena was famous, he concluded that these songs were neither survivals from Africa nor the sole creations of the Afro-Americans, but that they were the product of the acculturative contact of white and black in which African rhythms and styles of singing merged with forms, words, and melodies from the white culture to form a distinctive new type of song.

Not surprisingly, such ideas provoked considerable controversy on both the popular and professional levels. Reviews in the Negro press were often sharply critical, and one reviewer asserted that "Professor Johnson is trying to rob us of our spirituals." In the scholarly realm, Johnson's ideas were in conflict with the views of an eminent anthropologist in the field of black-white acculturation, the late Melville J. Herskovits of Northwestern University. Herskovits believed that survivals of African culture were numerous and that the African cultural past, rather than the historical contact of black and white in America, was the key to understanding the race problem. Today, fifty years after the St. Helena Island study was made, this controversy has not been completely resolved. The whole question is now enmeshed in black race politics and in the search by blacks for a new image of themselves and of Africa.

Meanwhile, Howard Odum had renewed his own interest in the portrayal of what he liked to call "the black folk." Over a period of three years he produced his famous trilogy about a character whom he called Black Ulysses: *Rainbow Round My Shoulder: The Blue Trail of Black Ulysses* (1928), *Wings on My Feet: Black Ulysses at the Wars* (1929), and *Cold Blue Moon: Black Ulysses Afar Off* (1931). The prototype for Black Ulysses was a one-armed Negro wanderer called Left-Wing Gordon whom Odum befriended and listened to for hour upon hour, but the books were a compound of Odum's own fertile imagination and Gordon's real-life narratives and songs. Odum projected much of himself into the writing, and he tried, with insight and compassion, to portray the joys and trials and degradation of life among the southern black people. He wrote with verve and poetic abandon, and he said that he enjoyed this writing more than any other. When asked whether the stories were truth or fiction, he would reply that it did not matter; even if some of the stories were fictitious, they revealed the truth.

A project in which the Institute played a facilitating role was a study of the use of phonophotography in folk music, by Milton Metfessel, who was a protégé of Professor Carl Seashore of the University of Iowa. Metfessel developed a machine in which a "phonelloscope" recorded sound waves on a film. It was one of the pioneer efforts in sound photography. The object was not to convert the waves on the film back into sound, but to use the film for the measurement of pitch and vibrato in the singing voice. Johnson took Metfessel to Hampton Institute in 1927, where Metfessel spent a couple of days recording songs sung by members of the Hampton Quartet. The results of this work were published by the University of North Carolina Press in 1928 under the title of *Phonophotography in Folk Music*. Metfessel concluded that his method could show clearly the extent of deviation of a particular pitch from the conventional musical scales and that black singers had vocal qualities that were different from white singers.

In addition, the Institute assisted in the publication of two books in the field of folk culture that were written by outsiders. One of these was *Folkbeliefs of the Southern Negro* (1926), by Professor Newbell Niles Puckett of the University of Mississippi. Fifty years later this work still stands as the best in its field. The other book, *The Negro Sings a New Heaven and a New Earth* (1930), was written by Mary A. Grissom, who had spent many years collecting the spiritual songs of the Negro. Both books were published by the University of North Carolina Press.

Five years after the publication of *The Negro and His Songs* the Institute's interest in Negro folk studies subsided, and during the succeeding forty-five years nothing more of any importance was published in this field. The studies of the Negro folk had accomplished their purpose; they had appeared at an auspicious time and had helped put the Institute on the map. Odum now shifted his attention to his more vital concern, regionalism, while Johnson returned to his original interest in the broader aspects of race relations and the status of the Negro in American society.

Race and Ethnic Studies

Although the Institute began in a period when the comparison of races by means of "intelligence" tests and other sorts of tests was a common pursuit among psychologists and educators, the Institute staff did not have any strong interest in this aspect of race studies. Odum often said, "I am interested in race differentials, not race differences." By "differentials" he meant the measurable social, economic, and cultural differences between black and white that were so much a part of the problem of relations between the races. A study by Graham B. Dimmick entitled "A Comparative Study of Growth in Physical and Mental Abilities of Mill and Non-Mill Children," completed in 1927 under the direction of Professor A. M. Jordan of the School of Education, made use of intelligence tests but was not concerned with racial comparisons. Apparently the only project concerned directly with race differences was Guy B. Johnson's doctoral dissertation, "A Study of the Musical Talent of the American Negro" (1927). Johnson applied the Carl Seashore Phonographic Tests of Musical Talent to about 3,000 Negro subjects of fifth-grade, eighth-grade, and college level in North Carolina, South Carolina, and Virginia and compared the results with the national norms which Seashore had developed. His experience in this study left him with a strong distrust of any test that purported to measure innate racial differences. The results of Johnson's study were published in the *Music Supervisor's Journal* (1928) and the *Journal of Comparative Psychology* (1931).

The great majority of the Institute's projects in the area of race and ethnic relations consisted of studies of the Negro and his status in American society. One important segment of these studies dealt with the socioeconomic aspects of Negro life. These studies were mostly master's and doctoral theses prepared by research assistants. Among the unpublished works in this area were "Life Histories of Rural Negro Teachers" (1927), by George E. Pankey; "Social-Economic Characteristics of the Mississippi Delta" (1930), by Virginia L. Denton; "Wage Differentials between Negro and White Workers in Southern Industry" (1934), by Charlotte Califf; "Mississippi: A Regional Social-Economic Analysis" (1937), by John M. Maclachlan; "A Social-Economic Analysis of a Mississippi Delta Plantation" (1938), by Raymond McClinton; "Agrarian Conflicts in Alabama: Races and Classes in a Rural State" (1939), by Olive M. Stone; "Rural Poverty and Relief in the Southeast" (1941), by Selz C. Mayo; "Recent Changes in Negro Farm Tenure'' (1941), by Robert J. Milliken; and ''The Negro Tobacco Worker and His Union'' (1941), by John Donald Rice. A published study that was particularly revealing was Roland B. Eutsler's ''Agricultural Credit and the Negro Farmer,'' in *Social Forces* (1931).

One study in the area of black socioeconomic life merits special mention because of its consequences forty years afterward. In 1934 John Beecher, now a distinguished American poet, wrote a term paper entitled ''The Sharecroppers' Union in Alabama'' for Guy Johnson's course on the Negro. It was based in part on the story of a black sharecropper who had been intimidated, jailed, beaten, and almost killed by ''the law'' because he dared to try to organize farm tenants into a union. Nate Shaw, as Beecher called him, was an unforgettable character—tough, fearless, wise, philosophical. The term paper was published in *Social Forces* in October 1934. Many years later Theodore Rosengarten ran across the article, did some sleuthing, found that Nate Shaw (whose real name was Ned Cobb) was still alive, and spent many hours with the old man, recording his rich recollections. The result was *All God's Dangers: The Life of Nate Shaw*, a fascinating book of personal history that became a best-seller in 1974.

The Great Depression of the 1930s stimulated a series of researches. Under the direction of Odum, Woofter, and Herring, the Institute staff engaged in twenty-four projects under the heading ''A State in Depression,'' which resulted in reports totaling about two thousand pages. Some of these projects related to the effects of the Depression on Negroes. However, for financial reasons, these reports remained unpublished, with the exception of an article by Guy B. Johnson, ''The Negro and the Depression in North Carolina'' (1933), and one by Gordon Blackwell, ''The Displaced Tenant Farm Family in North Carolina'' (1934), both of which were published in *Social Forces*.

The most significant work published by the Institute in the early years on the socioeconomic aspects of Negro life was Arthur Raper's book, *Preface to Peasantry: A Tale of Two Black Belt Counties*, which appeared in 1941. Raper, who was research secretary for the Commission on Interracial Cooperation, had served as a research assistant in the Institute while pursuing his doctorate in sociology. His dissertation, completed in 1931, was entitled ''Two Black Belt Counties: Changes in Rural Life Since the Advent of the Boll Weevil in Greene and Macon Counties, Georgia.'' The book was an elaboration of this study. Several years later, Raper, in collaboration with Ira De A. Reid, a professor at Atlanta University, produced another work in this field entitled *Sharecroppers All* (1941). These books, which served to focus attention on such pressing problems as farm tenancy, poverty, and migration, will be discussed in more detail in a later chapter.

Several studies of black community and institutional life were made in the early years. Among these were "The Negro in Durham," by Hugh P. Brinton (1930); "The Negro Churches of Chapel Hill," by Agnes Brown (1939); "The Negro in Greenville, South Carolina," by Joseph T. Drake (1940); and "Growth and Plan for a Community: A Study of Negro Life in Chapel Hill and Carrboro, North Carolina," by Charles M. Freeman (1944).

Another aspect of the field of race and ethnic studies that received prolonged attention from the Institute was the area of crime, the administration of justice, extralegal punishments, and the legal status of the Negro. Among the early studies dealing in whole or in part with Negro offenders that were made by research assistants and deposited with the Institute's manuscripts were "Types of Crime in North Carolina," by Francis S. Wilder (1926); "A Statistical Analysis of Crime in North Carolina," by Aileen S. MacGill (1926); "Case Studies of Delinquent Girls in North Carolina," by Margaret C. Brietz (1927); "Extent and Types of Juvenile Delinquency and Dependency in Durham, North Carolina," by C. Horace Hamilton (1927); "Backgrounds of Delinquent Boys in North Carolina," by Clyde V. Kiser (1927); "One Hundred Country Dwelling Negroes and Their Crimes in Durham, North Carolina," by Hugh P. Brinton (1928); and "A Study of Homicides in South Carolina, 1920–26," by H. C. Brearley (1928). Brearley later expanded his study of homicide and in 1932 the Institute subsidized the publication of his book, *Homicide in the United States*. This work put a spotlight on the exceedingly high rate of murder in the United States and on the disproportionate number of murders committed by Negroes. After examining the statistical evidence on court dispositions and sentences, Brearley concluded that blacks who killed were dealt with more severely than whites who killed.

Several years later Guy Johnson, after observing many courtroom trials involving Negroes, theorized that Brearley's conclusion was an oversimplification because it was based on the race of offenders only. He believed that if homicides could be categorized as black killing black, black killing white, white killing black, and white killing white, and if the dispositions of cases so categorized could be tabulated, some very important differentials would show up. No judicial statistics of this kind existed, but with the assistance of two former students Johnson was able to assemble offender-victim data from court records and other sources for several southern cities over a period of several years. The results tended strongly to bear out his hypothesis. In 1941 he published a paper, "The Negro and Crime," in which he presented a theory of the causation of Negro crime. The administration of justice itself was posited as one important factor because of the striking differentials in the punishment of intraracial as against interracial offenders. If Negro killed white, for example, the pattern of punishment was one of extreme severity; if Negro killed Negro, the pattern was one of high acquittal rates and lenient sentences.

A brilliant young graduate student, Harold F. Garfinkel, who had joined the Institute staff as a research assistant in 1940, wished to pursue the question of race and homicide further. Choosing ten counties in central North Carolina, he assembled data from court records, coroners' reports, and newspapers on all homicides in these counties over a period of eleven years, by the race, sex, and socioeconomic status of offenders and victims. He traced each indictment through the judicial possibilities: nol pros, acquittal, conviction, sentencing. He even compiled considerable data on the extent to which those who were sentenced to death were actually executed or escaped execution through commutation of sentence by the governor. All in all, Garfinkel made some of the most remarkable tabulations of criminal statistics ever compiled. His results amply filled in the gaps in Johnson's smaller study and left no doubt as to the reality of differentials in the administration of justice in terms of offender-victim categories of homicide. Garfinkel's master's thesis, "Interracial and Intraracial Homicide in Ten Counties in North Carolina, 1930–1940," completed in 1942, was a tour de force, but Garfinkel, ever the perfectionist, hesitated to see it published. In 1942 he entered military service. After the war he summarized his study in one paper that was published in *Social Forces* in 1949.

One of the early publications by Institute staff members was in the area of penology. This was *The North Carolina Chain Gang*, by Jesse F. Steiner and Roy M. Brown, which appeared in 1927. The book was primarily about black prisoners because at that time, North Carolina, like many other southern states, used prison labor in highway construction and maintenance, and Negroes comprised a high proportion of the prisoners who worked on the chain gangs. The book, which had considerable weight in the movement for prison reform in North Carolina, is discussed in some detail in chapter 8.

In 1928 Lawrence A. Oxley, who was the first black professional employee of the State Board of Charities and Public Welfare, made a study of prisoners who had been sentenced to death for capital offenses. Howard Odum helped to plan and guide the study, and the Institute assisted in preparing it for publication. Of the two dozen prisoners studied, all were black. Oxley used the case method, sketching the family background, education, and criminal record of each man and reporting on the results of physical and mental examinations. His monograph, *Capital Punishment in North Carolina*, was published by the State Board of Charities and Public Welfare in 1929. The bleak picture it presented of mental retardation, mental illness, malnourishment, and cultural deprivation was another jolt to the public conscience.

Another important publication in the Institute's first decade was Wiley B. Sanders's *Negro Child Welfare in North Carolina* (1933). It conveyed a stark picture of the problem of dependent and delinquent black children and the inadequacy of the facilities for coping with the problem in a humane fashion.

In 1924, when the Institute began, the pattern of extralegal punishment of offenders, especially black offenders, was still common enough in the South to constitute a disgraceful situation. Sixteen Negroes were lynched in the South that year, the lowest number since statistics on lynching had been compiled, but the number did not consistently decline for some time. Black victims numbered 17 in 1925, 23 in 1926, 16 in 1927, 19 in 1928, 7 in 1929, and 20 in 1930. An Institute research assistant, John Roy Steelman, made an extensive case study entitled "Mob Action in the South" (1928), but lack of sufficient funds prevented the Institute from proceeding with its publication.

The upsurge in lynchings in 1930 caused the Commission on Interracial Cooperation to set up the Southern Commission on the Study of Lynching, composed of prominent southerners of both races, to make a detailed analysis of the twenty lynchings of 1930. Arthur Raper, assisted by Professor Walter Chivers of Atlanta University, conducted the research. Two publications resulted. One was an eighty-page pamphlet, *Lynchings and What They Mean*, which summarized the findings of the study and presented the recommendations of the Commission.

The Institute's director, Howard Odum, played an advisory role in that work. The other publication was Raper's *The Tragedy of Lynching*, a detailed analysis that ran to some five hundred pages; it remains one of the best on the subject. The Institute was involved with Raper's book in two ways: one of its research assistants, N. Clifford Young, wrote the account of the North Carolina lynching of 1930, "A Case Study of the Tarboro Lynching," which became the basis of one of Raper's chapters, and the Institute subsidized the publication of the book by the University Press. The Southern Commission on the Study of Lynching also secured the services of James H. Chadbourne, a young assistant professor in the School of Law at the University of North Carolina, to explore the task of law in the punishment and prevention of lynching. Chadbourne examined the relationship of lynching and the administration of justice, evaluated existing laws on lynching, and discussed proposals for additional legislation that would strengthen the hand of the law. His book, *Lynching and the Law*, was published in 1933. The Institute had provided some funds for preliminary work and had borne part of the cost of publication. Thus the Institute had a part in several significant publications that are generally held to have played a part in helping to move the South toward the eradication of lynching.

The broader problem of the legal status of the Negro was approached a little later in a cooperative effort of the Institute and the School of Law of the University of North Carolina. Charles S. Mangum, Jr., a native of Chapel Hill who held a Doctor of Jurisprudence degree from the School of Law, undertook the tedious task of abstracting and commenting on state and federal constitutions, statutes, and judicial decisions in relation to the Negro. His book, *The Legal Status of the Negro*, published by the University Press in 1940, was a landmark in the field. Later Mangum turned his attention to the legal aspects of the problem of farm tenants and sharecroppers, and his second book, *The Legal Status of the Tenant Farmer in the Southeast*, published by the University Press in 1952, remains the best work on that subject.

Soon after the United States entered World War II, there was a period of intense racial tension. There were riots in Detroit, Mobile, and other cities, and rumors concerning Negro conspiracies and aggressions were common, especially in the South. Howard Odum made a comprehensive survey of attitudes and opinions and published a book entitled *Race and Rumors of Race* in 1943. The most fascinating chapter in the book, called "The Romance of the Eleanor Clubs," debunked the widely held notion that Eleanor Roosevelt had incited black domestic workers to desert their jobs in white households and to express extreme animosity toward their former employers. The readiness of black women to give up low-paying drudgery for the well-paid industrial jobs that the war effort had opened up to them for the first time was something many white people could explain only by assuming that some sort of general conspiracy was afoot. Odum showed that an intensive search had failed to turn up one iota of evidence that "Eleanor Clubs" actually existed. His book, widely and favorably reviewed, was a wholesome antidote to the rash of rumors that swept the South in the early 1940s.

Between the end of the folk studies and the coming of the era of desegregation, Guy Johnson's researches centered on the status of the Negro in American society and the probable course of race relations. His objectives were (1) to understand and interpret Negro life through a close acquaintance with the press, literature, organizations, and leaders of black society, and (2) to understand the dynamics of the race situation as a basis for projecting the probable course of change and demonstrating the need for the adoption of constructive public policies.

Among Johnson's publications that dealt with problems of the status of the Negro and with racial movements and strategies were the following: "Some Factors in the Development of Negro Social Institutions in the United States" (1934), "Negro Racial Movements and Leadership in the United States" (1937), "Patterns of Race Conflict" (1939), "Negro Leadership and Strategy" (1939), and "The Course of Race Conflicts and Racial Movements" (1955). His last professional paper in this area was "Race Relations: The Strategy of Violence," delivered at the 1968 annual meeting of the Southern Sociological Society.

The problems of social change, particularly with regard to segregation and desegregation, were also the subjects of Johnson's researches over a period of forty-five years. Among his publications prior to the era of desegregation were "A Sociological Analysis of the New Ku Klux Movement" (1923), "Is the Negro Accommodated or Assimilated?" (1928), "Changing Problems of Race Adjustment" (1934), "Does the South Owe the Negro a New Deal?" (1934), "Isolation or Integration?" (1935), "Educational Segregation and Race Relations" (1935), "Graduate Study for Southern Negro Students" (1937), "Pioneering for the New South" (1944), and "Civil Rights in the South" (1947). When southern state universities, beginning with the University of Oklahoma in 1948, were ordered to admit black students as the result of lawsuits brought by applicants who contended that the separate facilities for blacks were either unequal or nonexistent, Johnson began researches on desegregation in higher education. Over the next decade he visited a large number of institutions that were undergoing desegregation, made firsthand observations on the situation, and published six reports.

By 1955 at least fifty southern state-supported white institutions and an equal number of private institutions had begun to admit Negro students. Johnson attributed the extremely low incidence of episodes of violence during this desegregation process to several factors. Among these were the role of the Supreme Court, which limited the role of the politician; the South's drift toward more liberal ethical and social norms; the constructive role of the pioneer Negro students; the "personal touch" that had long been a part of the southern tradition; and the maintenance of separate social worlds between white and black, which appeared to be "the price of peace" during the transitional era.[4]

In anticipation of the landmark decision that the Supreme Court was to make in 1954 in the public school segregation cases (*Brown* v. *Board of Education of Topeka*), Johnson began in 1952 to study the probable consequences of such a revolutionary decision and devoted several papers to this subject: "The Impending Crisis of the South" (1953), "Segregation versus Integration and the Impending Supreme Court Decision" (1953), "A Sociologist Looks at Racial Desegregation" (1954), "Integration: A Human Relations Problem" (with Richard L. Simpson, 1957), and "Freedom, Equality, and Segregation" (1958). In the paper published in 1954, Johnson undertook to outline some of the results that might be expected in the process of public school desegregation. These included a long period of evasive policies and legislation designed to stall the desegregation process; a heavy increase in the number of private schools; increase in aggression and occasional violence against Negroes, with a real prospect that a series of reactionary social movements might crop up in various places in the South; some loss of jobs by Negro teachers, at least temporarily; development of official norms for equal treatment of white and Negro students; a heavy increase in the cost of public schools; and a tendency to minimize equal-status social contacts between white and black.[5]

As for the long-term consequences of desegregation, Johnson believed that the South would learn to live with them more quickly than the North would. However, the ideology of white supremacy was strong, and even after twenty-five years of desegregation the result, he felt, would be "something which falls short of the Negro's dream of full integration." He suggested that "white people will probably feel more relaxed about the situation than Negroes. . . . They will have substituted for the old philosophy of separate-but-equal a new philosophy of together-but-unequal."[6]

Although Johnson believed that the goal of equality could be achieved through the orderly processes of the American constitutional system and was opposed to violent or revolutionary approaches, his writings and public addresses on race relations often drew fire from suspicious citizens who believed that anyone who stood for equal rights for black citizens was probably a Communist. Over the years, and especially during the desegregation era, he accumulated a substantial file of anonymous letters laden with abusive language and threats of physical harm. More disturbing, however, was the effort by a member of the University Board of Trustees to remove Johnson from his job in 1947. The attempt was unsuccessful, but it served as a reminder that, as was pointed out in chapter 2, the subject of race was still "delicate."[7]

In the year before his retirement in 1954, Odum turned his attention to the problems of desegregation. He was taken by surprise by the Supreme Court's landmark decision in 1954—he felt that the court would not have the courage to abandon a doctrine which had prevailed since 1896—but he welcomed the decision because he viewed desegregation as an inevitable change in the way of the South. He planned a book on this subject, to be called *Agenda for Integration*, but it remained unfinished at his death in November 1954. However, he had written a paper that probably embodied much of what he planned to say, and this paper, entitled "An Approach to Diagnosis and Direction of the Problem of Negro Segregation in the Public Schools of the South," was published in the *Journal of Public Law* a few months before his death. It was a lengthy paper that examined fifteen "series of assumptions" concerning the crisis facing the South. It reflected both Odum's deep respect for the folkways as guardians of social stability and his commitment to the necessity of drastic social change. At the end, he pleaded for "statesmanship such as was made articulate by the founding fathers, . . . rather than relegating the problem to a simple moral or a complex national issue, or leaving it to vested frustration, political demagoguery, or intellectual exhibitionism."[8]

The junior staff of the Institute did considerable work in the field of

desegregation. Notable among these efforts were the following unpublished studies: ''The Integration of Negroes into the University
of North Carolina Law School,'' by James H. Vaughan, Jr. (1952);
''Change in Attitudes toward Segregation: An Experimental Study of
the Effects of a Religious Youth Conference in North Carolina,'' by
Janet D. Head (1955); ''Desegregation in Public Education: Selected
Aspects of Social Change,'' by Father James F. Muldowney (1957);
and ''The Resistance Movement to Desegregation,'' by James Vander
Zanden (1958).

In the meantime other members of the Institute staff were studying
the process of desegregation. A series of violent incidents and school
closings afforded opportunities for studying crisis situations and the
ways in which people adjusted to them. Ernest Q. Campbell, who had
earned his doctorate at Vanderbilt University and had joined the staff
of the Institute and the Department of Sociology in 1958, and Thomas
F. Pettigrew, a young psychologist who would later win distinction as
professor of social psychology at Harvard, collaborated on a study of
the turbulent situation in Little Rock, Arkansas. Their field work concentrated on the role of Christian ministers in Little Rock in the desegregation crisis, and they found that the performance of the ministers
often deviated widely from the Christian creed that they professed.
Their findings, which won national attention at the time, were published in a monograph, *Christians in Racial Crisis: A Study of the
Little Rock Ministry* (1959), and in a number of papers, including
''Race and Moral Crisis: the Role of Little Rock Ministers'' (1962).
They also analyzed the political situation in Arkansas and published a
paper entitled ''Faubus and Segregation: An Analysis of Arkansas
Voting'' (1960).

When the city of Norfolk, Virginia, closed its schools in 1959 in
response to court-ordered desegregation, Campbell turned his attention
to this new crisis situation and made an on-the-spot investigation.
Charles E. Bowerman and Daniel O. Price, of the Department of
Sociology, collaborated with him on the project. Their report, *When a
City Closes Its Schools*, published in the Institute's Monograph series
in 1960, was in frequent demand by school officials throughout the
South. The interest of Institute staff members in desegregation abated
somewhat after these studies, but occasional papers were published
in later years, such as ''School Desegregation and New Industry:
The Southern Community Leaders' Viewpoint'' in 1963, by Richard
Cramer (Department of Sociology), and ''Community Leadership for

School Desegregation" in 1972, by Robert R. Mayer (City and Regional Planning).

In 1961 the Institute obtained a grant from the United States Office of Education for a study of the educational aspirations of Negro adolescents. Bowerman, Campbell, and Cramer undertook the research. Over the next several years they collected data through interviews, observation, attitude measurements and other means, and in 1966 their findings were published as a volume in the Institute's Monograph series, *Social Factors in Educational Achievement and Aspirations Among Negro Adolescents*. This report, 590 pages in length, was one of the most comprehensive studies ever made in its field. Five years later the work of Glen H. Elder, Jr., represented a continuity in this area of research, as shown in such papers as his "Intergroup Attitudes and Social Ascent Among Negro Boys" and "Racial Conflicts and Learning." During the same period, a study of unwed mothers conducted by Bowerman, Halliwell Pope, and Donald Irish included extensive materials on unwed black mothers. Their report, *Unwed Motherhood: Personal and Social Consequences*, was published in the Institute's Monograph series in 1966.

One of the Institute's outstanding publications in the 1960s was M. Elaine Burgess's *Negro Leadership in a Southern City*, published by the University Press in 1962. Elaine Burgess had studied leadership in the black community in Durham, North Carolina, for her doctoral dissertation. Skill, insight, and empathy in her inquiries among Negro leaders in Durham resulted in an excellent dissertation and in a book that is considered one of the most valuable ever published on Negro leadership.

The most extensive project in the area of Negro studies undertaken by the Institute in the 1960s was a study of Negro political participation. In the era of the civil rights movement and the passage by Congress of the Civil Rights Act and the Voting Rights Act, this was a timely study. It was also significant in that it marked the first time that any department other than Sociology had originated and conducted an extensive program of research involving black Americans. The study was made possible by special grants beginning in 1961, and it was directed by James Prothro and Donald Matthews of the Department of Political Science. Several junior staff members of the Institute assisted in the program. This became the most extensive survey of Negro voting behavior and political participation that has been made. Prothro and Matthews began to present some of their findings in professional journals in 1962 and 1963. Among these articles were "Recruitment for Survey Research on Race Problems in the South" (1962), "Southern Racial Attitudes: Conflict, Awareness, and Political Change" (1962), "Social and Economic Factors and Negro Voter Registration" (1963), and "Political Factors and Negro Voter Registration" (1963). More than a dozen additional papers, written individually or jointly, were published later. The comprehensive summary of their work was their book, *Negroes and the New Southern Politics*, which was published in 1966. It was considered a landmark in the study of Negro political behavior, and it met with such demand that a paperback edition was issued in 1968.

Institute members in the Department of History were also active in studies involving the status of the Negro and its changes through time. Among some of the early publications resulting from projects conducted by junior staff members were *A Social History of the Sea Islands*, by Guion G. Johnson (1930); *Pro-Slavery Thought in the Old South*, by William S. Jenkins (1935); *Ante-Bellum North Carolina*, by Guion G. Johnson (1937), and *South Carolina Negroes, 1877–1900*, by George B. Tindall (1952). More recently Tindall, now a professor in the Department of History, has published two works that are concerned to a considerable degree with the changing status of the Negro: *The Emergence of the New South* (1967) and *The Disruption of the Solid South* (1972). In addition, a book by Joel Williamson, *The Origins of Segregation* (1968), attempts to throw new light on the beginnings of the system of legal segregation in the South.

In the Department of Psychology, the work of Institute staff members such as Harold G. McCurdy, John W. Thibaut, E. Earl Baughman, W. Grant Dahlstrom, and Chester A. Insko has included research on attitude formation, color prejudice, and the like. Of special importance is a book by Baughman and Dahlstrom, *Negro and White Children: A Psychological Study in the Rural South* (1968), in which they explored the dimensions of the psychological and cultural disparities between Negro and white children.

While most of the researches done by the Institute staff members in the area of race and ethnic relations have been concerned with the Negro or with black-white relations, other ethnic groups have not been entirely neglected. The earliest such study, "The Kentucky Mountaineer: A Study of Four Counties in Southeastern Kentucky," completed in 1930 by Harriette Wood, dealt with an area that had remained isolated and retained a great deal of its English cultural heritage. In

1938 Mildred Mell wrote "A Definitive Study of the Poor Whites of the South," which summarized what was known at that time about that subculture. In 1942 Oscar E. Hoffman, a research assistant from Wisconsin, completed a study entitled "Culture of the Centerville-Mosel Germans in Manitowoc and Sheboygan Counties, Wiconsin," which was a portrayal of cultural persistence and change in a contact situation. In 1946 Frederick B. Parker wrote an extensive demographic report, "Foreign Stocks in the Population of the Southeast: A Statistical Study of Nativity and Minor Racial Groups." All of these studies have remained unpublished.

One ethnic area that was of considerable interest to the research staff was the mixed-blood "racial islands" that existed throughout the Southeast and the South. These groups, usually quite small, represented varying intermixtures of white, Negro, and Indian stocks, and they were as a rule isolated, segregated, inbred, and culturally deprived. Many of them had identity problems because they had no generally accepted group names. One group was quite large, with a population in 1930 of about 12,000, a figure that had grown to about 30,000 by 1970. This was a group centered in Robeson County, North Carolina, which according to local legend descended from a mixture of Indians and the English who disappeared from Sir Walter Raleigh's ill-fated Roanoke Island colony in the late sixteenth century. They have been known by many names, the last four of which have been bestowed by the North Carolina General Assembly: Croatan Indians of Robeson County (1885), Indians of Robeson County (1911), Cherokee Indians of Robeson County (1913), and Lumbee Indians (1953). In 1935 a research assistant from that area, Ernest D. Hancock, wrote a thesis, "A Sociological Study of the Tri-Racial Community in Robeson County, North Carolina," in which he analyzed the relationship of the white, Negro, and Indian population groups in the county. Over a period of years Guy and Guion Johnson performed extensive field work in Robeson and adjoining counties on the history, social status, institutions, organization, and leaders of the mixed-blood community. At first a full-scale published report was envisaged, but for strategic and ethical reasons the Johnsons decided to withhold such publication. Several papers were presented to professional societies, and one paper, "Personality in a White-Negro-Indian Community" (1939), which was published contrary to the author's instructions, came close to causing Guy Johnson to be assaulted the next time he set foot in the Indian community.[9]

One other ethnic group that received some attention in unpublished studies by the Institute's junior staff was the Jewish people of the South. In 1938 William H. Levitt produced a study entitled "The Jews in North Carolina: A Study in Occupational Distribution." In 1950 Gladys E. David completed "A Preliminary Inquiry into the Jewish Culture as a Folk Society Surviving and Flourishing within the State Society," a study that was directed by Howard Odum and that was based on his well-known dichotomy of folk and state. In 1951 Solomon Sutker presented an extensive study of the Jewish community in Atlanta for his doctoral dissertation, "An Ethnic Elite in a Southern Metropolis: a Study of Jewish Position in Social Structure."

It should be noted that very few of the Institute's numerous studies in the field of race and ethnic relations have been concerned with the problem of a broad theoretical framework. A notable exception is Hubert M. Blalock's book, *Toward a Theory of Minority-Group Relations*, which appeared in 1967. In this work Blalock attempted to organize assumptions and hypotheses in the field of minority-group relations in such a way that they could be tested empirically.

Studies in Cultural Anthropology

Anthropology is the youngest of the major social science departments at the University. As an independent department it dates only from 1965, but teaching and research in this field began much earlier. From the beginning of the Department of Sociology at the University, Odum had in mind its expansion to include anthropology. Guy Johnson also had considerable interest in the subject, an interest that was enhanced when the renowned British anthropologist Bronislaw Malinowski spent several days in Chapel Hill on his way home from the Trobriand Islands in 1925. Johnson's study at St. Helena Island and his personal contact with several anthropologists, Clark Wissler in particular, led him to institute a course in social anthropology in 1930. In 1937, after a year of post-doctoral study in anthropology at Chicago and Yale, he introduced a second course in anthropology.

Johnson also had an interest in the prehistoric Indian cultures of North Carolina, and in 1933 he joined with a small group of amateur archaeologists to form the Archaeological Society of North Carolina. Among the charter members was a young man, Joffre L. Coe, then a high school student in Greensboro, who had trained himself in archaeology by intensive reading, correspondence, and field work. Later, when he became an undergraduate student at Chapel Hill and the Archaeological Society was undertaking its first site excavations, Coe supervised the field work, catalogued the artifacts, and brought them to the University. In 1939, with a modest subsidy and space allotment from the University, he formally organized the Research Laboratory of Anthropology and has been its director ever since. In 1948, after earning a graduate degree at the University of Michigan, he received a formal appointment in the Department of Sociology and Anthropology. He has been affiliated with the Institute from time to time ever since.

In 1940 a young man trained at Harvard, Robert Wauchope, came to the University to direct a Works Progress Administration archaeological project and to augment the offerings in anthropology. He did not stay long, being enticed away in 1942 by Tulane University, where he has had a distinguished career as director of the Middle American Research Institute, but one result of his tenure at Chapel Hill was the recognition of anthropology to the extent that within a few years the official name of its home department was changed to the Department of Sociology and Anthropology. In 1946 John P. Gillin joined the staff and served as administrator of the anthropology section until 1959, when he resigned to become dean of the Division of Social Sciences at the University of Pittsburgh. Gillin made a major contribution to the research capabilities of the University when he persuaded the administration in 1950 to acquire a set of the Human Relations Area Files, which had been developed at Yale University under the leadership of Professor G. P. Murdock. The rather heavy initial cost and the continuing annual fee for new materials were assumed by the University's library budget. For years the files were housed in Wilson Library and were under its supervision. In 1966 administration of the files was transferred to the Institute, and after the Institute moved to its present quarters in Manning Hall in 1970 the files were placed in the custody of the Institute. This valuable research resource is available for use by students and staff throughout the University, and it has provided source material for numerous scholars who are interested in cross-cultural studies.

Other staff members in anthropology were added from time to time, some of them remaining for only brief periods, but three of the early appointees settled down to make their careers at Chapel Hill: Coe, the archaeologist mentioned earlier, and two cultural anthropologists, John J. Honigmann (1951) and John Gulick (1955), both of whom owed their initial appointments to Institute funding. In 1965 anthropology became an independent department under the chairmanship of John Gulick. By 1974 it was a burgeoning department, with seven professors, two associate professors, and five assistant professors, offering about seventy courses. Most of its staff members are affiliated with the Institute, and several of them have pursued a series of distinguished studies under the Institute's sponsorship.

The researches of the anthropologists in the Institute may be divided for convenience into those that deal with American or domestic situations and those that deal with foreign situations. The most important projects within the first category are the researches on the culture of the South, directed by John Gillin, and the researches on the Eastern Cherokee, directed by John Gulick. Gillin, like some of his contemporary cultural anthropologists, was interested not only in studying "primitive" or undeveloped peoples, but also in applying the concepts and methods of cultural anthropology to the study of modern American communities. In 1946 the Institute received a grant from the Rosenwald Fund for Gillin's proposed studies of the culture of the modern South. Five communities, representing five different subcultural areas, were chosen for study. One of these, a North Carolina coastal community on Core Sound, was to be studied by Gillin himself. Doctoral candidates were responsible for the field work in the other communities. Vladimir Hartman studied a North Carolina mountain community, Morton Rubin was responsible for the study of a Deep South plantation community in Alabama, while Charles Peavy dealt with a "piney woods" community in southern Alabama. The fifth area was a textile town in Piedmont South Carolina, to which three scholars were assigned. Kenneth Morland studied the mill community, Ralph C. Patrick, Jr., studied the town itself, and Hylan Lewis, a young black sociologist from Atlanta University, observed the ways of the black people of the town. In addition, Gillin planned to write a summary volume on the culture of the modern South.

Although the whole series was not published as planned, the project resulted in a number of excellent dissertations and in several significant publications. Morton Rubin's *Plantation County* was published in 1951, Hylan Lewis's *Blackways of Kent* in 1955, and Kenneth Morland's *Millways of Kent* in 1958. Gillin's heavy involvement in other researches, particularly his studies of Latin American culture, plus his departure for the University of Pittsburgh in 1959, prevented the completion of the projected summary volume on the culture of the South. A paper that he published in 1951 in collaboration with Emmett J. Murphy, entitled "Notes on Southern Culture Patterns," was indicative of what such a volume would have attempted to do. The article presented the results of the field workers' efforts to delineate the content of the southern subcultures. A checklist headed "Some Characteristic Traits in Areas of the South," covering over two hundred items under such categories as technology, housing, food, labor, stratification, and religion, was used to determine the presence or absence of a given trait in each of the five subcultures. The tentative conclusion was that "it is impossible to say what is 'distinctively Southern' with any degree of finality":

> . . . Mountains and Coastal Fringe are quite unlike each other and in turn differ from the Plantation, the Piedmont, and the Piney Woods subcultures. In other words, when viewed in terms of content, the area of the South is not culturally homogeneous. And this is as we should expect, when varying environmental and historical factors are taken into account. In the light of these materials the question may be legitimately raised as to whether there is in actual fact a general Southern culture whereby the region may be distinguished from other parts of the Nation.[10]

In addition to this large-scale project during Gillin's tenure, several studies that deal with contemporary American problems have been made by the anthropologists on the staff of the Institute. John Gulick, who has a strong interest in urban anthropology, collaborated with sociologists Kurt Back and Charles Bowerman on an urban project in North Carolina and wrote, with Bowerman, *Adaptation of Newcomers in the Piedmont Industrial Crescent*, published as part of the Institute's Monograph series in 1961. Frederick Hafer has studied cooperation and conflict in a North Carolina Piedmont community; Shirley Witt has studied sociocultural adaptations in small North Carolina communities; Dorothy Clement has made an ethnographic study of race relations in a Durham school; and James Peacock has joined with Ruel Tyson of the Department of Religion to study Southern Baptist religious services.

In 1955 the Ford Foundation provided support that made it possible for the Institute to set up its Cross-Cultural Laboratory at the Cherokee Indian Reservation in western North Carolina. The purposes of the laboratory were described as follows:

(1) To provide field training opportunities for graduate students in anthropology at the University of North Carolina; (2) to focus and coordinate a variety of research projects by students and faculty members of the University and (if feasible) of other institutions, thereby facilitating the testing of hypotheses through the approaches of several behavioral sciences; (3) to provide information and insights which may be of help to the Cherokee communities themselves in the continuing adjustments which they must make to the society which surrounds them. . . .

Though the Cherokee reservation no longer constitutes an island of really exotic culture, it nevertheless has enough elements of ethnic distinctiveness to make it a suitable testing ground for cross-cultural analysis.[11]

This project under the direction of John Gulick, was carefully planned. It was formally presented to the Chief and the Tribal Council, to the Superintendent of the Reservation, and to the Commissioner of Indian Affairs, so that their cooperation was assured. Household location maps were prepared, contacts with key Cherokees were made, and staff living quarters were secured before the study itself was begun. Field work covered a period of three years and involved ten researchers, several of whom were from other institutions.

C. H. Holzinger, a doctoral candidate at Harvard, and R. P. Kutsche, a doctoral candidate at the University of Pennsylvania, conducted research in culture and personality among the conservative Indians of the Big Cove community. Ann Cofield, a graduate student at the University of North Carolina, made a sociocultural survey of the Painttown community. Raymond D. Fogelson, a graduate student at the University of Pennsylvania, made case studies of three conservative conjurors and applied projective tests to nonconservative Indians. Robert K. Thomas, a member of the Oklahoma Cherokee tribe and a doctoral candidate at the University of Chicago, spent almost a year in residence at Cherokee and prepared working papers on a variety of topics, such as social organization, kinship systems, and metalinguistics of the Cherokee language. Harriet J. Kupferer, a doctoral candidate at Chapel Hill, surveyed the attitudes of local whites toward their Indian neighbors and gave attitude tests to white and Indian school children. Several others were involved in the project from time to time. The director of the Institute reported in 1959 that "as of June 1, 1959, the work of the Laboratory had produced: 6 published papers, 5

papers read at professional meetings, 4 M.A. theses, and 14 substantive reports in manuscript, with two doctoral dissertations in progress and a third in the planning stage.'' John Gulick published three
papers in 1958, and in 1960 his summary volume, *Cherokees at the
Crossroads*, was published in the Institute's Monograph series. In
1962 Harriet Kupferer completed her dissertation, ''The Acculturation
of the Eastern Band of Cherokee to the 'Principal People,' 1960: A
Study of the Cultural and Social Groups of the Eastern Cherokee.'' A
revised edition of *Cherokees at the Crossroads*, updated by a chapter
by an Institute research assistant, Sharlotte Williams, was issued in
1973.

Among other Indian groups that received attention were the Catawba
of South Carolina. Charles Hudson began field work among the Catawba for his doctoral dissertation under a grant obtained by Honigmann and administered by the Institute, and the results were published
in Hudson's book, *The Catawba Nation*, in 1970. The prehistoric
cultures of the Indians of the Southeast have long been the subject of
attention by Joffre L. Coe and his assistants, who have been affiliated
with the Institute from time to time. The numerous surveys, excavations, and reports that Coe has made have established him as one of the
nation's foremost authorities on southeastern archaeology.

Several of the anthropologists on the Institute staff also had an
interest in studying cultures outside of the United States. Gillin had a
special interest in Latin American culture. He did field work in Peru,
Guatemala, Colombia, and several other countries, and being profi-
cient in speaking and writing Spanish, he gained a comprehensive
knowledge of several cultures. During his tenure at Chapel Hill, from
1946 to 1959, he had several special grants and leaves of absence that
enabled him to spend long periods in field research. During that time
he produced at least six books and monographs, four of which dealt
with Latin America—*Moche: A Peruvian Coastal Community* (1947),
The Tribes of the Guianas (1948), *The Culture of Security in San
Carlos* (1951), and *San Luis Jilotepeque* (1958)—and nearly fifty
published papers, half of which were concerned with Latin America.
His interests were wide-ranging—descriptive, theoretical, methodological, and practical—as suggested by the titles of a few of his
papers: ''Methodological Problems in the Anthropological Study of
Modern Cultures'' (1949), ''Parallel Cultures and the Inhibitions to
Acculturation in a Guatemalan Community'' (1940), ''Is there a Caribbean Culture?'' (1951), ''The Security Functions of Cultural Systems''

(1951), "Components in the Ethos of Modern Latin American Culture" (1955), and "Social Science and Foreign Policy" (1958). In addition to his teaching and numerous field trips, he found time to serve as a consultant to the State Department on cultural and political affairs in Latin America and to write a widely-used textbook, *The Ways of Men* (1948).

Another cultural anthropologist who studied exotic cultures was John J. Honigmann. Before coming to Chapel Hill he had done field work in Subarctic Canada. Shortly after joining the staff of the Department of Sociology and Anthropology and the Institute in 1951 he spent some months in Pakistan on a research contract between the State Department and the Institute for a study of intercultural communication through motion pictures. His report, "Information for Pakistan: Report of Research on Intercultural Communication through Films," was submitted to the State Department and filed with the Institute in 1953. His interest in Pakistan continued, and he published several papers, including "The Men's House in West Pakistan" (1954) and "Relocation of a Punjab Pakistan Community" (1954). In 1957–58 Honigmann held a Fulbright fellowship that enabled him to spend a year in Pakistan. As a result he published a number of papers in 1958, among which were: "Cultural Change and Personal Law in Pakistan," "The Public Idiom of Pakistan," and "Pakistan's Prospects of Development." In the same year his *Three Pakistan Villages* was published in the Institute's Monograph series.

Honigmann's attention then returned to the Canadian North, and he made studies of the Cree Indians and the Eskimo of the Great Whale River in northern Quebec and of other native groups on Frobisher Bay.[12] With research assistants he spent several years under a grant from the National Science Foundation, pursuing field work, observing the cultural adaptations of the Eskimo to new towns, and studying the changes wrought by the encroachment of the white man's culture. In the spring of 1967 he was at Inuvik in the Northwest Territories studying the incipient urbanization of the native people. From these field trips came a number of papers and monographs, among them "Notes on Great Whale River Ethos" (1959), *Foodways in a Musket Community* (1962), "Indians of Nouveau Quebec" (1964), *Canadian Arctic* (1968), and, in collaboration with Irma Honigmann, "Frobisher Bay Eskimo Childhood" (1964), *Eskimo Townsmen* (1965), and *Arctic Townsmen* (1970). Honigmann also contributed significantly to the general field of anthropology with his additional works, among them *Culture and Personality* (1954), *The World of Man* (1959), *Understanding Culture* (1963), *Personality in Culture* (1967), and *The Development of Anthropological Ideas* (1976).

John Gulick came to the Department of Anthropology and Institute staff with an interest in the modern Middle East and a growing interest in urban anthropology. He had already done some field work in the Middle East, and after joining the University he returned there to continue his studies of urban anthropology. He wrote extensively on the culture of villages and cities of the Middle East. His *Social Structure and Cultural Change in a Lebanese Village* appeared in 1955, and in 1967 his *Tripoli: A Modern Arab City*, based on field work done in 1961–62. Among other publications growing out of his research were "Baghdad: Portrait of a City in Physical and Cultural Change" (1967), "The Anthropology of the Middle East" (1969), and "Urban Field Work in Lebanon" (1970). In 1970–71, on a grant from the National Science Foundation, Gulick made a study of readiness for family planning among urban Iranian families, and in collaboration with Margaret E. Gulick, who had worked with him in the field, he produced three publications on the subject: "Varieties of Domestic Social Organization in the Iranian City of Isfahan" (1974), "Kinship, Contraception, and Family Planning in the Iranian City of Isfahan" (1975), and "Migrant and Native Married Women in the Iranian City of Isfahan" (1976).

Several other Institute affiliates from the Department of Anthropology have been active in researches on various aspects of exotic cultures. Julia Crane has studied socioeconomic development, migration, and depopulation in the Caribbean and has published a monograph, *Educated to Emigrate* (1971). In collaboration with Michael V. Angrosino, she has also written *Field Projects in Anthropology: A Study Handbook*, which was published in 1974. Steven Polgar has done extensive research in the cultural factors involved in health and family planning, both in the United States and in foreign areas. Terence M. Evans is studying the sociology of the kibbutz in Israel. Frederick D. McEvoy, who joined the staff in 1969 and resigned in the Institute's fiftieth year, did field work in West Africa and published several papers dealing with kinship, social organization, and migration, with special reference to Liberia. Robert E. Daniels has carried on research on food and nutrition in three East African societies, and Anthony E. Thomas has made an analysis of the use of oaths and ordeals in Kenyan courts.

James L. Peacock, who joined the staff in 1968 and has served as chairman of the department, has done extensive work on Indonesian culture. He has concentrated on the area of myths, drama, ritual, and symbolism, and has published several works, including *Indonesia: An Anthropological Perspective* (1973), *Rites of Modernization: Symbolic and Social Aspects of Indonesian Proletarian Drama* (1968), and *Consciousness and Change: Symbolic Anthropology in Evolutionary Perspective* (1975). He is also concerned with the problem of cultural evolution and has published a volume on the subject, *The Human Direction: An Evolutionary Approach to Cultural and Social Anthropology* (1970).

The work of several men who were formerly on the staffs of the Department of Anthropology and the Institute deserves mention. Charles J. Erasmus, who served for a short time beginning in 1960, was interested in the problems, possibilities, and limitations of technical assistance in improving life in the less developed countries. His book on the subject, *Man Takes Control: Cultural Development and American Aid* (1961), was favorably received. Richard Lieban, who was affiliated with the Institute for several years, beginning in 1963, did research in the Philippines and was instrumental in obtaining funding for a medical anthropology program in the Department of Anthropology. F. T. Cloak, Jr., who was a member of the staff for several years, beginning in 1967, used his studies in Trinidad as the basis for a theoretical excursion into problems of cultural evolution. He proposed a method "for discovering, establishing and analyzing developmental sequences by comparing contemporary sets of qualitative data." His monograph, *A Natural Order of Cultural Adoption and Loss in Trinidad* (1967), became the first in the Institute's Working Papers in Methodology series.

The role of the Department of Anthropology in the Institute has steadily broadened. It has eight staff members affiliated with the Institute, most of whom are carrying on cultural studies. The interests of the anthropologists have widened, and they occasionally undertake research in areas that have been the traditional preserves of other social scientists. Anthropologists in general now have less interest than formerly in what was known as area research—usually descriptive studies of particular ethnographic areas—and, while still concentrating on specific parts of the globe, they now put increasing emphasis on substantive topics, such as urban anthropology, language and culture, and educational anthropology.

After fifty years, studies of race and ethnic groups are now relatively less common than they were in the early years of the Institute, but they still occupy a significant share of the total research program. Studies of the folk, as Odum used the term, have virtually disappeared from the Institute's repertoire except insofar as some of the work of the cultural anthropologists overlaps with that field; but the Folklore Curriculum, an interdisciplinary unit that owed its creation in 1940 in some measure at least to the work of Odum and Johnson, preserves a lively interest in folklore under the leadership of Professor Daniel W. Patterson. With Odum the early folk studies were a means to an end, a prologue to a larger field of study that would encompass the folk and much more— regionalism. The next chapter examines the Institute's researches in regionalism and regional planning.

CHAPTER 6

Regionalism

Howard W. Odum had been fascinated with the phenomena of the southern region even before he went north to receive two doctorates in the related areas of psychology and sociology. One of his primary concerns in establishing *Social Forces* was to give the region a forum, and the same concern motivated him to set up the Institute for Research in Social Science two years later "as a tool for building the state and the region" on the bedrock of "the actual facts." He repeatedly defined the purpose of the Institute to be the "cooperative study of problems in the general field of the social sciences arising out of State and regional conditions."

It was in the field of the regional studies that Odum was to win his highest praise and to make a major contribution to the South. *Social Forces* and the Institute shared in this prestige and also made it possible. Both Odum and the Institute staff arrived gradually at the concepts of regionalism and regional planning. As the first decade of the Institute closed, Carl Sauer, anthropologist at the University of California at Berkeley, voiced a growing opinion among social scientists that the Institute was plowing virgin land. In a letter to Odum in 1934, he wrote, "I have watched for years with growing interest the publications emanating from your institute, as records of what is to my mind the most interesting experiment in social science in America."[1] He spoke of the regional studies as "folk-soil-study," and added, "We geographers and anthropologists have been talking about the concept of culture and the fact that culture is a spatial manifestation, but your group is about the only one that has done anything about it."

Sauer thought that however much Odum might grope and wander in an effort to come up with a concept of regionalism that would indeed correspond to the facts, he was doing something that would "in the end be methodologically helpful to all of us." Sauer took it for granted that the southern region was a "field that belongs to you." It was fortunate that Odum had realized the uniqueness of the area, Sauer continued, because "the South certainly has a quality of culture, vividness of problem, and historical personality that makes it an enviable ground for the social scientist. Personally I have long thought that the country's most interesting and most dramatic human problems, both past and present, were in the South.'' With an insight into Odum's writings that showed an intimate knowledge of Odum's attempt to spell out the differentiations that made the South a distinct region, Sauer commended the method, the goals, and the spirit of Institute research:

> I like the way you have insisted that you were dealing with the
> reality of the South, that life was and would be different in its
> problems in your part of the country from others, that it was your
> job to examine the personality of the South, and that you are
> going about this business of understanding by whatever means
> would get results. I think you have been right in not being too
> formal in your procedures; we are inclined to be a bit professorial
> in the social sciences, and you have not been particularly worried
> about appearing academic on all occasions. I like the method, the
> objective, and the spirit with which your group has been at work.
> I wouldn't swap it, personally, for all the social science theory or
> statistics in the country, because you are documenting a
> distinctive part of the American scene and, being concerned with
> how a distinctive part of the American people has lived in its
> distinctive land, you proceed properly, as you have done, to a
> consideration of how that people on its land may become a
> balanced integrant of the national economy.[2]

Odum's Social Theories

To understand Odum's approach to regionalism and the conceptual structure within which he built the theory of regionalism and regional planning, it is necessary to mention briefly the social theories on which he erected his frame of reference. His concepts of society and the interdependence of its parts, his views on the races of mankind and their symbiotic relationships, and his theories on folk culture were distilled from his personal observations of the behavioral processes as well as from the philosophies of his professors and from others in the field of the developing social sciences of the period. His early studies in the classics seem to have convinced him that balance was an important concept of societal well being. His other theories of the organic nature of society, of the inevitability of progress, of gradualism as the best strategy for obtaining social change, of pragmatism as the wisest approach to social action, and of the folkways and mores were undoubtedly outgrowths of the philosophies of social Darwinism current during the years of his graduate studies. His graduate work also taught him the importance of using scientific methodologies in pursuit of research.

The concept of balance that appears throughout his works is one he must have gleaned at first hand from the writings of the Greek and Latin philosophers, who had placed emphasis upon balance in the natural world, in government, and in art and architecture. Years before going to Clark University, Odum had already seen an imbalance in the South between whites and blacks, between landlord and tenant, between city and country, between the poor and the rich, between the educated and the illiterate. The South was out of balance with the rest of America: in its standard of living, in wage rates, in the money spent on education, in labor relations, in disregard for child welfare, and in the treatment of the black population. This early insight stayed with him throughout his career, and in 1945, just nine years before his death, Odum pointed out in a brief summary of his regional theories, included in the volume *In Search of the Regional Balance of America*, just how central to his thinking had been the concept of balance. In the foreword to the book, he wrote: "The conclusion is that the most dynamic problem in postwar America is of one part with the search for a better regional balance of people and resources everywhere."[3]

His graduate studies in the social sciences at Clark and Columbia universities greatly illuminated Odum's thinking on the nature of society. He gleaned new insights both from G. Stanley Hall at Clark and from Franklin H. Giddings at Columbia. At the time, it was customary for social scientists to look upon society as conforming to natural law and to view society itself as a living organism or as analogous to one, so that the whole of society would suffer if one portion of it was injured. Both economic underdevelopment and racial discrimination in the South were seen as organic violations that were damaging not only to the South but to the whole of national society. The social problems of the South were, in fact, an indication of the organic malfunctioning of society.

The concepts of the organic nature of society current at the time of Odum's graduate work were influenced by the applications of Darwinism to social theory. Adaptations of social Darwinism may be found in the writings, for example, of Hall and Giddings, and of Lester F.

Ward, Herbert Spencer, and William Graham Sumner, but Odum made his own adaptations. He tended to reject most of Ward's evolutionary concepts, which were employed to reinforce conservative thought, but he accepted much of social Darwinism as developed by Spencer and Sumner. Spencer and Sumner took different approaches to their views of the nature of society.[4] To Spencer the fact that society conformed to natural laws meant progress. He believed that while a large segment of mankind might suffer poverty and poor health, the evolutionary process meant that society was moving toward a higher form, and by implication, to a more blissful state in which fewer and fewer men would suffer: progress was inevitable. Sumner was less optimistic about the achievement of a more perfect society and concluded that the evolutionary process meant that men must cope somehow with the inherent dangers and sufferings in the battle for life. Both Spencer and Sumner, however, agreed that change must come slowly in order not to interfere with the wisdom of nature, but that progress would come nevertheless.

Odum probably drew as much of his belief in inevitable progress from the teachings of Christianity learned at his mother's knee as he did from social Darwinism.[5] He had faith in the inevitable triumph of good over evil, and he sought through his own research and that of the Institute to undergird this faith with scientific data. Just a year before his death, however, he was writing in *Social Forces* about the need for "adequate analyses of the changing structure of human society" that should replace "the concepts of natural evolution of the oversimplified linear theories of universal progress."[6] He had lived long enough and had made enough analyses of human society on his own to reject the assumption of his earlier years that society is progressing automatically to a happier state of well-being.

From social Darwinism came not only the well-pronounced theories of the organic nature of society and the inevitability of progress, but also their corollaries of gradualism as the proper approach to social reform, and pragmatism as the most effective technique of change.[7] Odum accepted to some extent all of these related theories in his studies of regionalism and the problems of the South, as did most American social scientists in their writings for more than half a century. Odum's approach to the solutions of the ills of society followed gradualism and pragmatism as the wisest policies not because haste and ill-conceived action would interfere with the laws of nature, but because gradualism was necessary in order to give social customs time to change slowly so that the changes would be acceptable to the people. He was a pragmatist, above all, in the techniques he followed in achieving his goals, but he termed the process functionalism, not pragmatism. His often repeated admonition to the research assistants in the Institute was "If the research is not functional, it won't work and is not sound theory."[8]

The work of William Graham Sumner, modified by the writings of Hall and Giddings, especially enlarged Odum's thinking on folk society. Hall, who was a leading proponent of Freudian thought in America, was also an advocate of the virtues of "natural man." He abhorred the destructive forces of civilization on both man and society. Odum accepted Hall's theories that every man is a compound of his genetic inheritance and his individual differences, that civilization tends to have a degenerative effect on the individual, and that men who have long associated together as in a racial group develop a "soul" characteristic of that group. Giddings was more optimistic than Hall about the effects of civilization on society, and Odum must have considered Gidding's theory of the "consciousness of kind" as another approach to what Hall defined as the racial soul.

It was from Sumner's analyses of folkways and mores that Odum gleaned most of his insights into the folk culture that he had carefully observed before going north to study. Sumner held that a folkway was a positively sanctioned behavior pattern characteristic of a given society and that the mores were practices that had crystalized from the folkways as a means of enforcing folk customs. In time, Odum developed his own concepts of folkways versus stateways, which he called customs arising from governmental processes, and still later folkways versus technicways, which he defined as recently evolved customs growing out of technology.[9] At times he suggested that the technicways were "tragically destructive in contemporary society,"[10] a position reminiscent of Hall's view of the evil effects of civilization.[11] Odum stressed the crucial need of state government to base its ways upon a thorough knowledge of the folk, and cited the rupture in southern society that had followed the Civil War as a case in point of governmental ineptitude. "To use . . . an illustration from the southern region," be wrote, "the folk society following the Civil War was more powerful and effective than the combined bayonets and governmental routine of the whole Nation. . . . It is generally admitted by the historians that scientific study of such folk society would have avoided many blunders both North and South."[12]

Odum also maintained that the scholar must above all be objective in his findings. He must rid himself completely of all biases and examine his research coldly in light of the data he collected. He must explore all possible sources of information and examine his own feelings with complete detachment so that he might present "the actual facts." Odum often told his graduate students that the Negro problem might easily be solved in time if only southerners would "look" at the Negro rather than "feel about him," a distinction Hall had made between feeling and observation. In an *American Epoch*, some reviewers felt, Odum had carried his concepts of objectivity and balance to such an extreme as to bewilder the average reader. He had presented the pro and con of almost every question he raised. "In the long run," wrote John Donald Wade in the *Knoxville* (Tennessee) *Journal*, Odum "leaves his readers as unsure as to what definitely is the main trend in the present South as they could possibly have been before picking up his book."[13] Here again, Odum was using a research technique he had learned from Hall, who had a bewildering habit of compiling a long and confused list of opposing values in order to present an unbiased approach to his data.

For all his lectures to his graduate classes at the University of North Carolina on the scientific method, on deductive and inductive reasoning, on the importance of formulating postulates, on objectivity, on the organic nature of society, and on balance, Odum's methodology in his works on folk culture was largely descriptive and episodical, much as the writings of Hall had been. But Odum strove valiantly to give an accurate folk portraiture, and in this he largely succeeded.

He had written in *An Introduction to Social Research*, which he and Katharine Jocher had begun in 1925, that "the premise of the volume is that there is no one special method of social research and that new and significant developments in methods of social research are now well on the way."[14] The authors then went on to discuss the case method, the survey, and the questionnaire as well as to point out the various disciplinary approaches to research. From there the authors progressed to "common-sense techniques," the importance of research personnel, and methods of exploring the sources. In his own work and in the research he supervised in the Institute, Odum sought to follow the instructions he and Katharine Jocher had laid out in their discussion of research techniques. To Odum, his trilogy on Black Ulysses was a demonstration of the case-history technique as well as a portraiture of black folkways. As Carl Sauer said in his letter in 1934, Odum was going about the business of understanding the southern region "by whatever means would get results."

Soon after the Institute was set up, Odum reported to the Board of Governors that methodologies in social science research were changing and implied that the Institute would follow these new techniques. His employment of a statistician as a research associate in 1927 indicated the direction that Institute research would take. From the beginning of the Institute, Odum had insisted that the research assistants take graduate courses in social statistics as a prerequisite for further research. While at Columbia as a student of Franklin H. Giddings, he had learned the importance of methodological techniques that emphasized the use of statistics. His decision to turn in the direction of quantitative measurements of data was the Institute's first step toward mathematical sociology and foreshadowed the organization of the Statistical Laboratory, which was to become later a vital aspect of the Institute's work. After the publication of *An American Epoch* in 1930, Odum wrote to Edmund E. Day of the Rockefeller Foundation that the publication of Institute research on the southern folk was "only the first stage of our regional studies,"[15] and, in applying for a third grant from the Rockefeller funds, he wrote to Sydnor Walker that "the old survey study is no longer the thing we want."[16]

Development of Regional Concepts

The concept of regionalism by no means originated with Odum. Sectional or regional identifications and diversifications are as old as human society. The terms *sectional* and *regional* can be pinpointed in literature from about the middle of the eighteenth century. In the United States the geographers, the historians, the federal agencies, the Census Bureau, and Congress itself had long been dividing the nation into districts, sections, divisions, and regions for arranging the details of American geography. For the federal agencies and for Congress as well, it was a device for administering programs, collecting taxes, and dispensing justice.

John W. Powell's "Physiographic Processes," published in 1895, was the landmark work that revolutionized thinking on the subject.[17] Frederick Jackson Turner, whose research on the American frontier popularized the concept of sectionalism among historians, paid tribute to Powell's influence, but Turner also had been influenced by his history professor, William F. Allen at the University of Wisconsin, who early in his research discerned the historical role of geographic sections in American history. Walter Hines Page, a North Carolinian and an editor of the *Atlantic Monthly*, also helped to popularize the concept and to clarify Turner's thinking when he invited Turner to prepare an essay for the *Atlantic* that would spell out the reasons for cultural differences in such geographic areas as Georgia, Minnesota, and Vermont. Everybody knows, Page maintained, that these areas are "as different as three individuals." The task he assigned Turner was to point up the differences.[18] By the 1920s the terms *sectionalism* and *regionalism*, often used as synonyms, were much in vogue among social scientists.[19]

Odum chose to use the term *regional* rather than *sectional* largely because *regional* was becoming at the time a somewhat more acceptable term than *sectional*, and perhaps more importantly because *sectional* had for more than half a century been used by historians and by political leaders in and out of Congress as a derogatory term to describe the South. The essential quality of sectionalism, Odum thought, was "the idea of separatism and isolation; of separate units with separate interests." Regionalism was different from sectionalism because "the very definition of regionalism implies a unifying function." He pointed out further in his discussion of the two concepts that

> the distinctions are clear between the divisive power of self-seeking *sections* and the integrating power of co-ordinate *regions* fabricated into a united whole. The premise of the new regionalism goes further and assumes that the United States must not, either because of its bigness and complexity or because of conflicting interests, become a federation of conflicting sections but a homogeneity of varying regions.[20]

This emphasis upon the need to direct sectionalism toward regionalism and to integrate the various regions into a national unit represents, according to some writers, Odum's major achievement. It was left to Odum and the Institute to define the terms in a way that would be acceptable and to give them credence as recognizable aspects of American civilization. After twenty years or more of his own research and that done in the Institute, the definition of *region* that Odum came to adopt, stated simply, was that a region was an area united by the quality or characteristics peculiar to that area. *Regionalism* was the principle of dividing geographic areas according to their unifying forces, namely their institutional life-styles, and *regional planning* was the process of giving due consideration to these unifying forces in the development of the area so that the people living there might experience minimum disruption.

In a volume on regionalism, *In Search of the Regional Balance of America*, which he edited with Katharine Jocher in 1945, Odum laid out step by step the research studies in the Institute that had led him to the concepts of regionalism. These concepts had at their core his philosophy of the role folkways play in human society. He listed his first publication in the field of folk culture, ''The Religious Folk-Songs of the Southern Negroes,'' which appeared in 1909, as the beginning of his search for a conceptual framework of folk, region, and society.[21] As previously pointed out, his early community studies of Negroes in Georgia and Mississippi, begun before his graduate work in the North, stimulated his interests in the South as a distinct region and in folk culture as a distinctive field of inquiry. ''To know the soul of a people'' and to understand ''the truest expression of the folk-mind and feeling'' remained a central theme in Odum's motivation and in his social theories throughout his life.[22]

Odum's writings in the field of folk culture continued at intervals, and as he relates it, ''When the Institute for Research in Social Science was established at the University of North Carolina, with the specific keystone of its program that of Regional Research and Study, immediately the Negro and the folk life became a first unit.''[23] He included among the volumes of research that he believed had first led him to advance his theories of regionalism and folkways his two volumes on Negro songs edited with Guy B. Johnson; his own trilogy of a Negro folk hero; Johnson's *John Henry* and Johnson's supervision of the sociological studies for the Myrdal study, *An American Dilemma*; Newbell N. Puckett's *Folkbeliefs of the Southern Negro*; Wiley B. Sanders's *Negro Child Welfare*; and two volumes by Arthur F. Raper, *The Tragedy of Lynching* and *Preface to Peasantry*.

Odum said that the second step in the erection of his social theories on regionalism was the Institute's examination of the ''whole culture life of the region'' reflecting ''the peculiar civilization which still transcends the stateways of government.''[24] Among the research publications of the Institute that had given him this perspective, Odum listed his own *An American Epoch*; two books by Rupert B. Vance, *Human Factors in Cotton Culture* and *Human Geography of the South*; two social histories by Guion Griffis Johnson, one on the South Atlantic sea islands and the other on antebellum North Carolina; Fletcher Green's *Constitutional Development in the South Atlantic States*; William Jenkins's *Pro-Slavery Thought*; and Julia Spruill's *Women's Life and Work in the Southern Colonies*.

The third step in Odum's conceptualization of the southern region came from the Institute's "materials for the study of practical social problems of economic and social policy, or of social planning whether of local or national import."[25] He listed such materials as Clarence Heer's *Wages and Income in the South*; two volumes by Harriet Herring, *Welfare Work in Mill Villages* and *Southern Cotton Mill Workers and Their Villages*; two volumes by C. K. Brown on transportation; Jesse F. Steiner and Roy M. Brown's *The North Carolina Chain Gang*; Brown's *Public Poor Relief in North Carolina*; Claudius Murchinson's *King Cotton is Sick*; T. J. Woofter Jr.'s *The Plight of Cigarette Tobacco*; and Arthur Raper's research on lynching and sharecroppers.

A fourth type of research that was illuminating to Odum in its delineation of regionalism was the cooperative study of St. Helena Island. The research involved five disciplines in the social sciences— anthropology, economics, history, psychology, and sociology—and emphasized cooperation of these fields in the development of methodology and theory. It was undertaken partly as "an objective in the development of social science, social research, and personnel within the given region."[26] It thus became clear to Odum that a multidisciplinary approach in the examination of a region was perhaps the best way to reveal all the intricacies of a folk society.

Recent Social Trends in the United States, a project in which Odum participated as assistant director with his friend William F. Ogburn, a sociologist from the University of Chicago, was a second example of cooperative research that opened up new insights into Odum's developing concepts of regionalism. It was the final link in the chain of studies that Odum said had helped him formulate his theoretical framework. President Hoover had appointed the Committee on Social Trends in December 1929, with instructions that it survey the nation and report on its social development. Besides Odum and Ogburn, other prominent social scientists such as Charles E. Merriam in political science, Wesley C. Mitchell in economics, and Shelby Harrison in social work, served on the Committee. In 1933 the Committee presented a two-volume report. Until that time, Odum had been chiefly engaged in thinking and writing about the southern region. The new work gave him knowledge of national development and prepared him to relate his folk-culture theories to the nation as a whole. Before moving toward "regional national planning," however, he had to synchronize and make practical applications of the southern regional studies to "larger composite regional studies," to apply the findings to teaching and additional research, and finally to relate the evolving concepts to regional planning.[27]

Odum's Southern Regions of the United States

Before undertaking a major research project in the area of regional national planning, Odum brought out his monumental *Southern Regions of the United States* in 1936, written under the auspices of the Social Science Research Council. In 1929 the Social Science Research Council had set up its Southern Regional Committee, on which Odum was invited to serve. The committee was to function for eighteen years.[28] In 1932 Odum requested the Board of Governors of the Institute to grant him a leave of absence for two years to direct the Southern Regional Planning Study, which was to be administered by the Southern Regional Committee. During this time he planned to "make the University of North Carolina his headquarters, continue as Director of the Institute without pay, and continue the work and planning of the further development of the Institute."[29]

At this same meeting of the Board of Governors, Odum also proposed to reorganize the Institute for Research in Social Science into a "Southern Regional Research Institute" with headquarters in Chapel Hill. In the discussion of this proposal that followed, it was undoubtedly Odum who stressed that "nothing in the discussion of this new plan was understood to indicate a change in policy except as a means of strengthening and enlarging the original regional objectives of the Institute and as enabling it to provide a long time program with reasonable security."[30] Six months after his original proposal in January 1932, Odum sent a memorandum to the Board pressing for a decision. "There is," he wrote, "considerable interest abroad in the development of a real regional institute for the study of regional cultures and interregional cultures with the recent added feature of regional planning." With a veiled implication that such an institute might be settled elsewhere, he added, "Whether such an institute would be at the University of North Carolina or in some other institution would depend, as I see it, entirely upon the University of North Carolina in its internal policy."[31] But the Board of Governors took no action on the proposal. On several other occasions while he was working on the Southern Regional Planning Study Odum proposed to the Board that the Institute be reorganized into a regional body, but he had no better success than with his first proposal.[32]

Odum had hoped to complete his part of the Southern Regional Planning Study, which he was to call *Southern Regions of the United States*, within two years, and he was embarrassed to find that the research required twice as long. After a year of research, he laid out the plan of the work to Wilson Gee, a sociology professor at the University of Virginia, who was working on a survey of social science research agencies in the United States:

> The program of the Institute for the next year or two is partly a continuation of present projects . . . and partly an extension of the Institute's coordinated program growing out of its past studies and out of the Southern Regional Study. . . .
>
> The studies of folk-regional culture, while basic to the theoretical backgrounds and evolution of regional cultures, have in mind primarily facts which are pertinent to regional planning and development of the South's capacity for education, social welfare, adequacy in all aspects of its life. Working upon the general studies here are Howard W. Odum, Katharine Jocher, Rupert B. Vance, Helen I. McCobb.
>
> Special aspects of regional culture study are those attempting to inventory for the first time the submarginal groups and areas of which the South is reputed to have such an abundance. This is more than the continuation of the earlier studies of folk-life and race; it is also a study of regional social pathology and of redefinition of many terms and assumptions of the past. Working upon these aspects are Howard W. Odum, T. J. Woofter, Jr., Rupert B. Vance, Lee M. Brooks, and Gordon Blackwell, who will also attempt to focus upon social waste in the South, selecting special aspects for unit by unit attack. Closely related will be a continuation by Dr. Woofter and Dr. Vance and others of the regional analysis of the Southeast, utilizing some twenty-seven subdivisions for social analysis and for an approach to planning.[33]

When *Southern Regions* at last appeared in 1936 it was a massive tome of nearly seven hundred pages, filled with charts, graphs, and statistical tables, almost encyclopedic in content but lucidly written and laid out in scholarly fashion. Odum acknowledged in the introductory note indebtedness to a large number of work memoranda prepared by the Institute staff.[34] The volume was certainly Odum's major scientific work. It went through four printings and was used in the universities of the South, in school systems, and in government offices. Years later, *Southern Regions* was said to have inspired a revolution, and Odum was called "the Eli Whitney of the modern South."[35] At Odum's death in 1954, an editorial in the *Washington Post* stated that "there was no one—unless it was Franklin Roosevelt—whose influence was greater than Odum's on the development of the region below the Potomac."[36] The *Post* singled out *Southern Regions*, "prepared in his cluttered study at the University of North Carolina," as his best known work, and declared that it "did as much to arouse the South economically as *Uncle Tom's Cabin* did to arouse the South sociologically before the Civil War."

Southern Regions was divided into two parts. The first part laid out the "objectives and framework" of the study and went on to list 258 distinctive characteristics of the South, a list that Odum liked to call a "social inventory." The first objective was to present a portraiture of the South: its geographic areas, its cultural diversities, and its behavior patterns. He sought to draw this portrait in a way that would reveal the place of the southern region in the nation and would at the same time dramatize the struggle of the South to develop a superior civilization despite the complexity of its culture and its "cumulative handicaps."[37] Here was a rephrasing of what Odum had been writing in *Social Forces* since its first issue and what he had been repeating to every graduate class in sociology since his arrival in Chapel Hill.

What was new was his projection of the study "upon a theoretical framework which would insure measurable reality in research and attainability in whatever programs might emerge." The theoretical framework he constructed emphasized that a regional analysis must:

1. give "a clear recognition of the history and theoretical significance of the region and of the power of the folk-regional society in modern culture";
2. give "reality to the southern picture" by "facing absolute facts rather than substituting rationalizations" and give the "measurement of conditions in terms of comparison with certain selected standards and with regional and national variations" but with the understanding that the "methodology

of evaluating such comparisons and differentials'' is part of the task;

3. give ''a fair picture of the major resources and forces which have determined the capacity of the southern regions.''

The third dimension of the theoretical framework had two requisites: ''first, an inventory of the natural resources . . . and, second, an appraisal of human resources . . . [available for] the development of a richer culture and social well-being.''

Several aspects of the southern picture, Odum admitted, were not measurable by statistical tables: tradition, opinion, conflict, arrangement of stateways and folkways. He hoped to give ''the dignity of cultural history'' to the South's ''chronological lag, its retarded frontier dominance, its agrarian culture, its youthful and immature population, its lusty vitality, its unevenness of life, and its marginal struggle for survival.''[38]

Most important of all, one objective of the study was to explore the southern regions as a laboratory for research and experimentation in social planning. Odum promised further research in these areas, and in later years he fulfilled his promise.

He could not close his statement of objectives and framework without attempting to settle the controversy over the terms *sectional* and *regional*. He thought sectionalism had a ''past constrictive power'' in contrast to the unifying attribute of ''the new regionalism.'' *Southern Regions* was, therefore, ''projected to feature the regional-national as opposed to the local-sectional emphasis.'' His regional premises consequently avoided ''any hypotheses of a self-contained or self-sufficing South'' and looked toward a greater degree of federal interest and participation on the part of the South.[39]

The second part of *Southern Regions* was Odum's attempt to synthesize his raw data within the framework he had spelled out in the first part. Here he added a new integral part to his original premise that regional-national cooperation was necessary to develop the region to the point of accepting social planning. Now he declared that the state must also be included to provide stability for a permanent action-agency.[40]

The second part of the book also had much to do with Odum's theory of balance. He saw the urgent need for a balance between the new and the old, the rural and the urban, the agrarian and the industrial, the folkways and the technicways, and he believed that it was only through social planning based upon an adequate examination and interpretation of the facts and forces of the region that a workable balance might be obtained. To acheive this, he said, scientific principles and practicable, workable techniques built upon factual inventories should be combined to erect a social action-agency that would lead the way to the development of a richer culture and social well-being. The implication was that each southern state should have its own social planning agency, perhaps a council, and that the region should look to the nation for a composite pattern of national planning. For years Odum had been lecturing and writing briefly about the importance of social planning, but here for the first time he came down hard on the side of cooperative state and national planning. Harvey Lebrun, writing in *Social Forces* in 1937, called *Southern Regions* a social philosophy, a technique, and a blueprint for relating a planning program based on scientific research and technical knowledge to practical social action.[41] Many years later, Harvey A. Kantor, professor of sociology at the University of Rhode Island, wrote that the valuable aspect of Odum's proposal was his insistence that the expert design the program but never overlook the folk psychology.[42]

Almost every member of the Institute staff and numerous graduate students as well were involved in some aspect of the production of *Southern Regions*. Odum had paved the way for the introduction of the work by writing a pamphlet, *The Regional Approach to National Planning*, for the Foreign Policy Association in 1935, and at the same time his colleague, Rupert B. Vance, wrote a second pamphlet for the Association, *Regional Reconstruction: A Way Out for the South*. A year later Vance brought out a pamphlet for the Public Affairs Committee, *The South's Place in the Nation*, and at the same time T. J. Woofter, Jr., prepared the first pamphlet for the Southern Policy Papers, *Southern Population and Social Planning*. These were just a few of the numerous articles and pamphlets in a variety of publications and journals by which Odum and the Institute staff helped to popularize the concepts of regional planning.

In 1936, the year *Southern Regions* was published, a teaching manual for use in the public schools was prepared by Lee M. Brooks of the Department of Sociology, and a graduate student from Texas, Harry Estill Moore (whose wife, Bernice M. Moore, was also pursuing a doctorate in the Department of Sociology), wrote another pamphlet in the Southern Policies Papers, *What is Regionalism?* Gerald W. Johnson, Odum's longtime friend, who was at the time an editor of the *Baltimore Sun*, issued simultaneously a brief, popular version of *Southern Regions* called *The Wasted Land* as a part of the Southern Regional Planning Study.

Criticisms of Regionalism

Although *Southern Regions* won acclaim as a major contribution to sociology, it was not without its critics. Even before the publication of the volume, Odum had found rising sectionalism within the Southern Regional Study Committee. "What is happening is a revivification of Turner's sectionalism," he wrote regretfully to George Milton, a liberal Democrat and editor of the *Chattanooga Evening Tribune*.[43]

A group of conservative southerners, sometimes called the Agrarians, had been at work since the late 1920s on still another philosophy of southern society, and they were ready to do ideological battle with Odum's concept of regionalism. Led by a few professors at Vanderbilt University, of whom Donald Davidson was probably the most outspoken, "Twelve Southerners" had issued a manifesto in 1930, *I'll Take My Stand*, that extolled the virtues of rural society. The statement of principles contained in the book's introduction was an ardent endorsement of "the Southern way of life against what may be called the American prevailing way."[44] While the manifesto was a blatant appeal to sectionalism, its authors did not see it as such. They were contending not against the other sections of America, the Agrarians said, but against the industrialization of the nation, which would lead in the end to "much the same economic system as that imposed by violence upon Russia in 1917." The ideal society, they insisted, was one "in which agriculture is the leading vocation, whether for wealth, for pleasure, or for prestige."[45] Donald Davidson maintained that the program Odum proposed could not circumvent "the political aspects of Southern economic and cultural problems" merely by calling itself "regional" instead of "sectional."

The Agrarians referred to the Chapel Hill "Regionalists" as being possessed of a "disassociated cynicism" that sprang, no doubt, "from their flirtation with alien doctrines." Fred C. Hobson, Jr., who has examined the impact of H. L. Mencken on the South in his *Serpent in Eden*, thinks the Agrarians' attacks upon "the North Carolina school of progressive liberalism" were similar to their attacks upon Mencken, who had been far more acrimonious in writing about the South than had Odum and the Institute.[46] Their references to the Regionalists as being possessed of an "agitating and crusading spirit" and their accusations that the Regionalists were toying with "alien doctrines" are strongly reminiscent of the attack of the *Southern Textile Bulletin* upon Odum and the Institute in the 1920s. But Odum, with his characteristic strategy of meeting criticism by turning the other cheek, invited Donald Davidson to air his views in an article for *Social Forces*. Davidson's article, "Where Regionalism and Sectionalism Meet," which appeared in October 1934, reiterated his position that there was little difference between regionalism and sectionalism, but it contained none of the Agrarians' suggestions that regionalism was subversive. Four years later, the University of North Carolina Press published Davidson's major criticism of regionalism, *The Attack on Leviathan: Regionalism and Nationalism in the United States*.

Among sociologists, the professors at the University of Chicago, who for years had been concentrating on the development of ecological concepts to deal with urbanism, were the most penetrating, even caustic, in criticism of Odum's regionalism. Louis Wirth, the theorist of the group, was selected at a conference on regionalism, held at the University of Wisconsin in 1949, to point out the limitations of regionalism. Wirth contended that "regionalism, which is the way of viewing social life in areal terms is, after all, only one possible perspective of human beings living together," and he added that to imply that regionalism was the only way was to distort reality. "Regionalism as a dogma," he warned, "can easily degenerate into a cult," and he strongly implied that this was what Odum and the Institute were promoting. There was, Wirth concluded, "no magic in the regional idea, but rather risk," for regional dogmatism would lead to "falsification of the facts."[47]

The most penetrating evaluation of Odum's *Southern Regions* has been made recently by his two sons, both of whom are involved in research into ecology as a new integrative discipline. Eugene P. Odum is Callaway Distinguished Professor of Ecology and director of the Institute of Ecology of the University of Georgia at Athens, and Howard Thomas Odum is a professor of environmental engineering at the University of Florida at Gainesville. Their *Fundamentals of Ecology*, first published in 1953, has gone through several editions. It was a revolutionary approach to the discipline because it insisted upon considering the ecosystem level as the beginning rather than the conclusion of research in ecology and because the authors selected energy as the common denominator that integrates a functional whole. For this and later research, the Odums were awarded the Prix de l'Institut de la Vie in Paris, France, in 1975. Eugene Odum received in 1977 the John and Alice Tyler Ecology Award given by Pepperdine University in California, which is generally considered to be the highest award in the United States in that field, and in this instance the award was presented by President Jimmy Carter in a ceremony in Washington.

In his acceptance address for the French award, published in *Science* in 1977, Eugene Odum briefly reviewed his father's concept of regionalism as a pioneer approach to regional social science that was "widely misinterpreted in those days as being merely an inventory device designed to upgrade 'backward' regions (such as the South in the 1930s)."[48] It was, on the contrary, "an approach to the study of society based on the recognition of distinct differences in both cultural and natural attributes" of different but interdependent areas. Regionalism as a major sociological theory "stalled," he explained, "because there was no appropriate linkage with natural science (applied ecology had not yet 'emerged' to that level of thinking) and because statistical methods of the day were totally inadequate to cope with the mountains of data collected by social science researchers." (Howard Thomas Odum agrees with this assessment.) Eugene Odum has also called attention to two recent regional studies that embody Howard W. Odum's ideas but that consider them from the basis of ecology and resources: *The California Tomorrow Plan*, by Alfred Heller, published in 1972, and *Ecology and Economy, a Concept for Balancing Long-Range Goals: The Pacific Northwest Example*, edited by Mark Westling and published in 1973.

Odum and Moore's American Regionalism

When *Southern Regions* was published, Howard W. Odum had promised further research on regionalism and social planning, and in 1938 he fulfilled his promise by writing with one of his graduate students, Harry Estill Moore, *American Regionalism: A Cultural Historical Approach to National Integration*. This volume received even higher acclaim than *Southern Regions*. As late as 1972 it has been called the classic book on the subject and "the most complete statement of regional thought yet produced."[49]

Odum and Moore clearly defined their terms and spelled out the difference between regionalism and sectionalism. They held that regionalism signifies an area which is "a totality composed of several areal and cultural units" which form a component of the nation whereas sectionalism "always assumes isolated, segregated areal divisions with potential completeness in themselves."[50] In summarizing the mass of data pointing to the organic nature of regionalism and its unifying force, Odum and Moore found that "the real theme of American regionalism is essentially that of a great nation in whose continuity and unity of development . . . must be found the hope of American democracy and, according to many observers, of Western civilization." The first step in realizing this hope, they said, is an understanding of the region "as a dynamic social reality," and to arrive at this understanding, it is necessary to investigate two major areas of inquiry: (1) "the American background with its extraordinary undesigned mastery of the continent and its pluralisms in time, geography, and culture," and (2) "the impact of modern civilization itself upon the changing nation." They believed that the nation was facing dilemmas and that it had arrived at this unfortunate situation "through logical sequence of cause and effect and especially through imbalance and unevenness in its regional developments and integration." Another significant aspect of these dilemmas was the impact of technology and urban civilization upon American society.[51]

The solutions they proposed were many-faceted. First, regionalism implied decentralization, which was vital to maintain a balanced growth rate. Cities with their concentration of wealth and power should not be allowed to grow at the expense of the outlying areas. Second, dispersion of resources created by centralization would bring about a better economic balance in the area and would establish unity, homogeneity, and comprehensiveness in regional development. In taking this position, the authors allied themselves with Lewis Mumford, whom they quoted as thinking that "regionalism is the antithesis to false cosmopolitanism." There was yet a third facet of the new regionalism, one Odum had stressed in his *Southern Regions*: its organic nature in which time, geography, and culture are integral parts of the whole. Thus the feeling of being at home in the region, emotionally secure as a result of this feeling, would help the people realize their potential and prevent the cities from absorbing resources and wealth.

Odum and Moore tested the validity of their assumptions by examining the "composite regions" of the nation. They found these regions to be six. The Northeast included the New England states and New

York, New Jersey, Pennsylvania, Delaware, Maryland, West Virginia, and the District of Columbia. The Southeast included Virginia, North Carolina, South Carolina, Georgia, Florida, Alabama, Mississippi, Louisiana, Arkansas, Tennessee, and Kentucky. The Southwest was composed of Texas, Oklahoma, New Mexico, and Arizona; the Middle States, of Ohio, Indiana, Illinois, Michigan, Wisconsin, Minnesota, Iowa, and Missouri; the Northwest of North Dakota, South Dakota, Nebraska, Kansas, Montana, Idaho, Wyoming, Colorado, and Utah; and the Far West, of Washington, Oregon, California, and Nevada.[52] The authors were aware that others before them had divided the states somewhat differently and that there would be objections to this classification—perhaps even that there was no possibility of devising a classification that would be suitable to a majority of students. What they tried to do was to set out the major societal regions, and in doing so they used three criteria:

1. The number of regions must not be too large.
2. The "measures of physiographic homogeneities, historical development, folk culture and institutions, the origin and character of its people" must be "commonly accepted as characteristic."
3. Each region must have in common "statistical indices of a socioeconomic nature compiled from an inventory of physical, technological, and social facts."[53]

Solutions of regional problems were not possible, the authors concluded, without a state-regional-national planning agency, but *American Regionalism* was brought to a close with only a suggestion of the structure for such an agency.

Regional, State, and Local Planning

It was at a symposium on American regionalism held at the University of Wisconsin in 1949 that Odum presented to a national audience of social scientists a work memorandum of the Institute for Research in Social Science outlining a national-regional-state network that was called "Administrative Levels of Social Planning Agencies in American Democracy." At the apex would be the United States Planning Agency, authorized by act of Congress, made up of nine members whose qualifications would be as high as those of members of the

Supreme Court. There would be one member from each of perhaps six regions and three members at large, and a central office and a staff of research and planning experts and sufficient Congressional appropriations "to include cooperative arrangements with State and regional agencies." The agency was to be a major one, "implying the highest prestige and most distinguished service." Odum outlined its functions as being threefold, and it is the third of these that has most recently attracted the most favorable attention: "To act as a buffer between the national government and the States and regions, and provide the necessary federal centralization necessary to effective decentralization."[54] The regional and state planning agencies were to be patterned after the federal agency and would work cooperatively to achieve the unity so necessary for the preservation of American democracy. Odum also visualized county and town or city planning agencies that would "cooperate with the regional, national, State, county, and district agencies on problems of intra-State concern."[55]

Had Odum lived longer than the five years left to him when he addressed the Wisconsin symposium, he might have put his considerable promotional powers to work to develop a climate in which Congress would at least consider the proposal, despite the trend of the New Deal toward greater centralization and despite a resurgence of the old sectionalism that led the National Emergency Council to label the South "the Nation's No. 1 economic problem."[56] Perhaps the greatest blow of all to the possibilities for regional planning was the approaching Cold War with Russia. One of the side effects of the Cold War was that popular thought came to link planning with communism. Social planning, it was held, was socialism and socialism was the next step to communism; and communism was a dire threat to the free enterprise system and therefore to "our way of life and Western Civilization."

In North Carolina Odum had somewhat better luck. The Institute for Research in Social Science had cooperated with the planning of the Tennessee Valley Authority almost from the beginning by lending the services of T. J. Woofter, Jr., and others. Relative to cooperation with TVA, Odum had written to Sydnor Walker of the Rockefeller Foundation in 1933 that "so far as I can now see, we have almost complete assurance that the work we do will be put to immediate practical use."[57] In 1935 Governor J. C. B. Ehringhaus appointed the North Carolina State Planning Board at Odum's suggestion and named Odum a member. The General Assembly later in the year approved the Planning Board as a state agency and located the office in Chapel Hill in

Institute headquarters. Two years later, by legislative act, the General Assembly declared the Planning Board to be a permanent "advisory agency of the State government." In 1947, however, the General Assembly failed to appropriate funds for the Board, and its activities ceased. No state administration has since asked for a state planning agency with the broad functions that Odum had outlined in the Institute's work memorandum on government planning agencies.[58]

It was not until Governor Robert Scott's administration (1969–1973) that the state was carved into subregions, each with broad authority to seek federal funds for support of a variety of developmental programs. North Carolina is now divided into seventeen subregions called Councils of Government, which are involved in a variety of activities that include reviewing local applications for federal funds, directing programs on nutrition, and setting up Councils on Aging, Emergency Medical Services programs, and mental health centers. For example, Triangle J Council of Governments, of which Orange County is a part, includes six counties and thirty municipalities. In 1975–76 it had forty-four full-time staff members and a budget of $1,899,693. Most of the staff members of the Councils of Government are professionally trained planners. In most instances, the funds are derived from a local-state-federal matching plan, the major portion of funds coming from the federal government.[59] It was this kind of planning program that Odum had been turning over in his mind even before he came to the University of North Carolina and before he set up the Institute for Research in Social Science, but never in his wildest imagination could he have foreseen the abundant flow of federal funds to state and local communities "as the way out for the South."

The policy of organizing subregions with similar characteristics, although these areas might cut across state lines, gained acceptance under the program of the War on Poverty during the Lyndon B. Johnson administration. Appalachia, for example, included all the impoverished areas in the mountainous regions of North Carolina, Tennessee, and other contiguous states. Since then other contiguous areas with similar problems of geography, economy, and life-style have been recognized, and some have organized planning agencies; for example, the Coastal Plains Development Commission serves North Carolina, South Carolina, and Georgia with the function of goal-setting and economic development.

The Institute for Research in Social Science had been steadily turning out research on regionalism since Odum and the Board of Governors first decided to concentrate upon some approach to planning. After the publication of the two major studies, *Southern Regions* and *American Regionalism*, *Social Forces* emphasized regionalism in four of its volumes (20, 21, 22, and 23, 1942–45).[60] During this period, among other published research designed for regional documentation were Margaret Jarman Hagood's *Mothers of the South* (1939) and *Statistics for Sociologists* (1941); Harriet L. Herring's *Southern Industry and Regional Development* (1940) and her *Part-Time Farming in the Southeast* (1937), which she wrote in collaboration with others for the Works Progress Administration; Ernest R. Groves's *The American Family* (1934) and *The American Woman* (1937); and Rupert B. Vance's *All These People: The Nation's Human Resources in the South* (1945), written with the collaboration of Nadia Danilevsky. It took Vance and Danilevsky seven years to complete their project, which was planned as a companion volume to *Southern Regions*.[61] The book was immediately hailed as a significant contribution to demography and established Vance as a major scholar in that field. Odum himself had also produced two more publications: *Understanding Society* and *The Way of the South* (1947).

The Regional Laboratory for Social Research and Planning

During this period, the Institute had also set up in Chapel Hill several important conferences on regionalism and planning and had established the Regional Laboratory for Social Research and Planning. One of the most important of the meetings was a summer work conference ''on the delineation of major regions and administrative districts in the United States basic to defense planning and post-war building of a strong nation,'' for which the Institute received a grant from the Carnegie Corporation.[62] Out of these meetings grew a need for a regional laboratory.

Odum often had declared that a research institute needed ''a living laboratory'' in which to carry on its work, and he had always pointed out that the southern region was the living laboratory for the Institute for Research in Social Science. But he also wanted a regional laboratory as part of the Institute, established in its headquarters in Chapel Hill. Such a laboratory was made possible in 1942 by a grant from the

General Education Board "for development of the permanent Workshop on Regional Research and Education."[63] As described in detail
by Odum in 1945,

> the regional laboratory as utilized by the Institute for Research in
> Social Science has actually consisted of three major levels. One is
> the South itself as the area from which materials are gathered and
> in which research is conducted. A second is the subregional
> laboratory of thirteen counties proposed as the central focus for as
> many concrete projects as practicable. The third is the physical
> laboratory and workshop and its correlated activities in Alumni
> Hall at the University of North Carolina.[64]

The Institute had, indeed, converted a portion of the fourth floor of
Alumni Hall into a small auditorium able to accommodate conferences
attended by one hundred or more persons. It had large wall maps
illustrating the regions of the United States, and appropriate literature
dealing with regional and planning processes was arranged on tables
nearby. The ideal regional laboratory, Odum pointed out, should also
contain a map room, a drafting room, a statistical laboratory, and small
workshops "in which from five to 15 persons can work together at
desks or around tables." The Institute's laboratory did contain all these
provisions, but the only commodious feature was the large conference
area.

In 1946 the Institute brought to the University a professionally
trained planner, John A. Parker, who held a master's degree in city
planning and a master's degree in architecture from the Massachusetts
Institute of Technology. Parker soon organized the Department of City
and Regional Planning as a distinct unit in the University structure.
With a grant from the Ford Foundation in 1957, the Institute established the Urban Studies Program under the direction of F. Stuart
Chapin, Jr., and in 1962 it became the Center for Urban and Regional
Studies. The Center maintained affiliation with the Institute until 1969.
A more detailed discussion of the program on urban and regional
planning will be given in chapter 10.

It was with justifiable pride that Odum could write in 1943 to the
administrative dean of the University, Robert B. House, that universities across the nation were following in the footsteps of the University of North Carolina in the area of regional planning. Yale had set up
a faculty committee on regional research and planning to explore the
development of New England. Harvard "borrowed Professor John

Gaus from Wisconsin as professor of regional planning.'' The state universities of Colorado, Wyoming, and New Mexico were "setting up university committees on regional research and cooperating in a program of regional planning.'' [65] To his old friend and supporter, Harry W. Chase, who had been president of the University at Chapel Hill, and was now at New York University, he wrote: ''We have in this folk-regional culture framework the most basic approach to societal reorganization that has been set up. You see I do not think much of it (!), but the main point of emphasis is that it is not Utopia, no ism, no one-road highway to perfection, but just a [sic] evolutionary approach.'' [66]

The division of geographic areas into regions and subregions is now such common practice that it is easy to overlook Odum's pioneering work in advocating the principle of regionalism, which stresses the wisdom of dividing areas according to the quality or characteristics peculiar to an area. If Odum were alive today he would rejoice that the plan for a regional division of governors such as the Southern Governors' Conference, organized in 1934, had spread throughout the nation, and he would be cheered by the recently created Coastal Plains Development Commission, which is the sort of planning group he had visualized. In reviewing Odum's ideas of regionalism and social planning in 1973, Harvey A. Kantor concluded that ''in the context of the early 1970s, it seems that his insights have renewed importance and speak pertinently to many of the problems of contemporary America.'' [67]

Government planners have found to their dismay that it can be destructive to overlook the life-style and interests of a region, whether it is in building publicly financed highrise apartments for the urban poor, laying out a new highway route, or planning a series of dams for a hydroelectric power plant. It is by a careful regard for the folkways, the stateways, and the technicways, examined patiently by the regional or subregional planning agency, that technological changes can be made peacefully and the people affected be given time to make adjustments in the institutional framework of society. These ideas were at the heart of all Odum's thinking and writing about regionalism and regional planning.

All the work and research that Odum had done since he founded *Social Forces* in 1922 and the Institute for Research in Social Science two years later had come to a head through the regional approach. He was convinced that regionalism was the way of the future to lead

America out of its multitudinous domestic dilemmas. He had always wanted the Institute to apply its research findings in a practical way and to explore through research "the actual facts" as a basis for alleviating the anguish of the present. From the beginning, therefore, the Institute sought through scientific research to shape practical tools for bringing the South into balance with the rest of the nation. Research, he insisted, must be of practical use in coping with the problems of society.

After Odum's death, regionalism in the Odum fashion became virtually extinct in the Institute's research program. However, studies of various aspects of southern life and culture continued to be, as they had always been, a concern of some of the staff members of the Institute. Most of the studies of folk and race that were cited in chapter 5 were southern studies, and more of these studies will be described in the chapters that follow.

CHAPTER 7

The South at the
Bottom of the Ladder

From first to last, Howard Odum held that "the study of man and his society *now* is the supreme scientific task at hand."[1] The region he wanted most to study was the South. He wanted the Institute to produce research that would show to the nation why the South was different from other parts of the country; why it was at the bottom of the economic ladder. As Odum began publication of the *Journal of Social Forces* and as he set the Institute in motion, the region was under fire as the "Sahara of the Bozart."

In 1917 H. L. Mencken had written an essay for the *New York Evening Mail* declaring that in the South there was not a critic, musical composer, painter, sculptor, architect, historian, sociologist, philosopher, theologian, or scientist, "not even a bad one between the Potomac mud-flats and the Gulf."[2] At the same time, the Federal Council of Churches was planning home mission projects in the field of southern industrial relations, and the economist Frank Tannenbaum, sometime professor at Columbia University, was pointing to the "darker phases of the South." The thrust of all the Institute studies leading to Odum's monumental books on regionalism was to confront these criticisms and to discover a "way out" for the South.

Why at the Bottom?

Was the South really at the bottom of the economic ladder? If so, why? The Institute's Board of Governors agreed with Odum's insistence that the staff should include an economist who would produce research to answer these questions. In 1927 the Board found their man in Clarence Heer of New York, who was soon at work examining the South's economic profile. His statistical analysis of southern incomes supported the general assumption that the South was, indeed, at the bottom. Incomes in the South were lower than elsewhere in the nation because of the preponderance of low-yield occupations. Southern agriculture was particularly low, yet 46 percent of the southern population was engaged in that occupation. Since manufacturing, on the whole, yields larger per worker returns than does agriculture, Heer thought that a shift to manufacturing would undoubtedly improve the economic picture. Despite the rapidly increasing flow of farm tenants to manufacturing, Heer found that the percentage of southern labor in industry was far below the rest of the country.

The industries into which southern workers were moving were textiles, lumber, and timber, traditionally ranked low in average earnings per worker. Heer suggested that to improve this situation "there should be a flow of labor from agriculture to manufacturing, a flow which should be comparatively rapid in view of the South's million or more tenant farmers with little in the way of capital investment to tie them to the land. There should also be some tendency for southern labor to migrate to the high wage industrial centers of the North."[3] He also saw the need for "a high order of economic statesmanship rather than . . . a supine policy of *laissez-faire*," and added that the positive measures needed, "if they are to succeed, must not neglect the South's two million farmers."[4]

With the Depression in the 1930s came New Deal assistance programs, and these, along with rapid development in technology during that period, brought help to the South in its struggle up from the bottom and also broadened the research opportunities for the Institute. Odum eagerly accepted the requests for research assistance that came from various federal agencies set up to cope with the Depression. All the studies completed during this period were grist for Odum's mill as he set to work grinding out data about the southern regions.

With funds from the Civil Works Administration, the Tennessee Valley Authority, the Works Progress Administration, the Federal Emergency Relief Administration, and other federal agencies, plus the cooperation of their staffs, the Institute began an ambitious program of research called "A State in Depression." The program was directed by Odum, T. J. Woofter, Jr., and Harriet Herring, with the assistance of additional senior staff members—Roy M. Brown, S. H. Hobbs, Jr., Herman Schnell, Edgar W. Knight, A. S. Keister, and others.[5] Among junior staff working on the project were Gordon Blackwell, Columbus Andrews, Mabel Bacon, Chester P. Lewis, W. H. E. Johnson, and Irene Strieby. The studies included "Public Administration in the Fifteen North Carolina Counties of the Tennessee Valley Area"; "Rural

Relief Families in North Carolina,'' which included a study of eastern and Piedmont counties; "The Problem of the Displaced Tenant Farm Family in North Carolina''; "Survey of Idle Land and Vacant Houses Available for Displaced Tenants in Wilson County''; "A Study of Three North Carolina Cities in Depression''; and several studies of the public school system, since the salaries of teachers and school budgets had been drastically cut by the North Carolina General Assembly. The studies of public schools included "State Centralization of the Public Schools in North Carolina'' and "A Study of Living Costs of North Carolina Teachers.''[6]

During the Depression years, the Institute examined many additional aspects of the southern economy: the ways the people made a living and the opportunities they had to get job training for advancement, patterns of agriculture that sentenced the workers to generations of poverty, the black farmer, migration of workers, discriminatory freight rates that worked against the South, wholesaling and retailing, changing occupational distributions in the South, social resources in the Southeast, regional variations in standards of living, and folkways as a cause of regional poverty.[7] Most of these studies went unpublished, but their findings were useful in the construction of Odum's *Southern Regions*, and their authors, as a rule, received master's or doctor's degrees for their work, as well as a stipend while they were doing their researches.

During this period, the Institute did publish at least fourteen studies that dealt with the social and economic forces that destined the South to lie at the bottom of the ladder. One of the first and best known was Rupert Vance's *Human Geography of the South* (1932), which had been preceded by his *Human Factors in Cotton Culture* (1929). Both were competent preludes to Odum's *Southern Regions* (1936).

In terms strongly reminiscent of Odum's early editorials in *Social Forces* and of his classroom lectures, Vance pointed out the "eclectic tasks'' that lay before the South if it were to assume its rightful place as an important region in the nation. The leadership in the forward march toward agricultural reform and industrial development would have to come from the intellectuals in the universities, "the more cultured of the industrialists,'' "some of the inheritors of the old traditions,'' and other public-spirited citizens. Their guide would be research and planning.[8]

The Southern Revolt against Imperialism

Vance's *Human Geography of the South* spurred the movement of protest already under way against the causes of the South's unfavorable economic and social conditions. The agitation for removal of the restrictive measures that were keeping the South at the bottom came from several directions.

In 1935 Benjamin B. Kendrick and Alex M. Arnett, both Georgia-born and both professors of history at the Woman's College of the University of North Carolina, published *The South Looks at Its Past* as one of the volumes in the Southern Regional Studies series being prepared under the sponsorship of the Social Science Research Council, also the sponsor of Odum's *Southern Regions*, which was to appear the following year. Kendrick and Arnett sought to focus on the roots of Southern backwardness, and they found the origins not only in the old plantation system but also in the repressive political and economic measures of Reconstruction and its aftermath. Kendrick was even more specific in 1941 in his presidential address to the Southern Historical Association. "The people of the South," he said, "who all their lives had suffered deprivation, want, and humiliation from an outside finance imperialism, followed with hardly a murmur of protest leaders who, if not directly, were nonetheless in effect agents and attorneys of the imperialists."[9]

This was a declaration far stronger than Vance had made in his *Human Geography of the South*. From his examination of the geographic, economic, and cultural conditions in the North and South, Vance determined that the type of organization needed to bring together natural resources and labor in the process of production had developed in the North sooner than it had in the South. From this view, he concluded, "the South remains largely a colonial economy." The reasons for this colonial status were to be found, he thought, "in the colonial system under which it was founded, the frontier zone into which it expanded, the plantation system to which it passed, and the cotton system with its tenancy which prevailed after abolition."[10] Others, like Kendrick, were to carry Vance's ideas of southern colonialism further and to use the term as a rallying symbol for southern solidarity.

It was not the Institute, however, that led the revolt against northern imperialism. It was Walter Prescott Webb who sparked it. Webb was a native of Texas who had taken both of his graduate degrees at the University of Texas and was a professor of history there when he challenged the South to present a united front against northern imperialism in his *Divided We Stand: The Crisis of a Frontierless Society*. The first edition of the book, which appeared in 1937, was a delineation of the fate that awaited America unless it worked to preserve democracy, and a prediction of the fate of the South and West unless these regions were rescued from "corporate fascism and business feudalism." The second edition, which appeared five years later, stated specific measures necessary to accomplish these goals: the dispersal of industry, the abolition of discriminatory freight rates imposed on the South, revision of the patent system to include supervision of licensing of patented machinery, and federal charters for interstate corporations.[11] Webb had given southern liberals concrete issues upon which to concentrate their efforts, but the liberals had already seized upon one of those issues before the second edition of his book was published. That one issue was discriminatory freight rates.

In the meantime, the Institute continued its research that had long been under way on the social and economic conditions of the South. Unlike most of the southern protestors, the Institute staff ferreted out a wide range of problems—farm tenancy, dependence on a one-crop system, exploitation of black workers, tax conflicts, poor housing, low wages, domination of "soft" industries such as textiles, lack of vocational training and business education, and political cronyism in the seats of the county and state government.

Claudius T. Murchison, an economist in the University of North Carolina School of Commerce, had written for the Institute in 1930 a short inquiry into the plight of the cotton crop, *King Cotton is Sick*, and in 1934 he pointed out the South's lack of specialty enterprises in an essay prepared for *Culture in the South*, edited by William T. Couch, director of the University of North Carolina Press. The lack of such enterprises, Murchison maintained, "leaves the South with the worst form of economic disadvantage, that is of having to exchange a few bulky staple products for the myriads of highly manufactured specialty goods which she must consume."[12] A few years later, in 1939, Walter J. Matherly, an economist from the University of Florida who had served on the Institute's Board of Governors in its early days when he was at the University of North Carolina, wrote *Business Education in the Changing South* as a unit in the Southern Regional

Planning Study, and throughout the 1930s both Odum and Vance continued to write about the South's low economic position in the national economy.[13]

At the same time, other articulate southern leaders had been stirred to revolt against the South's "colonial economy," and in the 1930s a body of protest literature had grown up about the issues. Movements toward consolidation of leadership led to the appearance of action organizations. The Southern Governors' Conference, for example, first organized as the Southeastern Governors' Conference, was created in December 1934 after an earlier conference at Warm Springs with President Roosevelt, who favored the idea of a governors' coalition.[14]

A few months afterward, in April 1935, Francis Pickens Miller, a progressive lawyer from Charlottesville, Virginia, called together a group "whose minds are open to facts and who are aware of their responsibility for discovering and serving the general public interest" and created the Southern Policy Committee.[15] The organization sprang from an effort of the Foreign Policy Association to set up a national policy committee that would deal with domestic issues. The organizational meeting was held in Atlanta, and as a result of this meeting, T. J. Woofter, Jr., a senior Institute staff member, prepared the first of ten studies in the Southern Policy Papers series published by the University of North Carolina Press. Woofter's paper was *Southern Population and Social Planning* (1936). The Institute staff produced two other papers: *How the Other Half Is Housed* (no. 4, 1936) by Rupert Vance, and the final paper, *What is Regionalism?* (1937) by Harry Estill Moore. Although the Southern Policy Committee was just the kind of action body that Odum had dreamed of for almost twenty years—southern leaders who would use the hard facts of Institute data on which to base a sound social policy—the committee must have been a disappointment to Odum because it soon ceased to be active.

Out of the Washington unit of the Southern Policy Committee, however, grew a report that stirred the South for years. It was the *Report on Economic Conditions of the South* published in 1938 by the National Emergency Council. The *Report* had been prepared under the supervision of Clark Foreman, formerly on the staff of the Southern Interracial Commission in Atlanta, who was now an official of the Public Works Administration. The *Report* was largely the work of a group of southern federal employees in Washington who were involved with the Washington division of the Southern Policy Committee. They based their findings for the most part upon the published research of Howard

Odum, Rupert Vance, and Walter Webb. The *Report* supported the South's indignation against colonial bondage and seemed to suggest that the Roosevelt administration was forthrightly behind a coordinated effort toward regional development. The president himself had said, after the *Report* appeared, "It is my conviction that the South presents right now, in 1938, the Nation's No. 1 economic problem." The phrase immediately caught on as another symbol of the backward South.[16] Leading southern politicians would have none of the talk about the South's being the nation's number one economic problem. They pointed with pride to what their forefathers had done to rebuild the South singlehandedly after the Civil War and declared anew that what the South needed most was to be let alone.

The controversy, which was aired on public platforms in the South from the church down to the smallest civic club, seemed to spur the Institute in Chapel Hill to turn out more and more articles on southern economic problems. The articles were written chiefly by Howard Odum, Rupert Vance, Harriet Herring, and Guy Johnson, and their graduate assistants, and covered industrial development, occupational opportunities, farm tenancy, the human and material resources of the South, Negro leadership and strategy, migration, better educational opportunities, and the importance of social and economic planning.[17] Odum himself reviewed the question in "Is the South the Nation's Number One Problem?" (an article for *Scholastic*, March 25, 1940), in which he implied that the answer to the question was both yes and no.

The *Report on Economic Conditions of the South* also had its impact on the Southern Conference for Human Welfare, whose organization had been contemplated as early as 1936 by Joseph S. Gelders, Southern Secretary of the National Committee for the Defense of Political Prisoners, who had at one time been a professor of physics at the University of Alabama. The plan had been to call a conference in Birmingham in the fall of 1938 to organize and to discuss the civil rights of workers and Negroes, and at the suggestion of President Roosevelt to launch a campaign against the poll tax. After the appearance of the National Emergency Council's *Report*, the organizing group also decided to include the problems of economic colonialism. William T. Couch, director of the University of North Carolina Press, was the program chairman, and Frank Graham, president of the University, became the first president of the Southern Conference for Human Welfare.

The meeting in Birmingham in November attracted a broad assembly of southern liberals and radicals, and the organization held together this coalition in diminishing numbers for almost a decade.[18] When it developed that the Southern Conference for Human Welfare was more concerned with political action than analysis of social conditions and that the coalition consisted chiefly of CIO unions and southern activists, academic liberals such as Odum and his Institute staff avoided affiliation.[19] President Graham was harassed for years because of his early affiliation with the Conference.

Odum had himself hoped to set up a southern development organization to carry out the recommendations he had made in his *Southern Regions*. Shortly after the appearance of *Southern Regions*, in June 1936, he conducted the ten-day Institute on Southern Regional Development and the Social Sciences at Chapel Hill, which he hoped would be the springboard for the organization of his long-dreamed-of council on southern regional development. He envisioned the council as an independent agency financed by contributions from foundations and individuals, but he was never able to establish it as a functioning organization, largely because other interest groups were competing with Odum and the Institute for a share of available funds. As he described the situation in 1938 in a letter to Prentiss M. Terry of Nashville, Tennessee, who was attempting to organize the Southern States Industrial Council, ''Between the Right Honorable FD[R], the Southern Conference for Human Welfare, and twenty other groups in the South that are literally taking the lead to do what the Council ought to do, I think I'll go heat-wave hay-wire.''[20]

In 1941, therefore, when George D. Palmer of the University of Alabama organized the Southern Association of Science and Industry, Odum and the Institute staff gladly offered to cooperate in research. In 1948 Gordon Blackwell, then director of the Institute, announced the completion of three research projects in a series of twelve contemplated for the Southern Association of Science and Industry.[21] The research had been done under Blackwell's direction, and the monographs were edited by Katharine Jocher and published in Richmond, Virginia.

The Decline in Southern Studies

Research on southern studies continued intermittently after 1950.[22] In 1945 Odum had published *The Way of the South: A Biography of the Southern United States* as a further interpretation of his *An American Epoch* and his *Southern Regions*. Funds were found to bring the data in *Southern Regions* up to date with the latest census returns, but the revisions were never completed.[23] Research staff affiliated with the Institute at times over the next twenty-five years undertook investigations in special aspects of the southern scene, but the Institute staff did not concentrate on the region as intensively as it had previously.

During 1951–52, several approaches to southern studies were published and others were under way. Milton S. Heath, professor of economics, published *Constructive Liberalism: The Role of the State in Economic Development in Georgia, 1732–1860*. Odum directed a doctoral dissertation by Walter M. North, "Change and Transition in the Southeastern United States," and another by George L. Simpson, which was published in 1956 as *The Cokers of South Carolina: The Social Biography of a Family*. Fletcher M. Green, professor of history, directed a doctoral dissertation on another topic in southern biography, "Thomas Butler King, Planter, Statesman, and Industrial Leader," by Edward M. Steel, Jr., and one by George B. Tindall, which was published as *South Carolina Negroes, 1877–1900*.

At this time, Daniel O. Price, who had written his doctoral dissertation on internal migration under the direction of Rupert Vance, returned to the Institute as a research associate in applied statistics and population. He was assigned the major responsibility for research on migration. Economists, including Clarence Heer, who had examined the southern economy in 1930, had generally considered migration to be a viable alternative to southern poverty, and Odum had wanted this field of research explored further. *Social Forces* had published Price's first article on migration in 1942 and two others followed in 1948 and 1951.[24] In 1951 he was also directing a major project, "Internal Migration in the United States, 1870–1940," in cooperation with the University of Pennsylvania under a grant from the Rockefeller Foundation. His summary of the cooperative project was published in the *American Sociological Review* in 1953, but thereafter, while associated with the Institute, he published only an occasional article on migration. His interests had turned to methodology, especially in the field of mathematical sociology. In 1965, however, he contributed a chapter, "Next

Steps in Studying Mobility and Mental Health," to a book edited by Mildred B. Kantor, a former Institute research assistant, and read a paper, "The Effects of Migration on the Educational Level of Non-whites in a Southern Area," before the Population Association of America.

Rupert Vance, who had served as president of the Population Association of America, also published several studies in the field of migration. Shortly before World War II, he testified before a regional congressional hearing on the topic "Interstate Migration of Destitute Citizens," presenting his evidence in a paper, "Probable Trend of Migration from the Southeast." In 1958 he contributed a chapter, "Prerequisites to Immigration: Elements of National Policy," to *Selected Studies of Migration Since World War II*, published by the Milbank Fund; and in 1965, a chapter on migration and urbanization to *Exploring Virginia's Human Resources*, published by the University Press of Virginia.

As Gordon Blackwell pointed out years later in recalling his administration of the Institute, the Board of Governors had every intention of continuing the southern studies,[25] but funds were not as readily available for this area of research as they had been previously, and the research interests of the staff tended to be elsewhere. In 1953, however, Blackwell listed no less than fifteen research projects under way in southern studies in economics, history, and sociology. In the same year he and Arthur J. Bachrach edited a special issue of *The Journal of Social Issues*, which they called "Human Problems in the Changing South."

A year earlier, the Institute's Board of Governors had considered an ambitious plan for a research project on the formulation and administration of regional development programs, under the direction of Frederic N. Cleaveland, an assistant professor in political science, with the cooperation of a faculty research team composed of professors in economics, city and regional planning, political science, and sociology. The proposal was the logical outgrowth of Odum's ideas on regionalism and came as the specific recommendation of a conference of state and regional agencies interested in regional development that had been held in Chapel Hill in November 1950 by the Institute and the Department of City and Regional Planning. The conference had concluded that "the University of North Carolina is strategically located and especially fitted to continue and expand its leadership in educational programs and research activities directed towards more effective development not only of North Carolina and the South but of regions generally.''[26] Funds to carry out the proposal as planned were not found but soon afterward a grant to begin the Urban Studies Program was available and the Board turned over most aspects of regional research to that division of the Institute.[27]

Although few of the research projects in southern studies that Blackwell listed in his annual report of 1953 were published, projects in this field were not abandoned. Rupert Vance, Harriet Herring, and George L. Simpson, until he left the Institute to become director of the Research Triangle Committee, continued research in the sociology of the South. Fletcher M. Green and later George B. Tindall, when he returned to the University as a professor, continued research in southern history, and Lowell D. Ashby, Ralph W. Pfouts, and Milton S. Health did research in economics. In 1960, for example, three papers were read by Institute staff at the annual meeting of the Southern Sociological Society, one by George Simpson, ''Industrial Growth and Recent Change in the South,'' and two by Vance, ''Social Concepts of the South'' and ''Double Image of the South.'' Lowell Ashby was continuing research on issues he had first examined in ''Regional Aspects of Cyclical Fluctuations,'' a paper he read in 1957 at the annual meeting of the American Statistical Association. In 1960 Ralph Pfouts read a paper, ''Consumption in the South Since 1930'' at the first annual Economic Conference on the South held in St. Petersburg, Florida, and in 1966 Fletcher Green edited and contributed an introduction and bibliography to a new edition of *Southern Wealth and Northern Profits*, by Thomas Prentice Kettell.

Daniel O. Price's annual report for 1960–61 reflected a shift in emphasis from southern studies. One of the continuing interests of the Institute, he wrote, ''is in urban and regional development with its research site being mainly the Piedmont area of the Carolinas, but the emphasis being less on what is intrinsically southern than on general organizational problems associated with urbanization, industrialization and the incorporation of a region into the larger society.''[28] The research interests of the Institute were clearly moving away from concentration on the southern region to a focus on analysis and theory relating to the ''larger society.''

In 1966, when the Board of Governors appointed an ad hoc committee to study the functions of the Institute for Research in Social Science, with James W. Prothro, professor of political science, as chairman, the first recommendation of the committee's report was that "the Director should be encouraged to develop large-scale inter-disciplinary research programs," and it cited as examples the Institute's own recent study of the changing position of the Negro, and the Center for Southern Studies at Duke University.[29] The committee was aware of the Institute's trend away from southern studies and the report made note of it:

> The difficulty has been that large-scale general support funds for research are no longer available. But funds for a broad research program are available. The Center for Southern Studies at Duke University, for example, might easily have been a Program of Southern Studies in the IRSS. This kind of program is broad enough to be of interest to all social science departments but it has a sufficiently specific·focus to secure large-scale support. . . .
>
> The fact that the Center of Southern Studies is not located in its "natural" home may turn into an advantage. That program is focused on a single geographic area, and the social sciences have reached the point at which such confinement could be theoretically crippling. The Institute could better develop a program of research with an analytical and theoretical focus, rather than a geographical focus, but with the problem one that is particularly important in and for the South. Something like a Program of Research on Intergroup Relations is an appropriate example. Such a research program would permit the Institute to continue its fine tradition of interest in and concern for the South, but it would also permit the pursuit of the cross-cultural, comparative research that is so important for the development of true generalizations.[30]

When James W. Prothro became director of the Institute in 1967, his annual reports, beginning with that of 1968–69, opened with a statement paying tribute to the work done in southern studies in the past: "Since its founding in 1924 by Howard W. Odum, the Institute has contributed significantly to the understanding of social problems in the southern United States. The hope is to continue this contribution by concentrating on basic research problems relevant to, but not restricted to, any geographic region."[31]

Prothro carried through with these intentions when the Institute received a substantial grant from the National Science Foundation to conduct the Southeastern Regional Surveys. The first and second of the three surveys were largely in the field of political science and will be discussed further in chapter 9. Out of Survey III, which was under the general supervision of Angell G. Beza, director of research services in the Institute, grew the first study in almost a decade of southern social patterns reminiscent of the research on the South during the administration of Howard Odum, although the methodology was different.

The pilot study of Survey III was under the direction of Glen H. Elder, Jr., and John Shelton Reed, Jr., of the Department of Sociology. It focused on the white southerner as a cultural minority.[32] Reed published two reports from data growing out of this survey: "Summertime and the Livin' Is Easy: The Quality of Life in the South," which was an address given at a conference on the changing South at Sweet Briar College in 1974 and published later that year in the *University of North Carolina News Letter*; and in 1975 a chapter, "New Problems, Old Resources: Continuity in Southern Culture," in a volume, *Group Identity in the South*, edited by Harold F. Kaufman and others. A larger work by Reed, *The Enduring South: Subcultural Persistence in Mass Society*, appeared in 1972[33] and was brought out in paperback edition by the University of North Carolina Press in 1974, but this study was the result of previous research unrelated to the Southeastern Regional Survey.

A scattering of other published research in what might originally have been considered the Institute's southern studies program also appeared as the first fifty years of the Institute drew to a close. Rupert Vance contributed a chapter and Richard L. Simpson and David L. Norsworthy coauthored a second chapter in *The South in Continuity and Change* (1965), edited by John C. McKinney and Edgar T. Thompson, a publication of the Center for Southern Studies at Duke University. Vance also contributed a chapter, "The South Considered as an Achieving Society," to a second publication of the Center for Southern Studies, *Perspectives on the South: Agenda for Research*, edited by Edgar T. Thompson.

A few others in the Institute for Research in Social Science also were occasionally publishing research on the South. In the late 1960s, Robert E. Gallman, an economist, published a series of articles on self-sufficiency in the plantation economy of the antebellum South, and in 1970 he was at work on farm efficiency and interdependence in the economic development of a region. In 1969 Maynard M. Hufschmidt of the Department of City and Regional Planning edited *Regional*

Planning: Challenge and Prospects; George Iden of the Department of Economics published with Charles Richter "Factors Associated with Population Mobility in the Atlantic Coastal Plains Region" in *Land Economics* in 1971 and was researching alternative strategies for southern economic development and poverty reduction. In 1973–74 two articles strongly reminiscent of Odum and research in the 1930s appeared, one by George B. Tindall of the Department of History, "Beyond the Mainstream: The Ethnic Southerners" in the *Journal of Southern History* (1974), which was his presidential address to the Southern Historical Association; and the other by Emil Malizia of the Department of City and Regional Planning, "Economic Imperialism: An Interpretation of Appalachian Under-Development," in *Appalachian Journal* (1973).

The Mill Village and Industrial Research

"Economic development," "reduction of poverty," and "the disinherited southerners" were all terms heard frequently in the early days of the Institute. As director of the Institute, Odum wanted to point out the causes for southern deprivations, and among the urgent problems he wanted to survey immediately were those involving industrial development. Among the first research assistants to be appointed by the Institute's Board of Governors at its organizational meeting in June 1924 was Roland B. Eutsler, who was asked to undertake research in industrial relations and economic problems.

At the second meeting of the Board, Professor A. M. Jordan of the Department of Education proposed "a project to study the effect of physical work on mental growth in rural and industrial communities." At the third session, the Board suggested employment of a research assistant for special study in industrial problems, and President Chase appointed a special committee on social industrial conditions to clear through the Institute.[34]

With the safeguard of a committee that would approve all research in this area, the Board thought it had sufficient protection against the manufacturers who might be defensive about academic probing into the textile industry. Howard Odum had already been under attack from the *Southern Textile Bulletin* because of the liberal stance of the *Journal of Social Forces*,[35] and his early efforts had failed to bring together civic leaders, educators, health officials, and industrialists to discuss ways to improve the southern textile industry. A project of that nature had been planned to take place in 1924–25 by Worth M. Tippy, executive secretary of the Commission on the Church and Social Service of the Federal Council of Churches, and Tippy had recruited Odum to set up a series of public conferences in strategic North and South Carolina mill towns. But the Federal Council of Churches was suspect by business, industry, and local church leaders themselves because of its aggressive advocacy of labor reforms. Had Odum not been eager to bring together the very leaders Tippy had suggested, in order to discuss in a spirit of goodwill the problems the Federal Council of Churches wanted to explore, he would have been too wise to align himself with an agency that had already aroused the suspicion of the textile manufacturers. When the proposed conferences failed to develop as both Tippy and Odum had hoped and the leaders of Spartanburg, South Carolina, had refused to participate, Odum wrote in distress to one of the professors whom he had recruited to handle local arrangements that it was "a constantly recurring source of suffering, really, to find that we who were born here of the same folk and who try to work so hard to eliminate the outside criticism of our section, as well as to work for its upbuilding, should constantly be misunderstood."[36]

Odum was convinced that basic research was needed to prove to mill owners that their paternalistic approach to mill labor was a denial of democracy and at the same time unproductive. Gerald W. Johnson, a liberal spokesman for the South and editorial writer for the *Greensboro Daily News*, had introduced Odum in 1922 to Harriet L. Herring, a personnel officer of the Carolina Woolen and Cotton Mills in Spray, North Carolina. Harriet Herring was from a successful agricultural family in Lenoir County and was a graduate of Meredith College with a master's degree from Radcliffe, and had also a year of training in industrial relations at Bryn Mawr. She was not an outsider, but "born here of the same folk," and therefore Odum thought she should be an acceptable investigator to the mill owners. Even before the Laura Spelman Rockefeller Memorial had confirmed its appropriation for the Institute, Odum had tried to recruit Harriet Herring. In December 1924, when he at last had her consent to join the Institute staff, he reported to the Board of Governors her willingness to come and he set out his plans to get the mill research under way. He said he would call a meeting of the Institute's Industrial Social Research Committee in January and ask the members to meet with representatives from North

Carolina College for Women, North Carolina State College, the University of North Carolina, the American Cotton Manufacturers Association, and the Southern Textile Social Service Association to take stock and go over the whole program for future industrial study. He proposed to lay before the meeting five research projects that he hoped the Board would approve: "Social Studies in the Mill Village Community," to be undertaken by J. J. Rhyne; "Cotton Cloth as a Type Study of the Evolution of Community," by Mary O. Cowper; "The Religious Factor in the Mill Village," by G. A. Hunnicut; "An Interpretation of Mill Village Organization in North Carolina," by G. A. Duncan; and "The Status and History of Organized Labor in North Carolina," by William Bloom.[37]

The Board approved Harriet Herring's appointment to begin with September 1925, and "an interim appointment of two months was made so that she might study the industrial situation of New England on her own expense."[38] On the subject of the proposed industrial conference the Board was silent. In the meantime, Odum went forward with his plans to recruit scholars from southern universities to the Institute's Industrial Social Research Committee. Although this committee probably never functioned as it was intended, Odum did create a committee composed of the two research assistants in industrial relations, Herring and Rhyne, and three University economists from the School of Commerce, D. D. Carroll, Walter J. Matherly, and Claudius T. Murchison. They prepared a memorandum for a study of the social and economic aspects of the southern textile industry that they presented to President Chase, and later instructed Harriet Herring to take it to the November 1925 meeting of the North Carolina Cotton Manufacturers Association to request approval and cooperation.[39] Officials of the Association rejected her request and the proposal never reached the whole membership. David Clark attacked the Institute's effort in the issue of the *Southern Textile Bulletin* for December 3, 1925, and praised the Association for "unanimously" denying the Institute's request for cooperation. He emphatically declared that the textile industry was none of the University's business and that the proposed research that would have been financed by Rockefeller money was "another form of attack by our enemies."[40]

Clark continued his assault for several weeks until news of the incident and of the Institute's proposed study broke in the state press. Some newspapers supported the position of the *Southern Textile Bulletin*, while others condemned Clark and the manufacturers for failing to work with the Institute.[41] Harriet Herring's approach to the cotton manufacturers could not have come at a worse time for the Institute. It came shortly after Clark had accused Odum and the *Journal of Social Forces* of promoting atheism, an attack in which conservative protestant ministers had joined. In the same year, a fight arose in the General Assembly over the Poole bill, which proposed to forbid teaching evolution in state-supported schools, a struggle in which the University played a leading role toward defeating the measure.[42] The Institute resolved the issue of the textile industry study by directing Herring's research into a survey of welfare work in mill villages.

Harriet Herring met with almost no opposition while conducting the study. She surveyed 322 North Carolina plants in 1926 and her work was published by the University of North Carolina Press in 1929 as *Welfare Work in Mill Villages: The Story of Extra-Mill Activities in North Carolina*. President Chase was pleased with the results and praised it as an example of the patient, reasonable research the Institute was undertaking. He sent about thirty copies of the book to textile manufacturers as evidence that neither the University nor the Institute had any hostile motives in wanting to survey manufacturing in North Carolina. Although Odum thought that Herring had probably been "over generous to the mill people," her findings revealed the depth of paternalism in the villages and the isolation of the mill workers from the communities in which they lived. Most of the mills, she found, had contributed largely to building the churches in which the mill workers worshiped and were the main support for the ministers. The ministers preached "a gospel of work, of gratitude for present blessings, and of patience with economic and social maladjustment as temporal and outside the sphere of religious concern."[43] She found that only 28 mills supplemented the budget for mill schools, but Carl E. Rankin, making a survey of mill villages for a doctoral dissertation at Columbia University some years later, discovered that "the mill manager or owner is not infrequently the superintendent of the school."[44] Of all the benevolent activities of mill owners for their employees, Herring found the most frequent to be supplying wood and coal at low prices. Next came supporting baseball teams—127 mills had teams—but only 49 employed community workers and only 10 had group insurance plans.

In the years that followed, Harriet Herring continued her research on the textile industries and published numerous articles, such as "The Beginnings of Industrial Social Work" in *Social Forces* (December

1926, March 1927), "Working Mothers and Their Families" in *Family* (1928), and "The Southern Mill System Faces a New Issue" in *Social Forces* (1930). In 1940, her *Southern Industry and Regional Development* was published as a part of the Institute's regional studies. She also continued her research long enough to see the textile industry finally abandon the tradition of providing housing for its workers, and she wrote about this new movement in *Passing of the Mill Village* (1949). For a period of about twenty years, Harriet Herring was the only member of the Institute staff who gave full time to industrial research.

While Odum was willing, as he wrote to his friend Professor W. C. Jackson of the North Carolina College for Women, "to retreat into the background" for a few years after the debacle with the Cotton Manufacturers Association in 1926, he did not capitulate. In 1928 the Institute gave some help to Broadus Mitchell, an economics professor at Johns Hopkins University, for field work and assisted in the publication of his *William Gregg: Factory Master of the Old South*. Nor did Odum encourage Institute assistants and graduate students to avoid controversial research in industrial development, although findings of their research were not always published. Charlotte Califf's "Wage Differential between Negro and White Workers in Southern Industry" went unpublished, as did Harry M. Douty's "The North Carolina Industrial Worker, 1880–1930," although *Social Forces* did publish in 1933 Douty's "Labor Unrest in North Carolina, 1932."

By the late 1940s others in the Institute were publishing in the field of industrial development. In 1948 Rupert Vance wrote a chapter, "Social Organization for the Use of Industrial Resources," in *Scientists Look at Resources*, a Bulletin of the Bureau of School Services, and in 1950 Milton S. Heath of the Department of Economics published "Public Railroad Construction and Development of Private Enterprise in the South Before 1861" in the *Journal of Economic History Supplement*. As late as 1952, Odum was supervising a doctoral dissertation, by Marjorie L. Tallant, entitled "Mill Village by the River: Changes in the Structure of the Southern Mill Village."

In the meantime, the School of Business Administration had set up its Institute of Industrial Relations in 1946 under the direction of Harry D. Wolf, the labor specialist in the School, who also served from time to time as a member of the Board of Governors of the Institute for Research in Social Science. The Institute of Industrial Relations was a coordinating agency of the School of Business Administration and the University Extension Division. Its function was to promote and direct educational programs in labor-management relations and workers' education.

While this was a valuable program, it did not attempt research that both Odum and Blackwell thought was needed in industrial relations. Accordingly, Blackwell discussed with Logan Wilson, provost of the University, the areas of research being neglected by the Institute for Research in Social Science and with his approval drew up a memorandum that stressed the need for a separate research institute in industrial relations to be located in the School of Business Administration, no doubt hoping to encourage the already existing Institute of Industrial Relations to undertake research as well as education. He sent copies of the memorandum to Wilson and to members of the Executive Committee of the Institute for Research in Social Science and placed discussion of the proposal on the agenda for the next meeting of the committee, to be held on January 31, 1952. The Executive Committee dismissed the suggestion with a general statement: ''In answer to questions concerning areas in social science research in the University which might logically come within the scope of the Institute and which may now be neglected, it was suggested that one criterion for Institute research be considered that of team research.''[45]

A year later, when the Institute undertook for the University a survey of behavioral science on the Chapel Hill campus, the report took note of the Institute of Industrial Relations under Wolf's direction, but also proposed as a focal area of research the establishment of a program on human relations in industry. The survey pointed out that funds had been allocated for such a program, and while ''this plan did not develop since a qualified person could not be obtained,'' the funds for this purpose had generated sufficient momentum for the School of Business Administration to develop the area. Work was under way to collect human relations cases from southern industry by a multidisciplinary faculty team.[46] The program, however, was never developed as laid out in Blackwell's memorandum, and years later when Blackwell looked back on his work as director of the Institute he recalled the program as one of his ''failures.''[47]

Research in human relations in industry, however, was not entirely neglected in the Institute for Research in Social Science. In 1949 the Department of Sociology had brought to the University a specialist in the field of human relations in industry, E. William Noland, as a research professor in the Institute. In 1953 *Social Forces* published his

"Industry Comes of Age in the South" and in 1960 his "Industrial Sociology and the Businessman." Institute professors in the Department of Economics and the Department of City and Regional Planning were involved in research in the area of industrialization, and Noland cooperated with both departments in several of their projects. In 1958 he was a joint author with Richard F. Calhoun and A. M. Whitehill of the Department of Economics in the preparation of *Human Relations in Management*.

In his annual report for 1962–63, Daniel Price, director of the Institute, mentioned "the development of urban and industrial communities" as one of the two major emphases of Institute research. Most of this research was being done by the Division of Urban Studies under the direction of F. Stuart Chapin, Jr., but the Departments of Sociology, Economics, and Geography were also participating. For example, Lowell D. Ashby of the Department of Economics contributed a chapter on trends in industrial development to *Urban Growth Dynamics* (1962), edited by F. Stuart Chapin, Jr., and Shirley F. Weiss.

Ashby continued his research in the general area of industrial development, as did also Ralph Pfouts and later Robert E. Gallman. Gallman's research on the service industries in the nineteenth century, in which he collaborated with T. J. Weiss, appeared in 1969 in *Production and Productivity in the Service Industries*, edited by Victor R. Fuchs as a volume in the series Studies in Income and Wealth, published by the National Bureau of Economic Research. Gallman was also concerned with the distribution of wealth in the United States, and published articles in that field.[48]

In the Department of Geography, Richard E. Lonsdale, an Institute affiliate and editor of *Southeastern Geographer*, wrote a brief article in 1968, "North Carolina Manufacturing: Trends and Future Prospects," for the *Quarterly Review* published in Charlotte by the First Union National Bank, and in 1969 he wrote "Deterrents to Industrial Location in the Rural South" for *Research Previews*, a publication of the Institute for Research in Social Science.[49] During the few years of his association with the Institute, he continued to produce several articles each year on southern industrialization. In 1971, for example, he wrote with Clyde E. Browning, "Rural-Urban Preferences of Southern Manufacturers" for the *Annals of the Association of American Geographers*.

Institute Research and Labor Relations

Institute research in industrial development could not ignore the labor that turned the wheels to produce development. It was, in fact, Odum's concern for labor and the social impact that low wages had upon the lives of the workers and their families that led the Institute into industrial research. The Institute's findings encouraged others outside the University to explore the field. Thirty years after the Institute began research in industrial and labor relations, the University of North Carolina Press published a composite study, *Human Relations in the Industrial Southeast*, by Glen Gilman, who had "never come under the personal influence" of the Institute but felt, nevertheless, that he must "give particular credit to Howard Odum, Harriet Herring, and Rupert Vance . . . for the understanding their studies had given him of the special circumstances that surround living and working in a human fashion in southeastern United States."[50]

In the Institute's early years, Odum had expected that Harriet Herring would explore some of these human questions in her study of mill villages and that she would have the assistance of Jennings J. Rhyne, a graduate student in sociology. When the hostility of the Cotton Manufacturers Association rebuffed the overtures of the Institute and changed the direction of the research, Rhyne set to work to study mill families in Gaston County in the North Carolina Piedmont. It was his native county, where he had lived for twenty-five years, and he knew most of the mill owners, the workers, and the men who ran the mill villages. He was himself a quiet, unassuming man. In the preface to his published research, *Some Southern Cotton Mill Workers and Their Villages*, he acknowledged the help of all his hometown friends and acquaintances: "I wish to express my appreciation of the cooperation and invaluable help received from mill superintendents, county officials, and all others who have contributed toward making this study possible."[51]

The emphasis of Rhyne's study was on labor patterns, and this was the very topic about which mill owners were most touchy. The mill owner's greatest fear was that his workers might be unionized; unionization meant higher wages and higher wages meant lower profits. Profits, the owners held, were already too low to make expanding the mills a feasible alternative. Profits had always been marginal in the textile industry in the South from the time the industry began developing in the late antebellum period. The mills had been built with the combined capital of bankers, merchants, farmers, and men of little means with a blind hope that if they could diversify the economy they might bring prosperity to the region and with it social and economic rehabilitation.

When Herring was confronted with the suspicion and hostility of the *Southern Textile Bulletin*, industrialization in North Carolina was on the threshold of realizing the dreams of those who had invested in its future. The one flexible component of manufacturing was the cost of labor. The cost of raw materials was not as heavy as was the price of machinery and the expenses of retooling when a mill changed, for instance, from the manufacture of cotton thread to cotton cloth. If the working hours were long, the wages low, and the laborers unorganized, profits might conceivably be high enough for expansion. New England manufacturers were beginning to move their plants away from unionized, high-priced labor into the South, where labor was cheap and defenseless. The southern states were competing for northern money in the effort of the ''New South'' to become industrialized. Any effort to unionize southern labor and any research related to conditions of labor were viewed as a threat by the mill owners, their administrative personnel, and in most instances by local and state governments.

When the American Federation of Labor tried to unionize mill workers in Charlotte, North Carolina, in 1921, the struggle ended in a victory for the manufacturers.[52] The strike had come during a downturn in business, and even those who might have sympathized with the hard lot of the mill worker thought the time was inopportune to press for higher wages and better working conditions. David Clark began his first attacks on Odum and the *Journal of Social Forces* at a time when the textile industry was suffering its worst depression in a decade, and when Harriet Herring approached the cotton manufacturers, textiles were still struggling for survival.

The Institute under Odum's leadership was genuinely concerned with the plight of mill workers—the long hours, the low wages, the exploitation of women and children, and the miserable mill villages. Odum thought that improvement of the lot of the worker would actually improve the industry itself by taking the paternalistic burden off the shoulders of the manufacturer and thereby improving chances for regional development. He was also irked by the caustic criticism of northern reformers, which he felt made the manufacturers hostile toward their labor and created obstacles toward development.

This was the situation in the textile industry and the position of the Institute director when Jennings Rhyne moved quietly back home to Gaston County to study labor management. He did his research in 1926–27, before the labor troubles in 1929 in Gastonia, but the research was not published until 1930. Rhyne's study was largely descriptive of the social, economic, educational, religious, and political aspects of the lives of cotton mill workers. It contained supportive data on most of these aspects of life. Rhyne also wanted to know what the workers thought of child labor, and he found that 62.5 percent of the 481 household heads interviewed were favorably disposed to the state law that restricted work to those fourteen years or older for a sixty-hour work-week (eleven hours a day for five days a week and five hours on Saturday).[53] Less than half (43 percent) of the workers interviewed approved of labor unions, and they were careful to point out that while the trade union was a good thing they opposed unionization by outsiders.[54]

When Frank Tannenbaum of Columbia University toured the South to observe its "darker phases," he declared that it were far better that textile workers "had remained on the farm and scratched the soil with their nails,"[55] but Rhyne found in his study, made soon afterward, that mill work actually gave the laborer a better wage than farm tenancy. His findings were also supported by Broadus Mitchell and George Mitchell, who thought that "the mill villages were a natural and necessary stage in industrial upbuilding" and that the mill village was actually bringing the farm tenant back into the work and council of the community.[56] "The family at the cotton mill is in much better financial condition than the tenant farmer family," Rhyne observed, and he pointed to a study that Professor E. C. Branson and J. A. Dickey had made in 1922 of farm tenancy in Chatham County, North Carolina, which showed that although the daily income of each person in a white farm tenant family was only fourteen cents a day, in a sharecropper family it was only eight cents a day.[57]

Unlike the works of northern critics such as Frank Tannenbaum and Paul Blanshard, the Institute studies of the textile industry had been somewhat favorable to the cotton manufacturers, but the Institute was again forced into confrontation with the manufacturers before Rhyne's research had been published.[58] The confrontation revolved around a meeting held in Greensboro in December 1927, organized by Blanshard, who was active in the labor movement and was at the time field secretary of the League for Industrial Democracy. He had tried in 1926 to get Odum's cooperation in undertaking a study of labor conditions in southern mills that he and the Federal Council of Churches had in mind, but Odum declined, saying that the Institute would conduct studies of mill labor if outsiders would let the labor controversies rest.[59] Blanshard also wanted access to the data from Herring's and Rhyne's projects, but again Odum declined. Blanshard, however, went forward with his own survey and published two articles in the *New Republic* in September 1927.[60] The articles were critical of the low wages of textile workers in the South, the long hours, the poor living conditions, and the lack of channels to force change.

After the publication of these articles, Blanshard began work on a meeting in Greensboro that he hoped would spark a labor reform campaign in North Carolina. Although Odum declined to participate, four young social scientists from the University did attend: Frank P. Graham, Thomas W. Holland, Harry M. Cassidy, and Gustave T. Schwenning. Among the reforms the conference called for were higher wages in the textile mills and a reduction in hours from sixty to fifty-four a week.

Shortly before the conference, Harry Cassidy, a young economist in the School of Commerce, wrote a letter to the editor of the *Chapel Hill Weekly* (December 9, 1927) disputing in diplomatic, even-handed terms the claim of the textile industry that mill wages were high in North Carolina. He pointed out that wages in North Carolina were substantially lower than in the North, although, in fact, higher than in South Carolina, Georgia, and Alabama. He also announced an address to be given on December 9 by T. A. Wilson, president of the State Federation of Labor, at the invitation of the Lecture Committee of the School of Commerce, and he invited the public to attend and submit questions. Two days later, the *Greensboro Daily News* (December 11, 1927) gave a favorable report on Wilson's address in Chapel Hill and commented editorially both on the labor statistics he had quoted and on the data contained in Cassidy's letter to the *Chapel Hill Weekly*. The *Greensboro Daily News*, usually supportive of the University and its faculty, concluded its editorial with the comment: "The information supplied here would indicate that Mr. Wilson is correct in his contention that [the term] 'average high' wages in North Carolina means little because it does not include a large proportion of the whole number of workers. But until more definite information is supplied on that point the state has a good deal to learn about the wages of the workers in the major industries.'"[61]

Odum had hoped that Institute research would be able to supply this definite information, but the outrage of the textile industry, stirred by David Clark in the *Southern Textile Bulletin*, had reached such a boiling point over the Greensboro conference that President Chase observed several months later to Haywood Parker, a member of the University Board of Trustees, "The question is rapidly becoming a serious one as to whether the University can try to render service of an expert kind in public matters without having to pay for it politically." [62] Any public contact, Chase continued, that the University had that went "beyond praising the status quo" was seized upon as another indication of Chapel Hill radicalism. In defense of the Institute, he wrote, "I don't know a better Christian gentleman than Odum, or a man with a greater passion for the South, and yet you know some of the things he [has] had to go through." Cassidy's letter to the *Chapel Hill Weekly* and the Lecture Committee's sponsorship of a lecture by the president of the State Federation of Labor, in addition to participation in the Greensboro conference, gave sufficient cause for a rumor to be started that the young economists in the School of Commerce were working secretly with labor organizations. Chase said that he had called the young men in and asked them to sign a statement denying the rumor. All of them had done so and Chase declared that he believed them.

David Clark had opened fire against the Greensboro conference and the University in the *Southern Textile Bulletin* on December 15, 1927, and on December 29 Thomas Holland gave him further cause for attack. Holland was a research assistant in the Institute for Research in Social Science whose project on the textile industry had been approved in 1926. Following the Greensboro conference he had attended a meeting in Washington, D.C., of the American Association of Labor Legislation and had discussed a paper on the new industrial South presented there by Broadus Mitchell, professor of economics at Johns Hopkins University. Holland was reported to have said that among the problems of southern industry were low wages and long hours, little protection for women workers, exploitation of child labor, and lax enforcement of such regulatory laws as did exist.

In the issue of the *Southern Textile Bulletin* for January 18, 1928, Clark accused Broadus Mitchell and "several from the University of North Carolina and North Carolina State College" of having attended both the Greensboro conference and the one in Washington to meet Paul Blanshard, and complained that "at both meetings vicious and untrue attacks were made upon the textile industry of North Carolina by men who are employed to teach in her colleges.'"[63] He kept up his assault through January and at intervals for more than a year. In one editorial he referred to Holland as a professor ''who is paid by the State of North Carolina for teaching,'' and later on in the same editorial he attacked Blanshard for his article in the *New Republic* that praised the work being done in the University.[64] The University, according to Clark, was actually becoming ''the refuge of radicals and socialists who are financed by a Northern organization known as the Laura Spillman [*sic*] Rockefeller Memorial Foundation.'"[65] The greatest menace to the nation, Clark declared, was ''the new fashioned professor who, while drawing a salary for teaching, feels that part of his duties is to cure all the ills of State and to regulate the conduct and the affairs of the public.'' These new-fashioned professors were radicals, communists, and atheists who were ''breeding'' in their classrooms ''a multitude of other radicals, communists and atheists.'"[66]

The pressure on President Chase grew so intense that he began to have anxieties about the Institute. In a letter to Haywood Parker in the spring of 1928, he said that he had noted a major change in the attitude of the public toward the University since about 1924, the date the Institute was established.[67] Because of this change, the faculty already had refrained from several research projects for fear of adverse reactions, and Chase felt that if hostility continued, the University might be forced to ''retreat within the walls of the campus.''

Two days before writing Parker, Chase had sent a confidential memorandum ''as a basis for discussion'' to Odum as director of the Institute, to D. D. Carroll, dean of the School of Commerce, in which Cassidy and Schwenning were employed, and to Frank Graham of the Department of History:

> The question has been raised—What are proper and what improper activities for members of a university faculty in the field of the social sciences? . . . It should be clear that no principle having to do with the freedom of teaching is under discussion. . . .
>
> A man who enters a university faculty in any of the fields of social science takes upon himself the obligation *to be a scientist*, and not a social reformer. The whole theory of university education in America draws such a distinction. . . .
>
> As a matter of fact men do engage in the advocacy of such causes as better educational facilities, the promotion of health and sanitation, civic improvements, church causes and the like, and there is no thought of impropriety. . . .

No faculty member has any right to allow his personal sym-
pathies for any controversial cause to involve his colleagues and
his institution in a situation that means general embarrassment, restricted educational opportunities for students and threatened
careers for his colleagues. . . . If his sympathy for such a cause
becomes sufficiently strong to raise in his mind a real conflict
with his institutional loyalty, he should obviously sever his
connection with the institution.

To what causes does the above apply? . . . In North Carolina
they certainly involve, for example, advocacy of particular forms
of taxation, of the organization of labor, of social equality between the races, of a socialistic regime, etc.[68]

The memorandum was probably meant as a warning, although Chase
had written to Haywood Parker that he might have to fire two or
three young faculty members.[69] While Graham and Schwenning stayed
on, Holland and Cassidy left Chapel Hill amid rumors that they had
been forced out. On July 15, 1928, the Raleigh *News and Observer*
broke the story that Malcolm M. Young, a recent honors graduate
of the University, had requested the United States Commissioner of
Education and the National Education Association to investigate the
situation. He had included in his request the case of Robinson N.
Newcomb, another Institute research assistant, who he claimed had
been "let out" the previous year because his study of Negro labor in
Winston-Salem had been too radical.[70] Young's request failed to bring
an investigation, but it did air the controversy over the freedom of
faculty members, including Institute staff, to endorse social change or
even to explore controversial social issues. Odum's position as Institute director remained unchanged: the times called for careful research
carefully pursued rather than for agitation.

While these traumatic events deterred Odum from mounting a major
study of southern labor conditions, the concern of the Institute in this
field of research continued. Before the furor over the Greensboro conference, the Institute had given funds to Robert A. McPheeters and
William H. Wicker for a study of workmen's compensation in North
and South Carolina and their report was published in 1926 in the *North
Carolina Law Review*. Almost two years afterward, Harriet Herring
prepared two feature stories for the *Greensboro Daily News* (October 27 and November 3, 1929), the "Metamorphosis of the Docile
Worker" and "Peace or War in Southern Textiles," and a year later
Rupert Vance contributed "The Southern Labor Supply" to the *Uni-*

versity Extension Bulletin, a publication intended for use in civic organizations. The same year Herring published "The Social Problem of Labor Organization Casualties" in *Social Forces*.

In 1931 the Institute assisted with the publication of the somewhat provocative research of George S. Mitchell, an instructor in economics at Columbia University, *Textile Unionism and the South*, and in 1933 *Social Forces* published "Labor Unrest in North Carolina, 1932," by H. M. Douty, a graduate student in economics whose work was directed by Harry D. Wolf. In 1934 Herring contributed a chapter, "The Industrial Worker," in William T. Couch's *Culture in the South*, and John Beecher, a graduate student in sociology, wrote "The Share Croppers' Union in Alabama" for *Social Forces*. In the same year, Robin Hood, a research assistant in economics, published in *Social Forces* his "A Bibliography on Southern Labor." In 1937 Odum himself delivered a lecture, "Industrial Relations and the Social and Economic Life of the South," before the Eighteenth Annual Industrial Conference at Blue Ridge, North Carolina, which was published in a summary of the conference called *New Factors in Industrial Relations*. Through these published studies, none of them definitive and all only mildly provocative, Odum was making good his promise to spell out the problems of labor relations through quiet, orderly research. Sporadic research in labor relations continued during the 1940s. Using data collected for their major work, *All These People*, Rupert Vance and Nadia Danilevsky prepared an article, "Population and the Pattern of Unemployment, 1930–1937" for the *Milbank Memorial Fund Quarterly* (1940), and in the same year published "How Can the South's Population Find Gainful Employment?" in the *Journal of Farm Economics*.

When E. William Noland became affiliated with the Institute in 1949 his major research on labor relations had recently been published: *Workers Wanted: A Study of Employers' Hiring Policies, Preferences, and Practices in New Haven and Charlotte*, which he had written in collaboration with E. Wight Bakke, Sterling Professor of Economics at Yale University and an authority on trade unionism. The research had been sponsored by the Committee on Labor Market Research of the Social Science Research Council, and although Noland had collected the data in Charlotte, the home of the *Textile Bulletin*, a few years after David Clark had accused Odum of being a subversive and of helping to initiate the Southern Regional Council,[71] *Workers Wanted* went almost unnoticed in North Carolina except in the professional field. In 1952 one of Noland's graduate students, George E. Baker, completed a doctoral dissertation on an analysis of the changing structure of southern industrial labor.

When Governor Luther H. Hodges came to office in 1954, he brought to public administration a long experience in the textile industry. Only recently he had retired as vice-president of Marshall Field and Company. He was concerned about the low per capita income of the state and, like Odum, he wanted to get at the root causes. He soon appointed a study commission to explore the reasons, and turned to the Institute and North Carolina State University for leadership. He appointed the Institute director, Gordon Blackwell, cochairman and made Harriet L. Herring and Lowell D. Ashby members of the commission. In 1955 the report was ready and was made widely available to the state press. Herring's research dealt with the factors in North Carolina's manufacturing industry that contributed to the low level of per capita income, and Ashby's was a report prepared with W. Allen Spivey entitled, "Per Capita Income Payments to Individuals, Their Nature and Reliability."[72]

During the decades of the 1950s and the 1960s Institute research in labor relations continued mainly in sociology and economics, but no major interdisciplinary research was undertaken. Among the research assistants in sociology working in labor-related programs without, however, a prime focus on labor were Raymond W. Mack, Alfred M. Denton, and Marjorie L. Tallant. Institute research professors engaged in labor research in the Department of Economics were Lowell Ashby, Ralph Pfouts, and Robert L. Bunting. Pfouts, writing with Franklee Gilbert Whartenly in 1957, published "Some Measurements of the Occupational Mobility of Labor" in *Econometrics*, and the next year Robert Bunting had an article in the same journal, "Labor Market Concentration." In 1960–61 Ashby published a major work on employment, *The North Carolina Economy, Its Regional and National Setting, with Particular Reference to the Structure of Employment*, and with Sang O. Park and the collaboration of the North Carolina Employment Security Commission and the Bureau of Employment Security of the United States Department of Labor, he completed a thorough research on unemployment compensation in North Carolina between 1936 and 1965, "A Study of Long-Range Benefit Financing and Fund Solvency." With Robert Bunting and Peter A. Prosper, Jr., Ashby also published in 1961 an article on labor mobility in three southern states in *Industrial and Labor Relations Review*. In 1968, just a year before his retirement from the Department of Sociology, Rupert Vance published "When Southern Labor Comes of Age" in *Monthly Labor Review*.

In the 1970s little research was being done in labor relations or management, although in 1972–73 Robert P. Strauss of the Department of Economics had under way projects on patterns of black employment and income and patterns of income distribution. Despite the intermittent researches in the Institute over a period of almost fifty years concerning the precarious position of nonunionized southern labor, North Carolina continues to this day as one of several southern states among the twenty in the nation with right-to-work laws permitting open shops,[73] and wages continue generally lower than the median for the nation.

Occupational Studies

Research into employment opportunities was a logical correlate to the Institute's studies in industrial development, labor relations, and labor mobility. It was closely tied to the big question in Odum's mind as he began the Institute: How can the inequalities in southern society be equalized? He welcomed the request from the Southern Woman's Educational Alliance that the Institute supervise during its first year the work of a young woman who would study vocational guidance for women and occupations available for rural women. It was not until 1936, however, that a graduate student, Ruth Y. Schiffman, undertook as her doctoral dissertation, "Occupations in the United States and the South," a survey of job opportunities in the South against the backdrop of national work patterns. For the next twenty years the Institute sponsored almost no research on occupational studies, although in 1940 Odum had given high priority in his Conference on the Measurement of Regional Development, held in Chapel Hill, to the encouragement of research on the needs and resources for development.[74] He hoped to see research on training leaders, skilled workers, and technicians "to translate natural resources into capital wealth."

When a major occupational project was next undertaken, it was an examination of a specific profession rather than a search for answers to problems of regional development through vocational training. The annual report of the Institute for 1959–60 announced as "the largest single new project" a grant of $84,000 from the United States Office of Education "to Professor Richard L. Simpson for a study of The School Teacher: Social Values, Community Role, and Professional Self-Image."[75] The study proposed to examine two important questions: (1) "Can existing programs produce the personnel to meet our growing need for school teachers?" and (2) "Do our programs of teacher education produce dedicated professionals, or do they produce people to whom teaching is only a job, perhaps a job to be abandoned after a few years?" For the answers to these questions, Simpson's study concentrated on two cities in the Southern Piedmont Crescent. Ten years later, in 1969, after many interruptions by research in other areas and a year in which he served as acting director of the Institute, Simpson made a final report to the Office of Education under the title "The School Teachers: Social Values, Community Role, and Professional Self-Image."[76] But he had not finished with the data and as the fifth decade of the Institute closed he was still at work on the self-image of the school teacher and voluntary deprofessionalization.

In addition to Simpson's study, the Institute produced a scattering of other occupational reports, a number of which were concerned with mobility. In 1964 Harry J. Crockett, Jr., prepared an article, "Social Class, Education, and Motive to Achieve in Differential Occupational Mobility," for the *Sociological Quarterly*, and a chapter, "Psychological Origins of Mobility," in *Social Structure and Social Mobility in Economic Development*, edited by Neil J. Smelser and Seymour M. Lipset. In 1965 the Institute staff produced two articles and a book on mobility. One of the articles was by Bruce K. Eckland, "Academic Ability, Higher Education, and Occupational Mobility," which appeared in the *American Sociological Review*, and the other was a chapter by Richard L. Simpson and David R. Norsworthy on the changing occupational structure of the South in *The South in Continuity and Change*, edited by John C. McKinney and Edgar T. Thompson, sociologists at Duke University. The book on mobility, *An Empirical Examination of the Relationship of Vertical Occupational Mobility and Horizontal Residential Mobility*, was by Edgar W. Butler.

Had Odum lived to read the chapter by Simpson and Norsworthy in *The South in Continuity and Change*, he might have been overcome with despair. The authors found the South to have a "persistent economic lag behind the rest of the nation" not only in low income, but also in underrepresentation of southern workers in the higher occupations.[77] In 1965 as in 1924, the South was the most agricultural region in the nation and its farmers were the poorest. Its industrialization had brought in the kind of soft manufacturing and unskilled services that call for the fewest craftsmen and the lowest number of white-collar and professional jobs. Whites had benefited most from the progress that had been made and southern Negroes were "in some ways more disadvantaged than ever in the region's occupational structure."[78]

Although formal research in occupational structure had come late in the history of the Institute, the field had not been neglected in contributions to *Social Forces*. In the fifty-year history of the Institute, the professional journal that it helped to maintain had published some seventy articles on occupations, occupational choice, mobility, and structure. Some of the articles were by former Institute assistants, among them Raymond W. Mack, Richard L. Simpson, Charles B. Nam, and Fred E. Katz.

Studies of Southern Farm Problems

Howard Odum was so deeply troubled by the low wages and lack of vocational opportunities for southern workers that he did not include southern farm problems in his first list of projects to be explored by the Institute, although he had a deep and personal concern for the plight of the farmer, because he himself had come from a farm background. The first published research of the Institute on southern agricultural problems came in 1929 with *Human Factors in Cotton Culture*, the doctoral dissertation of Rupert B. Vance. Vance considered his work to be an attempt "to state in terms of cultural anthropology the problem of the psychological equipment of the human factors in cotton culture."[79] He found that an economic harmony existed between the spinner, the cotton buyer, the landlord, the supply merchant, and the cotton farmer that tended to benefit all except the farmer: "The cotton farmer's income often just balances his upkeep from the landlord or a supply store."[80] Life for the tenant farmer, and especially for the sharecropper, was below the poverty line. The cotton culture complex bred two sets of attitudes peculiar to southern cotton and tobacco tenants: a shiftless attitude toward the lands on which they lived, and a tendency to rove from one farm to another in search of a better landlord, better land, better housing, better education, and better health conditions. As a sociologist, Vance contended that "for farming to survive in America it must be a satisfying way of life" as well as a means of economic subsistence, but that "the future of the small cotton farmer is precarious at best."[81]

Within the next seventeen years, the Institute was to produce nine books, twenty-five published articles or chapters in books, and twenty-one manuscripts on southern farm problems. Among the best known of the books were *Black Yeomanry*, by T. J. Woofter, Jr.; *King Cotton Is Sick*, by Claudius T. Murchison; *Part-time Farming in the Southeast*, by Harriet L. Herring and others; *The Wasted Land*, by Gerald W. Johnson; *Preface to Peasantry*, by Arthur F. Raper; *Sharecroppers All*, by Arthur F. Raper and Ira De A. Reid; and *Mothers of the South: Portraiture of the White Farm Tenant Woman*, by Margaret Jarman Hagood. Among the best known articles were "The Negro and the Farm Crisis" (1928), by T. J. Woofter, Jr.; "The Rural Tax Problem" (1929), by Clarence Heer; "Agricultural Credit and the Negro Farmer" (1930), by Roland B. Eutsler; "The Displaced Farm Tenant Family in North Carolina" (1934), by Gordon W. Blackwell; "Problems of Reintegration in Agrarian Life" (1937), by Harry E. Moore and Bernice M. Moore; and "Poor Whites of the South" (1938), by Mildred Rutherford Mell—all published in *Social Forces*. In the meantime both Odum and Vance were publishing articles on southern farming in the Depression in a series known as "The South Today" that was published in twelve southern newspapers through the Southern Newspaper Syndicate, preparing reports for the National Resources Committee, and writing position papers for United States congressional hearings on the issue "Rural Distress and Relief in the Southeast."

Arthur Raper's books on tenancy and sharecropping were among the most widely noted of all the Institute's research on southern farm problems. The research for *Preface to Peasantry* began when Raper was an assistant in the Institute and continued after he received his doctorate from the University in 1931, when he became a member of the staff of the Commission on Interracial Cooperation, in Atlanta. It was published by the Institute in 1936. The study had originally been planned as a comparison of conditions in a Black Belt county in Georgia that had suffered a substantial population decrease since 1920 with conditions in another county that had retained its population. In this way Raper hoped to determine the cause of the migration of Negroes from the Black Belt to the cities of the South and North. As the New Deal unfolded, the Interracial Commission wanted to determine how these programs were affecting the population in the same

two counties, Green and Macon, that Raper had examined as an Institute researcher. The survey resulted in one of the best analyses of
farm tenancy that had been made. The book opened with a photograph
of black farm workers atop two loads of freshly picked cotton on the
way to the gin. The picture was labeled, "The Black Belt's Riddle—
To Whom Does This Cotton Belong: To the Tenant Farmer Who Grew
It, To the Landlord Who Furnished the Tenant, Or To the Banker Who
Financed the Landlord?"

Raper's findings were similar to those made by Vance's earlier study
of the cotton culture complex. To gain a firsthand knowledge of tenancy, Raper had lived for a time in the two counties, interviewed more
than three hundred tenant families, gone hunting and fishing with
them, gone to their churches on Sunday, and hung around the supply
stores at night. He found the poorest people on the richest land in the
two counties. The old plantation system was crumbling, and its col-
lapse was a "preface to peasantry." The independent renters and small
owners were emerging as a new type of American farmer, "almost as
poor as the sharecropper" and at the same time "almost as independent as the plantation owner."[82] They were a fatalistic people, dependent upon the supply store and the banks, living within the framework
of crippled institutions and upon soil rapidly being exhausted. Raper
held that "the average white farm family has been lowered rather
than raised by the assumption that the Negro must be kept servile,
dependent, and landless." He concluded that the cotton culture might
be revitalized by mechanization, but that more important than mechanization would be a "change in the prevailing philosophy." A constructive land policy and a change in the attitude of people toward
people seemed the best hope.[83]

Sharecroppers All, by Arthur Raper and Ira Reid, published by
the Institute in 1941, reached much the same conclusion, but extended beyond the sharecropper to include all deprived workers in
"essentially feudalistic" southern communities: chain-store clerks,
salesmen, insurance agents, taxi drivers, filling-station operators, the
city's casual laborers, and domestic workers. In words reminiscent of
Odum's early editorials in *Social Forces*, Raper and Reid saw the
South as "problem and opportunity, proud and pitiful—a land of un-
limited possibilities and of unrelieved privation."[84] They argued that
the South had been victimized by national policy and politics that
imposed tariffs and a colonial status that in turn reinforced the South's
economic feudalism, the one-party system, the white primary, and the

poll tax. The result had been ''the disinheritance and disfranchisement of nearly all the Negroes, a majority of the whites, and of the region itself in national affairs.''[85] The crux of the South's inadequacies was its ''rural, industrial, and racial problems,'' and the greatest of these was racial.[86] ''One of the most obvious reasons for the social retardation of the South,'' the authors concluded, ''is the unwillingness of the white man to face the fact that his own fate and the fate of the region as a whole are inseparable from the fate of the Negro.''[87]

Sharecroppers All was the last major research on farm problems sponsored by the Institute, although for the next thirty years the senior research professors occasionally turned out monographs or articles related to the rural South. In 1941, the same year that *Sharecroppers All* was published, Rupert Vance prepared a chapter, ''Interrelation of Population Trends and Land Tenure in the Southeast,'' for *The People, the Land, and the Church in the Rural South*, published by the Farm Foundation of Chicago. Two years later, Margaret Jarman Hagood's ''Statistical Methods for Delineation of Regions Applied to Data on Agriculture and Population'' appeared in *Social Forces* and her ''Development of a 1940 Rural-Farm Level of Living Index for Counties'' in *Rural Sociology*. In 1946, Rupert Vance and Gordon Blackwell published a monograph, *New Farm Houses for Old: Rural Public Housing in the South*.

In 1954 the Richardson Foundation of Greensboro, North Carolina, gave the Institute a small grant to study ''part-time farming and related community factors in the State.'' The research team was composed of Gordon Blackwell, Harriet Herring, S. H. Hobbs, Jr., and George L. Simpson, and the study, ''Part-time Farming in North Carolina,'' was completed the following year with the help of Albert Schaffer, a research assistant.[88] By this time the reorganization of research to focus on behavioral science studies had turned the Institute away from emphasis upon agriculture and the plight of the farmer. Technological development had decreased the number of sharecroppers and tenants in southern agriculture and these displaced people were moving out into industry and service in the North and Middle West.

Not until the arrival in 1968 of Professor Henry A. Landsberger from Cornell University did the Department of Sociology again have a senior faculty member in the Institute who was concerned with farm labor, although his chief research in this field had focused on Latin America, especially Chile and Mexico. In 1969, however, he read a paper, ''Social and Political Preconditions for Cooperatives among

Poor Farmers in the United States South,'' at the Conference on Social Prerequisites for Agricultural Cooperation at the Institute for Development Studies, held at the University of Sussex in Brighton, England. He was also at work with Cynthia Hewitt on peasant movements in Latin America, and was editor of *Latin American Peasant Movements*, published that year by Cornell University Press. In 1973 *Rural Unrest: Peasant Movements and Social Change*, of which he was editor, appeared, to which he contributed two chapters, one on the general topic of peasant unrest and the other on the English peasant revolt of 1381.

Research on Taxation Policies

Howard Odum had seen as one of the inequalities bearing down upon the unequal people in the South the variations in the tax structure that appeared to favor the large landowner. Government, he contended, should serve the needs of all the people and not exploit any group for the benefit of a chosen few. With these thoughts in mind, Odum and the Institute's Board of Governors decided in 1927 to undertake a series of studies on taxation and agreed to enlist specialists in economics and law to direct the research. They found the economist in Clarence Heer and the lawyer in Millard S. Breckenridge of the University law school. To Breckenridge they assigned a bright young professor of law, Edwin M. Perkins, as assistant.

Soon after coming to office in the late 1920s, Governor O. Max Gardner invited the Institute to participate in a study of taxation undertaken by the North Carolina Tax Commission, and Clarence Heer undertook that responsibility. In 1929, before he presented his first reports to the Tax Commission, Heer published a series of three articles, "Decisions and Rulings—North Carolina" (June and December 1928, November 1929) and a fourth article, "The Public Dollar" (October 1929), in the *Bulletin of the National Tax Association*. In 1930 he completed "Taxation of Public Service Corporations" for the *Report of the Tax Commission to Governor O. Max Gardner* and in 1932 he completed Part II of the *Report* with the assistance of Hugh P. Brinton and Robin Hood.[89]

During his research for the Tax Commission, Heer was also directing Hershal L. Macon in preparing a history of the North Carolina tax system from 1877 to 1935, as the counterpart to Coralie Parker's *The History of Taxation in North Carolina during the Colonial Period*,

1663–1776, which the Institute had helped finance in 1928. Heer was also undertaking an analysis of state and local finances as "an approach to the problem of securing inter-regional equality in the matter of tax burdens and uniformity in standards of local governmental services through a rational allocation of functions, financial burdens, and revenue resources as between the state and its subordinate political units."[90] Out of these studies grew two articles, "Comparative Costs of County Governments in the South" in *Social Forces* in 1932, and the chapter entitled "Taxation and Public Finance" for the report of the President's Committee on Social Trends, of which Odum was a research director. After completing his research for the North Carolina Tax Commission, Heer was made research director for the Interstate Commission on Conflicting Taxation and research consultant for the American Legislators' Association. When he completed this work, he returned to Chapel Hill in August 1934, only to be released again briefly by the Institute for a three-month special research project on "the changing status of public employment" in cooperation with the Commission of Inquiry on Public Service Personnel.[91] Soon afterward, Heer became a professor in the School of Commerce and concluded his research for the Institute.

Edwin M. Perkins from the School of Law published as an Institute research project a series of articles on tax issues in the *North Carolina Law Review* between 1933 and 1935, beginning with "Tax Injunctions and Suits to Recover Taxes Paid under Protest in North Carolina" and including two articles on "the regressive sales tax" that the state had passed to bolster its revenue during the Depression, and another entitled "The Power of Congress to Levy Taxes for Distribution to the States."[92]

Not until the 1950s did the Institute again turn its attention to the tax structure. Governor Luther H. Hodges had appointed not only a commission to study per capita income in the state but also a commission for the study of revenue structure. The Commission on Revenue Structure turned to the Institute and the School of Business Administration for assistance in setting up its Conference on Economic and Social Factors in the Development of North Carolina. The Institute provided leadership and financing for the conference in the winter of 1955 and early spring of 1956. Six of the eight faculty members who participated in the conference were members of the Institute staff: Lowell D. Ashby, Milton S. Heath, Harriet L. Herring, James C. Ingram, E. William Noland, and Ralph W. Pfouts. All of the papers were widely publicized in the state press and Ashby's articles, "Government Taxing and Spending: Development of the Last Decades and Current Problems," appeared in the *American Economic Review* in 1957. This conference seems to have been the last major effort the Institute made to study problems of taxation. In 1973, however, Clyde E. Browning of the Department of Geography read a paper at the annual meeting of the Association of American Geographers, "The Property Tax and Public Policy: A Neglected Opportunity for Geographic Research," which was published in the Association's *Proceedings* in the same year. An article such as this would have pleased Odum.

Those who followed Odum as directors of the Institute were committed in varying degrees to his view that the prime object of research was to serve society and more specifically, to gather data that would point the way for the South to climb up from the bottom into the enjoyment of all the social and economic benefits of full partnership in the flourishing nation. Gordon W. Blackwell, who followed Odum as director in 1944, frequently referred to "the need for conscious attention to the problem of application of research findings," and remarked that "indeed this has been set forth as one of the main functions of the Institute."[93] When James W. Prothro became director, he stated the function of the Institute more in terms of understanding than in application, but to Odum these terms might easily have been synonymous. To understand a situation certainly implied to Odum a moral responsibility to take action, and Odum would have had no quarrel with Prothro's opening statement in his annual reports: "The purpose of the Institute for Research in Social Science is to advance understanding of human behavior. Although additions to knowledge may be regarded as self-justifying, such additions—particularly in the social sciences—may be expected to lead to the social, economic, and political improvement of the human condition."[94]

Research during Odum's administration had explored the reason why the South was at the bottom of the nation's economic ladder: the lack of industrial development and the short-sighted policy toward their laborers of those industries that were located in the South, the need for low-income labor to move out of a feudal system in search of higher-paying jobs, the job opportunities open to southern labor, the system of farm tenancy that created the anomaly of tying agricultural workers with the lowest income to the richest land, a tax system that placed the greatest burden upon those least able to pay. But these were only a few of the problems Odum thought were keeping the South at the bottom. He was convinced that continued research would expose other crucial social issues and would bring the leaders of the South to see these problems as obstacles to progress and thus set in motion the forces of change.

CHAPTER 8

Research in Social Problems and Social Policy

Howard Odum maintained that the South was kept at the bottom of the ladder not only by economic practices but by social problems as well, which were in large measure the result both of public policies and of folk culture. The region could rise only if men of goodwill became aware of these facts.[1] With this knowledge, southern leadership, he fervently hoped, would take action to correct the inequalities and bring a better balance to the southern region. Odum was acclaimed throughout the nation, at his death in 1954, for having directed the research of the Institute toward digging out the root causes of the South's problems, and because of this research the Institute was hailed as a monument to the accomplishments of "a great and good man."[2]

Odum had experienced the inequalities in the South. As a young man, he had seen in Bethlehem, Georgia, where he was born, and in Toccopola, Mississippi, where he had taught in a rural school, the harsh realities that tied generation after generation of poor whites and poor blacks to a life of bare existence. He had seen in his schoolroom children in rags, guilty of slovenly work and inattention, given frequently to petty thievery. Like his friend Morris Mitchell, who was also a Southerner and who taught in a rural school in the southern Piedmont of North Carolina, he knew that there were hidden causes that set these children against society. As Mitchell related it, "invariably such causes were to be found—hookworm or tuberculosis, parental abuse, bad associates, overwork in the fields, ignorance in the home, low intelligence, or malnutrition."[3]

During the two decades of Odum's administration as director and well afterward, the Institute undertook such projects on social problems as the role of public welfare, child care and development, delinquency and crime, marriage and the family, family planning and birth control, women's roles, recreation, community organization, and housing. For a short time during Gordon Blackwell's administration, the Institute also attempted a program of research interpretation, which Odum had always felt was crucial to promoting an understanding of these problems among the southern people.

Blackwell, who followed Odum in 1944 as director of the Institute, shared Odum's conviction that basic research would play an essential role in showing the South the "way out" of its problems. Voicing the generally ebullient attitude of most physical and social scientists at that time, he declared in 1945, "We are . . . learning that the ways of men, their social organization and their institutions, can be consciously directed toward more effective achievement of agreed-upon goals. There logically follows, then, the need for a constant search for more knowledge . . . in order that our efforts and our plans may become increasingly effective."[4] Directors of the Institute who followed Black-well were less sanguine than he about the potentials of social engineering, but affiliates of the Institute, especially in community health and in urban development, continued to explore social issues through the end of the Institute's first half-century.

Public Welfare

Public welfare was one of the first social issues that the Institute faced when Odum and the Board of Governors laid out the program. Odum was ready with research proposals that had grown out of the work of the School of Public Welfare, which he had organized in 1920, and the articles he had published in the *Journal of Social Forces*, which he had founded in 1922. In the opening volume of the *Journal*, he devoted three of its eight departments to welfare and social work, and in later issues he occasionally published a leading article on social policy.

In 1925, just one year after the creation of the Institute, with the assistance of D. W. Willard of the University of Washington at Seattle, Odum presented the Board of Governors with a volume on public welfare ready for publication, *Systems of Public Welfare*, which the University of North Carolina Press brought out. The next year Odum followed up with a second book, *An Approach to Public Welfare and Social Work*, and in 1928 the Institute published two additional volumes: *Social Work and the Training of Social Workers*, by Sydnor Walker of the Laura Spelman Rockefeller Memorial, and *Public Poor Relief in North Carolina*, by Roy M. Brown, a research associate in the Institute who was later to become chairman of the Department of Public Welfare and Social Work. These books were followed in the next year by Harriet Herring's *Welfare Work in Mill Villages*, which was discussed in chapter 7. During 1928 and 1929, Odum, Katharine Jocher, and Harriet Herring published six articles on welfare. Odum was also making public addresses on public welfare and social work, among them "The County Unit as a Basis of Social Work and Public Welfare in North Carolina" at the National Conference of Social Work in 1926, and "Human Factors in Social Science Research and Social Work" at the New Jersey Conference on Social Work in 1928.

Roy Brown's *Public Poor Relief in North Carolina* traced the history of relief in the state, but the major portion of the work concentrated on current conditions. The state constitution of 1868 had removed poor relief from the courts of pleas and quarter sessions and placed it under jurisdiction of the county commissioners, and there it had remained until an act in 1917, strengthened in 1919, created the State Board of Charities and Public Welfare and authorized the formation of county departments in charge of county superintendents of public welfare. The indoor relief cases were cared for in county homes, or almshouses, supervised by the county superintendents. Most of the superintendents had less than a high school education, and a large number were illiterate. Before their employment, some county superintendents had been tenant farmers, carpenters, jailers, policemen, and even moonshiners.[5] The job soon became prey to the political spoils system.

The county homes had long been places to dump the unwanted and the defenseless, the elderly whose relatives did not want to or could not afford to provide for them, the feebleminded, orphans, delinquents, and often women prisoners. A survey of county homes made in 1922 by Harry W. Crane, director of the Bureau of Mental Hygiene and Health in the State Board of Charities and Public Welfare and later a professor of psychology in the University, found that feeblemindedness often perpetuated itself in the county homes. The biennial report of the State Board for 1920–22 cites a case in the Nash County Home where a woman and her daughter had arrived "a generation ago." The girl was feeble-minded and grew up in the county home. There she gave birth to ten children. Two of the children died, and six were placed for adoption. Two remained in the home, and "one of these, a young woman about twenty-four years old, is the mother of four children, including twins only a few months old."[6]

The outdoor poor-list (those receiving aid who were not in institutions) was also administered by the county superintendents. The numbers served by outdoor relief far exceeded those cared for in the county homes. Brown discovered that while some of the counties had made "a beginning of the application of social casework methods to the investigation of requests for aid," very rarely had the county superintendent even conceived of using the outdoor poor-funds for rehabilitation.[7] But it would be a bit ludicrous, Brown thought, to undertake any kind of constructive casework on the basis of the two or three dollars a month that were sometimes the amounts of the dole. He was encouraged by the state's insistence on "somewhat adequate grants for mothers' aid cases," and he hoped in time "the same common-sense method in dealing with all relief" would suggest itself to the counties. As for the county homes, which were "a part of the political spoils systems," he would abolish them, consolidate them, or follow the example of Vance County, which turned its county home into a hospital with a ward for county home inmates.

With the coming of the Depression and the enactment of federal assistance programs, county homes in North Carolina began slowly to disappear.[8] The federal programs were welcomed by the Institute staff. Between 1930 and 1932, Odum was at work on "Public Welfare Activities," which was to appear as a chapter in *Recent Social Trends in the United States*, published in 1933 as the report of the President's Committee on Social Trends, of which he was a codirector. He and his staff accumulated a mass of data for his chapter in the volume.[9] Odum spoke of his hopes for social security in an address, "Social Security and Public Welfare in the '30's," given at the second annual institute of the North Carolina State Employment Service, held in Chapel Hill in 1936. About this time, Lyda Gordon Shivers, a graduate student in sociology in the University and later chairman of the Department of Sociology in the University of North Carolina at Greensboro, produced as her doctoral dissertation an excellent composite picture of public welfare in the South, "The Social Welfare Movement in the South: A Study in Regional Culture and Social Organization," which unfortunately still remains unpublished. An Institute study on the important role played by the North Carolina Conference for Social Service in advocating social welfare reform was published, however, in 1942. This was Virginia Wooten Gulledge's *The North Carolina Conference for Social Service: A Study of Its Development and Methods*.[10] Many Institute staff members, among them Odum, Katharine Jocher, Harriet Herring, Roy M. Brown, Wiley B. Sanders, and later, Gordon W. Blackwell and the staff of the School of Social Work, participated in the conference either as officers or committee chairmen.

With the increase in federal welfare assistance to the states during the Depression a growing concern arose in the nation as to the effectiveness of the welfare program. The Institute staff, including Margaret Jarman Hagood, Fred Bunting, Robert Hodges, and Virginia Lynn Denton, under the supervision of Roy M. Brown, then chairman of the Department of Public Welfare and Social Work, was busy with research to determine the impact of the program on dependency. Virginia Denton coordinated the research in her doctoral dissertation in social work in 1941, "An Introductory Study of Inter-relationships among Federal, State, and Local Public Relief Administrations."

The American Public Welfare Association turned to the Institute in two major instances for an examination of the federal program of Aid to Dependent Children (ADC). The first survey was undertaken by Gordon W. Blackwell and Raymond F. Gould, and their *Future Citizens All* was published in 1952. The project was the first comprehensive survey made of the effectiveness of the federal program. A popular assumption among those opposed to ADC was that it encouraged illegitimacy, but the study found that while 11 percent of children among the ADC families in the survey had been born out of wedlock prior to the family's receiving aid, only 3.4 percent were born out of wedlock after aid was granted.[11] The study also found that ADC was meeting one of the prime objectives of its establishment: the program was operating successfully to keep children in their homes. An additional dividend of the program was that ADC children turned to delinquency at a rate lower than the estimated national rate for all children. This fact, the authors concluded, was "impressive indirect evidence of satisfactory social adjustment of the vast majority of these ADC children."[12]

The second survey of ADC was an analysis ten years later by Daniel O. Price, director of the Institute, and M. Elaine Burgess, who had received her doctorate in sociology from the University and was later to become a professor of sociology in the University of North Carolina at Greensboro. Their research was published in 1963 as *An American Dependency Challenge*. Burgess and Price used the questionnaire developed by Blackwell and Gould in order to obtain comparable data, but the new study went beyond this to obtain additional information on housing, living conditions, family background, illegitimacy, types of problems faced, and general assistance to families. It also examined in more detail than the earlier study such variables as race, urban-rural residence, educational level, and types of crises. It was found that most of the dependent children were growing up in homes with their own mothers and that there was little evidence of child abuse or misuse of funds. Like Brown in his earlier Institute study on public welfare in North Carolina, Burgess and Price found that dependent families tended to continue their dependency in successive generations. Of the families receiving assistance, 40 percent had grown up in homes that had received assistance; 70 percent of the children had not finished high school; and only 2 percent had gone beyond high school. The authors concluded that financial assistance through ADC was not enough to solve these problems. The need was for "a new emphasis on prevention and rehabilitation, more adequate financial assistance for those in need, better protection and education of the children, and more and better prepared social work personnel." But even these reforms were not enough. There was also a need for "more meaningful coordination of services in the areas of health, education, vocational training, testing and guidance, and community work projects."[13] The study was widely acclaimed and in several instances might have served as a blueprint for the War on Poverty, which President Lyndon B. Johnson was soon to launch. Although the War on Poverty addressed itself to some of the recommendations of the study, it was dismantled too soon, under the Nixon administration, to determine whether the authors' proposed remedies would in fact help to solve the increasing problems of public welfare in America.

When Arthur E. Fink became chairman of the Department of Public Welfare and Social Work in 1945, he quickly moved to develop an accredited school of social work that could sponsor carefully supervised field training. He and his staff, among them Floyd Hunter, Alan Keith-Lucas, and Albert Johnson, became involved from time to time in research associated with the Institute. Fink's best known publication is his textbook, *The Field of Social Work*, first published in 1942 and in 1974 published in its sixth edition. When the book first appeared it was called "a lucid, able exposition" for the nonprofessional field.[14] The revision published in 1949 was considered "a notable addition to the literature of social work."[15] Fink revised the various editions in collaboration with his staff and others in the field of social work. Among staff members who participated in revisions and who were also affiliated with the Institute were C. Wilson Anderson, Morris H. Cohen, Maeda J. Galinsky, and H. Carl Henley. As a senior member of the Institute, Fink also wrote a history of institutional care of children in North Carolina, which except for one article, still remains unpublished. Floyd Hunter's research was in the field of sociology, although he did collaborate with Isabelle K. Carter in the preparation of a manual for field work.[16] The research done by Alan Keith-Lucas was on institutional care of children, and it will be referred to later in this chapter. Social work faculty listed as senior research affiliates of the Institute in 1974 were Morris H. Cohen, Andrew Dobelstein, Maeda J. Galinsky, H. Carl Henley, Erwin H. Plumer, and John B. Turner.

Child Welfare and Development

Research in child welfare was one of the six areas proposed for investigation at the first meeting of the Institute's Board of Governors in 1924. A. M. Jordan, a professor in the Department of Education, was given responsibility for its development, and at the next meeting of the Board he proposed a study of the effect of physical work on the mental growth of children in rural and industrial communities. At the third meeting, he requested permission to make a visit at the expense of the Institute to the Child Welfare Station of the University of Iowa, and the request was granted.

The concern of the Institute for a research project on the effect of physical work on the mental development of children arose from the findings of a graduate student, L. H. Jobe, in the Department of Education. Jobe had conducted his research in 1920 under the direction of Lester A. Williams, professor of school administration. Williams had been a member of the University faculty since 1913 but in 1922 went to the University of California at Berkeley. He had been active in the Graduate Club at Chapel Hill, an organization composed both of faculty and of graduate students, and he had prepared the club's report in 1922, "a survey of the fields at present unworked, or only partially worked, in which outstanding research could be done," in which he pointed out that the South was almost a virgin area for research.[17] Odum published the report, "The South as a Field for Sociological Research," in the second issue of the *Journal of Social Forces*. The report parallels so closely Odum's own thinking, first presented formally at Emory University before he came to Chapel Hill and later at Chapel Hill in the establishment of the Institute for Research in Social Science, that Odum undoubtedly must have had a hand in preparing the Graduate Club report.

Williams had suggested in the report that it was possible that the South had "an unusually large proportion of subnormal children in its schools both white and black," and he based his assumption on preliminary studies that suggested "that this is the true situation."[18] The preliminary study to which he referred was that of his graduate student Jobe, whose data he later summarized in an article for *Social Forces* in 1925, "The Intellectual Status of Children in Cotton Mill Villages." In 1920 Jobe gave IQ tests to school children in a southern mill village and found that according to the tests 34 percent were at or below borderline intelligence. Later Jobe tested the children in a second mill village some distance from the first and found "almost exactly two-thirds of the group below normal intellectual capacity."[19] While Williams pointed out that mere random sampling was not sufficient to show that a surprisingly large proportion of children in mill villages were at the borderline or feeble-minded levels, he did ask the question, "Is it true that our cotton mill village population is a stratum of low grade intelligence in our social order?" And he called for extensive research to determine the facts.

It was against this background that the Institute Board authorized Jordan to begin the research necessary to answer the questions that Jobe's research had raised. Work was already under way in the Institute when Williams's article appeared in *Social Forces*, and the article soon came to the attention of the mill owners and the *Southern Textile Bulletin*. David Clark, editor of the *Bulletin*, led the attack and broadened "the fight," as he called it, to University students who set out under "egotistical professors" to study the social and economic ills of North Carolina. He denounced the "Meddling Departments" in the University that were responsible for the studies and said that they were "financed partly by New York money."[20] Clark maintained that Williams's article had held North Carolina up to ridicule throughout the nation and that the mills would eventually be driven out of the state as they had been driven out of New England by radical university professors unless the "Meddling Departments" in the University of North Carolina ceased their activities. By this time, "Meddling Departments" had come to Clark and his followers to include the Institute for Research in Social Science. At one point in the controversy, a reporter from the Raleigh *News and Observer* interviewed Clark and reported that "he expressed no doubt that the manufacturers can and will cause the legislature to cut the appropriation of the University if they persist in making studies unwelcomed to them," but Clark denied having made such a threat.[21] The controversy raged on for several months and later merged into the dispute over the Institute's proposal, discussed in chapter 7, to study the mill villages.

The Institute went on, nevertheless, with the proposed research on the effect of physical work on the mental development of children. The project was carried out under the direction of A. M. Jordan with the help of Graham B. Dimmick, his research assistant. Dimmick made his study in Winston-Salem. His report was a comparative study of growth in mental and physical abilities of mill and nonmill children. A year later, in 1928, Jordan summarized his own research in a manuscript, "Mental and Physical Growth of Children in Different Occupational Groups."[22] While Jordan and Dimmick explored only a few variables affecting childhood growth and abilities, they recorded retardation at 4.5 percent, a far lower rate than Jobe's study had predicted.

Some twenty years later, Clarence J. Gamble, a geneticist with an international reputation for his work at Harvard University and the University of Pennsylvania, stimulated an Institute study of the startling rejection rate (14 percent in 1942 and 48 percent in 1944) of North Carolina draftees in World War II for reasons of mental illness or retardation, and he financed a study of sterilization in North Carolina done by Moya Woodside.[23] He later sent Elsie Wulkop, a medical social worker, to North Carolina to explore the facts behind these statistics. As a result, A. M. Jordan made two additional studies of the intelligence levels of the school children of a rural (Orange) and an urban (Forsyth) county, and these findings, at Gamble's urging, led to the organization of the Human Betterment League of North Carolina. James G. Hanes, president of Hanes Hosiery Corporation at Winston-Salem, and A. M. Jordan were among the founders of the League.[24] Hanes served as treasurer of the organization until his death in 1972.

The Institute also encouraged a number of other research projects on child welfare. Among the first of these was a study of child labor by Katharine DuPre Lumpkin and Dorothy Wolff Douglas, which was published in New York in 1927 as *Child Workers in America*. In 1933 the Institute published a study by Wiley B. Sanders, professor in the Department of Social Work and Public Welfare, *Negro Child Welfare in North Carolina*.

In 1945 the Institute entered into a project of a combined research-planning nature with the Committee on Security and Services for Children, of the North Carolina State Planning Board. As outlined by Gordon Blackwell in his "Report of the Director for 1945," the project was designed to provide basic information and recommendations for administrative decisions and legislation on child welfare. The program was financed by the Institute through a grant from the Parents' Institute and was under the direction of W. Curtis Ezell, but the inadequacy of funds to sustain both the project and the State Planning Board made the implementation of these ambitious plans impossible.

The Institute's emphasis on regionalism for a time turned attention away from research on children, but in 1960 the Executive Committee of the Institute had before it three such proposals. The first was a request from Alan Keith-Lucas of the School of Social Work for support of a study of the child care institution as a factor in rehabilitating family life. The second was a proposal from three professors from the Department of Psychology, E. Earl Baughman, William Grant Dahlstrom, and Halbert Robinson, for a study of the personality development of southern rural children. The intention of the research staff was to use Efland, North Carolina, as a laboratory "because of the possibility of studying both white and Negro rural children in a community where the researchers [had] developed excellent rapport."[25] The third request came from William P. Richardson of the University Division of Health Affairs. His research proposal was on handicapping conditions in North Carolina children, which was being sponsored by the North Carolina Health Council, and partial funding had already been obtained.

Although the Institute did not immediately adopt these proposals, chiefly for lack of funds, research in these areas moved ahead. The research proposal that Keith-Lucas presented had already been jointly approved by the School of Social Work and the Group Child Care Project of the Southeastern Child Care Association. Keith-Lucas was to direct the study with the cooperation of his associate in the School of Social Work, Alton M. Broten. The idea for the study had originated with the organization of the Group Child Care Project in 1956. The governing board of the Group Project, representing twenty-nine child-care institutions in six southern states, had approached the School of Social Work and asked that consultative teaching and research services be provided for the institutions on a fee basis for a trial period of three years. The Group Project was now asking that the Chapel Hill consultants undertake a further research project while continuing the consultative services. In 1958 the Chapel Hill consultants had produced the first book of readings for houseparents produced in the United States. The Group Project now was in need of empirical data by which to assess the advisability of returning children from child care institutions to their rehabilitated families. In 1960 more than 90 percent of children in child care institutions, formerly called orphanages, were not orphans. They were children either from broken homes or from homes where there were social problems. Members of the Group Project believed that a new study might conceivably revolutionize the "concept of the uses of child-care facilities and of short-time child-parent separations, as well as provide indications of the tools and structures needed to overcome family disorganization."[26]

Although the Institute did not find the necessary financing for the research project as proposed by the Group Child Care Project, the Children's Bureau of the United States Department of Labor gave funds for a one-year pilot project. The manuscript containing the results is available in the Chapel Hill Workshop files in the School of Social Work.[27] In 1962 Keith-Lucas brought out his study of church-related children's homes, *The Church Children's Home in a Changing World*, and his associate director, Alton Broten, also published that year *Houseparents in Children's Institutions*. The central theme of Keith-Lucas's study was that the children's home, to fulfill its real function, must serve the entire family. Broten's book was called "an invaluable tool in improving the quality of care for children."[28]

As in the case of the proposal from Alan Keith-Lucas, the Institute was unable to find the necessary funds for the research proposal from Baughman, Dahlstrom, and Robinson of the Department of Psychology, but it did provide clerical and computer assistance. The psychologists were able to obtain their own funding, and their success in doing so marked a trend among University professors, which has continued to this day, of seeking their own outside funds for research rather than turning to the Institute for financial assistance. The study was an examination of personality development of elementary school children in the rural South and attempted to determine the variances, if any, between black and white children. The focus of the research was on achievement behavior, intellectual development, social deviation, and the influences of home, peer group, and school on the children's development. The study was published in 1968 in Baughman and Dahlstrom's *Negro and White Children: A Psychological Study in the Rural South*, which won the Anisfield-Wolf Award in race relations.

At the same time, other clinical psychologists were doing research in child development. Beginning in 1960 and continuing for almost a decade, Halbert B. Robinson was listed as a member of the research staff of the Institute from the Department of Psychology. With the assistance of his gifted wife, Nancy M. Robinson, who had obtained her doctorate in psychology from Stanford University and was employed in work with retarded children at Murdoch Center, in Butner, North Carolina, he published research in the field of child development. Their best-known work produced during this period was *The Mentally Subnormal Child: A Psychological Approach*, published in 1965. At the same time, Halbert Robinson was busily engaged in setting up the Child Development and Mental Retardation Institute in the University and soon afterward the Frank Porter Graham Child Development Research Center, which is associated with the public school system of Chapel Hill and Carrboro and now occupies expanded facilities in the Frank Porter Graham Elementary School.[29]

Harriet L. Rheingold, who came to the Department of Psychology from the National Institute of Mental Health, where she was acting chief of the section on early development, was also doing pioneer research in the field of child development and infant behavior. From the time of her affiliation with the Institute upon her arrival in 1964, she produced over the next ten years numerous articles on the social behavior of the human infant, sometimes in collaboration with other psychologists. In 1967 she edited with Harold W. Stevenson and Eckhard H. Hess *Early Behavior: Comparative and Development Approaches*, to which she also contributed a chapter, "A Comparative Psychology of Development." In 1969–70 she published six articles, three with Carol O. Eckerman, on childhood behavior in social relations, among them "The Social and Socializing Infant" in *Handbook of Socialization Theory and Research*, edited by David A. Goslin. In 1973 she published "To Rear a Child" in *American Psychologist*, and as the first fifty years of the Institute's history came to a close, she was working with Eckerman on proposals for unifying the study of social development, which were published in 1975 in *Friendship and Peer Relations*, edited by Michael Lewis and Leonard Rosenblum.

Earl S. Schaefer, professor of maternal and child care in the School of Public Health, and an affiliate of the Institute, was also doing research in the field of social development. He contributed a chapter, "Factors That Impede the Process of Socialization," to *The Mentally Retarded in Society: A Social Perspective*, edited by Michael J. Begab and Stephen A. Richardson. His other research on the social aspects of childhood education will be cited in chapter 10.

While Robinson, Rheingold, and Schaefer concentrated on new

areas of research in infant and early childhood development, the senior faculty of the Institute in various other departments and schools in the University had been exploring the field of development and socialization since the early 1950s. Dahlstrom, who came to Chapel Hill in 1953, and Baughman, who came in 1954, had already begun exploration of research on developmental attitudes of southern children. Daniel O. Price, director of the Institute, reported in 1960–61 that he had been looking for funds to undertake a major study in development and socialization. Despite his failure to obtain financing, Price announced that the Institute had projects under way in sociology and psychology that placed an emphasis on socialization;[30] but almost no research was being explored comparable to that to be done later by Rheingold. The next year he reported that Eugene Robert Long of the Department of Psychology had published "Additional Techniques for Producing Multiple-Schedule Control in Children" in the *Journal of Experimental Analysis of Behavior* (1962).

These research projects on infant and child development undertaken by Institute affiliates contributed to the revolutionary approach to the study of human processes characteristic of research in the behavioral sciences following World War II. Other behavioral science research conducted at the Institute will be discussed later in this chapter and in chapters 9 and 10.

Delinquency and Crime

The Institute's concern for child welfare and development led to corollary studies in delinquency, criminology, and penology. Social scientists were generally of the opinion, as the Institute began its work, that children brought up in a caring environment would develop into good citizens and that deprived children were likely to turn to delinquency and crime. Howard Odum considered Wiley B. Sanders to be the Institute's authority in the area of juvenile delinquency as well as in child welfare. Sanders's first published research on delinquency, *Juvenile Court Cases in North Carolina, 1929–1934*, which he wrote with W. Curtis Ezell, appeared in 1937 and was a cooperative study with the North Carolina State Board of Charities and Public Welfare. After his retirement, Sanders was able in 1970 to complete his definitive work, *Juvenile Offenders for a Thousand Years*, which dealt with the treatment of wayward children from Anglo-Saxon times onward.

To collect the data for this volume he had taken two leaves of absence for research in England.

Over a period of sixteen years, between 1926 and 1942, the Institute published five books on criminology and more than two dozen articles. In addition to Sanders, this work was directed by Jesse F. Steiner, until he left for Tulane University in 1927, and later by Lee M. Brooks, one of Steiner's graduate students who later became a research professor in the Institute. In 1927 three research projects on delinquency were completed, which remain in manuscript: "Case Studies of Delinquent Girls in North Carolina," by Margaret C. Brietz; "Extent and Type of Juvenile Delinquency and Dependency in Durham, North Carolina," by C. Horace Hamilton; and "Background of Delinquent Boys in North Carolina," by Clyde V. Kiser. Both Hamilton and Kiser went on to distinguished careers in sociology outside the field of juvenile delinquency. In 1928, H. C. Brearley, one of Odum's students, completed his doctoral dissertation, "A Study of Homicides in South Carolina, 1920–1928." Odum was so impressed with this study that he persuaded Brearley to enlarge its scope. The result was Brearley's book, *Homicide in the United States*, which was discussed in chapter 5. This work stood for years as the best American book on homicide. Although Brearley was not a member of the Institute staff, Odum arranged in 1932 for the book to be published by the University Press under the auspices of the Institute. Two other graduate studies on delinquency followed: Mary Katharine Fleming's "A Follow-Up Study of Juvenile Court Cases in Orange County, North Carolina" (1930), and Robert King Bailey's "A Follow-Up Study in Juvenile Delinquency: The Careers of Eighty-Eight White Boys Committed to Jackson Training School by the Durham, North Carolina, Juvenile Court (1922–1935) and Their Post-Adjustment" (1938). A third project, the North Carolina Youth Survey, coordinated by Gordon W. Lovejoy for the National Youth Administration, dealt indirectly with delinquency by pointing out how to avoid trouble by providing recreation facilities and wholesome activities for youth. The report was known as "Paths to Maturity: Findings of the North Carolina Youth Survey, 1938–1940."

One of the few Institute projects on delinquency to be published was Edgar W. Butler's "An Action and Research Program in a Delinquent Girls' Residential Treatment Center," which appeared in the July-August 1966 issue of *Police*. In 1970 Glen H. Elder, Jr., listed among his research projects for affiliation with the Institute a study of age composition and rehabilitation in a correctional setting.[31] Several proposals on the study of delinquency came before the Institute's Board of Governors at various times but were dropped for lack of funding.[32]

Most of the Institute's research projects in criminology were done between 1926 and 1942 as master's theses or doctoral dissertations that remained unpublished. Among them were "The Administrative Cost of Crime with Special Reference to Durham County, North Carolina," (1926), by Lee M. Brooks; "Types of Crime in North Carolina," (1926), by Francis S. Wilder, which showed a preponderance of assault and battery cases, a condition that had prevailed since colonial days;[33] "Liquor Law Violations in Durham and Person Counties, North Carolina" (1927), by Clyde V. Kiser; "One Hundred Country Dwelling Negroes and Their Crimes in Durham, North Carolina" (1928), by Hugh Penn Brinton; "Mob Action in the South" (1928), a voluminous study by John Roy Steelman; another lengthy study, "Crime in North Carolina" (1931), by Lena Mae Williams; "A Study of Some Reformatory Systems for Women Offenders in the United States with Particular Reference to the Industrial Farm Colony at Kinston, North Carolina" (1934), by June Rainsford Butler; "A Sociological Study of Police with Special Reference to Personnel Selection" (1937), by James Payne Beckwith; and perhaps the longest thesis (498 pages) ever submitted to the University for a master's degree, "Inter-Racial and Intra-Racial Homicide in Ten Counties in North Carolina" (1942), by Harold Garfinkel.

The Institute undertook two studies of the North Carolina penal system, and one brief study of the chain gang by Jesse F. Steiner and Roy M. Brown, which was ready for publication in 1927. The University Press decided that the study needed further research, however, and sent the manuscript out for appraisal. When Odum learned of this move, he wrote an indignant letter to L. R. Wilson, director of the Press:

> I still think as I suggested to you the other day with reference to the publication of the study of the chain gang. If we cannot publish the normal, wholesome, and constructive results of the Institute, we ought to come to an understanding about it now. If here at home we are to be apologized for and shot at from all sides by snipers, and if then, on the other hand, the foundations do not wish to give us enough money to let us do the thing well, I am for telling Dr. Ruml frankly that we ought not to have any more money. That is, if what we are doing here is

not wanted and is no good at home; and if, on the other hand,
they propose to hand us out something, just enough to make
us drive ourselves to death, I am sure most of us have
better work to do.[34]

Wilson had wished to forestall attacks that he feared would surely
come if the Institute published the chain gang report as the first volume
in a series on crime in North Carolina that Odum was proposing. The
series was to include research that had been under way since October
1925 on "the nature and amount of crime, the conditions under which
crime is produced, the cost of crime, case histories of criminals, the
administration of criminal justice, methods of penal treatment, and
crime prevention." The Press went forward with the publication of
The North Carolina Chain Gang, but the other manuscripts in the
series remain unpublished. The findings of the chain gang study were
explosive, as Wilson had realized, but the book did not cause anything
like the furor that was raised by the Institute's attempt to study labor
conditions within the textile industry.[35]

The study showed that the number of prisoners in the county convict
road camps was almost double that in the state prison. The number of
prisoners within the period of one year who were sentenced to county
camps "outnumbered those sent to the state prison by more than 10 to
1."[36] The research staff was told by the state prison officials that
"those unfit for hard labor are committed to [the state prison] while the
strong and able-bodied are required to work out their sentences on
the county roads."[37] The law permitted commitment to labor on the
county roads up to a maximum of ten years. The research staff found
that many of the chain gang prisoners had been convicted for petty
offenses, but that some were serving time for such serious crimes as
rape, first degree burglary, assault with intent to kill, and manslaughter.

The study sought to refute the idea that there were economic advan-
tages in the continuance of the county chain gang, and in this position
the research staff had the support of Ellison Capers, secretary of the
Board of Public Welfare in South Carolina, who wrote that his board
was seeking to abolish the chain gang system in that state. "Wherever
we have had the full cooperation of the county supervisor and the
county board of commissioners, in so far as the adequate keeping of
records is concerned," wrote Capers, "it has been proven conclusively
that the chain gang system is an economic loss."[38] Steiner and Brown
found that in North Carolina "the average county official in charge

of such prisoners thinks far more of exploiting labor in the interest of good roads, than of any corrective or reformatory value in such methods of penal treatment. . . . No thought is given to the education of the illiterate or to the reformation of those not yet hardened to crime.''

The study also pointed out that in the eighteen states outside the South that had once used prisoners for work on the streets or county roads, all had abandoned the practice, partly on account of the colder climate in the North and West and the earlier development of manufacturing industries in those areas, ''and partly, no doubt, due to an earlier development of a sensitivity on the part of the public to the degrading spectacle of men working in public in chains.''[39] The study also found that the persistence of the chain gang in the South was due to the presence of the Negro. It was ''this race that [had] furnished the bulk of the prisoners'' in the past and ''that still furnishes the large majority of the prisoners used in these gangs today.''[40] To the average North Carolinian, these would have been fighting words had not Governor T. W. Bickett, who was keenly interested in penal reform, said emphatically only a few years earlier, ''As for the county chain gang system, it is hopeless. The only thing to do is cut off its head.''[41]

It was partly as a result of the chain gang study that the Institute was involved in a second study in the field of penology. Many leaders were urging prison reform, and Governor O. Max Gardner appointed a prison commission to study the matter soon after he took office in 1929. Howard Odum was asked to direct the study, and several assistants from the Institute participated in the research. His report was presented to the governor in 1930.[42] It contained many recommendations for reform, including the abolition of the convict labor system. Reform was slow, but eventually a number of Odum's recommendations were implemented. The Institute, through Odum's leadership and the involvement of several research assistants, had played a major role in the movement for prison reform.

The Institute's only effort at research on rehabilitation came in 1952. Alexander Heard of the Department of Political Science and Richard McCleery, a research assistant, proposed a study to be done in cooperation with the University Extension Division on ''the effect of adult education in North Carolina prison camps.'' The proposal hoped to initiate a program of adult education in sixty of the eighty prison camps in North Carolina. The Executive Committee of the Institute's Board of Governors approved a one-year pilot study to be carried out in six camps, but it postponed the larger program until funding could be found. Within a year McCleery had completed a report, "Our Six Prisons: A Pilot Study of Adult Education in Six Prison Camps in North Carolina," under the joint direction of Heard and Charles B. Robson, who was chairman of the Department of Political Science.[43]

McCleery's next research was a brief project in criminology directed by Lee M. Brooks of the Department of Sociology, again with the sponsorship of the Extension Division. McCleery's doctoral dissertation in the Department of Political Science, "Power, Communication, and the Social Order: A Study of Prison Government," dealt with the process of institutional change from authoritarianism toward democracy. The dissertation was done under the direction of the Political Behavior Committee, whose work is discussed in chapter 9. The American Political Science Association presented McCleery's dissertation its Birkhead Award.

For more than a decade after McCleery's work, the Institute did no research in criminology, but it renewed its interest in 1970, when Richard J. Richardson of the Department of Political Science came to the Institute as a research professor.[44] In 1971 Richardson's *Public Attitudes toward the Criminal Justice System and Criminal Victimization in North Carolina* was published by the Governor's Committee on Law and Order, for which he was a principal investigator. The research for the committee had been done in collaboration with four assistants: Thomas Denyer, Skip McGaughey, Darlene Walker, and Owen J. Williams. They also collaborated with Richardson on an article for the magazine *North Carolina* (1972), "Some Views by the People on Police, Prisons, and Courts," and on one for *Research Previews* (1972), "Public Attitudes and the Legal Justice System." In 1973 Richardson produced with others a monograph for the Administrative Office of the Courts, *Delay in the Superior Courts of North Carolina: An Assessment of Its Causes*, and presented in *Research Previews* with M. Kuykendall and D. Walker a brief statement on a similar topic, "Judicial Activism: A Measure of Intrasystem Conflict." Richardson then began an examination of public attitudes toward the legal justice system and the political impact of delay in the courts.

In 1971 Donald R. Gill from the Institute of Government became affiliated with the Institute as a senior staff member. His research was on the Mecklenburg Criminal Justice Pilot Project, for which the Institute of Government had received a funding grant. In 1973 he submitted the *Interim Report on the Second Phase of the Mecklenburg*

Criminal Justice Pilot Project to the National Institute of Law Enforcement and Criminal Justice and to Region IV of the United States Department of Justice. In 1974 the Institute of Government also published two research projects by Anne D. Witte, of the Department of Economics, *Work Release in North Carolina: The Program and the Process* and *Directory of the Department of Corrections Organization.* The same year Alvin L. Jacobson from the Department of Sociology reported in *Research Previews* on a twenty-year perspective of crime trends in southern and nonsouthern cities. While these approaches to the study of crime and punishment were significant in themselves, they did not constitute the systematic study of criminology that Odum and Steiner had envisaged as they were setting up the Institute in 1924.

Marriage and the Family

Early in its program the Institute had been concerned not only with research concerning the optimum environment for child development and socialization but also with the conditions of marriage and family life that would make such an environment possible and thereby reduce delinquency and crime. Jesse F. Steiner was the first professor of sociology at the University to teach a course on the family, and after he left, his place was taken by Ernest R. Groves.

With the arrival of Groves from Boston University in 1927 as a research professor, publications in the field burgeoned. By 1944, at the close of the second decade of the Institute, Groves had turned out eight books on marriage and the family and thirty-four articles published in a variety of journals, both professional and popular. He continued to publish until his death in 1946. His first book after coming to Chapel Hill was *American Marriage and Family Relationships* (1928), written with William F. Ogburn of the University of Chicago. In 1933 came a lengthy publication, *Marriage: A Text for College Men and Women*, which was widely used as a basis for college curricula on the family. Then followed in rapid succession *The American Family* (1934), *The American Woman: The Feminine Side of a Masculine Civilization* (1937), *Christianity and the Family* (1942), *Sex Fulfillment in Marriage* (1942), and *Conserving Marriage and the Family: A Realistic Discussion of the Divorce Problem* (1944).

Writing on a subject that might easily have disturbed Bible Belt southerners, Groves nevertheless avoided being labeled a "teacher of smut,'' a term that was hurled at English Bagby, a professor in the Department of Psychology, in 1932 by the Tatum Petition because of his lectures on Freudian psychology.[45] Groves's writings were based upon his wide knowledge of the field and upon his own spiritual values, which were rooted in Judeo-Christian philosophy. History and anthropology revealed, he contended, that the family is the basic unit of society, institutionalized for the prime purpose of child nurture. Details of structure have varied from time to time in response to changing economic and social conditions, Groves pointed out, but the ideal family would always be composed of father, mother, and children. He recognized, however, that happy marriages could exist without children, that sexual fulfillment was a requisite for the ''good'' marriage, and that unhappy marriages might better end in divorce. In 1927 he began a series of articles, published annually for several years in the *American Journal of Sociology*, noting the forces at work in American society that were having an impact on the family.

In their eagerness to conserve the American family and to interpret the pathologies of family life, both Groves and his wife, Gladys Hoagland Groves, engaged in informal marriage counseling and also published short articles in popular magazines. Their chief effort, to train marriage counselors and develop family life education among citizens in general, led to the organization in 1934 of the Groves Conference on Marriage and the Family, which was held annually in Chapel Hill for many years and attracted family life specialists from across the nation.

In 1950 Reuben Hill, professor of sociology at Iowa State College, joined the Department of Sociology at the University and became a research professor in the Institute in the area of marriage and the family. He became associate director with Gladys Groves of the annual Groves Conferences, and after a few years the directors began rotating the conferences to other university campuses in order to obtain broader citizen participation. Hill also became active in the organization of the North Carolina Family Life Council, which was getting under way when he arrived in Chapel Hill, and like Groves, he too wrote articles for popular magazines—for example, ''How to Enjoy Being a Father,'' which appeared in the June 1949 issue of *Better Homes and Gardens*. Soon after his arrival in Chapel Hill, Reuben Hill's major research, *Families under Stress: Adjustment to the Crises of War Separation and Reunion* (1949), became recognized as a significant contribution in the field. In 1951 he published his revision of Willard Waller's *The Family* and directed the Puerto Rican Family Life Study for the University of Puerto Rico with the assistance of two graduate students, David Landy and Joseph Stycos.[46] In 1955 *Family, Marriage and Parenthood*, which he edited with Howard Becker, was entering its second edition.

In 1951 Hill's "Inter-disciplinary Workshop on Marriage and Family Research" appeared in the winter issue of *Marriage and Family Living*. This article was a description of the content and methods of the workshop held in 1950 by the National Council on Family Relations in cooperation with the Committee on Human Development of the University of Chicago "to train researchers from eleven different disciplines in a common language, stressing family development and structure-function approaches to family study." Hill pointed out that in the past most family research had been "random, scattered, and subject to faddish imitation."

In the March 1955 issue of *Social Forces*, Hill evaluated and summarized trends in marriage and family research. While he maintained that he regarded "the most valuable service research renders to be that of keeping teachers and counselors modest and humble in the assertions they make in teaching and counseling," he thought that "family research has been limited for a number of years by its own value framework, a framework which emphasizes family stability as the major end of family processes." Most textbooks and writings on marriage and the family, therefore, had made "patterns of conventionality, appeasement, and harmony at any cost appear desirable for success in marriage."[47] Since family research had now become respectable as an area of scientific inquiry, researchers in this field had at last "gained elbow room within which to function." They were free to test hypotheses scientifically, free to engage in theoretical speculation, free to design decisive experiments, free to discard the "shackles" of "taboos and ancestral superstitions." These new approaches made family study "researchable by more rigorous definition of concepts and by methods of data collection which can provide analyzable data."[48]

Before Hill left the University in 1957, his research assignment in the Institute had been enlarged to include methodology as well as family research. Shortly after he left for the University of Minnesota to head his own research institute, he published with two of his coworkers, Mayone Stycos and Kurt W. Back, *The Family and Population Control*.

Hill was replaced by Charles E. Bowerman from the University of Washington in Seattle. During his first year in Chapel Hill, Bowerman's research was in the area of parent-child relations. With Donald P. Irish he did research on the adjustment of the adolescent to a stepparent, and with John W. Kinch he studied the changes in their orientation to their parents of children from the fourth to the tenth grades. By 1959 Bowerman had added urban studies to his field of research and was working with John Gulick of the Department of Anthropology and Kurt W. Back in sociology on a survey centering on the acculturation of newcomers to the city. In 1962 he continued research in parent and peer orientation, working with Donald Irish and Halliwell Pope on a survey of unwed mothers, and with Ernest Q. Campbell and Richard Cramer on educational aspirations and performance among southern Negro youth. His graduate courses in sociology continued to be in the field of marriage and the family, but his research covered a wider span of interests.

When Bowerman, after having served as chairman of the Department of Sociology, left the University in 1970 to become professor of sociology in Washington State University at Pullman, he was succeeded by Glen H. Elder, Jr., who received his doctorate in sociology from the University in 1961 and returned to the University in 1967 in the Department of Sociology. Soon afterward Elder became affiliated with the Institute. His research was focused on youth within and outside the family complex rather than upon the general interests that had occupied Ernest Groves, the pioneer in the field of marriage and the family. His doctoral dissertation was published in 1962 under the title *Adolescent Achievement and Mobility Aspirations*. In 1970–71 he had five research projects under way that illustrate the change in emphasis in family studies in the Institute from the time of Groves and Hill. Among them were "Economic Deprivation and Personality Development," "Socialization and Ascent in a Racial Minority," and "The Relative Influence of Adults and Peers on Youth."[49] In 1974 he published his second major study, *Children of the Great Depression: Social Change in Life Experience*, and was working on a project related to the family as a unit, "Social Change in Family and Life Course."

Family Planning and Birth Control

In the meantime, an entirely different aspect of family-related studies got under way with the arrival in 1965 of J. Richard Udry, who had a joint appointment in sociology and public health. He became affiliated with the Institute the following year. His research interest was listed in the annual report of the Institute for 1966–67 as the biosocial aspects of reproduction. The annual report for the following year listed six of his research articles already published or forthcoming. Four of the articles were prepared in collaboration with Naomi M. Morris, professor of maternal and child health in the School of Public Health, and dealt with research seldom mentioned in an earlier generation in college classrooms on marriage and the family, for example, "A Method for Validation of Reported Sexual Data," in the *Journal of Marriage and the Family* (1967), and "Daily Immunological Pregnancy Testing of Initially Non-Pregnant Women," in the *American Journal of Obstetrics and Gynecology* (1967). In 1972–73 Udry was also collaborating with Morris in the publication of articles on research in the area of contraceptive pills, and with C. L. Chase, L. T. Clark, and M. Levy on the possible use of mass media advertising to increase the use of contraceptives. In 1974 the third edition of Udry's *The Social Context of Marriage* was published.

Elizabeth J. Coulter of the School of Public Health and Betty E. Cogswell of the School of Medicine, who was also connected with the Carolina Population Center, were likewise involved in research in various aspects of human reproduction. The Institute's annual report for 1969–70 listed three papers that Cogswell had read at professional meetings; one of these was "What Parents Owe Their Children: Myths About Socialization," presented at the Family and Society Conference sponsored by the Merrill-Palmer Institute in Detroit. Coulter is mentioned in the annual report for 1970–71 as coauthor with Sidney Chipman, Earl Siegel, Donald Thomas, and Robert Tuthill of a study entitled "Factors Associated with Involvement of Low-Income Women in Public Family Planning Programs," published in the *American Journal of Public Health* in 1970. Both Cogswell and Coulter are currently continuing their research in these and related areas. Cogswell published two articles with M. B. Sussman in 1972 on changing family and marriage forms, and Coulter worked with H. B. Wells and L. S. Wienir on a report, "Completeness and Quality of Response in the North Carolina Marriage Follow-Back Study," that appeared in *Vital and Health Statistics* in 1973.

The work of Karl E. Bauman in human reproduction is listed for the first time in the Institute's annual report for 1972–73. One of the three articles he published during that academic year was "The Poor as a 'Perfect Contraceptive Population' and Zero Population Growth," in

Demography (1972). The following year he collaborated with J. Richard Udry on four projects on unwanted births, including "Five Million Poor Women and Unwanted Births: An Evaluation of the Five Year Family Planning Plan," which appeared in *Health Services Report* in 1973. Bauman also reported on a four-year project he had undertaken with R. R. Wilson on contraceptive practices of unmarried university students, the results of which appeared in the *American Journal of Obstetrics and Gynecology* in 1974. In 1972–73 the annual report of the Institute listed eighteen members of the School of Public Health as senior research faculty. Of this number, eight were working in the area of social biology, human reproduction, and family planning.

Several members of the Department of Sociology were also doing research in health-related areas of reproduction in the 1960s and 1970s. For example, Edgar W. Butler in collaboration with Jeanne C. Biggar delivered two papers on fertility at professional meetings in 1967, and Bruce K. Eckland published five articles on social biology in 1972, including "Evolutionary Consequences of Differential Fertility and Assortative Mating in Man" in the fifth volume of *Evolutionary Biology*, edited by Thomas Dobzhansky and others. In 1974 the *Journal of Marriage and the Family* published Peter R. Uhlenberg's "Cohort Variations in Family Life Cycle Experiences of United States Females."

During this period Steven Polgar of the Carolina Population Center, who had a joint appointment with the Department of Anthropology, was also writing about family planning and birth control. The Institute's annual report for 1968–69 lists six of his research projects either published or in press. He wrote an essay on health for the *International Encyclopedia of the Social Sciences* (1968), and with F. S. Jaffe he wrote an article, "Evaluation and Record Keeping for U.S. Family Planning Services," in *Public Health Reports* (1968). In 1973 he contributed an article, "Cultural Development, Population, and the Family," to the *Symposium on Population and the Family* for the United Nations, edited the "Commentary" section of *Human Organization* (1973), and published a summary article, "The Objectives and History of Birth Planning," in the *International Journal of Health Services* (1973).

Women's Role

Although research in the Institute in the field of marriage and the family had not neglected the role of women, it had paid scant attention to the feminine personality, or to women's needs and aspirations. Too often, especially in the early research, as Hill's comment on the status of research in family studies had implied, women's role was viewed from the point of view of "ancestral superstitions." The woman, like the Negro, had a fixed place in society, and society was best served by her keeping that place.

From the early days of the Institute, Odum had been concerned with research about women. In a memorandum to the Board of Governors for the meeting of December 1924, Odum noted that "an unusual opportunity for an excellent piece of work is open from January to July as a part of our larger study of leadership." Rochelle Gachet, "a native of New Orleans and Phi Beta Kappa graduate of Newcomb and Tulane," who had considerable experience in "statistical and research work," was prepared to "make a study of women in the South who [had] achieved leadership in any of the professions, and their cultural background, educational training, success, attitudes of communities, geographical distribution, and other important factors."[50] But the Board was cool to the suggestion. "In the case of Miss Rochelle Gachet," the minutes read, "it was the sense of the Board that her preparation and the type of project proposed would not be consistent with the commitments already made by the Institute and with its probable facilities for the future."[51]

Cordelia Cox was already at work, using Institute facilities, on a study for the Southern Woman's Educational Alliance of vocational opportunities for women in Durham and adjoining counties. When she went on to Virginia at the end of the year in 1925 to continue the survey, she left behind in the Institute files three manuscripts: the first was "Notes on Vocational Guidance," the second was entitled "Rural Occupations for Women," and a third pointed out the need to incorporate vocational guidance in rural elementary education.[52] The Southern Woman's Educational Alliance wished to continue the study in North Carolina and again turned to the Institute for help. The Board of Governors voted to assign two of its women assistants, Clyde Russell and Kathryn Norman, "to do the cooperative work." The Board also agreed to supervise their work and offered them the use of the Institute Ford if the Alliance would provide their stipends.[53] Out of their study came Clyde Russell's "The Rural Working Girl in Durham, North Carolina," which, however, went unpublished.

The first published article on the status of women done by a research assistant in the Institute was Guion Griffis Johnson's "Feminism and the Economic Independence of Women" in the *Journal of Social Forces* in 1925.[54] The article discussed the demands of the feminists for full employment as the only way to freedom and the best way for both men and women to be happy. The two chief doctrines of the feminists were the economic independence of women and birth control. In 1928 Harriet Herring examined the situation of mill families, and her "Working Mothers and Their Children" appeared in *Family*.[55] A year later Mary Phlegar Smith's essay, "Legal and Administrative Restrictions Affecting the Rights of Married Women to Work" was included in *Annals of the American Academy of Political and Social Science*.[56]

Three books on the roles of women that grew out of Institute research in the late 1930s are still in current use. The first is Ernest R. Groves's *The American Woman: The Feminine Side of a Masculine Civilization*, which appeared in 1937. It was a lengthy book and one of the first by a family-life specialist to point out that American culture assigned women a status of inequality. It was welcomed by the feminists and by professional organizations for women such as the American Association of University Women. Kathryn McHale, director of the Association, reviewed *The American Woman* for *Social Forces* and pronounced it "widely interpretive, and above all . . . expert and revealing in critical thinking." The book, she said, "traces the progress of women in a setting which shows how sweeping in American culture has been the dominance of man. The bulk of the book is devoted to the influences that have contributed to two related currents: one, the increasing encroachment upon the special privileges of men by gifted women leaders; the other, the social changes, the economic and intellectual developments, affecting both sexes, which have brought men and women closer to equality."[57]

The second Institute study to deal specifically with women's role was Julia Cherry Spruill's *Women's Life and Work in the Southern Colonies*, published in 1938. It required ten years of careful historical research. Spruill examined the everyday life of colonial southern women, their role in the settlement of the colonies, their homes and the work they did, their social life, their education, their activities outside the home, and their status in the eyes of the law and of society in general. The research was appraised by more than one historian as "the finest study . . . on the history of women in the world by any author." Spruill found that marital discord had existed "in appalling amounts" and that the only recourse for most unhappily married women had been to slip away secretly and thereupon to be advertised in the newspapers by their husbands between notices of runaway slaves and horses for sale. Although a few daughters of the aristocracy were educated in Europe, tutored at home, or taught in neighborhood schools, the majority of colonial southern women were illiterate. Despite their lack of education, many women were successful in business, mainly as widows who sometimes had complete charge of the affairs of their deceased husbands, whether this involved a plantation, a tavern, or a general store. Both by custom and by common law, however, the colonists "generally agreed with the *Spectator* (No. 295) that 'separate purses between man and wife' were as 'unnatural as separate beds.'"[56]

The third of the Institute's studies in this period that dealt with the role of women was Margaret Jarman Hagood's *Mothers of the South: Portraiture of the White Tenant Farm Woman*, published in 1939. The research was part of the studies on regionalism upon which the Institute was concentrating at that time, and it was intended to be not so much a project about women as an inquiry that might serve as a detailed analysis of one aspect of the regional scene that showed social waste in the South. Hagood found that white tenant farm women are the victims "of a long-continued cash crop economy; they undergo extreme social impoverishment . . . and they bear the brunt of a regional tradition—compounded of elements from religion, patriarchy, and aristocracy—which subjects them to class and sex discrimination."[59] The study was based upon interviews and schedules obtained from more than one hundred white tenant farm women in thirteen Piedmont North Carolina counties, which were compared with an equal number from the Deep South—Georgia, Alabama, Mississippi, and Louisiana. Although the author found variances in details, the basic conditions were similar. "From truncated childhoods, with meager preparation, they begin prematurely the triple role of mother, housekeeper, and field laborer. . . . And yet they function—producing and caring for families and crops."[60] Her findings disagreed with the alarmists among the eugenicists who deplored the high fertility in low economic groups such as farm tenants because of "the transmission of innate, biological inferiority." On the contrary, Hagood insisted that the survival and achievement of the white tenant farm women surveyed in her study "can be interpreted as evidence of the existence of inherent quality, vitality, and endurance in the people" coupled with "certain facilitating factors and enhancing values of rural life."[61]

Since the publication of the studies by Groves, Spruill, and Hagood, the Institute has undertaken no major study of the role of women in American culture. In 1946, however, Faye Elizabeth Hancock prepared a lengthy research report for her master's thesis in sociology, "Occupational Opportunity for Southern Women," based on the 1940 United States Census. In summarizing her findings, she called for "a more equal status of women with men, freedom of choice to work, a broader range of occupational selection for both white and Negro women, better wages and working conditions."[62] From that time forward, the Institute, for the most part, left the examination of women's role to its staff members who were engaged in family research. Bruce Eckland, however, included a section on the status of American women in the Southeastern Regional Survey II, which he directed in 1970, and is presently at work on a related project, "Explorations in Equality of Opportunity." Others in the Department of Sociology have occasionally examined the role of women. For example, Richard L. Simpson, from the Institute's senior staff, with his wife, Ida Harper Simpson of the Department of Sociology at Duke University, wrote an article on career-oriented women, "Occupational Choice Among Career-Oriented College Women," for *Marriage and Family Living* in 1961, and in 1969 prepared a chapter, "Women and Bureaucracy in the Semi-Professions," for the volume *The Semi-Professions and Their Organizations*, edited by Amitai Etzioni.[63]

Influenced, no doubt even if subconsciously, by the rise of the women's liberation movement, senior Institute faculty in the School of Library Science, the Departments of Psychology, History, City and Regional Planning, and the Center for Alcohol Studies and the School of Business Administration have given some attention to studies related to women. In 1972 Kenneth D. Shearer and Ray L. Carpenter from the School of Library Science published "Sex and Salary Survey: Selected Statistics of Large Public Libraries in the United States and Canada" in the November issue of *Library Journal* and followed up their study with "Sex and Salary Update" in the January 1974 issue of the same journal. Also in 1972 the *Journal of Counseling Psychology* published George S. Welsh's "On the Relationship of CPI Femininity and Intelligence."

The last academic year of the Institute's first half-century came to a close with the publication in professional journals of at least seven articles on various aspects of sex roles. Benson Rosen and Thomas H. Jerdee from the School of Business Administration published "The Influence of Sex on Role Stereotypes on the Evaluation of Male and Female Supervisory Behavior" in the *Journal of Applied Psychology*. The next year another article by these authors on sex role stereotyping appeared in the same journal and still another in the *Harvard Business Review*, "Sex Stereotyping in the Executive Suite." The *Journal of Marriage and the Family* carried two articles in 1973 by Edward J. Kaiser, of the Department of City and Regional Planning, prepared with the assistance of E. W. Butler and R. J. McAllister, on the relative ability of males and females to adapt to "residential mobility." In the same year John A. Ewing and Beatrice A. Rouse of the Center for Alcohol Studies completed four studies on therapeutic abortion and the effects of drug use on women, including "Marijuana and Other Drug Use by Women College Students: Associated Risk-Taking and Coping Activities" in the *American Journal of Psychiatry* and "Therapeutic Abortion on Psychiatric Grounds: A Follow-Up Study" in the *North Carolina Medical Journal*. The nearest approach to a biography of a woman leader was David M. Griffith's "Catherine II: The Republican Empress," which appeared in *Jarbücher für Geschichte Osteuropas* in 1973. Apparently the time had not come for affiliates of the Institute to undertake major research on women's role in American culture, although elsewhere the history of the women's movement and the issues facing American women were attracting considerable attention. Several affiliates of the Institute, however, outlined plans to examine some of these issues in 1975. Benson Rosen was planning to continue with his research on sex roles in organization and family life, and several new projects were in hand: "Working Wives and Family Income: A Policy Paradox of Equality," by Edward Bergman; "Sex Stereotyping of Reporter's Bylines and Reporting," by Richard R. Cole of the Department of Journalism; "Breast Cancer and Female Labor Force Participation," by Jo Anne Earp of the School of Public Health; and "Women's Auxiliaries to Black Railroad Labor Unions, 1930–1950," by Genna Rae McNeil of the Department of History.

Recreation

While most research personnel today would not consider public recreation to be a social problem, Harold D. Meyer certainly did. Meyer, who came from Georgia with Howard Odum to join the University in 1920, remained in the Department of Sociology, and at intervals was a member of the Institute staff until his retirement in 1965. He was teaching courses in social problems at a time when public recreation was beginning to be considered an important instrument of social adjustment. His students frequently quoted one of his favorite sayings: "The family that plays together stays together." He developed the Curriculum in Recreation as a division in the Department of Sociology. In 1967 the program was transferred to the School of Education under the direction of H. Douglas Sessoms, and in 1973 it became the Curriculum in Recreation Administration in the University College of Arts and Sciences. As an undergraduate, Sessoms had been one of Meyer's students, and later he earned his doctorate at New York University.

Meyer joined the Institute staff in 1954 as a professor in the area of recreation for the aging.[64] In the same year he edited a pamphlet for the North Carolina Recreation Commission, *Recreation and Community Groups in North Carolina*. Previously he had published with Charles K. Brightbill *Community Recreation: a Guide to Its Organization* (1948), and in 1955 the authors revised the book and published it as *Recreation Administration: A Guide to Its Practices*. In 1955 he also edited *Recreation for the Patient*, the proceedings of the second annual Regional Conference on Hospital Recreation. In 1957 he prepared two more pamphlets for the North Carolina Recreation Commission, *Recreation in the Hospital Setting* and *The Philosophy of Recreation for the Aging*, and also contributed an article, "The Adult Cycle," to *Recreation in the Age of Automation*, edited by Paul F. Douglas for the American Academy of Political and Social Science. After Meyer's retirement, the Institute undertook no further research in the area of recreation.

Community Organization

Although Jesse Steiner was responsible for research on family life as long as he was associated with the University, he was not as enthusiastic as Harold Meyer about recreation as a means of family solidarity. In fact, Steiner's major research expertise was in community organization. He had prepared an article, "Community Organization: A Study of Its Rise and Recent Tendencies," for the first issue of the *Journal of Social Forces*, and the following year he wrote a series of three articles for the *Journal*: the first on the way community organization can affect social change, in which he stated that "social control of community life is both practicable and necessary";[65] the second on community organization and the crowd spirit; and the third pointing out how Home Service standards of the Red Cross could be modified to meet conditions in small cities, towns, and rural communities. In 1924 he prepared another series of three articles on community organization for *Social Forces*, investigating how a community becomes disorganized, field training in community organization, and theories of community organization. In 1927 he published yet a third series of three articles, which dealt chiefly with organization in rural communities.

In 1928, the year following his departure from Chapel Hill, Steiner's classic book, *The American Community in Action*, appeared. It contained not only Steiner's theory of community organization but also case studies prepared by research assistants in the Institute who had taken his University courses in that field. Among them were J. J. Rhyne, Harriet L. Herring, and Guy B. Johnson. "Our modern problem," Steiner had written in 1923, "is to determine how ever-growing numbers of people interrelated and dependent upon each other in an infinite variety of ways can live together harmoniously and satisfactorily. Future progress depends upon man's ability to work out more effective ways and means of controlling the social process."[66] He thought that the problem of community organization was educational rather than administrative: "A community where welfare of all its members is made the goal of intelligent action must be made up of people emancipated from the petty provincialisms and narrow prejudices that are still so widely prevalent." While he strongly recommended the community council as an effective instrument for working together for the common good, he warned that there was no magic in such an organization unless the council was "the expression of a real desire to get together." During World War II, when the national administration stressed the urgent need of the American people to work together for the common goal of victory, the Office of Civil Defense relied on Steiner's theories for direction in organizing citizens' councils, although his writings on community organization had been published almost two decades before.[67]

In the years following Steiner's departure, several community studies were undertaken by the Institute, but most of them still remain in manuscript. Among them were "Problems of the Small Town in North Carolina" (1931), by Ina V. Young; "West Southern Pines: An Episode in Negro Self-Government" (1933), by Joseph Herman Johnson; "A Social Study of High Point, North Carolina" (1933), by Sara M. Smith; "A Sociological Study of the Tri-Racial Community in Robeson County, North Carolina" (1935), by Ernest D. Hancock; "Growth and Plan for a Community: A Study of Negro Life in Chapel Hill and Carrboro, North Carolina" (1944), by Charles Maddry Freeman; and "The Patterns of Village Life: A Study of Southern Piedmont Villages in Terms of Population, Structure, and Role" (1944), by Vincent Heath Whitney.

With the arrival of Gordon W. Blackwell as director of the Institute in 1944, a renewed interest in research on community organization appeared. It was while Blackwell was chairman of the Department of Sociology of Furman University in Greenville, South Carolina, from 1937 to 1941 that he became interested in community organization, as a staff member of the Greenville County Council for Community Development. In his first annual report as director of the Institute, Blackwell noted that "several studies to provide a sociological understanding of southern communities" were under way. One of these was made at the request of the Restudy Committee on Religious Education of the Presbyterian Church of the United States as part of an analysis to help the church evaluate its programs. The work was being done by senior staff (Blackwell, S. H. Hobbs, Jr., and Lee M. Brooks) with the help of two research assistants, Solomon Sutker and Sara Smith.[68] In 1949 the results of these studies appeared in *Church and Community in the South* by Blackwell, Brooks, and Hobbs. It summarized the literature on rural and urban community studies and analyzed the results of ten surveys in church-community relationships made especially for the study. Blackwell also announced in his first report the addition to the staff of John Gillin, who came from Duke University to the Institute and the Department of Sociology and Anthropology as a professor in anthropology, intending to "initiate an anthropological study of selected southern communities."[69] The research projects accomplished under Gillin's direction have been discussed in chapter 5.

Realizing the opportunities before the Institute for pioneering new procedures, Blackwell also reported after his first year as director that there were "many other State and national contacts of value" that would put the Institute in "a position to stimulate effective use of

research in the field of community development."[70] One of the first of
the studies to be published after Blackwell's arrival was *Building
Atlanta's Future*, by John E. Ivey, Jr., Nicholas J. Demerath, and
Woodrow Breland. This research was prepared as "a junior high school
textbook for the Atlanta city schools to describe the resources, potenti-
alities, problems, and constructive ways ahead for the South's leading
metropolitan center." In 1948 Demerath prepared a community development monograph, *Economy and Population of Hickory, North
Carolina: A Master Plan Study*, but his interest soon turned to research
in complex organizations. Blackwell himself worked on a text on
community organization in America, which his administrative duties
never allowed him time to complete,[71] but some of this research appeared as lectures or articles in professional journals. For example, he
published "Community Structure and Community Organization" in
the *Journal of Educational Sociology* in 1949, and presented a paper,
"A Theoretical Framework for Sociological Research in Community
Organization," at the University of Tennessee and later at Columbia
University.

In 1953 one of Blackwell's graduate students, Floyd Hunter, formerly director of the Social Planning Council of Atlanta, published his
doctoral dissertation, *Community Power Structure*, which is possibly
the best known of the community organization research projects to
come out of the Institute. In discussing the book years later, Blackwell
called it "a real breakthrough . . . plainly one of the best books in
sociology in that ten year period."[72] He related how Hunter had decided to come to Chapel Hill, and told "what had happened to him" in
Atlanta in 1948. Hunter had "taken a stand for [Henry] Wallace"
as president on the Progressive Party ticket and had himself run for
the Senate on that ticket against the well-known Georgia senator,
Richard Russell. After he lost the election, and lost his job as well, he
approached Blackwell and said he wanted to begin work toward a
Ph.D. in sociology. Blackwell was "skeptical," afraid he was "a social
action man and would not even get a degree." But Hunter came to
Chapel Hill with his wife and four children. When he was ready for a
dissertation topic Blackwell said to him, "I think the next breakthrough
in community organization is going to be in community power structure." Blackwell had found only two references to power structure in
his examination of the literature. The one that impressed him most was
from Robert Merton. The idea appealed to Hunter, and after he had
laid out the plan the Institute gave him funds for field travel to inter-

view leaders in Atlanta. He "turned up this wealth of empirical data that he conceptualized very skillfully," Blackwell said, and he considered that Hunter's work "affected political science as much as sociology."[73]

Among other community studies completed during the period of Blackwell's directorship were *North Carolina Associated Communities: A Case Study of Voluntary Subregional Organization* (1953), by Harriet L. Herring and George L. Simpson in cooperation with the Tennessee Valley Authority; *The Urban South* (1954), edited by Nicholas J. Demerath and Rupert B. Vance with the assistance of Sara Smith and Elizabeth M. Fink; and *Community Organization: Action and Inaction* (1956), by Floyd Hunter, Ruth Connor Schaffer, and Cecil G. Sheps. After Blackwell's departure in 1957, the area of community organization was left to the Urban Studies Committee under the direction of F. Stuart Chapin, Jr. The work of that committee will be discussed in chapter 10. In 1970, however, Berton H. Kaplan, professor in the School of Public Health with a joint appointment in anthropology, published *Appalachian Community: A Community in Transition*, which he had written for the University of West Virginia Center for Appalachian Studies. He had previously completed a project, *Urbanization and Health in an Appalachian Community*.

Housing

Soon after Gordon Blackwell became director of the Institute, two housing studies were begun.[74] The Institute had long been aware that housing, especially in the rural South, was an index of the economy and of the poverty of the region. Herring and Rhyne had described the miserable housing of the majority of mill workers in North Carolina in the 1920s, but it was not until 1936 that a brief account of the wretched conditions of tenant farm housing appeared as a pamphlet in the Institute's Southern Policy Papers, *How the Other Half is Housed: A Pictorial Record of Sub-Minimum Farm Housing in the South*, by Rupert B. Vance. Odum's *Southern Regions of the United States* contained only four brief references to housing, but he did point out the need to consider rural housing. Among the 273 "objectives" listed in *Southern Regions*, he included "programs of rural housing and rural electrification" as item 261. It is likely that he assumed that housing would take care of itself if the urgent needs of the South were met, including "the whole problem of land use and planning and of optimum programs of agricultural production."[75]

By the time Blackwell arrived, however, public housing was being discussed as an important component of public policy. In November 1944 Blackwell reported to the Institute's Board of Governors that "the two housing studies now being completed are significant since housing is now a major field of interest and will be for the next few years. The Institute is cooperating with the FPHA and the Bureau of Public Administration of the University of Alabama in a study of Rural Public Housing in the South by Dr. Vance and Dr. Blackwell with the assistance of Howard McClain; and in a study of Subsistence Homestead Projects in Alabama by Dr. Wager."[76] Blackwell's summary of the Institute program for 1944 also contained a proposal for an inquiry into housing deficiencies in the South that he hoped would soon become possible. The study would examine both rural and urban housing for whites and Negroes. It would outline "already existing facts concerning housing deficiencies in the South, together with field work in selected cities, towns, and rural counties to bring the data up to date." The intent of the study would be "to awaken the South to the importance of housing and newer housing developments and to provide basic data on which policies of private and public housing groups might be projected for the postwar period."[77] The Institute was unable, however, to find funds to proceed with such an ambitious program.

The studies in cooperation with the Federal Public Housing Authority in Alabama that Blackwell had applauded in his report for 1944 were carried to completion and published. In addition, Nicholas J. Demerath published two articles on housing, "Measuring Housing Quality" in the *Journal of Housing* (1948) and "Housing Needs and Housing Standards" in *Land Economics* (1949). In 1956 Kurt W. Back and Howard Stanton published "Public Housing Attitudes Tested through Role Playing, Picture Matching" in the *Journal of Housing*. Further research in the area of housing was left for the consideration of the Urban Studies Program as an ancillary aspect of the urban process.[78]

Research Interpretation and Application

Less than a year after becoming director of the Institute, Gordon Blackwell stressed the urgency of interpreting the research under way to the people of the state and the region.[79] Before the meeting of the Board of Governors on November 7, 1944, Blackwell circulated a statement on the "1944 Program" in which he called attention to the fact that "during its 20 years of existence, the Institute has cooperated in publishing more than 80 books and monographs, while four times as many articles have resulted from Institute studies. In the files of the Central Office are some 250 manuscripts, classified under more than 40 specific fields of research, growing out of the Institute program." Without hesitation he declared that "the University has one of the finest, best equipped centers for research and training in social sciences anywhere in the country."[80]

In his report to the Board of Governors on the 1944 program, he also stated that he believed that the Institute's new subregional laboratory, composed of ten counties surrounding Chapel Hill, was not sufficiently comprehensive to carry out the full research responsibilities of the Institute. What was lacking was a facility or program that could interpret the results of Institute research to the people of the region and train personnel to make these interpretations so that the Institute's research might be useful in the implementation of state and regional social policies.[81] Blackwell sought the Board's approval of this new project, and in doing so he was careful to point out the differences between social action and social interpretation. Certainly the Institute should not become a social action agency; its primary functions were research and training. Yet "research undertaken with or for social action agencies, both public and private, may lead more directly to effective social engineering and planning" without "threatening the freedom and impartiality upon which scientific research must be based." To bolster this position, Blackwell turned to the past record of the Institute: "Howard W. Odum, who founded the Institute and directed its program for 20 years, has always maintained that the soundest contributions to social theory can be made through this approach." His words to the Board were strongly reminiscent of Odum's insistence that a major purpose of the Institute had always been "to gain knowledge that could be put right to work helping North Carolina and the South."

When the Board convened on November 7, 1944, Blackwell was ready with a concrete plan to implement the unmet need of social interpretation. It was a two-pronged program, aimed at (1) development of resource education and (2) training in planning. Resource education would involve "the promotion of translation and use of research materials in education, with resources broadly defined within a regional framework." He thought that the work being carried on by John E. Ivey, Jr., executive secretary of the Committee on Southern

Regional Studies of the American Council on Education, was typical of the kind of resource education needed by the Institute. Ivey had been responsible for promoting, planning, and carrying through two conferences on resource education at Gatlinburg, Tennessee, in 1943 and 1944 that had been recognized by national educational authorities as outstanding achievements in the field.

Training for planning as a means of interpreting social research could be found in only six universities in the United States at the time,[82] and most of these programs lacked sufficient emphasis upon the social sciences. No southern university had such a program. As Blackwell envisioned it, the Institute staff would serve as a nucleus, supplemented by other University social science departments and other divisions and schools in the Greater University. The training program would be administered under a committee of the Graduate School, with the implication that the training curriculum would lead to a graduate degree but would also include an undergraduate curriculum, and courses in the General College and in the Extension Division, and certainly that it would involve research. The proposal occasioned one of the most lively debates in which the Board had ever engaged,[83] but in the end, the Board accepted "in principle a program of resource education and training in planning." It delayed appointing Ivey to direct such a program until 1946, when funds became available.[84]

In the meantime, the Institute was already at work tabulating the resources of the southern region under the direction of Blackwell, Odum, Edith Webb Williams and others, for the Southern Association for Science and Industry.[85] Odum was in the second year of an ambitious work on southern leadership with the assistance of nine research assistants, including Mildred Mell, Anna Greene Smith, W. B. Twitty, Leslie Syron, and Ruth Lynch, all of whom later received graduate degrees for their work.[86] Blackwell was working on a study of college teaching of the social sciences in the South, initiated by the Southern Association of Colleges and Secondary Schools. Paul Wager, assisted by Mavis Mann, was exploring county planning and resources in cooperation with the State Planning Board, while Rupert Vance, in collaboration with Nadia Danilevsky, was studying human resources in the South. S. H. Hobbs was completing a revision of his earlier study on North Carolina resources, and Harriet Herring had recently produced *Industrial Development in North Carolina* for the State Planning Board.

Blackwell also initiated a cooperative project with state agencies on resource education in North Carolina, and after a meeting of agency representatives on June 9, 1945, the committee decided that the next step was to discuss with Governor Gregg Cherry the advisability of his creating a state agency for resource education.[87] This the governor did in July. The new State Commission on Resource Use Education was composed of representatives of approximately fifty agencies and organizations within the state and began work in July 1946, with John Ivey as executive secretary. The Institute's Board of Governors had by this time approved his appointment to the staff as a result of a grant from the General Education Board. After Ivey's appointment, Blackwell reminded the Board that the function of training for planning was still lacking in the program. This lack was made up in the fall of 1946 with the arrival of John A. Parker, who organized the Department of City and Regional Planning.[88]

To obtain tools for research interpretation as well as for training, the Institute had employed Marjorie Nix Bond to prepare with S. H. Hobbs, Jr., a book on North Carolina resources, *North Carolina Today*, for use in the eighth-grade social studies classes in the North Carolina public school systems. Bond also prepared a textbook for the junior high school level with Rupert Vance and John Ivey, based on Odum's *Southern Regions* and Vance's *All These People*, which she called *Exploring the South*. A book mentioned earlier in this chapter, *Building Atlanta's Future*, by Ivey, Demerath, and Breland, was the third book in the Institute's interpretative series for the junior high school level.

Eager to get on with the job of training, Blackwell had assisted in the organization of the North Carolina Council for the Social Studies, and in the summer of 1945 the Institute cooperated in setting up the Institute for Education in Human and Natural Resources as a graduate training program for health educators, social studies teachers, and eighth grade teachers.[89] Blackwell also welcomed, "in the field of business and industrial application of research," the recently created Bureau of Business Services and Research in the School of Commerce.[90] At the same time, Harry B. Williams, an Institute research assistant, was working in cooperation with North Carolina State College on an analysis of the role and techniques of the county agricultural agent. Following the practice that Odum had used from the beginning of the Institute, Blackwell set up conferences to interpret resource education, such as the Conference on Regionalism in World Economics under joint sponsorship with the Institute of World Economics in April 1945. He also brought in outside experts, like David E. Lilienthal, director of the Tennessee Valley Authority, to lecture on planning, and Talcott Parsons, professor of sociology at Harvard, to lecture on the theory of social change.

In December 1947, having worked for a year and a half as director of the Division of Research Interpretation, Ivey appeared before the Institute's Advisory Board to report on the projects under way. He explained that the Division of Research Interpretation had two functions, (1) "the actual translation of research information into form and language that the layman can understand," and (2) "research in methods of interpreting research—the best media for communication," and stated further that "projects may be divided into those of direct University concern—of which there are 39 at the present time—and projects with outside groups, of which there are now 50 being carried on in 14 different states."[91]

Ivey's interest in discovering the best means of research interpretation had led him to cooperate with the University Communications Center, and in January 1948 he obtained jointly with the Communications Center a contract from the Office of Naval Research for a project in radio communications that would explore various aspects of mass communications.[92] Daniel O. Price and Harry B. Williams from the Institute staff also worked on this project. In discussing the research years later, Blackwell said, "This was an early thing that later came to be a big thing in social science and communications research."[93] The Institute also undertook a study for Jonathan Daniels, editor of the Raleigh News and Observer, on the readability of the newspaper and the educational levels of the population served by it.[94]

To further enhance the program of resource education, the Institute established a graphic arts section to develop visual methods of presenting research data.[95] Although the graphic arts section was a significant aid in research interpretation, especially in preparation of exhibits for the Regional Laboratory, which by this time had expanded into a library as well, and in drawing charts for Institute publications, the difficulty of retaining competent personnel led to its discontinuance in 1953 upon the departure of William Hubbell, who had ably served as head of the section for several years.[96] The library was also closed and became incorporated with the Louis Round Wilson Library in 1957, soon after the arrival of the new University librarian, Jerrold Orne, who held that departmental libraries weakened the purpose and function of the central library.

At the meeting of the Institute's Executive Committee on October

15, 1948, Blackwell announced that John Ivey had resigned to become the first director of the Southern Regional Education Board in Atlanta. Blackwell assumed the responsibility of completing the findings of the State Commission on Resource Use Education and arranged the conference that presented the findings.[97] He recommended the employment of a new staff member to work half-time for the Institute and half-time for the Bureau of Community Services of the University Extension Division. In this way, research interpretation slowly came to a close as a unit in the Institute's program.

At the same meeting of the Executive Committee, Blackwell recommended that a search be made for a social psychologist to take the position left open by Ivey's resignation. He thought that there was a need for such a professional on the Institute staff. Moreover, the chairman of the Department of Psychology, Frederick Dashiell, was heartily in favor of such an arrangement. For this appointment, John W. Thibaut of Harvard came to the University, where he continues to this day with research and teaching. Blackwell also recommended that Cecil G. Sheps, who had a doctorate in medicine from Manitoba University and a master's degree in Public Health from Yale and was currently on the staff of the School of Public Health at the University, be invited to join the Institute staff as a research associate. Since Sheps had the endorsement of Dean Edward G. McGavran of the School of Public Health, the Executive Committee readily accepted Blackwell's recommendation.

As the appointments of Thibaut and Sheps indicated, Blackwell was rapidly gathering a multidisciplinary staff that would move the Institute into a broad approach toward research in human behavior involving the skills of all the social sciences. For almost thirty years the research of the Institute had focused on digging out the root causes of the South's social problems. If in some instances the research on specific problems was inadequate and failed to get at the basic issues, the fault lay not in the failure of the Institute to point out the goals of society in a region like the South, but in the lack of funds, and sometimes the lack of personnel, to pursue the projects in depth, and also sometimes in the failure of public opinion to support the findings of such research as the Institute was able to produce.

Institute directors who came after Blackwell were less enthusiastic over applied research than he was, and Institute researches began to reflect the growing interest of staff members in social theory and in the testing of hypotheses within the framework of current theoretical orientations. By the late 1950s, examination of social problems, especially in sociology, seemed to be no longer academically acceptable, and some of the younger members of the Institute staff scoffed at the research on the ground that such concerns were irrelevant to scientific inquiry. The Department of Sociology continued, however, to offer the course on American social problems that had been one of the most popular in the undergraduate curriculum since its establishment in 1920. In 1973 Duncan MacRae, Jr., Kenan Professor of Political Science and Sociology, and a research affiliate of the Institute, published three articles in which he stressed the significance in research of evaluating the goals of society as well as the behavioral processes. The assumptions embodied in these articles later appeared in MacRae's book *The Social Function of Social Science* (1976). Nevertheless, from the time of the Behavioral Science Survey in 1954 to the close of the Institute's first half-century in 1974 the research of its affiliates was more concerned with the processes of human behavior than with the problems of society. Before the survey was undertaken, Institute research on behavioral processes was already under way and thereafter led increasingly in that direction.

CHAPTER 9

Behavioral Science Research

In the late 1940s projects in the Institute for Research in Social Science began to extend beyond southern studies and social problems to the area of the behavioral sciences. As defined by the committee appointed to survey the scope of behavioral science in the University of North Carolina in 1953–54, behavioral science included "as many areas as scientists can usefully investigate" by "application of methods of science to problems of human behavior."[1] By the time the survey was made, the senior staff at the Institute had been increased by the arrival of a group of young scientists whose training had been influenced by social theories and methodology growing out of the rapidly developing technology of the late 1930s and World War II.

The Beginnings of Behavioral Science Research

Gordon W. Blackwell, the Institute's director, who had obtained his doctorate in sociology from Harvard, had met there another graduate student in sociology, Nicholas J. Demerath, who joined him in Chapel Hill. Other additions to the faculty in the Department of Sociology were Reuben Hill of Iowa State College, who had a doctorate from the University of Wisconsin and excellent credentials in the changing methodological approach to research on marriage and the family; E. William Noland of the University of Iowa, who had a doctorate in sociology from Cornell University and whose research specialization was in human relations in industry; and Harvey L. Smith, who had a doctorate from the University of Chicago and whose research interests lay in the social aspects of health and medical care.

John W. Thibaut, the social psychologist whom Blackwell had brought to the Institute and to the Department of Psychology in 1953, had a special research interest in the psychology of small groups. Dorothy C. Adkins, a psychometrician, had become chairman of the Department of Psychology and had been largely responsible, with some help from Institute funds, for bringing to the University L. L.

Thurstone and his wife, Thelma, after their retirement from the University of Chicago.[2] In 1952 Thurstone established a psychometric laboratory in the Department of Psychology similar to the one he had set up at the University of Chicago. Other psychologists interested in the behavioral sciences who were already in the department or were added as funds became available usually became affiliated with the Institute; among them were W. Grant Dahlstrom, Earl Baughman, George S. Welsh, and John H. Schopler, clinical psychologists; Harold G. McCurdy, whose research interests lay in small groups and in personality; and Halbert Robinson and later Harriet Rheingold, who were specialists in child psychology and infant behavior.

At the same time other social science departments were beginning to acquire faculty members trained in quantitative methodology and behavioral science. In the School of Business Administration, Lowell D. Ashby was involved in research on economic indices and Ralph W. Pfouts was pursuing studies in econometrics. The Department of Political Science joined Blackwell in encouraging Alexander Heard to return to Chapel Hill with the promise of Institute affiliation. Heard had been a student at the University of North Carolina and had gone on to take his doctorate at Columbia University. He had assisted V. O. Key in the preparation of *Southern Politics in State and Nation*, which appeared in 1950, as a new approach to the study of politics. In addition to Heard, the Department of Political Science had James W. Fesler and later Frederic N. Cleaveland as specialists in public administration. In 1955 the department added Robert E. Agger, whose research was in urban and political studies. In 1949 F. Stuart Chapin, Jr., joined the teaching staff of the Department of City and Regional Planning, and he at once affiliated with the Institute for research in urban studies. These social scientists and others in anthropology, the School of Public Health, and the School of Journalism, and an occasional one in history were all concerned with the developing methodologies of the behavioral sciences.

More than twenty years later, when recalling his tenure as director of the Institute at the time it was moving in this new direction, Gordon Blackwell said that his graduate work at Harvard led him "to feel that as strong as the Department of Sociology was at Chapel Hill, and it was one of the strongest in the country . . . by the early '40s things were happening in the field in which the Department needed to keep abreast."[3] By the late 1940s, the Institute was on the way toward a new approach in behavioral science and empirical research.

Odum had started the Institute with the high hope of being able to bring together the social sciences to work cooperatively, but he was constantly frustrated in his attempt, and by the early 1940s the Institute was almost exclusively a research agency for sociology. But during the 1950s, "as a social science research institute," Blackwell said, it had become "very strong," and "it was as good perhaps as you could find in the country." The Institute as then organized "demonstrated a pattern," he recalled, that seemed attractive to other institutions:

> You remember when President Conant of Harvard paid a visit, and I think . . . maybe gave a lecture in Chapel Hill, and Paul Buck, his Provost, was with him. Buck brought President Conant over to see Dr. Odum to talk about sociology and the Institute. I'll never forget Buck saying, "Mr. President, now this is the kind of thing you should do in sociology at Harvard." And it was not long before they created the Department of Social Relations which brought together social psychology, sociology, and anthropology. Now this model, although we had it only in research, they brought into a teaching department, and combined both teaching and research. They also formed the Laboratory of Social Relations. I think this is an interesting historical note. That visit, in my opinion, helped move Harvard into the new Department of Social Relations.[4]

The Institute at Chapel Hill as organized around behavioral science also became a model for other research centers, including the one at Florida State University set up by Charles M. Grigg, who had been a doctoral graduate in sociology at Chapel Hill during the period when the Institute was focusing on behavioral science.

The Behavioral Science Survey

Blackwell began in 1948 to move the Institute rapidly into research on behavioral science. His annual report for 1948–49 spelled out a seven-point program in this direction:

1. Further extension of the Institute staff in the several social sciences. . . .
2. Development of an integrated team approach in several interdisciplinary projects. . . .

3. Initiation of an interdisciplinary faculty seminar to develop common terminology and theoretical orientation for research on some problem of common concern.
4. Development of opportunities for graduate research assistants in the Institute to participate in informal discussions or interdisciplinary seminars as a means of broadening their understanding of research methodology and theory applicable to interdisciplinary problems in the social sciences. . . .
5. Consideration of the advisability of a 3-day conference on selected problems in interdisciplinary social science research to commemorate the twenty-fifth anniversary of the founding of the Institute. . . .
6. Development of a social science forum series with local and visiting speakers bi-monthly or quarterly, so selected as to represent various research points of view in the several social sciences. . . .
7. Exploration of ways by which the Institute can be of greater direct assistance to State agencies through gratis or contract research, while at the same time assuring that service research does not handicap more basic research as the fundamental concern of the Institute.[5]

Blackwell undoubtedly discussed this change in emphasis with Howard Odum, who at the time was Kenan Professor of Sociology and a research professor in the Institute. Odum must have been gratified to see his dreams of a research staff with a strong social science orientation at last being realized, but he must also have insisted that the Institute retain its service-research orientation, if not for the South, at least for the state.

Blackwell pressed forward on the implementation of his behavioral science proposals. He reported to the Executive Committee in November 1949 that "an interdisciplinary group from psychology, anthropology, sociology, social philosophy, mathematical statistics, etc., were already meeting regularly to lay the groundwork for this important project."[6] In 1950 he announced a working conference on a unified science of human behavior that would meet in February 1951 in Pinehurst, North Carolina, for a week of discussion, with John Gillin, a professor of anthropology and research professor in the Institute, as conference chairman, and he certainly must have been assured that the focus on behavioral science was beginning to materialize when the University obtained an interim grant of $100,000 from the Ford

Foundation "for scientific research in human behavior and social relations."[7]

The Behavioral Sciences Division of the Ford Foundation continued to strengthen the resolve of the Institute to concentrate on research in behavioral science by following up the interim grant with two additional ones. In the spring of 1953, the Ford Foundation invited several universities to submit proposals for a self-study of the behavioral sciences and made grants of $50,000 to each university for that purpose. Chancellor Robert B. House appointed the Behavioral Science Survey Committee to undertake preparation of the proposals for the University of North Carolina. The committee turned to the Institute for direction, and Daniel O. Price was made director, and James D. Thompson, a recent doctoral graduate in sociology, was appointed executive secretary of the self-study.[8] After the various universities had filed their self-study reports, the University of North Carolina was chosen as one of five to receive substantial grants of more than $1 million each to develop their proposals.

In their investigations with the committee in 1953–54, Price and Thompson found that at the University of North Carolina "the viewpoint that human behavior can be studied empirically so as to achieve verifiable generalizations is coming to be accepted up to a point. Yet members of other groups on this campus have doubts about the scientific nature of behavioral science."[9] The behavioral sciences themselves seemed to be divided into two areas:

> The social sciences at Chapel Hill have in the past been separated
> into two clusters, with sociology, anthropology, and psychology
> on the one hand and economics, history, and political science
> on the other. There has not been much effort to bridge the gap
> between the two. . . . An examination of footnote references
> in texts and similar materials will also show that social scientists
> tend to acknowledge ideas and data presented by others in the
> same cluster of disciplines, but rarely mention those in the other
> cluster.[10]

The recommendations of the Behavioral Science Survey Committee fell within four areas: employment of existing resources, new facilities needed, additional personnel needed, and financial needs. The committee stated that the existing resources at the University would strengthen the behavioral sciences if more research time were made available to faculty members, increased continuity given to research effort, independent research supported and encouraged, graduate training improved, the organization of the Institute for Research in Social Science modified, and a faculty committee appointed "to implement a curriculum in behavioral science . . . although at this time we would *not* advise the authorization of a major in the behavioral science curriculum."[11] In almost every instance, the new facilities needed by the University, according to the committee, were those that would enhance the ongoing programs of the Institute. They included a small-group observation room, a subregional field laboratory (a group of contiguous counties in the Piedmont Crescent), an urban studies laboratory, a cross-cultural laboratory (three counties in Western North Carolina), a "world area laboratory" in Ecuador, an econometrics center with research assistants and fellowships, a survey research facility, and work space for graduate students.[12]

Suggestions for modification of the Institute concerned "(1) scope and content of research programs and (2) organization, including (a) administrative structure and control and (b) staff membership regulations and privileges."[13] The primary function of the Institute should be encouragement of research and graduate training in social and behavioral science, and its resources should be devoted to support of the best research proposals in the field: "The Institute seems the best adapted organization in the University to facilitate multidisciplinary team research, and it should continue to support such research though the final criterion for choosing projects to be sponsored should be excellence as measured by scientific standards." The survey committee also remarked that the University Research Council and its Social Science Section had "responsibilities that partially overlap with those of the Institute," but stated that "we believe that both have a place in the University structure. The Research Council is primarily an allocative body, and is not likely to play an active and direct role in stimulating research."[14]

Focal Area Research

The report of the Behavioral Science Survey Committee listed six focal area statements which summarized "activity in behavioral science at the University of North Carolina" that had "implications for research, for training, and for service." At the same time the report expressed the hope that these statements would point the way to the planning of future activity in broad programmatic terms. The focal area statements, listed without any implication of a schedule of priorities,[15] were

1. *Human development and adjustment*
   Linguistics
   Personality
   Family Behavior
   Psychiatry

2. *Group functioning*
   Group problem solving
   Small group and complex organizations

3. *Demography and social epidemiology*
   Demography
   Urban processes
   Behavioral science in the field of health
   Community health

4. *Economic and industrial behavior*
   Economic behavior
   Human relations in business

5. *Socio-political behavior*
   Political behavior
   Race and ethnic relations
   Mass communications

6. *Cross-cultural studies*
   World areas and national cultures
   Religious behavior

Gordon Blackwell considered the year following the behavioral science self-study to be "one of transition in organizational structure and in financing." To indicate the multidisciplinary affiliations of the senior staff, he listed the members by departments—thirty-three members from fourteen disciplines, with sociology having ten, the largest number.[16] Pointing out that the Institute's Board of Governors and, ideally, the program itself had always been interdisciplinary, Blackwell remarked on the difference in the approach of Institute projects in the early days from that currently being pursued. He explained that Odum "saw the need for an interdisciplinary research institute that would emphasize projects and problems, not separate disciplines, and that would take as its major field of research the South as a region, not as a section. He saw, too, such research beginning with the community, extending into the State, and from there embracing the region.'' During Odum's directorship the Institute usually had one specialist in a research area, but now, said Blackwell, ''the practice increasingly is to have an interdisciplinary committee (focal area group) engaged in research planning and in developing a conceptual framework within which separate projects may be more cumulative in theory building.''[17]

Since the Behavioral Science Survey had recommended that the Institute assist research in certain focal areas considered of current importance in social science, Blackwell's annual report for 1954–55 organized the current projects under those focal areas. Instead of the six focal areas recommended by the survey, however, the projects were listed under fifteen areas:[18]

1. Cultural contacts and change in foreign areas
2. Demographic studies
3. Economic behavior
4. Family behavior
5. Social science aspects of health and medical care
6. Human relations in business and industry
7. Mass communication
8. Personality studies
9. Political behavior
10. Race and ethnic relations
11. Russian studies
12. Small groups and complex organization
13. Southern and North Carolina studies
14. Urban studies
15. Methodology and theory

Within these fifteen focal areas the Institute staff had published during the year thirteen books and monographs, thirty-seven articles, three brochures, eleven chapters, and two pamphlets, and had completed fifty-four additional manuscripts.[19]

With such a mass of research in a variety of fields under way, it is understandable that the Institute could not at once reduce projects to five or six focal areas, nor immediately implement the recommendations of the Behavioral Science Survey. But Blackwell was able to report in the year following the survey that four focal areas had developed integrated research programs with an organizational structure.

These were the Political Behavior Committee, the Urban Studies Committee, the Organization Research Group, and a cluster of projects on social science aspects of health and the health professions.[20] The senior staff had been increased to forty-one, a new department had affiliated, and the services of the Social Science Statistical Laboratory were increasingly in demand. The laboratory had been expanded in 1950, and Daniel O. Price was appointed director and George E. Nicholson of the Institute of Statistics was made associate director.[21]

The four focal areas that Blackwell announced as having been organized with a committee structure had actually been set up or were in process before the Behavioral Science Survey was undertaken. These four continued to be the only organized focal areas to function during the remainder of Blackwell's administration and to continue into Price's administration. Blackwell was able gradually to reduce the number of projects outside the focal areas, but the number fluctuated according to the criteria that Blackwell listed in 1956 as pertinent to all Institute research: "significance to behavioral science, significance in potential application, appropriateness for UNC, availability of competent staff within the faculty, and availability of financial support."[22]

The first annual report that Daniel Price made in 1957–58 as director of the Institute summarized the approach to research that had been under way during most of Blackwell's administration and that was to continue through most of his own: "While much of the Institute research is carried on through the several specially financed focal areas, which have been set up to facilitate cooperative and interdisciplinary research, it should be emphasized that a large part of the research in the Institute is of the individual project type. More than 30 of the 48 senior staff members are carrying on some 65 projects unrelated to any of the focal areas."[23] This approach to research in behavioral science continued to the end of the Institute's first half-century.

The Research Triangle Institute

While the Institute program in the behavioral sciences was being developed, the groundwork was being laid for a cooperative research center outside the University campus that came to be known as the Research Triangle Institute. The Research Triangle Institute was indirectly an outgrowth of dreams that Howard Odum had had for many years of creating an organization that would be concerned with research on southern resources and industrial development. He had first proposed such an organization in 1932 to the Board of Governors of the Institute for Research in Social Science and again in 1938 at a conference on southern regional development held in Chapel Hill soon after the publication of his *Southern Regions of the United States*. It was to be called the Council on Southern Regional Development, suggestive of the Southern Growth Policies Council of the 1970s. He eventually abandoned the plan but returned to it in the closing years of his life.

When the Ford Foundation began expanding its program into the behavioral sciences, Odum wrote to the associate director, Robert M. Hutchins, suggesting that the foundation fund six or eight regional university centers for research in "human relations, organization, and control."[24] This correspondence may have influenced the Ford Foundation in its decision to allocate grants to various universities chosen on a regional basis for self-surveys in the behavioral sciences and to single out the University of North Carolina at Chapel Hill as a representative of the southeastern region. This study and the additional grant that it brought for enrichment of the behavioral science programs at Chapel Hill have been discussed earlier in this chapter, and will be referred to again in chapter 10.

Odum's third approach to a regional research center came in July 1952 in the form of a work memorandum to the administration of the Consolidated University of North Carolina, proposing the creation of an institute in the humanities and in the social and physical sciences in which the three branches of the University (the University of North Carolina, North Carolina State College, and the Woman's College of the University of North Carolina) would participate. He suggested that the institute be called "The North Carolina Center for Research in Institutions and Administrative Organization" and that its purpose be "for integrating the work of the several institutions on the University level," including two state-supported Negro colleges, the Agricultural and Technical College at Greensboro and North Carolina Central College at Durham.[25] He thought the institute should be located near the Raleigh-Durham Airport. He followed up his proposal with two additional memoranda and two appraisals of resources required for research institutes and regional centers. In the last years of his life, Odum, with Blackwell, attended a dinner in Chapel Hill at the invitation of Governor Luther H. Hodges at which the idea of the Research Triangle development was first presented by Romeo Guest, an industrialist of Greensboro, North Carolina.

Unfortunately, Odum did not live to see the fruition of his dream and the location of a research center on five thousand acres near the Raleigh-Durham Airport that came to be called the Research Triangle Park. The Research Triangle Institute opened in 1960 in the Robert M. Hanes Memorial Building, the first building erected on the 288-acre campus assigned to the new Institute in the park. The Institute had developed from the Research Triangle Committee, which Governor Hodges appointed in the spring of 1955. The committee was incorporated on September 25, 1956, as a nonprofit agency. The incorporators were Governor Hodges in his capacity as chairman of the Board of Trustees of the Consolidated University of North Carolina, President William C. Friday of the Consolidated University, President A. Hollis Edens of Duke University, and Norman A. Cocke, chairman of the Duke University Board of Trustees.

By October 1, 1956, George L. Simpson, one of Odum's protégés and a senior staff member of the Institute for Research in Social Science, was appointed director of the Research Triangle Committee, and he immediately named an advisory committee on which Blackwell, director of the Institute for Research in Social Science, was a member. About two years later, Simpson and his associates proposed a three-stage approach to development of the research park. The Research Triangle Committee incorporated and changed its name to the Research Triangle Foundation and continued as a nonprofit corporation, and on the same day, December 29, 1958, the Research Triangle Institute was chartered as a nonprofit organization to be administered by the Consolidated University of North Carolina and Duke University but to be operated as a separate institution with a separate board of trustees. The third step was to incorporate the Research Triangle Park as a profit-making organization.[26] The Research Triangle Park immediately gave the Research Triangle Institute half a million dollars to employ staff and begin operation. Gertrude Cox, director of the Institute of Statistics at North Carolina State College, was employed to establish a statistical division of the Research Triangle Institute, and George R. Herbert, formerly associate director of the Stanford Research Institute in California, was employed as president of the Research Triangle Institute. Simpson later became chancellor of the University System of Georgia.

The charter authorized the Research Triangle Institute ''to establish and operate, in close proximity to or in conjunction with research facilities" of Duke University and the University of North Carolina a center "for research in the physical, biological, medical, mathematical, agricultural, economic, and engineering sciences, and thereby to promote the educational and scientific purposes of the universities."[27] The charter also directed the Institute to "encourage, foster, conduct, and contract to conduct investigations and research" in these sciences and to "publish and disseminate . . . appropriate information and data."

The Research Triangle Institute began with the support of both government and industry. Its services have expanded through the years until contract research has grown by many millions of dollars. It has maintained a close relationship with its corporate parents, Duke University and the University of North Carolina. The two universities and the Research Triangle Institute have shared facilities, and the Institute from time to time has turned to the faculties at Duke and North Carolina for assistance in planning and development of key research programs.

This was the kind of thriving research organization that Odum had seen in his dreams as the best means of giving the South the necessary thrust to rise up from the bottom of the nation's socioeconomic ladder. The Institute for Research in Social Science in Chapel Hill, Odum's first effort at a research center, had been involved only incidentally in the development of the Research Triangle Institute, but had it not been for the initial push from Odum, Simpson, and Blackwell the Research Triangle Institute might never have been realized. After the creation of the Research Triangle Institute, Duke University, the University of North Carolina, and North Carolina State College joined to create in the Research Triangle Park the Triangle Universities Computation Center, which houses computational facilities that have been a welcome resource for the Social Science Statistical Laboratory in the Institute for Research in Social Science in Chapel Hill.

"A Center of Excellence in Science"

By 1966 the four focal area programs growing out of the Behavioral Science Survey of 1954 had spun off into independent or semi-independent programs. Price was resigning as director of the Institute for Research in Social Science to go to the University of Texas, and an ad hoc committee was appointed to study the functions of the Institute and to make recommendations for the future.[28] At the same time, a University committee was preparing a proposal for the creation of a "center of excellence in science."

In a memorandum to the ad hoc committee, a research professor in the Institute cited the changes within the University and the increased availability of outside funds for independent research as causes for the decline in the importance of the Institute and the decrease in organized focal areas of interdisciplinary research:

> If its [the Institute's] relative importance in the total functioning
> of the University has declined during the past few years, I
> believe this is primarily due to the growth of the several
> departments, development of informal mechanisms for inter-
> disciplinary collaboration, increased support for research from
> the University, and increased availability of outside sources of
> research support enabling individual faculty members to obtain
> their own financing and conduct their research in relative
> independence of the facilities of the Institute.[29]

But the committee did not recommend abandonment of interdisciplinary research. On the contrary, it reached the conclusion that enhancement of this type of research would regain for the Institute its former role as the "active center of research life for the social sciences." To this end, the committee recommended that the Institute encourage interdisciplinary research and seek out a director "who will be interested in the development of a large-scale interdisciplinary research program under Institute auspices." Expanding the concept of focal area research in behavioral science recommended by the Behavioral Science Survey, the committee looked toward collaboration of the social sciences with the physical sciences:

> Another example [in addition to research on intergroup relations]
> of the kind of interdisciplinary collaboration the Institute might
> hope to stimulate would be a program of studies of the place
> of science and technology in the contemporary political
> intellectual scene. This is an interdisciplinary problem of
> tremendous significance for the South as it increasingly takes its
> place in the mainstream of our national life. In such an endeavor,
> social scientists at UNC could collaborate fruitfully with our

colleagues in the natural sciences and develop the kind of
program which has appeared at Columbia, Princeton, and a
number of foreign universities.[30]

To facilitate research, if only in the area of the social sciences, the
Institute needed to update its data processing equipment and skills.
With the increasing emphasis on quantitative research in all of the
social sciences, the Institute's Social Science Statistical Laboratory,
which had been a valuable facility for data processing in the past, was
"no longer adequate by itself for the needs of social scientists." The
committee therefore recommended that the Institute budget provide for
the development of a computer programming staff, a computer terminal device, and line costs for transmission of information to and from
the computer center at the Research Triangle. The committee also
made recommendations "that would more specifically contribute to
interdisciplinary research," such as (1) the development of a data bank
to store data from local projects and from other studies especially
related to developing areas, including the South, and (2) the appropriation of a modest sum for a series of seminars on interdisciplinary
research that could be attended by scientists from inside and outside
the University.[31]

The development of a computer facility and the data bank took
several years to implement, but the interdisciplinary seminars were
under way in 1967, the year that James Prothro became director of
the Institute, and significantly, the first seminar, which was on general systems theory, was presented by Howard Odum's younger son,
Howard T. Odum, then a member of the University's Department of
Zoology.[32] The second seminar, on law and social science, was organized by a former Institute research assistant, Berton H. Kaplan, who
had become a professor in the School of Public Health.

While the ad hoc committee was evaluating the functions of the
Institute, a University committee composed of representatives from
nine departments (Chemistry, City and Regional Planning, Economics,
Information Science, Physics, Political Science, Psychology, Sociology, and Statistics) was preparing a proposal for a multimillion-
dollar grant from the National Science Foundation under its Science
Development Plan for Colleges and Universities. The grant of almost
$5 million, which was made the following year (1967), was for the
achievement of an "Academic Center of Excellence in Science."[33] It
made possible the implementation of the major recommendations of

the ad hoc committee and turned the Institute away from its chief emphasis upon focal research and in the direction of establishing a major computation and data facility for quantitative analyses. A supplementary grant from the National Science Foundation brought the total amount to $6,537,000, of which the Institute's share was eventually $789,000, or 12 percent.

The expansion of the Social Science Statistical Laboratory and its data center will be discussed later. Research in two focal areas mentioned by Blackwell must now be examined.

The Organization Research Group

In 1949 Gordon Blackwell and Nicholas Demerath began an interdisciplinary seminar on basic theory of human behavior that was attended by members of the faculty in anthropology, statistics, psychology, social philosophy, and sociology. As described by Blackwell in his report to the Board of Governors on December 9, 1949, "The group is now attempting to construct a vocabulary and to determine what is involved in the development of theory."[34] Out of this seminar ultimately grew tbe Organization Research Group, frequently referred to as ORG. This group had probably the longest life of any of the organized area committees and produced a large number of research manuscripts. By the time of the Behavioral Science Survey in 1953–54, representatives from the faculty in political science had joined the group and the group itself had divided into two parts, complex organization research and small group research.

As described by the report of the Behavioral Science Survey Committee, there were six continuing members in the Organization Research Group, with Demerath serving as chairman, and two others who participated from time to time.[35] In 1953 the Organization Research Group was formally established "as a means of developing a long-range program of research in complex social organization." The Behavioral Science Survey report stated that of the four organized focal area committees, the Organization Research Group appeared "to be more cohesive and tightly knit than any of the other groups. . . . Furthermore, the group began with a body of theory and research method at least partially developed and tested by its members."[36] The research staff of the group in 1953 came from the fields of sociology, social psychology, statistics, and public administration.

The report of the Behavioral Science Survey explained that the objective of the Organization Research Group was to outline a "concentrated long-range program of research and graduate training which would join various methodological and empirical considerations now largely discrete but nevertheless amenable to synthesis on a theoretical basis."[37] It conceded that at first glance, the concept that one focal area could profitably encompass research on both small groups and complex organizations might seem illogical, but it argued that to dispel this doubt it was only necessary to "recall the importance of complex administration forms in contemporary affairs, and the part of the ubiquitous small group in mediating associational requirements and personality needs—in government, business, education, religion, health and welfare, work and play."[38] The Organization Research Group had interests in "various types of human association, both voluntary and constrained, ranging in size from very small to moderately large: from the relationships of two persons to the formidable structure of a great corporation." The focus of the Organization Research Group, however, would not be to reduce complex organizations to a summation of their small groups, but to determine whether "certain principles or 'laws' may be found applicable to both organizational and group behavior."[39]

With the organization of a multidisciplinary seminar in 1949, as already noted, the Institute was able to begin functioning promptly when in 1950 the Human Resources Research Institute of the United States Air Force gave a substantial grant for a three-year study, "Human Factors in Air Force Base Efficiency." The Air Force grant marked the beginning of a flow of large federal grants to the Institute that facilitated a variety of studies. The research for the Air Force was an ideal project for testing the assumptions of the informal group working on complex organization theory. In reporting to the Institute's Board of Governors in December 1950, Gordon Blackwell gave details of the development of the Air Force project:

> An Institute on Research in Human Resources has been set up at
> Maxwell Field, Alabama, under the direction of Raymond
> Bowers, a sociologist. Last summer Dr. Demerath [Institute
> for Research in Social Science] served that Institute for two
> weeks on a team of consultants engaged in research planning.
> Professors Noland [Institute for Research in Social Science] and
> Demerath are cooperating with the Air Force in the sociological

aspects of this proposed project and are now abroad to make first-hand observations and conduct pilot studies for the Air Forces in Korea.[40]

At the conclusion of the project in 1953, Blackwell summarized the results as an achievement in multidisciplinary research as well as an advancement in organizational research. He wrote:

A theoretical model applicable to analysis of the functioning of a complex instrumental organization has been hammered out as a group project, drawing upon functionalism in sociology, the concept of informal structure as developed in public administration and business management; motivation, morale, and leadership theory in social psychology; and interaction theory in sociometry. Currently the group is working on theories in small group organization and in clinical psychology in an effort to strengthen the theoretical model for complex organization analysis. Also further attention is being devoted to development of experimental designs for both laboratory and field research with psychologists proving to be particularly helpful.[41]

The research staff working on the Air Force project summarized the results of the study for the Behavioral Science Survey Committee as the development of ''a theory of organization capable of dealing in a uniform way with the functioning both of small groups and of large organizations.'' Acknowledging the theoretical contributions of Talcott Parsons, R. F. Bales, and Chester Barnard as well as their own original research experience, the Organization Research Group identified three principal processes of organizational action relating to productivity: coordination, integration, and harmonization. A ''cycle of organizational action'' was a feature of the theory. The cycle had four main phases: planning and replanning, directing, producing, appraising and reporting.[42] More than twenty-two published articles and technical reports spelled out the findings of the research group.[43]

With the completion of the Air Force study, the Institute was able to obtain additional funding from the Ford Foundation and the Office of Naval Research for another three-year project in the focal area of small groups and complex organizations. Demerath again acted as chairman for the Organizational Research Group. Other senior staff members included three social psychologists—John W. Thibaut and Milton Rosenbaum from the University of North Carolina and Edward E.

Jones from Duke University—and Frederick L. Bates, who had joined the Department of Rural Sociology of North Carolina State College after receiving his doctorate in sociology from the University of North Carolina in 1953. The junior staff consisted of six assistants from the fields of sociology, psychology, and business administration. The major objective of the project was to develop an integrated application of field and laboratory methods to the subject under study. Edward Jones and his research assistant, Richard deCharms, explored perceptual factors in group solidarity; John W. Thibaut and his assistants, Lloyd Strickland and Arthur Lee Miller, worked on innovation, conformity, and organizational change; Thibaut, Rosenbaum, and Demerath, with their assistants, William Kapner, R. Robb Taylor, Elizabeth F. Goding, Richard Stephens, and A. F. C. Wallace, concentrated on the area of structural factors in role and organizational performance; Thibaut developed methodology in measurement of achievement and affiliation motivation, and Bates in position, role, and status.

At the close of the academic year 1955–56 and the conclusion of the research project for the Navy, Demerath left the University of North Carolina to become chairman of the Department of Sociology at Washington University in St. Louis, where he established a social science research institute; Thibaut took a leave of absence for a year at the Center for Advanced Study in the Behavioral Sciences at Palo Alto, California; and Bates joined the staff in hospital administration at Cornell University and later went on to chair the Department of Sociology at the University of Georgia. Edward Jones became chairman of the Organization Research Group; deCharms was made a senior staff member, and he was joined by two new members, William Catton in sociology and Kurt W. Back, a social psychologist in the School of Public Health.

In the meantime, the laboratory for small group research recommended by the Behavioral Science Survey had been constructed on the fourth floor of Alumni Building. It was a small area carved out of Odum's Regional Laboratory, with two-way viewing areas for the observation of interaction in a group situation.[44] With the completion of the new social science building, Hamilton Hall, in 1970, the facilities for small group research were greatly enlarged. The laboratory is used to demonstrate research methods to University classes in sociology and psychology and to observe and attempt to classify the behavior of subjects. After his return from Stanford, Thibaut became chairman of the Organization Research Group, and Catton, who had moved on to the University of Washington in Seattle, was replaced by Ernest Q. Campbell. The Group Psychology Branch of the Office of Naval Research made a generous grant to intensify the study of structural factors in group interaction, and research continued in social perception as well as in structural factors.[45]

By 1960 the annual summary of Institute research no longer devoted several pages to a description of work in progress by the Organization Research Group, although the report did mention that laboratory research on small groups was still under way and that Thibaut continued as chairman.[46] By this time, staff members in other focal areas, including the Urban Studies Committee and the program in the social aspects of health, were also doing research in the field formerly undertaken only by the Organization Research Group. By 1965 Thibaut was no longer listed as chairman of the Organization Research Group, but his research focus continued in the general area of small group research. Several years later, other disciplines also became involved in small group research. One example is the work of Barbara Wasik from the School of Education, who produced an article with J. T. Simmons, "Management of Small-Group Behavior Within a First-Grade Classroom," in *Proceedings of the American Psychological Association* in 1971.[47] As the fiftieth year of the Institute drew to a close, Thibaut was still publishing articles on mixed-motive relationships and the resolution of conflict.[48]

In recalling his attempt to develop multidisciplinary research in the Institute, Gordon Blackwell years later said that this type of research has always been "very difficult to achieve."[49] He was not sure whether the goal was achieved better in the cultural community studies directed by John Gillin, in which sociology and anthropology cooperated, or in the projects of the Organization Research Group, in which several disciplines joined. He thought Thibaut's research greatly strengthened the Department of Psychology and helped it to obtain funds and to increase faculty. "That," Blackwell said, "is the kind of contribution that an Institute should make to its University." The research that Thibaut and Harold H. Kelley of the University of Minnesota did for their *The Social Psychology of Groups*, published in 1959, made a lasting contribution to the theory developed by the Organization Research Group. In 1975 Thibaut published with Laurens Walker of the University of North Carolina School of Law another significant contribution to organizational research, *Procedural Justice*, which was an analysis of the social psychology of legal processes.

The Political Behavior Committee

Blackwell believed that the attractiveness of Institute affiliation was a factor in Alexander Heard's decision to return to Chapel Hill. Soon after his arrival in the fall of 1950, Heard had organized the Political Behavior Committee. The committee was established in the Institute as a result of a grant of $15,000 from the University's interim fund from the Ford Foundation. Its purpose was to spur the development of "a long-range program in political behavior research that would interest faculty members and graduate students in several departments."[50] The committee was a multidisciplinary one with representatives from the faculties in anthropology, business administration, history, political science, psychology, sociology, and statistics. At first there were difficulties in communication, but the committee slowly achieved "a general agreement upon a frame of reference for investigating political behavior" and "worked out a uniform pattern for the design of research proposals and presentation of research ideas."[51] The members did not attempt to work as a research team but rather acted as a consulting group, critically reviewing research proposals and progress reports, challenging and sharpening the presentations. On some projects, however, several members did work together.

Research in political science had changed directions dramatically since the founding of the Institute in 1924. It was no longer primarily concerned with the "external characteristics of governing institutions,"[52] or with the government documents containing laws and rules, and it was now focusing on the field of public administration and on observable behavior in the political and administrative processes. During the 1930s and 1940s research in political science had begun to show concern for voting behavior, the analysis of elections, and public opinion research. It was this kind of research that the Political Behavior Committee wished to consider and possibly refine.

The committee was especially influenced by the thinking of the seven-man Committee on Political Behavior of the Social Science Research Council, which was set up in 1949 with V. O. Key as chairman and of which Alexander Heard became a member, and by the six-week summer seminar that the committee held in 1951 on research in political behavior.[53] The Social Science Research Council Committee agreed that it would follow two methodological procedures: the political process (repetitive patterns of action by key actors in the political system), and quantitative comparative analysis.

While keeping in mind the methodology of the committee from the Social Science Research Council, the Political Behavior Committee in the Institute made no attempt to develop a unit of related research projects within a narrow theoretical framework, but preferred to sponsor research already under way or completed either at Chapel Hill or elsewhere. Such a research program, the committee thought, would show cumulative results in time and would fit neatly into the continuum of research in the political process described by Oliver Garceau in his essay, "Research in the Political Process (1951)."[54] The Institute committee decided to concentrate on four foci that would fall within Garceau's continuum, two related to the individual-citizen pole of the continuum and two at the opposite end of the pole, one of which dealt with motivation, which Garceau had not identified as a separate cluster. These four foci were political participation, motivation in political behavior, political organization, and decision-making.

From its establishment, the Institute's Political Behavior Committee had sponsored four research projects financed by a three-year grant from the Ford Foundation.[55] They concerned the Farm Security Administration, North Carolina county politics, national power and policy structures, and money in politics.[56] The Farm Security Administration Study dealt with behavior of a federal administrative agency operating in a controversial area of public policy, and it attempted to determine how this behavior was conditioned by the need to maintain political support in order to perform its lawfully designated function. It was basically a study of political organization and decision-making.

The project on North Carolina county politics was a study in two parts, one conducted by a political scientist and the other by a sociologist, which combined all four of the foci. The two parts were worked out cooperatively and were closely integrated in data gathering and analyses. The study was also conceived as a counterpart of the Detroit Area Studies done by the Institute of Social Research at the University of Michigan. Through frequent consultation with the Michigan Institute, the Political Behavior Committee in Chapel Hill was able to "weave into the County Politics Study much of the conceptualization developed in the Detroit Area Studies so that these two separate undertakings [could be] complimentary and their results cumulative."[57] As the study progressed, the research team found that precise generalizations emerged concerning the nature and extent of political participation in the rural counties being studied, the motivation for participation and activity, and the structure of attitudes that led to involvement.

The third project, which was related to national power and policy, was directed by Floyd Hunter, a sociologist on the Political Behavior Committee, and represented an attempt to apply on the national level the theories he had developed in his *Community Power Structure*, which had been published in 1953. The basic hypothesis of the project on national power structure was the assumption that "at the national level in the United States, decisive actions are brought to bear on policy formulation and power execution by men who are identified with dominant urban centers."[58] Hunter assumed that at the national level, as in the community, power structures both inside and outside government exist that apply pressure on policy development. When completed, the study would make a major contribution, the Political Behavior Committee thought, toward the understanding of two of its focal interests: political organization and the process of decision-making.[59]

All four of the primary research foci were involved in the project on money in politics, which was directed by Alexander Heard. The objective of the study was to spell out the role that money plays, "first in the behavior of citizens in the electorate; secondly, in the behavior of governmental and political party officials; and thirdly, in the processes through which citizens and their officials are related to the making and execution of public policy.[60] The dominant working hypothesis was that "in the United States, power structures use money in politics to influence government policies."[61] Heard's pioneer research was published in 1960 as *The Costs of Democracy*.

The research staff participating in these projects varied from time to time. In 1954 ten senior members of the Institute were involved, including three from the Department of Political Science: the chairman of the committee, Alexander Heard, in the field of political parties and comparative politics; Frederic N. Cleaveland in public administration; and Robert E. Agger in state and local government. Other participants were Floyd Hunter from the School of Social Work in the area of community organization; four from the Department of Sociology and Anthropology, George L. Simpson in the area of regionalism, Rupert B. Vance in demography and stratification, Daniel O. Price in social statistics, and John Gillin, who had examined the process of government in Latin America; one from the Department of Psychology, John W. Thibaut, who was doing research in small group behavior; and Arthur Whitehill from the School of Business Administration, who served as a specialist in personnel relations.[62]

These ten, with the aid of one or more research assistants each, began the work laid out by the Political Behavior Committee, and a few carried on their work for a decade or more. All except Vance, who remained in the Institute until his retirement in 1969, and Thibaut, who is still active in research and teaching, went on to other universities or to offices in other research agencies. Heard resigned as chairman of the Political Behavior Committee in 1957 to become dean of the Graduate School at the University of North Carolina, and later he became chancellor of Vanderbilt University.[63] Floyd Hunter resigned to pursue independent research.[64] And Paul W. Wager, who had been in the first group of research assistants in 1924 and had become a professor of political science, returned to the senior staff to work with Robert Agger and others on a project on leadership and decision making. At the same time, Donald R. Matthews was invited to participate in the Political Behavior Committee. He had been brought to the Department of Political Science under a grant from the Falk Foundation in 1957, to replace Heard after Heard had assumed duties at the Graduate School. Before Heard had left the chairmanship of the Political Behavior Committee, work on a five-year research plan had been outlined and funds were being sought for implementation.[65] Some of these funds came, for a six-year period, from two successive grants from the Falk Foundation to the Department of Political Science.

The academic year of 1957–58 was a productive one.[66] Robert Agger, one of the most prolific writers of the Political Behavior Committee, was at work on two projects, one on the circulation of political elites and the other on comparative community politics. The previous year he had published two monographs with Vincent Ostrom on political participation in a small community, and he occasionally published as many as five articles yearly. Hunter had completed his manuscript on top American leadership and during the year had traveled to cities in the Far East, Asia, and Europe in a study of international power structure. Federico Gil, who had recently become affiliated with the Institute, had done field work in Chile and Cuba for his study of political parties and elections in Latin America. Frederic Cleaveland had completed the final two monographs of a series of seven on science and state government that was financed by the National Science Foundation, and Richard McCleery's doctoral dissertation on prison government, directed by Rogert Agger, had won the Birkhead Award of the American Political Science Association.

The research of the Political Behavior Committee was recognized as some of the most important being done in the Institute. Several years later it was incorporated into the Department of Political Science as the Political Studies Program, under the direction of Donald R. Matthews. The program was made possible by grants from the Maurice and Laura Falk Foundation. In 1966 the ad hoc committee appointed to study the function of the Institute praised the work of the Political Behavior Committee as "a key factor in North Carolina's leadership in the 'behavioral revolution' within political science."[67]

Public Administration

In addition to the Political Studies Program, another spin-off from the Political Behavior Committee was the establishment of a program leading to a master's degree in public administration, which is presently directed by Deil S. Wright.[68] Wright joined the Department of Political Science as professor in 1967 and immediately affiliated with the Institute. He received both his master's degree in public administration and his doctorate from the University of Michigan and came to Chapel Hill from the University of California at Berkeley.

The establishment of the program would have been a gratification to Howard Odum, the Institute's founder, and a vindication of his plan for a school of public administration that he initiated in 1932. In his early editorials in the *Journal of Social Forces*, before the establishment of the Institute, Odum had written of the importance of enlightened public administration as a basis for good citizenship. Government, he insisted, should serve the needs of the people and not exploit them for the benefit of the few. This had been E. C. Branson's incentive in organizing the North Carolina Club and in conducting surveys of county government. With the establishment of the Institute, the Board of Governors expanded the county surveys and soon had a staff composed of S. H. Hobbs, Jr., Paul W. Wager, and several research assistants. The next step toward development of research in public administration was in the area of municipal government.

In 1925 Edward Woodhouse was added to the Institute's senior staff to survey municipal government, and he immediately set to work on a survey of Winston-Salem at the request of Mayor William A. Blair. In 1927 the Board of Governors assigned Woodhouse a full-time assistant, Mary Phlegar Smith, who was to help "complete and edit Mr. Woodhouse's source book on municipal government in North Carolina," complete "records and research begun on small towns in North Carolina," arrange "a symposium of municipal folk to determine on next steps for research in this field," and help "Mr. Woodhouse keep up the North Carolina Municipal Association's work in gathering information."[69] Also in 1927 the Institute published Paul W. Wager's *County Government in North Carolina*.

Five years later, under Odum's guidance, the Institute was responsible for the establishment of a short-lived school of public administration. The first mention of the school in the minutes of the Board of Governors appeared June 29, 1932, with the passage of a motion "that the Institute cooperate with and assist the School of Public Administration to such extent as agreed upon by the President and Director with Dr. W. C. Jackson, Dean of the new School." The plan for the school had been in Odum's thinking for some time. In 1930, when he drew up a proposal to the Rockefeller Foundation for a grant of $1 million over a ten-year period (1930 to 1940), one of the six goals of the plan was "to reconstruct and enlarge a school of public administration and citizenship." Although the foundation declined to make so large a grant, Odum persisted with his plan for a school of public administration and obtained Jackson's consent to serve as dean. President Graham seemed hesitant to put into the University budget a request for funds for the school, and Odum wrote, pressing for the support: "The Rockefeller Foundation is basing its plan to give us the minimum five-year renewal partly on the understanding that there was an appropriation of $5,000 especially recommended by the Governor for this particular task. . . . It seems to me that we are really obligated to go ahead and develop this School."[70]

At the time, W. C. Jackson was a professor of history and government and was vice-president of the Woman's College of the University of North Carolina at Greensboro. He was well known and respected in the state. Despite Odum's difficulty in obtaining guaranteed funds for the School of Public Administration, Jackson did in fact come to Chapel Hill, and the school was established to begin work in the fall of 1932. The School of Public Welfare, which Odum had launched with high hopes when he first came to the University, was dismantled as such, and social work became a division in the new School of Public Administration. A brochure on cooperation between the University of North Carolina and Duke University, which Odum had a hand in preparing in 1935, referred to the joint effort between the Division of Social Work in the School of Public Administration and the

Duke University School of Medicine as "one of the most promising developments in the state and region."[71]

By 1935, however, Jackson had returned to Greensboro as dean of administration and later chancellor of the Woman's College. Odum assumed responsibility as dean of the School of Public Administration but the school ceased to exist soon afterward.[72] President Graham had never been convinced of the need for a school of public administration and supported instead the Institute of Government, which had been created by Albert Coates, a member of the faculty of the School of Law, although the foci of the two programs were different. The Institute of Government was concerned with in-service training of public officials and with giving assistance to local and county governments and state departments and boards, whereas the School of Public Administration hoped to engage in graduate teaching and research in many facets of public life. Cooperation between the Institute for Research in Social Science and the Institute of Government was worked out when Gordon Blackwell became director of the Institute for Research in Social Science, particularly in the Urban Crescent Project in the late 1950s. In 1973–74 two staff members from the Institute of Government were affiliated with the Institute for Research in Social Science.[73]

Five years after the close of the School of Public Administration, Odum prepared a private memorandum outlining "President Graham's Nullifying Activities" in which he listed as his first grievance Graham's failure to support requests for foundation grants for the School of Public Administration. Graham's arguments against the school "were that such a school of public administration was no longer in line with present trends" and that "the University was not organizing around schools." As a refutation of Graham's appraisal of trends in political science, Odum noted that "in less than a year the Harvard School of Public Administration had been endowed and strong centers in one or two other places had been developed."[74]

One of these places was the University of Alabama. When its Bureau of Public Administration turned in the 1940s to the Institute for Research in Social Science in Chapel Hill for assistance, the Institute gladly cooperated. In his first report as director in October 1944, Gordon Blackwell listed among the cooperative relationships between the Institute and other research and planning agencies a request from the Bureau of Public Administration at the University of Alabama.[75] His report for 1945 noted the completion of Paul W. Wager's project on subsistence homesteads for the Alabama bureau and announced a second project under way: "Paul W. Wager, with Donald Hayman as a graduate assistant, has undertaken an analysis and evaluation of the administration of natural resources in the State [North Carolina]." This was part of a seven-state project "arranged jointly by the Tennessee Valley Authority and the Bureau of Public Administration of the University of Alabama."[76] The volume by Vance and Blackwell, *New Farm Homes for Old*, already mentioned, was also a part of the same project.

James W. Fesler, who had taken his doctorate at Harvard in public administration in 1935 and had joined the Department of Political Science at the University of North Carolina about the same time, also became involved in the Alabama project. The University of Alabama Press published two of his reports for the Bureau of Public Administration.[77] In 1948, as a senior member of the Institute staff, he was writing about public administration in a democracy and directing two research assistants: Jonathan Marshall, in a study of interstate regional planning involving the Colorado River Compact, and Mary S. Albert, in a study of intergovernmental relations in agricultural planning.[78] When Fesler left the University in 1949 to chair the Department of Political Science at Yale University, the Institute's Board of Governors felt his leaving was a great loss to the Institute and to the University.

Blackwell had not given up Odum's or his own plans to develop the field of public administration. In 1946, while discussing plans to set up the Department of City and Regional Planning, Blackwell had written to Chancellor House, "It is clearly understood by all that the curriculum will be part of the projected program for training in public administration."[79] By this time Fesler had been directing research in public administration for almost ten years, but Blackwell saw the new Department of City and Regional Planning as another approach to practical training in the field. Fesler's place in the Institute was filled by the appointment in 1951 of Frederic N. Cleaveland as research associate in public administration. With the arrival of Alexander Heard and the organization of the Political Behavior Committee, Cleaveland at once became a productive member of the group, and later served as chairman of the committee.[80] One of his best-known publications is *Science and State Government*, published in 1959.

In 1966, with the cooperation of Donald B. Hayman, a professor in the Institute of Government, Cleaveland established the two-year graduate program in public administration known as the Master of

Public Administration Program, which is designed to train students for leadership and management in public service. The program is offered by the Department of Political Science in cooperation with the Institute of Government. From the beginning, several professors teaching in the program have been affiliated with the Institute for Research in Social Science. After almost thirty-five years, Odum's dream of a well-defined program in public administration had been realized, and it had been achieved in part through the efforts of the Institute of Government.

The Comparative State Elections Project

The establishment of the Political Studies Program and the master's degree program in public administration within the Department of Political Science were only two of the significant developments related to the interests of the Political Behavior Committee. Another was the support of a continuing research program in the political process. One of the recommendations of the ad hoc committee appointed in 1966 to study the function of the Institute was the continuation of interdisciplinary research with "a program of studies of the place of science and technology in the contemporary political and intellectual scene."[81] After James W. Prothro, professor in the Department of Political Science, was appointed director of the Institute in 1967, comprehensive study of political behavior continued to flourish.

As Prothro became director, the Institute received a major grant from the Ford Foundation for a study of national elections through statewide electoral analyses. The grant was to run for three years, with Prothro serving as project director and David M. Kovenock as study director. Kovenock had come to the Institute staff for this purpose in June 1968 from the Department of Political Science at Dartmouth College. The project called for an examination of thirteen states.[82] It was the first major study to examine in detail the question of whether political behavior in state elections tended to have an impact on the vote for the presidency. It was hoped that the interview schedule could be designed to point up topics influencing American public opinion, voting behavior, and party politics at the state and national levels, since analyses of these topics might determine whether state and local issues did in fact influence the vote for president.

State election analysts, who were university professors trained primarily in political science, met in Chapel Hill in April 1968 for a two-day session to assist in designing the research. The field interviewing was to be done by Louis Harris Associates and the data was to be published in three volumes: an election data book, an analysis of the elections in the thirteen states, and an analysis organized around theoretical concerns.[83] The field interviews were completed during the academic year of 1968–69, and the thirteen state election analysts were in Chapel Hill during the following summer analyzing data and writing monographs to be included in the published research. In 1970 the Ford Foundation gave an additional grant for completion of the study. Prothro's annual report for 1972–73 announced that the first volume would be ready for publication the following year as a three-part monograph entitled "Explaining the Vote: Presidential Choices in the Nation and States, 1968." The project also had in preparation three additional monographs that varied somewhat from the original plan: "a comparative analysis of voting for President, Governor, and U.S. Senator; a study of ethnicity and political behavior; and a databook on political attitudes in the nation and the states." In the meantime the project's data files had been shared with several dozen scholars at other institutions; they were released publicly in 1974 by the Institute's Social Science Data Library. In 1971–72 the Center for Political Studies of the Institute for Social Research at the University of Michigan invited the project personnel of the Institute at Chapel Hill to collaborate in drawing up the design and performing the analytical work for a study of the 1972 election.[84] David M. Kovenock continued as a research director for the Comparative State Elections Project and in 1972–73 was the principal director with Philip L. Beardsley of a project on public opinion and national priorities.

By 1974 two parts of the three-part study on explaining the vote had been published by the Institute under the authorship of Kovenock, Prothro, and their associates. The Institute had also published two other volumes of the Comparative State Elections Project, one on political attitudes, by Merle Black, David M. Kovenock, and William C. Reynolds, and another on electoral choice, by Gerald C. Wright, Jr.[85]

The Southeastern Regional Surveys

The studies for the Comparative State Elections Project were only a part of the Institute's program related to "the place of science and technology in the contemporary political and intellectual scene'' envisioned by the ad hoc committee of 1966. In 1967, when the University received the National Science Foundation grant ''for support to achieve an academic center of excellence in science,'' a portion of the grant was ''for the use of the Institute for adding computer facilities, computer personnel, and the establishment of a Southeastern regional survey unit.''[86] With these new funds and the much-needed new computer facilities provided by the grant, the Institute was ready to undertake the programmatic emphases suggested by the ad hoc committee in 1966. The use of the new funds for computer facilities will be discussed later.

The director of the Institute appointed a steering committee composed of representatives from the Institute and the Departments of Political Science and Sociology to discuss and erect a theoretically significant design for the proposed Southeastern Regional Survey. The first decision was to subdivide the research into three surveys that would be carefully constructed, and the second decision was that each survey should focus on a different aspect of the broad problem of social, political, and economic development. Since data on trends could not emerge in the short three-year span of the grant, it was decided that each survey would have a different focus and that together they would ''constitute a coherent body of work and establish base lines for future surveys.''[87]

Southeastern Regional Survey I began in the fall of 1968 with professors Thad L. Beyle and Robert G. Lehnen of the Department of Political Science as codirectors. It focused upon developmental patterns in five southeastern states in the areas of socioeconomic patterns, institutional government, politics, and policy, with the aim of relating these developmental patterns to attitudinal patterns at both the mass and elite levels. By the time of the next annual report of the Institute (1968–69) the survey was being called ''an omnibus public opinion study of three major problem areas: (1) the degree and range of contact of a typical citizen with governmental authority; (2) the structure of cognitive and affective dispositions of these citizens regarding governmental authorities; and (3) the relationship of a citizen's policy preferences to forms of political behavior.''[88] The survey employed the services of Louis Harris and Associates to conduct a one-hour interview with 1,500 adult Americans in March 1969. The sample was stratified by economic regions and racial composition to allow comparisons of attitudinal and behavioral variables between economic regions in the

South, the Atlantic Metropolitan Area, the Great Lakes–Northeast, the Midwest, and the West.

Some of the findings of Survey I were published in 1972 in *The American Governor in Behavioral Perspective*, edited by Thad L. Beyle and J. Oliver Williams. Among those in the Institute who contributed to the volume were Beyle, Lehnen, and Deil S. Wright. The chapters dealt with governors and bureaucrats, planning and governmental activity, gubernatorial transition in a one-party setting, public views of state governors, the intergovernmental system, and executive leadership in state administration. In 1976 the most definitive use of the survey data appeared in *American Institutions, Political Opinion, and Public Politics*, written by Robert G. Lehnen, who had been codirector of the survey with Thad Beyle.

Southeastern Regional Survey II began field operations in the fall of 1969 under the direction of Bruce K. Eckland of the Department of Sociology. It was a follow-up of 5,200 high school students in 44 schools that had participated in a survey conducted by the Educational Testing Service in 1955. That study, called "A National Study of High School Students and Their Plans," had surveyed 40,000 high school students. Eckland's survey in 1969 had four primary objectives:

> (1) to document and identify factors related to the flow of talent in and out of the Southeast and other regions of the U.S.;
> (2) to investigate the sources of variation in educational and occupational achievement of a representative sample of young adults who in 1955 were sophomores in the nation's public schools; (3) to provide national norms on former public school boys against which to compare data recently obtained from the alumni of a large private boy's school; (4) to provide a large body of social, demographic, and psychological data for several ancillary studies, of which the most important is an investigation of the status of American women.[89]

After a year of field work, Survey II had collected follow-up data on approximately 3,000 men and women comprising a representative sample of those who had participated in the study in 1955, and the foci of the survey had been narrowed to "(1) sources of variation in achievement in the transition from school to work and (2) the relationship between fertility, blocked mobility, and the status of American women."[90] The project was now frequently referred to as the Exploration of Equal Opportunity Study. With additional funding from the United States Office of Education and the National Institute of Mental Health, analysis of the data was under way during 1971–72. In 1973, with the assistance of Karl Alexander, Eckland completed the report on the first focus of the survey, and it was published by the National Institute of Education as *Effects of Education on the Social Mobility of High School Sophomores Fifteen Years Later.* At the same time, Eckland was continuing to examine "explorations in equality of opportunity" that related to the aspects of the survey dealing with the status of women. The results of that research were published in 1978 as *Wives and Workers*, which was written in collaboration with Karl Alexander, Pamela Cain, and David Gibson.

Southeastern Regional Survey III, financed with funds from the National Science Foundation, focused on North Carolina. It was supervised by Angell G. Beza, director of research services in the Institute. Field work began in 1970. The survey was designed as a general household sample of North Carolina. The sample as planned consisted of 1,200 households stratified by regions (mountains, northern Piedmont, southern Piedmont, northern coastal plain, and southeastern coastal plain) and size of population.[91] Interviewers were recruited by faculty members from Appalachian State University at Boone, the University of North Carolina at Asheville, the University of North Carolina at Charlotte, East Carolina University at Greenville, and the University of North Carolina at Wilmington. The survey had four sections: social indicators, a poll of current issues, a pilot study, and a general section open to questions from all Institute faculty members and from the survey staff.[92] Beza directed the section dealing with social indicators, and Gordon B. Cleveland and Earle Wallace of the Department of Political Science supervised the North Carolina poll on current issues. The pilot study concerned the white southerner as a cultural minority and was directed by Glen H. Elder, Jr., and John Shelton Reed, Jr., of the Department of Sociology.

Survey III pioneered in drawing a sample by using the 1970 Census of Population and Housing on computer tape.[93] The sample and the interviewing staff were used by three other studies being undertaken by government-related agencies: a survey of crime victimization sponsored by the Governor's Commission on Law and Order, a study of social indicators of the aged sponsored by the Governor's Commission on Aging, and a survey of outdoor recreation sponsored by the State Planning Division of the North Carolina Department of Administration. The data from these three studies were made available for faculty and student use through the Social Science Data Library of the Institute, while the data from the survey of North Carolina was presented through a series of reports published in the Institute's *News Letter*. The raw data were made available for use by faculty and students on the campuses of the University of North Carolina at Chapel Hill, Asheville, Charlotte, and Wilmington, and also Appalachian State University and East Carolina University.

The Social Science Statistical Laboratory

The largest share of funds to the Institute from the National Science Foundation grant of 1967 had not gone to the Southeastern Regional Survey but rather went to upgrade the facilities of the Social Science Statistical Laboratory. It has previously been mentioned that the Social Science Statistical Laboratory began in embryonic stage about 1930 with the appointment of T. J. Woofter, Jr., as social statistician on the Institute staff. The Institute's first investment in computing machinery was the purchase of a manual adding machine, which rested on a table in Woofter's office. Additional but meager equipment was added as the regional studies developed in the 1930s and early 1940s. In 1945 Howard Odum pointed out in his summary of the development of regionalism the importance to research of such a facility as the one in the Institute with its automatic machines and calculators.[94]

In 1950, six years after becoming director of the Institute, Gordon Blackwell worked out a joint arrangement with the Institute of Statistics[95] and the Institute for Research in Social Science for the establishment of the Social Science Statistical Laboratory. After the laboratory had been in operation for a year he outlined in his annual report to the chancellor the functions of the agency:

(1) to advise on all phases of quantitative methodology, using consultation from staff in the Institute of Statistics; (2) to provide editing, coding and computing services; (3) to serve in a liaison capacity with the sorting and tabulating units of the Institute of Statistics at State College; (4) to conduct research designed to develop and test new quantitative concepts and techniques. . . . The Laboratory assisted on several projects and gave consultation to eight social scientists in the University dur-

ing the year. Expanded staff and increased operations are anticipated for next year. At present, the Laboratory is developing a
method for using punched cards in Guttman's scale analysis.[96]

In 1952 Blackwell proposed the establishment of a "Sample Survey
Research Division" in the Institute that would include making opinion
polls, but it was not until 1954 that the Survey Operations Unit was
made the joint responsibility of the Institute of Statistics and the Institute for Research in Social Science. It was supervised by an administrative committee of four, two from each institute, and it was directed
by John Monroe, a statistician, with the part-time assistance of Stacy
Adams, a social psychologist. The unit operated on a self-sustaining
basis with funds administered through the Chapel Hill section of the
Institute of Statistics, of which George E. Nicholson, Jr., had become
director. During 1956–57 the unit conducted four separate contract
studies, including a study of bus riders for the Norfolk, Virginia,
Public Relations Institute and a study of smoking habits for the American Tobacco Company, as well as having planned an omnibus survey
of a random sample of North Carolina households.[97] Funds for operation of the survey unit undoubtedly decreased, and the following year
the Institute was exploring the possibility of transferring the work
to the Research Triangle.[98] It was not until the National Science Foundation grant became available in 1967 that the Statistical Laboratory
was able to give significant help with survey operations and opinion
polls.

By 1955 Daniel O. Price had replaced John Monroe as director of
the Statistical Laboratory, and George E. Nicholson, Jr., was serving
as associate director. During 1955–56, the laboratory provided services
to eighteen projects, including a study of fertility in Puerto Rico,
which was under the direction of Reuben Hill; a University of Alabama
project on training dentists; and data collection and computing services
for the North Carolina Board of Higher Education.[99] By 1957 Price
had become director of the Institute, and the laboratory services were
carried on by Josef Perry, a graduate student.

In 1959 the Statistical Laboratory was confronted with a challenge
in "the forthcoming installation of the Remington Rand 1105 Electronic Computer" in Phillips Hall, the home of the Department of
Mathematics and the Institute of Statistics, which was being enlarged
to accommodate the multi-ton machine. Price did not see the huge
electronic computer as a threat to his small punchcard operation, but

rather as a potential area of development for the Statistical Laboratory. He wrote in his annual report for 1958–59 that

> because of the complexity of social science data, we feel that social scientists must learn how to adequately use electronic computers in their research. The large number of variables involved in determining social behavior and the difficulties of manipulating these variables by ordinary methods exert pressure on social scientists to utilize machines that can handle large numbers of variables with facility. Also social scientists are beginning to see some of the possibilities of using these computers in new ways to do things not previously possible. The main development in this area has been in the simulation of social situations. If social scientists are able to simulate a social situation with reasonable accuracy, then we have set up a pseudo-experimental situation and the sort of situation from which future behavior can be projected.[100]

The installation of a computer on campus, the cooperative attitude of the computer staff, the presence of people from the Bureau of the Census working with the computer, and the presence of basic data tapes from the Bureau of the Census opened up, Price thought, an unusual opportunity for the outstanding group of social scientists in the Institute. He regretted, however, that "at the present time we are unable to grasp the opportunity presented by this combination of factors," but he did state that "we are making plans to develop these opportunities at the earliest possible date in conjunction with an expanded program of methodological training and training in the field of demography."[101]

By January 1960 the Institute's Social Science Statistical Laboratory had added three IBM data processing machines, and this new equipment led, in turn, to an increased use of the laboratory—3,500 hours in all during the academic year 1960–61. The laboratory had quickly become an educational resource for graduate training in research methods in the Departments of Political Science, City and Regional Planning, and Sociology and Anthropology, and by researchers in the University's Division of Health Affairs. The object of the laboratory had been to operate on a self-supporting basis without making a profit, but Price hoped that the next year would "bring an allocation of University funds to aid in support of this facility." By the close of the academic year 1962–63, the laboratory was serving faculty and graduate students in sociology, political science, statistics, business administration, psychology, journalism, education, medicine, public health, and dentistry. Angell G. Beza was also appointed during this year as full-time supervisor of the Statistical Laboratory.[102] From this position Beza rose to director of research services in the Statistical Laboratory and later became associate director of the Institute. By 1965 the functions of the Statistical Laboratory had expanded to include research design, data analysis, data management, and education.

The ad hoc committee appointed in 1966 to evaluate the function of the Institute included in its recommendations that (1) provisions be made for the development of a computer programming staff, (2) funds for computer time be allocated to the senior staff of the Institute just as research assistants are allocated, (3) funds be budgeted for a computer terminal device, and (4) continued maintenance be provided for the existing card-processing facilities for small-scale research. The committee concluded, "We feel that to continue its data-processing assistance to faculty members, the Institute needs to devote more of its resources to the provision of computer programming assistance and equipment. . . . Computer time is now as essential to Institute research as research assistants were when they were first provided through state funds."[103]

Therefore, when the National Science Foundation awarded the University nearly $5 million in 1967 for the creation of "a center of excellence in science," most of the funds allocated to the Institute went for the purchase of computer facilities and the employment of computer personnel. In his annual report for 1967–68, James W. Prothro, who had recently been appointed director of the Institute, summarized the work under way to develop the Statistical Laboratory into a center of excellence:

> During the year, plans were completed for the acquisition of an IBM 1130, which will provide both an in-house computer capability and a terminal linked with the IBM 360/75 computer at the Triangle Computation Center in the Research Triangle. The financing for this equipment, through NSF funds, involved cooperation between the Institute and the Departments of Political Science and Sociology.
> . . . The Institute has provided student instruction in the use of unit-record equipment for many years; it will provide instruction in computer usage when the computer is installed.[104]

The laboratory offered a short course in computer programming during the year, and ninety-nine faculty members signed up for the sessions. About thirty faculty members requested assistance in some phase of their research and four hundred students used the services of the laboratory. It was during this year that Angell Beza became director of research services, a position whose primary concern was providing assistance to faculty and students in the collection of data (study design, questionnaire and interview schedule construction, and sampling) and in the research use of the statistical data that the Institute received from the Bureau of the Census. Peter Harkins, whose academic training was in political science, became director of the Statistical Laboratory. By the next year, the computer facilities and services had become fully operational.[105]

The laboratory expanded still further in 1971–72 through the replacement of the IBM 1130 computer by an IBM 1403 high speed printer, a card-read-out punch, and a control unit. This hardware was connected to the University Computer Center in Phillips Hall by way of a cable and two-channel stretcher and through that facility to the Triangle Universities Computation Center. These changes made it possible to double the "maximum throughput" of the former equipment.

In 1970–71, the Student Data Processing Assistance Service was organized to emphasize further the Institute's long-standing role of training students in data analysis and use of data processing equipment. Kenneth A. Hardy, a graduate student in sociology, was appointed part-time director. This service became the Educational Services Unit of the Social Science Statistical Laboratory in 1971–72, and Hardy was appointed to succeed Peter Harkins as director of the laboratory. The merger of Educational Services with the Statistical Laboratory increased the number of users of the laboratory facilities, and the noncredit instruction by Institute staff continued to expand. Another function of the Educational Services Unit was to develop data files for instructional use and to assist faculty in introducing that material in their courses. The provost and an ad hoc committee reviewed this service in the spring semester of 1972 and concluded that "these educational services were of major assistance to the departmental teaching programs and . . . without them, costly duplication of efforts by the departments and less efficient services would result."[106]

In 1972–73 the Educational Services Unit again expanded its assistance to students and faculty by providing in-class instruction to approximately 750 undergraduates in courses in sociology, economics, and political science and to graduate classes in economics, history, journalism, library science, political science, sociology, and social work. The result of this training was that more users of the laboratory's computer terminal were becoming self-sufficient. To increase its training role and at the same time provide better services to its users, the laboratory also obtained hardware facilities that provided a fast turnaround arrangement with the University Computation Center, which speeded the completion of research tasks. The laboratory acquired three teletypewriters and a graphics cathode ray display terminal. The programming staff also developed improved programs for data editing and reformatting, produced user-oriented documentation for frequently used programs, and prepared a series of short memoranda entitled "Programmer's Aides."

Educational services continued to be a unit of the Social Science Statistical Laboratory until 1974–75, when it was made a separate division of the Institute. Ellen S. Vasu, whose doctoral work was done at Southern Illinois University, joined the Institute staff as director of the division in July 1974, with a joint appointment in the Department of Psychology.

The Social Science Data Library

The proposal that led to the National Science Foundation grant for a "center of excellence" also envisioned the creation within the Institute of a social science data center. In stating the case for the grant the proposal had said:

> A major means of research facilitation in the coming years
> will be the Institute for Research in Social Science Statistical
> Laboratory and Data Center. . . . The Data Center will combine
> in one location, adjacent to the Statistical Laboratory, the
> Yale Human Relations Area Files; the Louis D. Harris Political
> Data Center...a North Carolina county and city data bank
> including continuous series of demographic, political, and
> other detailed data; data from various faculty research projects;
> and all data gathered through the Southeastern Regional
> Survey. . . .[107]

When funds became available in 1969 for the employment of a director of the proposed data center, Richard C. Rockwell, who had been a student of Daniel O. Price at the University of Texas and had recently completed his doctorate in sociology there, joined the staff of the Institute as director of data libraries, with a joint appointment in the Department of Sociology. The data center, later formally named the Social Science Data Library, had access through the Louis D. Harris Political Data Center to a membership in the Inter-University Consortium for Political Research as well as to the survey data of Louis Harris and Associates. During 1969 the Statistical Laboratory also obtained membership in the Roper Center's association of colleges and universities known as the International Survey Association. The membership was financed by the Department of Sociology out of National Science Foundation funds and by the School of Journalism from Journalism Foundation funds.

In October 1970, when the Institute moved from Alumni Hall to Manning Hall, the Harris Political Data Center was moved from Caldwell Hall, where it had been housed since coming to the University, and the Human Relations Area Files were moved from the Louis Round Wilson Library, and they were incorporated into the Social Science Data Library. With a grant from Wilson Library and the State Library in Raleigh, the Data Library purchased the 1970 Census tapes, and through a much larger grant from the North Carolina Department of Administration it established the Census Data Service from the vast files of Census data available only on computer-readable magnetic tape. The Census Data Service provides information to state and local government officials as well as to the faculty and students of the University.

In 1971–72 the Data Library acquired the DATA-TEXT programming system from Harvard University, which could process multipunched data far more effectively than systems previously in use at Chapel Hill. Another significant development in the Data Library during the year was the creation of a system that permitted the location of needed data with greater ease. Throughout the country the speedy location of materials in data libraries was then at a "primitive level." "We anticipate," wrote Prothro, "that this system or a variant of it will become the national standard for data libraries."[108]

By 1972–73 Rockwell had prepared "An Introduction to the DATA-TEXT System," a user's manual for the new system, which had been installed in July 1972. The new system was soon in daily use by researchers in the area through the Triangle Universities Computation Center. The data librarian, Sue Dodd, compiled an annotated list of data holdings that ran to some three hundred pages, and supervised the completion of an integrated file of technical characteristics of data sets. By working with the Research Triangle Institute and Duke University, "so that the massive data base could be acquired and duplication avoided," the Data Library had almost completed the Census data base, and the Institute's annual report for the year stated that use of that data base was at a high rate—for example, "2,231 jobs were run using one program library on the Census data base between April 30, 1972, and June 20, 1973."[109]

In 1974 Elizabeth M. Fischer, who had received her doctorate at the University of Michigan, was appointed associate director of the Social Science Data Library, with a joint appointment in the Department of Sociology. She became director of the library in 1976–77, when Richard C. Rockwell, who had come to the library as director in 1969, left to become a visiting fellow at the Boys Town Center for Study of Youth Development in Omaha.

From the establishment of the Social Science Statistical Laboratory in 1950 through the administrations of Daniel O. Price and James W. Prothro, both of whom expanded its services, the functions of the laboratory developed so rapidly that they eventually became separate divisions within the Institute structure. By 1974–75 these divisions were the Social Science Statistical Laboratory, under the direction of Kenneth A. Hardy; Research Services, directed by Angell G. Beza; the Social Science Data Library, directed by Richard A. Rockwell and Elizabeth M. Fischer; and Educational Services, directed by Ellen S. Vasu.

In 1954 the Behavioral Science Survey had recommended that the Institute concentrate its major research on a limited number of areas in the behavioral sciences. While the Institute attempted to do so, the varied interests of its faculty affiliates made such concentration inadvisable. Nevertheless, work went forward on four recommended areas that were already under investigation at the time of the survey, and significant developments in theory and methodology were achieved in those focal programs. The Organization Research Group refined theory in complex organization and small group research. The Political Behavior Committee expanded its research to spin off two distinct programs in the Department of Political Science: the Master of Public Administration Program and the Political Studies Program.

These contributions to social theory and these developments of innovative techniques of research made between 1950 and 1974 came partly as the result of two major self-examination surveys undertaken by the University of North Carolina. They were, as outlined in this chapter, the Behavioral Science Survey in 1953–54 and the Proposal for a Center of Excellence in Science in 1966. In addition to the research discussed in this chapter, other focal areas of behavioral science research undertaken during this period in the Institute for Research in Social Science have yet to be examined. These additional areas include urban studies, the social science aspects of health, community health, world areas, mass communication, and related areas such as methodology and education.

Urban, Health, and Other Studies

By 1970 the Institute was rapidly becoming "a center of excellence in science." The expansion of the facilities and the services that grew from the work of the Social Science Statistical Laboratory had been a major factor in the development of such a center, and the work of the Organization Research Group and the Political Behavior Committee had likewise played an important role. The Urban Studies Committee, research in the social science aspects of health, and research in community health likewise added their share, as did research in two other focal areas recommended by the Behavioral Science Survey—world areas, and communication in the mass media. Outside the focal areas, research in other fields, among them the social aspects of education, theory, and methodology, also increased the prestige of the Institute as a research agency.

The Urban Studies Committee

The Urban Studies Committee, which initiated the Urban Studies Program, was established in the Institute in 1953.[1] At first the committee was composed of four members, three in city planning and one in public administration. Later an economist, a second political scientist, and a sociologist joined the group. At the time almost no theoretical framework of urbanization had been developed and most research in the field had been case studies. The Institute committee, therefore, attempted to relate the interests of each member to a "value-behavior-outcomes" approach to urban processes. In this way a clear pattern of common interests in four or five major areas of investigation began to emerge.

Previous Institute research in the general field of urbanism and demography had already been undertaken—for example, the southern community studies in anthropology directed by John Gillin; Vance's *All These People*; the study of Atlanta by Ivey, Demerath, and Breland; the study of the urban South by Vance and Demerath; Hunter's examination of power structure in Atlanta; and some thirty-five case studies of cities undertaken in the training program of the Department of City and Regional Planning.

The first substantial funding for urban studies came in July 1951 when the Institute received several contract research grants: the United States Air Force contract for a study of daytime and nighttime distribution of population in selected domestic industrial cities and for a study of foreign city planning, and a contract with the Housing and Home Finance Agency and a grant-in-aid from the United States Public Health Service for a study of the impact of the Savannah River industrial development project of the Atomic Energy Commission.[2] The Savannah River Project was directed by F. Stuart Chapin, Jr., an associate professor in the Department of City and Regional Planning, who in 1949 had been appointed a research associate in the Institute. Chapin had a master's degree in planning from the Massachusetts Institute of Technology and research experience with the Tennessee Valley Authority, and before joining the Department of City and Regional Planning he had been city planner of Greensboro, North Carolina.[3] The Savannah River Project, first suggested by an Institute research assistant, continued from 1951 to 1953, and the final report, "In the Shadow of a Defense Plant: A Study of Urbanization in Rural South Carolina," was written by Chapin, Alfred M. Denton, Jr., John C. Gould, and Theodore W. Wirths. These four researchers also prepared an interim report for the Housing and Home Finance Agency, "Development of Guides for Urbanization in Rural Areas Affected by Building of Large Industrial Plants."

Building on its report on urban processes for the Behavioral Science Survey of 1953–54, the Urban Studies Committee established a fortnightly seminar that over a two-year period explored selected areas within the values-behavior-outcomes framework. By 1956 the committee consisted of thirteen senior Institute staff members from the fields of anthropology, city and regional planning, economics, law, political science, psychology, and sociology. Six graduate students also served on the committee as research assistants. During the year the committee emphasized three kinds of activities: (1) initiation of research by individual members of the committee within the theoretical framework that had been developed, (2) continuation of faculty seminars to review research in progress, and (3) continued development of plans for a long-range program of research in urban studies.[4]

The Urban Studies Program

The long-range plan came to realization in April 1957 with a five-year grant of $1 million from the Ford Foundation, and Chapin became director of the program. The project was designed in three parts: the first and most significant concerned research and graduate training in the Piedmont Urban Crescent; the second, the advancement of communications between universities in the South engaged in urban research, was to be handled by the Institute under the direction of Frederic N. Cleaveland; and the third, research interpretation for local action groups, was to be the responsibility of George H. Esser, Jr., in the Institute of Government. The program opened in the academic year of 1957–58 with sixteen staff members at the faculty level, eleven research assistants, and three secretaries. It was housed in parts of three separate buildings, but the following year it obtained Evergreen House in the central campus area, where one portion of the program continues to this day.

As early as 1932 in his *Human Geography of the South*, Rupert B. Vance had defined as the Piedmont Industrial Crescent a region extending along the railroad and major highway system through the Piedmont between Washington and Atlanta. The Urban Studies Program was concerned with a portion of this area between Raleigh, North Carolina, and Greenville, South Carolina, which it called the Piedmont Urban Crescent. The central theme of the study was urban development. The areas to be examined were "the economic growth potential of the Crescent, the political and institutional factors affecting this growth, the problems this growth portends and the alternatives open to the area in solving these problems." The project areas were:

1. Economic Studies of the Piedmont Crescent.
2. Leadership Patterns and Community Decision-Making in Cities of the Piedmont Crescent.
3. Power Structure Studies of the Piedmont Crescent and the Intercity and Intracity Aspects of Interaction.
4. Newcomers to Urban Centers: Why They Move and Their Socio-Political Enculturation in the City.
5. Role of the Planner in Urban Development of the Piedmont Crescent.
6. Livability Qualities of Urban Development in the Piedmont Crescent.

7. Metropolitan Development Problems in the Piedmont Crescent and Alternative Approaches to Their Solution.[5]

During the first year of the program, baseline statistical descriptions of the four principal city-clusters in the Crescent were completed and five North Carolina cities (Greensboro, High Point, Lexington, Thomasville, and Winston-Salem) were chosen as test demonstration areas where more detailed studies of economic, population, and land development characteristics were made.[6]

The first year of operation also saw the development of a graduate training program focusing on both degree and course offerings. An apprentice system of research training in urban studies was developed, in which the research assistant worked under close supervision of the faculty on a particular study related to one of the project areas. As he progressed in skills a part of the project area was assigned to the student as his own responsibility, and finally the student usually prepared his report in the form of a thesis or dissertation for which he received a degree. The Graduate School accepted the doctoral program in the Department of City and Regional Planning in the fall of 1961 largely as an outgrowth of research and training resources of the Urban Studies Program. By the close of the fifth year of the Ford Foundation grant, twenty-six master's theses and four doctoral dissertations had been completed.[7]

As the program developed, the project areas were expanded from seven to fifteen and involved twenty faculty members, mainly in city and regional planning, economics, political science, sociology, and anthropology. The laboratory locale was the Piedmont Urban Crescent, which consisted of twelve North Carolina counties, extending from Wake on the east to Mecklenberg and Gaston in the southwest, and four South Carolina counties, extending from York County to Greenville County. The projects were grouped into four general study areas:

(1) one relating to the growth potential of the Crescent cities as a cluster of centers in an urbanizing region and particularly the economic variables affecting the growth outlook; (2) another relating to the leadership in this region—corporate, governmental and civic—and the political behavior of leader groups on urban issues and problems; (3) a third on the attitudes of people living in cities in this region with respect to various aspects of urban growth, their perception of problems, and their participation in political action aimed at solving problems; and (4) an

investigation of the physical extent of growth and an analysis of key factors which appear to influence the direction and intensity in which cities grow and spill out into the countryside.[8]

During the last two years of the Ford Foundation grant, the funds were sufficient to make the baseline studies of the Piedmont Crescent. Additional income became available through state funds, other grants, and contracts to develop other areas that were identified in the program supported by the grant from the Ford Foundation.[9]

As the fifth year of the Ford grant came to a close, the Urban Studies Program began work on additional aspects of the training and informational phases of the program. From the time of its organization, the Urban Studies Committee had conducted interdisciplinary group meetings and held box-luncheon discussion sessions in an effort to formulate a conceptual framework of the urban process. These group sessions developed into experimental seminars and into the Urban Studies Colloquium. In 1960–61 a six-member faculty steering committee and four research assistants laid plans for a formal interdisciplinary seminar to be held the following year on the subject "Control Processes and Urban Development." Research participants had already begun to publish articles in the area of their inquiries, and in 1960 the Urban Studies Program began publication of the series Urban Studies Research Papers.[10] In December 1962 these studies were summarized in a volume entitled *Urban Growth Dynamics in a Regional Cluster of Cities*, edited by F. Stuart Chapin, Jr., and Shirley F. Weiss, which contained chapters prepared by their associates.[11] Reviewing the book for *Social Forces*, Hope T. Eldridge of the University of Pennsylvania said of the symposium, "It is from studies of this sort that we may hope eventually to find the keys to both classification and prediction." The work "ends by rewarding the reader, not only with considerable knowledge about the area under analysis, but also with a sense of new understanding and sharpened insight into the urban process."[12]

At intervals during the five-year research period, the southern regional phase of the Urban Studies Program under the direction of Frederic Cleaveland sponsored a series of research meetings throughout the South that were attended by social science faculty with an interest in urban research. The faculty members were brought together in small meetings to discuss their own work and research in progress in the field. The meetings usually culminated in an interdisciplinary summer seminar on urban research held in Chapel Hill.[13]

The Urban Studies Program as laid out in 1957–58 required more than the projected five years and extended into a sixth. At the conclusion of the research program in 1962, the Institute for Research in Social Science created the Center for Urban and Regional Studies. F. Stuart Chapin, Jr., was appointed director and Shirley F. Weiss became associate director.

The Center for Urban and Regional Studies

The Center for Urban and Regional Studies was an extension of the original Urban Studies Committee and an outgrowth of the Urban Studies Program. As the Center began its work late in 1962, research continued in the project areas that had been studied during the earlier period. A series of in-depth investigations that emphasized theoretical research began on "methodological problems of describing in measured and systematic form the growth of urban centers and in exploring theoretical issues in modeling growth processes."[14]

The Center continued, as the Urban Studies Program had previously, to stress research and research interpretation through seminars and special sessions with visiting scholars. It also continued its training program but no longer directed the research of students working toward graduate degrees because of the expiration of the Ford Foundation grant that had made this phase of the program possible.[15] As in other Institute programs, the Center performed its functions with a staff made up of faculty who had appointments as senior members of the Institute and graduate research assistants from social science departments who had affiliation with the Institute as research assistants. In addition, the Center employed student assistants to work on an hourly basis at such tasks as computer programming, coding, mapping, and typing. In 1968–69, the Center staff consisted of twelve research professors and associates, eight research assistants, fourteen hourly assistants, and four secretaries. The budget for the year for eight research projects amounted to $380,530 derived from six sources, including the United States Public Health Service, the National Science Foundation, and the Ford Foundation.[16]

The Center also continued to regard the cities of the Piedmont Urban Crescent as its research laboratory, but as the work of the Urban Studies Program and later of the Center itself aroused both national and international inquiry, research activities expanded to other metropolitan areas and to cities as a whole. For example, during the academic year 1967–68, the Center was visited by two French delegations, specialists from three British university research centers, a group from Holland, and the rector of a West German university. This was the second year that a British social scientist had spent several weeks at the Center.[17]

The focus of research in 1969, the last year that the Center functioned as a division of the Institute, was on six studies: (1) residential development process and decisions, by Shirley F. Weiss, Edward J. Kaiser, and Randolph J. Burby, III; (2) new towns, also by Weiss, Kaiser, and Burby; (3) activity patterns in the black community, by F. Stuart Chapin, Jr., Edgar W. Butler, J. L. Robson, F. C. Patten, and Asta C. Cooper; (4) simulation of urban activity patterns, by George C. Hemmens; (5) household moving behavior and the choice of the place of residence, by Edward J. Kaiser, Edgar W. Butler, and Ronald J. McAllister; and (6) household activity patterns and community health, by F. Stuart Chapin, Jr., Philip G. Hammer, Jr., and L. A. Fischer.[18]

The study of residential development used the Greensboro–Winston-Salem, North Carolina, locale as a laboratory and used lake and reservoir areas throughout the Southeast for special analyses. The chief concern of the project was to follow residential land development decisions from original ownership through to the fully developed residential area. This step-by-step examination made it possible for the research team to evaluate the impact on residential areas of public works such as transportation, extension of sewer systems, and schools and also the effect of residential growth on public works programs. The team designed a series of three models to simulate predevelopment land transactions, the developers' location decisions, and household behavior in the decision to move and to select a place of residence.

This exploratory work led to a $1.1 million grant from the National Science Foundation to assess resident and local official attitudes toward living qualities in some fifteen new towns as compared with those of residents and officials in fifteen more conventional residential communities nearby. The study was an exploratory project on the evaluation of recent experience in the development of new towns to provide for urban growth. Again, this was an examination of the development process and the decisions leading to it rather than of the processes and decisions involved in extending existing urban centers. When this study was completed and published in 1976 as *New Communities*

U.S.A.,[19] it was hailed as "the most significant and comprehensive set of information ever collected on new communities in the United States" and as "enormously helpful" in making a better case for a national growth policy.[20]

The other four studies dealt with various aspects of household activity and behavior and represented some aspects of research that had been under way since 1963. Household behavior in the choice of a place to live was viewed as part of the "larger phenomenon of household moving behavior in cities." The Center therefore undertook a national survey into factors affecting household moves. In 1966 the National Academy of Science funded a national sampling study for the Center, to explore factors affecting civilian residential mobility. Later the National Science Foundation gave the Center a grant to recontact households falling within the 1966 sample, to determine the importance of availability of health and medical care facilities in past and proposed moves.

In 1964 Chapin began a new research program that emphasized household activity patterns. This work borrowed a time-and-motion technique from industrial management and used it to examine how and where different segments of a metropolitan population allocate time to their daily round of activities. A Community Health Service grant from the United States Public Health Service in 1965 made possible a comprehensive pretest in the Minneapolis–St. Paul metropolitan area. In 1968 a similar study was made of metropolitan Washington, D.C. The study was basically a time-budget analysis seeking to identify activity patterns of members of urban households during a typical weekday and a weekend day. This analysis supplied among other data the use of medical, recreational, and other local facilities. The study was also designed to fit into the other urban studies on residential mobility and household behavior.

The study on activity patterns in the black community, begun in 1968–69 under a grant from the Ford Foundation, used the same survey methods as the other household studies, to which it added "participant observation methods." The focus of the study was to determine the daily activity patterns of family and teenage groups in the ghetto neighborhood. By comparing living patterns in the ghetto with those in the suburbs, the study hoped to pinpoint problems that could be expected to occur in open neighborhoods and to determine how these problems might be minimized.[21] In a complementary study undertaken in 1971 under a grant from the National Institute of Mental

Health, another participant observation and survey project focused on a low-income white community in the process of decline. Field experiences from the study of the black community were published in *Hard Living on Clay Street* (1973), by Joseph T. Howell, and the survey analysis of the white community appeared in *Across the City Line: A White Community in Transition* (1974), by Chapin and R. B. Zehner. The series of studies in this ten-year research program were published in Chapin's *Human Activity Patterns in the City: What People Do in Time and Space* (1974).

As a part of the project on activity patterns, George C. Hemmens, who is now chairman of the Department of City and Regional Planning, undertook to develop techniques for simulation of urban activity patterns. Using transportation survey data from Buffalo, New York, and constructing activity sequences from travel patterns, he built tools for simulation of urban behavior. By testing hypotheses about the relationship of socioeconomic characteristics of households and their daily activity patterns, his aim was "to use the simulation technique in an experimental fashion to test hypotheses about the interplay between household activity patterns and the urban environment."[22]

As the Center's projects developed, the staff were able from time to time to report their preliminary findings at professional meetings, to contribute chapters to books on urban development, and to prepare urban studies monographs that were then published by the Center. In 1969, the last year of its affiliation with the Institute, the staff from the Center published seventeen papers of this nature.[23] In roughly a twenty-year period ending in 1976, research projects of the Urban Studies Program had appeared in twelve books brought out by commercial publishers and in about fifty monographs published by the Center for Urban and Regional Studies.

The Center for Urban and Regional Studies as an Independent Agency

In 1969 the North Carolina General Assembly passed legislation authorizing a program in urban affairs for the Consolidated University of North Carolina and provided funds for its establishment. The program was to be operated through the Office of the Vice President for Research and Public Service and provided for an office staff in urban affairs at the University of North Carolina at Charlotte, North Carolina

State University at Raleigh, and the University of North Carolina at Chapel Hill. This legislation made possible the permanent staff and central office that the Center for Urban and Regional Studies had long felt to be one of its important needs and enabled it to become an independent research center separate from the Institute for Research in Social Science. A cordial relationship, however, continued to exist between the two University-related agencies. Senior staff in the Center might also have an affiliation as senior research members of the Institute. In 1973–74, for example, three staff members from the Center were also members of the Institute research faculty: Raymond J. Burby III, Francis X. Mulvihill, and Robert B. Zehner.[24] Others who participated in Center activities, such as F. Stuart Chapin, Jr., Edward J. Kaiser, and Shirley F. Weiss, who were members of the faculty of the Department of City and Regional Planning, were also listed as senior research faculty in the Institute.

As soon as the Center acquired state funding, recruitment and hiring of five full-time staff members (three professional and two clerical positions) began, and the headquarters of the Center was located in Hickerson House adjacent to the central campus in Chapel Hill. The new director of the Center was Jonathan B. Howes, who came from Washington, D.C., where he had been director of the Urban Policy Center of the National Urban Coalition. David J. Brower was chosen as director of urban services. He came from Indiana University at Bloomington, where he had been assistant director of the Center for Urban Affairs. Francis X. Mulvihill, who was completing his doctoral work in sociology from Michigan State University, was appointed director of research interpretation. F. Stuart Chapin, Jr., who had recently been selected as Alumni Distinguished Professor of Planning in the Department of City and Regional Planning, continued as research director to see the household activities studies through to their completion. Two other former members of the original staff, Shirley F. Weiss and Edward J. Kaiser, were appointed associate research directors.

The research function of the Center was to continue as before, but with a major difference. The new state funds permitted the Center to determine its own research priorities "rather than having the research program dictated by the availability of funds" from contract research or funding by outside agencies. The new funds also permitted a communications and service program that the Center had long been contemplating. The service program would to some extent implement the research of the Center. "Opportunities for testing the research theories and models developed in the Center's research program,'' wrote Jonathan Howes in his first annual report, ''will be developed in cooperation with state agencies and local governments.''[25]

In October 1971, William C. Friday, president of the University of North Carolina system, appointed the Urban Studies Advisory Council, which was composed of forty leaders from state and local government, community groups, and the public at large who were concerned with urban problems in North Carolina. The associate vice-president for research and public service in the University system was appointed chairman of the council, which was given the function of coordinating the separate campus programs of urban studies. The budget authority for the programs, however, was transferred in 1972 from the president's office to the respective campuses.

Of the several program foci recommended to the Institute by the Behavioral Science Survey of 1953–54, the Urban Studies Committee is the only one that was able to expand its program and services into a division within the Institute that later became an independent agency supported by state funds. The Program of the Social Science Aspects of Health and the Health Professions, the fourth of the foci under discussion, became a separate function in the Division of Health Affairs just as public administration later became a distinct division in the Department of Political Science.

Research on Social Science Aspects of Health and the Health Professions

Even before Howard Odum had organized the Institute for Research in Social Science, he had been writing in the *Journal of Social Forces* about societal factors that produced ''unequal people with unequal opportunities.'' In the May 1923 issue, he discussed the problems of democracy and asked if ''the rights and opportunities of the physically and mentally deficient, with unequal situations on every hand'' might be one of the five major problems preventing ''equal opportunity for the development of every individual.''[26] His interests, however, in race and folk culture, industrial relations, farm tenancy, and other social problems that were at the root of southern poverty prevented his immediate pursuit of research in the field of health.

Almost every detailed study of the South produced in the Institute between 1924 and 1944 had mentioned the debilitating diseases common to the South—pellagra, hookworm, typhoid, malaria—as factors contributing to poverty.[27] Although no more than half a dozen research memoranda on health had been undertaken before Gordon Blackwell began his administration as director in 1944, some pioneer work had been done earlier. For example, Margaret Jarman Hagood prepared in 1939 the first report on what the Institute was later to call the "social science aspects of health" when she wrote "A State Experiment in Contraception as a Public Service," describing the contraception program of the North Carolina State Board of Health. The article was published in the *Journal of Contraception* in 1939. The next year, William P. Richardson, director of the local Tricounty Health Department and later professor of family medicine in the School of Medicine at the University, published with Donald S. Klaiss, a research assistant in sociology, "Prevention, the Health Department, and the Practicing Physician" in the first volume of the *North Carolina Medical Journal*.

After the addition of Cecil G. Sheps to the Institute's senior staff in 1948, health-related research was reported annually and continued to be reported throughout the remainder of the Institute's first fifty years. In 1949 Blackwell's annual report listed three published articles by Sheps and John J. Wright, professor of public health administration, giving information about the North Carolina Syphilis Studies, a state-sponsored research project.[28] A year later the Institute listed nine published studies by Sheps and others. In 1951 Sheps, Wright, George D. Newton, and Ruth M. Connor, a sociologist, published "Hospitalization Arrangements for the Indigent of North Carolina" in *Public Welfare News*, and two graduate theses were completed as part of an exploratory investigation of problem drinking in North Carolina. Several senior sociologists, among them Lee M. Brooks and E. William Noland, had directed the studies on alcoholism under a grant from the North Carolina Alcoholic Rehabilitation Program. Blackwell himself was becoming increasingly interested in health studies as a significant aspect of an integrated approach to the socioeconomic factors in community development. In 1950 he had written "A Social Scientist Looks at the Health Council Movement" for *Public Health Nursing*, and in 1953 he wrote an editorial for *Social Forces*, "Behavioral Science and Health," pointing out the interdependence of the behavioral sciences and medicine.[29]

At the close of the academic year 1953–54, Blackwell was able to report that a recent major development in the Institute's research program had been the expansion of studies relating to social factors in health and medical care.[30] Two important projects in the field had been completed that year. Frank M. LeBar, under the direction of John Gillin, professor of anthropology, had completed a contract project for the Veterans Administration, a study entitled "Socio-cultural Aspects of the Transference of Patients from Psychiatric Hospital to Home Community." The second project was "The Community Health Study of Salem, Massachusetts," directed by Cecil G. Sheps, research professor of health planning, and Floyd Hunter, associate professor in the School of Social Work. The project was financed by the Health Information Foundation, which wanted to test two hypotheses: (1) that cultural changes occur with least conflict and confusion along lines of established community patterns, and (2) that a community can solve most of its health problems through action programs if the citizens are aware of health needs and competent, democratic leadership is available. Ruth Connor Schaffer, a sociologist, was appointed a research fellow for the study, and two graduate students, Harry W. Martin in sociology and Ester Hunter in anthropology, were engaged to assist with field work, while two other graduate assistants, Emily Wilson and James Dinsmore, processed data gathered in the community by the field workers. The staff formulated eight additional hypotheses, and the study itself was a research approach to the processes of stratification and social action. The report was published in 1956 by the University of North Carolina Press as *Community Organization: Action and Inaction*, under the authorship of Floyd Hunter, Ruth Connor Schaffer, and Cecil G. Sheps.[31] The book was dedicated to Katharine Jocher, assistant director of the Institute. Before the publication of the study, Sheps had left the School of Public Health in the autumn of 1952 to become general director of the Beth Israel Medical Center and professor of community medicine at Mount Sinai Medical School in New York City.

Upon the addition of Harvey L. Smith to the senior staff in 1952, the Institute began the development of the social science aspects of health as a focal area of research. Smith had received his doctorate in sociology from the University of Chicago, and he came to Chapel Hill from the Russell Sage Foundation, where he had been at work on a two-year research project for the development of a framework for the study of the health professions with special reference to psychiatry. The Russell Sage Foundation awarded the Institute a two-year grant to begin a project on social research in health and the health professions, to be directed by Smith under the joint sponsorship of the Institute director and the administrator of the Division of Health Affairs.[32]

During the first year of the grant the program was well under way. Two studies were completed: "Organizational Problems and Community Interrelationships of New Hospitals," by Smith and John Scott, and "An Evaluation of the Handling of Psycho-Social Factors in the Comprehensive Clinic," by Smith and Kerr White. George Ham of the Department of Psychiatry had begun a seminar on interdisciplinary research on paranoid schizophrenia, and John Honigmann from the Department of Anthropology had joined Smith in giving lectures to public health students in the social science aspects of maternal and child health and in nutrition. At the same time, Smith was beginning a survey of the social organization of North Carolina Memorial Hospital and a study of sociocultural components of health in a mountain community in western North Carolina. In addition, the Institute staff worked with Smith and the School of Nursing on a proposal for a four-year project to determine the best ways of including psychosocial materials in the basic nursing curriculum.

In 1954 these activities brought a favorable comment from the Behavioral Science Survey, which noted the progress being made by the School of Public Health, the School of Medicine, North Carolina Memorial Hospital, and the Institute for Research in Social Science in the application of social science concepts to the field of health. The survey report noted that there was a staff of no fewer than fifteen behavioral scientists assembled at the University, "some already explicitly involved in medically relevant social research," all of whom with few exceptions were members of the senior staff of the Institute.[33]

The survey report also described varied social aspects of health with which Smith's research was dealing—for example, that of viewing illness itself as a form of social action that needs to be related to the human contexts involved, such as family, home, community, and work. The research project planned to develop a social-scientific frame of reference for understanding the sick person in the clinic and to refocus the content of life histories for medical case records so as to include the patient's life situations that might have a bearing upon his specific disorders. A "socio-biogram" was being developed, which combined a patient's medical, psychiatric, and social history materials in parallel columns so that each set of data might be considered in relation to the others. The research was likewise concerned with the importance of studying the social organization for medical practice, the hospital as a social institution, medical career specializations, and analyses of the therapeutic milieu.[34] The report mentioned that within the general clinic of North Carolina Memorial Hospital, Smith and a research assistant, Harry W. Martin, were "engaged in a program of research and teaching aimed at developing clinical considerations concerning the life situation of patients."[35] Smith had also been invited to collaborate with clinic physicians in lectures on the social and emotional aspects of illness that were presented in teaching sessions scheduled throughout the ten weeks that each group of medical students was assigned to the clinic.[36]

Since these changes and suggestions for reorientation in the Division of Health Affairs were encompassed in the brief period of two years, it was inevitable that they would arouse apprehensions among some of the older medical staff members, who may have felt some anxiety in the face of the new approaches to illness and clinical care.[37] But in later reminiscences of his administration as director of the Institute, Gordon Blackwell recalled the pioneer work of Harvey Smith in relating the behavioral sciences to the field of health and medicine, and remarked that Smith went quietly about the task of developing this new field of research, so that he was able to carry out the program with a minimum of friction.[38]

At the conclusion in 1954 of the original grant from the Russell Sage Foundation, a grant from the Commonwealth Fund made it possible for Smith to continue his program. In addition to himself and his secretary, Smith's staff now consisted of two research fellows, four research assistants, and two graduate students in sociology who were doing research under his direction. From the beginning of his association with the Institute for Research in Social Science, Smith had conducted a graduate course in the Department of Sociology on the sociology of health and the health professions. In 1956 his research and the training of social science students in the health field were focused on four areas:

1. Social and cultural factors in health and illness, with special emphasis on problems of family and community organization.
2. Studies in the area of social organization, primarily studies of hospital and of ward organization.
3. Studies in the organization and development of medical professions.
4. Studies of the clinical uses of social data, dealing with the application of social science to the clinical problems of medicine and psychiatry.[39]

Smith's work in proving the significance of the behavioral science approach to health was so successful that four years after he began his researches in Chapel Hill in 1952, he was appointed director of the Social Research Section of the Division of Health Affairs, a position that he was still holding in 1974 as the first fifty years of the Institute came to a close.

In 1957 Smith added another important program to the Social Research Section, following a grant from the National Institute of Mental Health for a five-year training program for social scientists in the field of mental health. The grant was for the establishment of a pilot program for specialized training in the social aspects of mental health and illness. It was an experimental program and the only one of its kind in the nation. Six students who were research assistants in the Institute participated in the first year of the project under Smith's direction in close collaboration with the Department of Psychiatry. Two members of the faculty in psychiatry joined the teaching staff of the program and participated in establishing a three-year clinical training sequence in the context of psychiatry as a second aspect of the program.[40] By 1958 the number of students in the program had doubled. As the five-year program was drawing to a close, the National Institute of Mental Health renewed the grant for another five years and the program continued through the close of the Institute's first half-century, although the social science aspects of health ceased after 1966–67 to be one of the focal areas of Institute research.

In 1957, the same year that Smith organized the pilot program in mental health training, the Department of Sociology and Anthropology accepted the sociology of health as an area of specialization for a doctorate in sociology. Among the graduate students who entered this program and went on to careers in sociology or in the field of the sociology of health were Alfred Dean, Betty E. Cogswell, Berton H. Kaplan, Fred Katz, Ann Carol Maney, Harry W. Martin, Ida Harper Simpson, and Jean H. Thrasher. In 1966 the ad hoc committee appointed to evaluate the Institute's overall program reported that "Harvey L. Smith's program in the sociology of health and the health professions" had been well established under Institute auspices and was now administratively located in the Division of Health Affairs as the Social Research Section.[41]

The results of research done under the Institute program and later under the Social Research Section of the Division of Health Affairs were published chiefly as articles in professional journals or as chapters in books related to the contribution of the behavioral sciences to the field of health. Several books, however, were published as a result of this research.[42] The chief contribution of research in medical sociology has been in the training of social science personnel, in the orientation of medical students to the behavioral science aspects of health care, and in the recognition by the medical profession that the family and the community have a profound effect upon illness.

In the late 1960s, two other health-related agencies not directly affiliated with the Institute for Research in Social Science were set up. The first was created in March 1966 as the Institute for Environmental Studies, with Daniel A. Okun, a professor in the School of Public Health, as director. The purpose of the Institute for Environmental Studies was to train graduate students for teaching, research, and practice in the fields of environmental health. Some of the schools and departments affiliated with the Institute for Research in Social Science also participated in the Institute for Environmental Studies, and occasionally faculty from the new institute joined the institute for the social sciences as senior research professors.

In 1968, when Cecil G. Sheps returned to the University, the Health Services Research Center was established in the Division of Health Affairs and Sheps became its director. When Sheps became vice-chancellor for health affairs in 1972, Gordon H. DeFreise was appointed director of the Health Services Research Center the following year. The research of the Health Services Research Center generally involves six broad categories, among them the organization and delivery of health services, health planning, and health planning development. The Center has utilized the services of the Social Science Statistical Laboratory in the Institute for Research in Social Science and has its own cathode ray tube in Manning Hall, which facilitates its use of the Institute's computing facilities. The two agencies have jointly supported several computing and data processing activities.

Research in Community Health

The Behavioral Science Survey, completed by the Institute in 1953–54, pointed out the "almost unprecedented" research opportunities that abounded at the University of North Carolina because of the availability of prominent social scientists interested in the field of community health and the existence of the School of Public Health with its eleven departments dedicated to the philosophy that public health has as close ties with the social sciences as with the medical sciences. The need was for additional staff to do the important research that had to be done to bring the field of community health out of its incompletely developed state into realization of its full potential. The survey report estimated that research in community health was at the same point in development that clinical research had been fifty years before and that it had as great an opportunity as clinical research to make a contribution to health care within the next fifty years.[43]

At the time the survey was being made, the School of Public Health was planning to augment its earlier studies of morbidity statistics by further studies of the effect of health problems upon the family, the structure of the family, and the family life style. The School added social scientists to its staff as funds became available, and in most instances these new staff members became affiliated with the Institute. They began the task of testing theories of social change within the context of community health. Among the new staff members was J. Richard Udry, a specialist in demography and biosocial reproduction, who came to the School of Public Health in 1965 with a joint appointment in the Department of Sociology. A year later Karl E. Bauman arrived to work with Udry. In 1967 Berton H. Kaplan, who had a doctorate in medical sociology from the University of North Carolina, also was added to the staff. These community health specialists were later joined by others, and fourteen of the faculty in public health were associated with the Institute by 1974.[44] Among the projects under way at this time were Elizabeth J. Coulter's study of socioeconomic factors in illness, mortality, and health services; Arnold D. Kaluzny's study of hospital innovation; Jane B. Sprague's study of determinants of innovation in health care organizations; and J. Richard Udry's family planning evaluation project. Some of these studies were referred to in chapter 8 in the discussion of family planning.

It was not until 1975 that Berton H. Kaplan and John C. Cassel from the School of Public Health prepared the first volume of a series to be published by the Institute on the correlation between life-style and health. Cassel, a graduate of the University of Witwatersrand at Johannesburg, South Africa, had been a student in the first course that Smith gave in the Department of Sociology, and Kaplan had been a trainee for several years. Their *Family and Health: An Epidemiological Approach*, published by the Institute, contains four studies that attempt a quantitative documentation of the relationship between family structure and function and the health of family members. After almost twenty years of testing carried on by Kaplan, Cassel, and their colleagues, the authors were prepared to demonstrate quantitatively that "susceptibility to many diseases and disorders (somatic as well as emotional and behavioral) is influenced by the interplay between psycho-social stress and the protection against stress provided by adequate family and social support.''[45]

As the Institute's first half-century came to a close, six different divisions in the University, in addition to the School of Public Health, that were associated with the Institute had under way projects related to the social aspects of health.[46] For example, in the Carolina Population Center, Saroy Pachauri was examining the maturity of the newborn with special emphasis on the effect of maternal nutrition on birth weight. In dentistry, Caswell A. Evans, Jr., was evaluating the Health Company, of Soul City, North Carolina. In economics Richard Scheffler was studying health manpower and Boone A. Turci was making a socioeconomic analysis of fertility and family size. In psychology, Mark I. Appelbaum, with Vaida D. Thompson, prepared a monograph, *Population Policy Acceptance: Psychological Determinants*, which was published by the Carolina Population Center. In the School of Medicine no fewer than twelve faculty members were at work on some aspect of the problems listed by the Behavioral Science Survey in 1954, among them Joseph F. Aponte, on analysis of the impact of social stress events; Aponte with Willard K. Bentz, Francis T. Miller, and others, on rural mental health; Betty E. Cogswell, on family response to disability; and Samuel M. Putnam, on the relationship of the black church to health care delivery through a neighborhood health center. In sociology Bradford H. Gray was at work on the practice-structure of physicians with regard to race and career process.

World Area Studies

Initiation of the program of health studies was undoubtedly one of Gordon Blackwell's major achievements as director of the Institute, but he also began other programs, one of which was a study of world areas, a field that had been recommended by the Behavioral Science Survey as a focal study. Research in world areas began in the Institute with the appointment of John P. Gillin as a professor of anthropology. In announcing his addition to the staff in September 1946, Blackwell had reported that Gillin would "continue his research in Latin America, and . . . assist in developing cooperative research and training relationships in the social sciences'' between the Institute and a university at Bogota, Colombia.[47] After Guy B. Johnson returned in 1947 from Atlanta, where he had gone on a leave of absence to direct the first years of the Southern Regional Council, he began offering through the Department of Sociology and Anthropology the first course given in the University on the peoples and cultures of Africa. Johnson, who was a research professor in the Institute, made two extended trips to Africa before his retirement in 1969, observing race relations in Southern Africa, Basuto culture, and education in East and West Africa.[48] The Institute extended its research in world areas with the arrival of two other anthropologists, John J. Honigmann in 1951, whose research was concerned with Eskimo and Pakistani cultures, and John Gulick in 1955, whose focus of research was the Middle East. (The anthropological research carried on in the Institute has already been discussed in chapter 5.) It should also be pointed out that visiting scholars from the Far East were affiliated with the Institute from time to time. For example, in 1955–56 two fellows of the Rockefeller Foundation were in residence: Professor Hae Young Lee from the University of Seoul, Korea, and Professor Kiyohide Seki of Hokkaido University, Japan.[49]

Beginning in 1952 the Institute undertook a series of studies on the Soviet Union. Under a contract from the United States Library of Congress, John A. Parker and Maurice Frank Parkins of the Department of City and Regional Planning completed a manuscript on Soviet theory and practice in regional planning. By the next year Parkins had finished *City Planning in Soviet Russia* under an Institute contract grant from the United States Air Force, and the book was published by the University of Chicago Press.

In his annual report for 1953–54, Blackwell remarked that the Soviet studies were a world area focus ''which it is hoped other parts of the University will develop as well,'' and he pointed out that the world area studies themselves were ''one indication of the Institute's broadened field of interest.'' The Behavioral Science Survey, which was being conducted at this time, outlined in its final report several reasons for encouraging world area research:

> One part of the interest in world areas and national
> cultures is to develop effective methods for studying these
> contemporary social units. . . . It is expected that studies of
> total national cultures can contribute information respecting not

only the discrete activities carried out by people in nations but also insight into how those activities support and determine each other to make possible national life. . . .

Another interest in contemporary culture on this campus concerns the impact of American culture throughout the world. Our public, private, and unorganized means of influencing foreign minds and customs have not been examined systematically to bring out whatever latent generalizations about social change they can produce.[50]

The survey report stated that the Soviet studies program had two purposes: "to prepare future citizens of North Carolina and elsewhere to understand better the world in which they live, and, second, to prepare some of them for further specialized training in Russian studies." The relation between the United States and Russia might "alter in character," but the report expressed the confident expectation that "our citizens will continue to find use for a knowledge of Russian national culture."[51]

The Soviet studies done under contract for the federal government continued for a period of about ten years. Most of that time, John A. Parker was director of the research. At the close of the first three years of the research, in addition to Parker, the program had one research associate, one research fellow, and three research assistants. By 1959, however, the staff had increased until ten of the forty-five senior staff members in the Institute were involved; in addition, the program included two research fellows, four graduate assistants, and a bibliographer. By this time, a majority of the staff working on the Soviet program had been brought to Chapel Hill especially for this specialized research and had no teaching affiliation in the University. James H. Blackman from the Department of Economics had joined Parker as codirector of the program, and the focus of research was listed in the Institute's annual report as "Analysis of Production Processes in the Soviet Heavy Machine-Building Industry, Phase II" and "Inputs to Selected End Products."[52]

Most of the research completed in Soviet studies was recorded in unpublished monographs, but in 1957 one project by John A. Parker and others, *Analysis of Production Processes in the Soviet Heavy Machinery-Building Industry: Interim Report, Phase I*, was among several monographs produced by the Institute that year.[53] The following year, Blackman and others, with Parker as director of the team study, completed two monographs that were published by the Institute, and Stephan G. Procuik, a senior member of the Institute staff, published in Ukrainian a series of articles in *Ukrainian Word* (Paris) in 1958 under the collective title "The Basic Tasks of the Study of the USSR" and contributed four additional articles to various European and American magazines on aspects of Russian industrialization.[54]

In the meantime, the Department of Political Science had fulfilled Blackwell's hope, expressed in 1954, that others in the University would extend the studies in world areas. In 1958 Robert Arthur Rupen, whose research interest was in Outer Mongolia, joined the department and affiliated with the Institute as a research professor. In 1958 and 1959, Rupen published four articles in professional journals, including "Inside Outer Mongolia," which appeared in *Foreign Affairs*. In 1964 his *Mongols of the Twentieth Century* appeared, as did two articles on the Mongolian People's Republic. Other Institute staff members in political science and economics were doing research in Soviet studies. They included William R. Keech and Joel Schwartz in political science and Steven Rosefielde in economics.[55]

Out of concern for research in Russian and Slavic studies grew the Committee on Russian and Eastern European Studies, founded in 1966 largely through the efforts of faculty in the Department of Political Science. The functions of the committee were to stimulate multidisciplinary research in Russian, Soviet, and East European studies, to enlarge the University library holdings in these fields, to promote the exchange of scholars and students with institutions in these regions, and to coordinate activities with Duke University through the Joint Advisory Committee on Slavic Studies, which consisted of representatives from both universities. Although the Committee on Russian and Eastern European Studies was not affiliated with the Institute for Research in Social Science, some members of the committee, Rupen, Swartz, Lonsdale, and Griffiths, among others, were senior staff members of the Institute and their research continued throughout the remainder of the Institute's first fifty years.

Hispanic American studies, as the Department of History listed the courses in this field in the 1920s, had been a major research interest of William Whatley Pierson, Jr., at the time the Institute was founded. The first publication in this field by a member of the Institute research staff was "The Monroe Doctrine and the Panama Congress," by Guion Griffis Johnson in *Studies in Hispanic-American History*, edited by Pierson in 1927. The first full-time research assistant working in Hispanic American history under Pierson's direction was David A. Lock-miller, whose study "The Second United States Intervention in Cuba, 1906–1909" won him a doctorate in history in 1935. After Pierson became dean of the Graduate School, Federico G. Gil was brought to the University in 1943 to strengthen the Latin American Studies program in the Department of Political Science. Political science, which had originally been a division in the Department of History and Government, had been established as a separate department in 1935.

Gil was one of the most prolific scholars in the field of world areas. He became a member of the Political Behavior Committee, which Alexander Heard organized in 1950, and the importance of his work was noted in the Behavioral Science Survey. Although the committee was working within the Institute, Gil was not officially listed as a member of the senior research staff until 1958.[56] The next year the Institute listed six publications that Gil had produced. In 1966 he published *The Political System of Chile* and contributed chapters to books edited by others—for example, "Cuban Politics and Political Parties, 1933–53" in *Background to Revolution*, edited by Robert Freeman Smith. As the fifth decade of the Institute came to a close, Gil was engaged in research for a study of leftist political groups in Latin America.

One of Gil's major contributions to the world area studies was the organization of the Institute of Latin American Studies. In 1962 he turned to the Institute for Research in Social Science for help in financing research assistants. While the Institute's Advisory Committee was eager to assist the new Institute, it hoped that the needed assistance might be found in the University Research Center. "If sufficient support comes to the Institute of Latin American Studies to permit Federico Gil to support research assistants," ran the Advisory Committee minutes, "Institute [for Research in Social Science] assistantships will be allocated to someone else."[57] The purpose of the Institute of Latin American Studies was to sponsor research, provide special training such as that for Peace Corps volunteers for assignment in Latin America, and establish collaborative relationships with scholars in Latin America. In 1968 the Administrative Board noted that "plans are currently under way for a joint undertaking between the Institute for Research in Social Science and the Institute of Latin American Studies to sponsor cooperatively with the University of Chile a ten-year program of research."[58] It is interesting to recall in this connection that the Behavioral Science Survey had recommended that the Institute set up a world area laboratory and chose Ecuador as the ideal location.

The cooperation of the two institutes and Gil's research and knowledge of Latin American affairs attracted other scholars to Chapel Hill. John Danhouse Martz III, who completed his doctorate in political science at the University in 1963, remained at the University as director of the Institute of Latin American Studies and research associate in the Institute for Research in Social Science. He later served as chairman of the Department of Political Science. In 1972 Martz's research on Ecuador was published as *Ecuador: Conflicting Political Culture and the Quest for Modernity*. In 1974 he was studying campaigns and elections in Venezuelan politics from 1958 to 1973. Three other political scientists with interests in Latin America were also publishing research during this period: Robert T. Daland, on Brazil; James W. Prothro, on Chile; and Enrique A. Baloyra, on Venezuela.[59]

At this time, research on Latin America was also under way in the Department of Sociology, the Department of History, and the Institute of Government. In sociology, the work of Henry A. Landsberger on peasant movements in Chile and Mexico has already been mentioned. In history, Joseph S. Tulchin and Ron L. Seckinger were involved in research on Latin America. Tulchin's interest was in student reform. He was also editor of *Problems in Latin American History* and series editor for the first volume of *Cross-Currents in Latin America*. Seckinger's work was on Brazil. His "A projectada alianca gracolombiana-rioplatense contre o Brazil: um documento inedito" appeared in *Mensario do Arguivo Nacional* in 1974. He then began work on a new research topic, "The Brazilian Monarchy and the South American Republics, 1822–1831." In the Department of Economics, Ann D. Witte contributed an article in 1973 to the *Journal of Developmental Studies* on employment in manufacturing in Mexico and Brazil.

The late 1940s also saw the beginning of research by Institute staff in other world areas besides the Soviet Union and Latin America. Studies were published by members of the Departments of Anthropology, Economics, Geography, History, Political Science, and Sociology, and by the Carolina Population Center. The first Institute publication on Africa appeared in 1949 in *Social Forces*: "The South African Native: Caste, Proletariat or Race?" It was written by Leo Kuper of Durban, South Africa, a graduate student in sociology and anthropology. No further Institute research on Africa appeared until William G. Fleming of the Department of Political Science became a senior staff member in 1965, specializing in African international systems and political development. In 1966 the *Administrative Science Quarterly* published his "Authority, Efficiency, and Role-Stress: Problems in the Development of East African Bureaucracies," a paper that he had given at the annual conference of the African Studies Association. In 1967 he presented a paper on planning for political development at the Congress of the International Political Science Association in Brussels, and in 1969 his "International Attitudes of Ghana and Uganda" appeared as a chapter in *Linkage Politics*, edited by James N. Rosenau. Stephen S. Birdsall of the Department of Geography presented a paper in 1969 to the Southeastern Division of the Association of American Geographers, "Utilitarian Modifications to Land Rent Determination," which used western Kenya as an example, and in 1972 he published in the *Bulletin of the American Geographical Society* a selected list of published literature on urban geographic studies of East Africa. Three anthropologists were also publishing research on Africa. Their work has been discussed in chapter 5. In the Carolina Population Center, David G. Stillman had under way a project on population policy that used Togo and Ghana as two cases for analysis.

Other Institute staff members were writing between 1950 and 1974 about Western Europe and the role of the United States in foreign affairs. An important publication in this area was by William Nelson Parker, from the Department of Economics, whose *Coal and Steel in Western Europe*, written in cooperation with N. J. G. Pound, appeared in 1957. Several years elapsed before another Institute staff member, James C. Ingram, also in economics, completed research on the international economy. He appeared before a hearing of the Joint Economic Committee in the first session of the Eighty-ninth Congress (1965), and his report, "Strengthening the Dollar-Exchange Standard," was published in *Guidelines for International Monetary Reform*. The following year his book, *International Economic Problems*, appeared and received recognition in Western Europe as well as in the United States.

After Andrew MacKay Scott joined the Department of Political Science in 1958, he published steadily on a number of aspects of American foreign policy. In 1967 he affiliated with the Institute as a research professor. His important book, *The Functioning of the International Political System*, appeared that year. Prior to his affiliation, he had written with Earle Wallace, also of the Department of Political Science, *Politics, U.S.A.*, whose third edition appeared in 1969. Another book by Scott, *Competition in American Politics*, was published in 1970, as was also *Insurgency*, which he had written with five other political scientists. In 1974 he was at work on a project on undirected processes and international politics, and he had previously published two articles applying theories of organization and communication to the field of political behavior. In the 1970s four other political scientists affiliated with the Institute also were publishing research on international affairs: Edward E. Azar, Jurg Steiner, Alan J. Stern, and James W. White. Azar's research examined international tensions and small state hostilities; Steiner's, conflict resolution in Switzerland; Stern's, the Italian Communist Party; and White's, contemporary problems of Japanese politics.[60]

While the political scientists were writing about political behavior in many parts of the world, the historians affiliated with the Institute were dealing primarily with domestic affairs, except for David M. Griffiths, who was writing about Russia in the time of Catherine II, and Ron L. Seckinger, as previously noted, whose research was on Brazil. In the fall of 1974, however, Joan W. Scott, whose field of specialization is France, became an Institute affiliate. Her book, *Glassworkers of Carmaux: French Craftsmen and Political Action in a Nineteenth-Century City*, which won the Herbert Baxter Adams Prize of the American Historical Association, opened the door for further research, and she has since begun a comparison of workers and elites in the woollen industry in nineteenth-century Reims.

In sociology two Institute affiliates were involved in research in world areas in the 1970s. Henry A. Landsberger's work on peasant movements in Latin America has already been mentioned. In 1973 he edited *Rural Unrest: Peasant Movements and Social Change*, in which he wrote two of the chapters, one in collaboration with his wife, Betty. Daniel Chirot published that year an article on the sociology of servile behavior, "A New Analysis of the Romanian Middle Ages (1300–1800)," in the journal *Southeastern Europe*.

As the Institute approached its fiftieth year, it inaugurated in 1973, with a grant from the Office of Education, still another approach to world area research, the Comparative Urban Studies Program. Frank J. Munger became director of the program and Susan E. Clarke was made his research assistant. The program was designed to integrate the international concerns of Institute members with the Institute's traditional interests in urban studies. It was developed as a nondegree multidisciplinary graduate-level curriculum and it provided assistance to faculty members in expanding and revising courses with a comparative, cross-national approach to urban analysis. In addition to formal courses, the program offered summer language tutorials in Spanish and Portuguese for faculty and graduate students, established a comparative urban data archive, and created a library and a slide collection of about eight thousand slides, which are available to the University and the community for use in presentations on urban issues. The slide collection is maintained by the Institute's Educational Services Division. The researches stimulated by the Comparative Urban Studies Program and published in the Institute's Comparative Urban Studies series include *Social Change in a Southern Province of Iran*, by Ali Paydarfar; *Urban Ethnic Conflict*, edited by Susan E. Clarke and Jeffrey Obler; and *The Urban Impact of Internal Migration*, edited by James W. White. The Comparative Urban Studies Program soon became a part of the Institute's basic research agenda, and in 1976 Susan E. Clarke was appointed director of the Institute's Division of Research Services.[61]

Studies of the Social Aspects of Education

While the study of world areas began relatively late in the development of the Institute, the social aspects of education were among its first concerns. The research undertaken in education, however, was meager, and except for the study of the effect of child labor on intelligence undertaken by A. M. Jordan and his research assistants in the early 1920s, the Department of Education, later the School of Education, undertook few research projects within the Institute until late in the Institute's first half-century. The few studies that were done—for example, Roy W. Morrison's "Some Inequalities of Educational Opportunities in North Carolina Public Schools" and Gustave E. Metz's "Social Factors and School Progress," both completed in 1928—went unpublished. Many years later, when Gordon Blackwell reviewed the studies that had been under way during his administration as director of the Institute, he mentioned with regret that he had been unable to stimulate much cooperative interest with the School of Education.[62]

Howard Odum believed strongly in the importance of education as a major instrument for leading the South out of its heritage of racial bigotry and economic backwardness. In an address delivered before a joint meeting of the Commission on Institutions of Higher Education and the Commission on Curricular Problems and Research, which met in Atlanta, Georgia, in 1940, Odum declared that education in the secondary schools in the South was "about the most important topic which it is possible to consider." One of his basic assumptions was that the realistic education of American young people must be accomplished "in close harmony with their American and regional environment" and that "the objective of this education must be mastery of the physical, technical, and cultural forces which sweep down upon us, and . . . this mastery must be turned to human-use ends through a regular democracy which shall guarantee the continuity of human development through a superior mankind and more adequate human society." [63]

Katharine Jocher, who worked with Odum as assistant director of the Institute longer than any other administrator, wrote of him after his death that "to Howard Odum the way forward was through education." He considered it strategic to interpret to popular audiences as well as to professional ones the results of the basic research in which the Institute was engaged. In a democratic society, he held, it was crucial that the people know "the facts," and knowing them, he thought, the people would act wisely in making the decisions "to build in America a 'society at its best.' " [64] As Katharine Jocher recalls her association with him, "Odum must have made hundreds of . . . addresses throughout the South, talking to teachers wherever he could." He also saw "the need for an expanding higher education in which the university would make every effort to adapt itself to a modern world of technology and change." He insisted that social scientists must "take the leadership in coordinating the social sciences with the humanities and the physical sciences since they themselves are a part of the scientific revolution." [65]

Odum also encouraged other Institute staff members to apply their areas of specialization to the educational scene. For example, in 1932 Ernest R. Groves wrote an essay entitled "Parent Education" for the *Annals of the American Academy of Political and Social Science*. He prepared a series of articles in the 1940s that gave bibliographies on marriage and the family for teachers and specialists in the field, and popular articles on educational principles and processes in such magazines as *Ladies Home Journal*. Guy B. Johnson wrote on education, segregation, and race relations, and Gordon Blackwell on the interaction of education and community in a democratic society. Lee M. Brooks, with Ruth G. Lynch, prepared an article for *Social Forces* that

stressed the importance of including information about consumer problems and the cooperative movement in the curricula of southern Negro
colleges.

When Gordon Blackwell replaced Odum in 1944 as director of the
Institute, he too was in frequent demand as a speaker on problems of
education. He perceived as keenly as Odum did the important role of
education in the development of American society during the scientific
revolution into "a society at its best." The situation under Blackwell's
administration was much as it had been under Odum's: "more sociology relating to education" than education seeking cooperation with
sociology and the Institute.[66] As a technique for presenting educators
the social science data collected by the Institute and in the particular
hope of "mediating the results of the regional research in the field of
education," John E. Ivey, Jr., and Blackwell developed the concept of
"research interpretation," as previously discussed. Ivey's project was
a short-term effort,[67] but Blackwell himself carried on the attempt to
mediate Institute research into education by serving on boards, such as
the Southeastern Adult Education Association, and by organizing the
high school social science teachers in North Carolina.

Other Institute staff members outside the School of Education from
time to time undertook studies related to the social aspects of education. The Institute's annual report for 1954–55, for example, contains
a list of three published articles in this area, among them "The Press
and Public School Superintendents in California," by Roy E. Carter,
Jr., in *Journalism Quarterly*, and a chapter, "The Culture of the
American Community and Public School Education," by John Gillin
in *Anthropology and Education*, edited by George Spindler. In 1957
Blackwell prepared the summary comments for the *Final Report of the
Southern Regional Conference on Education beyond the High School*,
a survey that had been conducted under the auspices of the Southern
Regional Education Board. The following year, the Southern Regional
Education Board gave the Institute a grant of $10,000 for a study of the
administration of research in institutions of higher education that was
to be made by Daniel O. Price, who had just become director of the
Institute. Also in 1958 a grant of $7,000 from two foundations made
possible a study of the effects of school closing in Norfolk, Virginia,
by three Institute sociologists, Charles Bowerman, Ernest Campbell,
and Daniel Price. The largest single grant that the Institute received for
research relating to education came in 1959 as funds became available
from the Office of Education for Richard L. Simpson to make his

extended study of the schoolteacher, which was, as previously mentioned, a study in both educational and occupational sociology. In the annual report for 1961–62 the director of the Institute listed "The School Teacher" as one of the three major studies under completion that year.

Other sociologists in the Institute and occasionally a member of the School of Public Health continued to write in the field of education. For example, in 1965 Rupert Vance contributed a chapter, "Education and the Southern Potential," to *The Southern High School*, edited by George Peabody College for Teachers, and in 1968 Bruce K. Eckland published an article from data collected for his study of Phillips Exeter Academy, which was more fully explored in his monograph, *The Spirit of Exeter*, published in 1971. In 1972 Eckland prepared a workshop report, *Sociological Theory and Research in Education*, for the National Research Council, and in 1973, with the assistance of Karl Alexander, he prepared a final report for the National Institute of Education, *Effects of Education on the Social Mobility of High School Sophomores Fifteen Years Later*, as a part of his work on the Southeastern Regional Survey. During this period Glen H. Elder, Jr., a specialist in the field of family research, was publishing such articles as "Peer Socialization in School" in *Educational Leadership* (1969) and "Continuation Schools and Educational Pluralism" in the *Journal of Secondary Education* (1969). During 1972 and 1973, Earl S. Schaefer, professor of maternal and child health in the School of Public Health, wrote a series of seven papers on childhood and infant education that were published as chapters in books edited by others or as articles in professional journals.[68]

It was not until 1969 that a faculty member from the School of Education, Robert E. Heiny, affiliated with the Institute. In 1970 his essay "The History of Special Education: Outline of a Social Philosophy Perspective" was published in the *Encyclopedia of Education*. By 1971–72 five of the faculty from the School of Education had become Institute affiliates, and several of them published research papers during the year. Among them were John C. Brantley, "Psycho-Educational Centers and the School Psychologist" in *Psychology in the Schools* (1971); William P. Hawkinson with E. A. Errickson, "A Response to Field Workers: An Introduction to an Alternative to Schools" in the *Peabody Journal of Education* (1972); and Barbara Wasik with J. L. Wasik, "Response Strategies of Culturally Deprived Children" in the *Journal of Experimental Education* (1971). As the

Institute's first fifty years came to a close, its affiliates included six professors of education, who were working on such research projects as cultural diversity, cross-modality support for decoding ability, modes of school organization and classroom patterns of influence and adaptation, systems of schooling and behavioral interventions, cooperative behavior in preschool children, and effects of attention focusing—all projects that hardly would have been thought of fifty years earlier.

The hesitation of the School of Education to associate itself with the Institute was largely a result of the Institute's requirement for many years that the school or department from which a senior staff member came must release him from a portion of his teaching load in order to give him time for research. As the Behavioral Science Survey pointed out in 1954,

> Some departments within the social sciences have openly
> and actively encouraged research by faculty members, while
> others have been less active in this regard. The pressures of
> undergraduate enrollment, the views of some early adminis-
> trators, and the tendency of budgetary planning to become
> unimaginative and traditional have led in time to fairly rigid
> patterns for the allocation of funds and staff time in departments.
> The Department of Economics, for example, has not participated
> extensively in the program of the Institute for Research in Social
> Science. . . . The need for research time has not been built
> into the department's budget over the years, and it is unable
> to relieve staff members from teaching duties on the scale
> that is possible in some other departments.[69]

The School of Education had been faced with the same budgetary restrictions as the Department of Economics, and despite the efforts of Carson Ryan when he was dean of the School of Education to change the situation, he was unable to do so.

The University Extension Division, however, cooperated with the Institute for more than three decades. Louis R. Wilson, who had set up the Extension Division and was still its director when the Institute was organized, was supportive of the Institute and a member of its first Board of Governors. The Extension Division encouraged Institute senior staff to prepare correspondence courses for extension classes in order to introduce the social sciences throughout the state, and it also published for Institute staff short pamphlets on social issues as study guides for various women's organizations. Once these women's groups were made aware of the issues through pamphlets written by Odum, Vance, Brooks, Meyer, and others, they often were prepared to support social legislation as it came before the General Assembly, and in more than one instance gave the necessary impetus for passage.[70]

Pointing out that the Extension Division was the major bridge between the University and its constituents, the Behavioral Science Survey noted the close relationship between the Extension Division and the Institute. During Russell M. Grumman's administration as director of the Extension Division, this relationship continued to expand. For instance, the Institute cooperated with the Bureau of Community Organization within the Extension Division by conducting some of its research activities, and it assisted the Bureau of Economic and Social Surveys in collecting pertinent data on North Carolina that was made available to the public through library loan packets, the University *News Letter*, and various bulletins.[71] These and other bureaus within the Extension Division continued to cooperate with the Institute for many years. Today the only relationship the Institute has with the Extension Division is through the acting director, Dwight C. Rhyne, who is an Institute affiliate engaged in research on a systematic evaluation of adult education programs.[72]

Research in Mass Communication

One of the major functions of the Institute as stated in the University of North Carolina *General Catalogue* in the 1940s was "to serve as a center for cooperation with other agencies toward the development and testing of procedures for making this research of more functional value." This had indeed been a compelling motivation for Odum as he set up the Institute in 1924, and it was the prime concern of Blackwell in supporting the Research Interpretation Division within the Institute in the late 1940s. John E. Ivey, Jr., director of research interpretation, initiated cooperation with the University Communications Center, and as mentioned in chapter 8, he obtained a small federal grant for research. Cooperation between the Institute and the Communications Center, which was under the direction of Earl Wynn, continued for several years and at various times thereafter. For example, in 1953 Blackwell listed in a memorandum on research contemplated for the next five years a project by Robert Schenkkan on the effectiveness of selected communication media.[73] In the late 1960s Wesley H. Wallace was the only Institute affiliate from the Communications Center; his research proposal was for an oral history project.

The report of the Behavioral Science Survey in 1954 listed mass communication as one aspect of an important focal area in sociopolitical behavior and observed that with the addition of television in 1954 the Communications Center might help to solve one of the problems that "has disturbed our most thoughtful faculty members." This problem, as stated by Gordon Gray, president of the University, "concerns the relative separation of the scholarship, research, and thought that are the very heart of the University from the great bulk of the people of the state."[74] The survey report acknowledged that the "mass media have assumed unquestioned importance in informing the members of societies of political and social events," but noted that their "effects in persuading" were not as clear and deserved further investigation. The report recommended the development of two closely related programs of investigation: "one of *persuasive* aspects of communications, the other on *informational* aspects." The research techniques of the two programs would be similar but their objectives sufficiently different to require separation. The purpose of a two-part program of this nature was to coordinate laboratory and field studies as well as to conduct research on methodology and theory that would be a service to the University's radio and television facilities.[75]

Upon the addition of Roy E. Carter, Jr., to the staff of the School of Journalism in 1954, research in methodology and theory got under way. Carter had been trained in the behavioral sciences and was prepared to conduct the research proposed by the Behavioral Science Survey.[76] During the first year of his affiliation with the Institute, he began research projects on methodological research in mass communication, content analysis procedure for the study of newspaper treatment of the school desegregation question, and the press and the medical profession in North Carolina. In the same year, he made two reports to the United States Information Agency, "Experiments in Pretesting Printed Materials" and "Filipino and Indian Students' Radio-Listening Habits and Reactions to Voice of America Broadcasts."[77] In 1955 the School of Journalism and the Institute jointly sponsored the duplication of Carter's "Field Methods in Journalism Research," which later appeared in a textbook on research methods.

By 1958 Carter was no longer with the School of Journalism, but communications research continued under the direction of John B.

Adams, Wayne A. Danielson, and a few years later James J. Mullen. Norval Neil Luxon, dean of the School of Journalism, was a member of the Institute's senior staff for several years, and Joseph L. Morrison for two years. As the journalism faculty increased so did interest in research as well as teaching. By 1974 seven faculty members were Institute affiliates.

John B. Adams came to the University in 1958 and was appointed dean of the School of Journalism after Danielson, who had followed Luxon as dean, left for the University of Texas. Adams completed a research project, "Effects of Reference Group and Status on Opinion Change," in 1961, the first year of his affiliation with the Institute, and it appeared in *Journalism Quarterly*. Each year for a period of more than ten years as an affiliate of the Institute, he produced from one to five articles that were published in American and occasionally in European professional journals.[78] He was especially interested in the coverage of foreign news, and in one academic year, 1964–65, he delivered three addresses and produced an article on the subject, and edited "Articles on Mass Communication in U.S. and Foreign Journals" for the *Journalism Quarterly*.[79] James J. Mullen, a professor of journalism in the field of advertising, affiliated with the Institute in 1961 and like Adams continued each year to complete research projects. In 1974 he was exploring the effect of the use of humor on the credibility of advertising. He occasionally collaborated with Adams in research; in 1969–70, for example, they prepared a study of the "sleeper" effect in political news and advertising communication.

In 1969 three others in the School of Journalism became affiliated with the Institute and turned out research in theory and methodology: Michael E. Bishop, Maxwell E. McCombs, and Donald L. Shaw. In 1970–71 Bishop was doing research on communication behavior in an Appalachian community, and in 1972 he produced five articles, some in collaboration with others, dealing with communications, the editorial function and societal stress, and the communication crisis in developing nations. McCombs examined incidental learning from broadcasting, cooperated with Prothro and Kovenock on the Comparative State Elections Project, published "A Scientific Method for Reporting" in *Journalism Quarterly* in 1970, and investigated the agenda-setting function of the mass media. Shaw edited *Journalism Abstracts* for the Association for Education in Journalism, as Wayne Danielson had done in 1962–63. In 1971 he also worked with Mary E.

Junck on a project concerning the news world of the nineteenth century, and for several years he continued the project as a study of "newspaper symbols of public thought" between 1820 and 1860.

In 1972–73 Thomas A. Bowers, Richard R. Cole, and Eugene F. Shaw also became affiliated with the Institute. Bowers's project was an analysis of newspaper coverage of political advertising in the 1972 campaigns; Cole's, the narcotizing dysfunction of the mass media; and Shaw's, the urban man in politics. As the Institute approached its fiftieth year, Bishop, Bowers, Cole, McCombs, Mullen, and Donald Shaw continued their research work, contributing articles to professional journals and preparing chapters for books, such as McCombs's "Mass Communication in Political Campaigns" in *Current Perspectives in Mass Communication Research*, edited by Philip Tichenor and F. G. Kline.

The former members of the Behavioral Science Survey Committee of 1953–54, which had recommended that research into mass communication become a part of the Institute's foci, must have been gratified with the research in the School of Journalism. In the twenty years between the publication of the Behavioral Science Survey and the Institute's fiftieth anniversary, numerous aspects of previously unexplored theory and methodology had been approached. The methodological procedure also had changed vastly from descriptive, speculative techniques to quantitative ones that found the Institute's Statistical Laboratory indispensible.

Research in Theory and Methodology

From its beginning in 1924, the Institute had stressed the role of theoretical concepts and the refinement of methodology in research, but refinement of techniques, especially in the area of mathematical analyses, developed slowly. In psychology, J. F. Dashiell was giving a graduate course on contemporary psychology that dealt chiefly with changing concepts in that field but had little to do with methodology except in his specialty, animal behavior. In 1926 the Department of History began a noncredit short course on historiography for graduate students, which was conducted by Wallace E. Caldwell with the assistance of others in the department. By the time of the Behavioral Science Survey in 1954, the Department of History was listed as one of a few in the University that offered a course in methodology. Since 1954 the course has been divided into one on American and another on European historiography. In 1970 an Institute senior staff member, Robert E. Gallman, who is an economic historian in the Department of Economics, wrote an illuminating chapter, "Fundamental Concepts of Statistical Studies as Applied to History," for *Approaches to American Economic History*, edited by George Rogers Taylor, for many years professor of economic history at Amherst, with the assistance of Lucius F. Ellsworth.

Howard Odum, prodded by Sydnor Walker of the Laura Spelman Rockefeller Memorial, whose interest was in social work, had an early concern for the development of skills in research among the Institute assistants. In 1928, at Odum's request Walker prepared a monograph, *Social Work and the Training of Social Workers*, for use in the School of Public Welfare. The following year, with the assistance of Katharine Jocher, and primarily with the needs of the Institute in mind, Odum produced *An Introduction to Social Research*, which was discussed briefly in chapter 6. Odum and Jocher, and later Blackwell and Jocher, offered for many years a seminar on methods of social research in the Department of Sociology. When T. J. Woofter, Jr., joined the staff as the Institute statistician, Odum was pleased that the Institute was now in a position to place greater emphasis on quantitative methodology. Woofter's *Race and Ethnic Groups in American Life* (1933) dealt sketchily with racial concepts, and it was not until William S. Jenkins' *Pro-Slavery Thought in the Old South* was published two years later that an Institute project attempted to analyze racial prejudice in America, although the analysis was in a political and intellectual rather than a behavioral science framework.

Regionalism was perhaps the major complex of social concepts produced by the Institute before 1950. It is discussed in some detail in chapter 6. Odum insisted that his conceptual framework on regionalism began as early as the founding of the Institute, when research on folk and race was under way. He maintained that the folkways of a region even more than its public policies were responsible for shaping and modifying the stateways and later the technicways. All the research turned out in the Institute prior to the publication of his *Southern Regions of the United States*, Odum contended, had been grist for his conceptual mill as he ground out the theories of regionalism. Along the way he had been helped in shaping these concepts by the work of

Rupert B. Vance, Harriet Herring, Katharine Jocher, Guy B. Johnson, T. J. Woofter, Jr., and his graduate students, Harry E. Moore and Margaret Jarman Hagood.

It was Margaret Hagood, now a member of the Institute's senior staff, who produced the lengthy *Statistics for Sociologists* in 1941, which laid out a more sophisticated methodology for quantitative research than Woofter had approached. The work quickly became the leading textbook in that field, but the next year Hagood left for Washington to work in the Department of Agriculture; so that it was not until Gordon Blackwell became director of the Institute that research became more quantitative and less descriptive and "organic" than previously. Blackwell had been exposed to Talcott Parsons's concepts of functionalism and social change while obtaining his doctorate at Harvard, and to Pitirim A. Sorokin's concepts of social dynamics and sensate culture as well. Years later Blackwell, when asked to point out what he considered to be his major contributions to the Institute while he served as director, listed among others (1) his ability to help the Department of Sociology and the Institute "move into some of the newer areas of sociology which were developing" and (2) his ability to initiate a multidisciplinary approach to research. He said further that

> I think by the early '40s that things were happening in
> the field and that . . . through the Institute we were able to get
> some things going, some different kinds of empirical research,
> some kinds of statistical research which were considerably more
> sophisticated than, say, Dr. Woofter's research in the '30s on
> subregions—which was a pioneer thing—but by the mid '40s
> the role of methodology and statistics was really moving.
> . . . [The Institute] aided the social sciences to move into
> new areas such as the sociology of health, social psychology,
> political behavior, and city planning. These are just some of
> the things that I would hope are achievements.[80]

These new fields required new concepts and new methods of research procedures. The trend toward the formulation of hypotheses, the testing of hypotheses, the definition of terms, quantitative analysis, the erection of mathematical models, and the derivation of complicated formulae based upon mathematical theory, which only highly trained mathematicians could construct and interpret, began to penetrate the social sciences and even to spill over occasionally into the humanities. As early as 1925, R. D. W. Connor had given sound advice to his research assistant, Guion Johnson, as she collected data for her social history of North Carolina: "Count everything that you possibly can, and include one or two tables in every chaper. Historians are going crazy over statistics."[81] While history was one of the last of the social sciences to move into quantitative analysis, the trend started decades before quantitative methodology was generally accepted in the discipline.

As Blackwell pointed out, the movement toward more precise formulation of concepts and more accurate measurement of data gained strength in the Institute in the late 1940s, and the process was accelerated by multidisciplinary research in the behavioral sciences. Blackwell brought research proposals before the Board of Governors for evaluation, and since the Board was composed of members from various social science departments, the process of evaluation was itself multidisciplinary. The Behavioral Science Survey in 1954 listed some of the difficulties encountered in the screening process: the danger of "acceptance of the lowest common denominator in theory and method due to variations in stage of development of the several social sciences"; "competing interests between basic research, applied investigation, therapy, and training due to differences between disciplines and the nature of sponsorship of the project"; and "semantic difficulties."[82] When a major difference of opinion arose, the custom was to appoint an ad hoc committee composed of members of disciplines related to the area of the proposed research. The committee would discuss and evaluate research ideas and suggest ways of strengthening research design, data collection techniques, and the tabulation and analysis of data. The committee then would report back to the Board with a recommendation and disband unless otherwise instructed.

With the organization of research in the focal areas of the behavioral sciences, however, most of the focal areas set up standing committees that continued to function over a period of years. For the most part, the committees arose spontaneously to meet the need of a closer exchange of ideas among scholars of different disciplines with similar or related research problems. The Behavioral Science Survey listed among these committees at work in 1954 the Political Behavior Committee, the Organization Research Group, the Urban Studies Committee, and the Human Relations in Industry Group.[83]

Although the procedures for the development of theory and methodology varied with each committee, the process usually involved (1) a statement of the research interests in the general area of the project by each social scientist represented on the committee, (2) an agreement on semantics, (3) a continued discussion of the inventory of interests until a more refined statement of major areas of interest and particular aspects of these interests had been achieved, (4) the development of guidelines for building a systematic theory, and (5) finally a discussion and evaluation of methodology.

In the case of the Organization Research Group, the majority of the members had already been associated for several years on the Air Force Base Project, which had examined human factors in Air Force base efficiency. The group consequently began with a body of theory and research method that had already been partially developed and tested by its members. But much testing and elaboration of both theories and methods yet lay ahead. Those involved in the discussions and in the research that followed devoted years to their research interests, using the knowledge gained in each new study to formulate the next problem. This method of pyramiding research to refine theory and method was used in the Institute especially by those exploring individual mental abilities, personality, the dynamics of problem solving, interactions in small groups, cultural change, the urban and political processes, and similar studies.

The Behavioral Science Survey in 1954 pointed out that the most urgent need for the facilitation of new research and the further development of research already under way was the establishment of a local field laboratory and a world laboratory, and the modernization of the existing Social Science Statistical Laboratory. The first order of implementation that the Institute undertook concerned the Statistical Laboratory, as discussed in chapter 9. More than one Institute director considered the facilities and services of the laboratory to be the factors contributing most to the Institute's increased usefulness and prestige.[84]

The purchase of modern equipment for the Statistical Laboratory and the employment of qualified personnel to give instruction in programming and computer use as well as advice on methodology opened a new era in the Institute's service to the University. It was now possible to train undergraduates as well as graduate students in computer techniques regardless of whether their professors were affiliated with the Institute and to acquaint them with some of the techniques of quantitative analysis. If this fascination with the ever-developing new machinery for quantitative methodology sometimes led the Institute's governing board to overlook theoretical research or the research in social problems that had once engaged almost the entire attention of the Institute, the directors could always point to the increasing number of professors, schools, and departments affiliated with the Institute. Occasionally a member of the board would almost plaintively ask if the Institute ever intended returning to some of its early concerns in social policy, only to be reassured that it would indeed.[85]

The Social Science Research Council in New York, which had on occasion turned to the Institute for personnel for some of its projects and to which the Institute had not infrequently turned for assistance, must have received similar queries. As early as the 1950s the Research Council had foreseen the role that mathematics would play in sharpening methodological techniques, and in 1953 it appointed its Committee on Mathematics in Social Science Research, which reported five years later. The report of the committee cautiously warned that "some students will tend to overstress their mathematical knowledge, to use techniques instead of thought, and to limit themselves to problems that can be solved mathematically." The report also emphasized that the role of mathematics in social science was not "a temporary development" but a continuing one.[86]

In time, most of the social science departments affiliated with the Institute began producing methodological monographs applying mathematics to their areas of interest. In 1951–52 Daniel O. Price assisted Margaret Jarman Hagood in revising her *Statistics for Sociologists*, and he also prepared a short article on the use of margin-punched cards in scaling social data. At the same time Blackwell obtained a small foundation grant to set up a seminar on social theory. In 1954–55 almost a flood of articles and papers dealing with methodology, from highly selected aspects to broad generalizations, began to appear in Institute publications.[87]

From this time forward, scarcely a year passed without the publication of articles either in theory or in methodology by the senior staff. The articles came from almost every discipline affiliated with the Institute. In 1955–56 more than a dozen projects in theory and methodology were under way. Among them were two personality studies by E. Earl Baughman; a development of a method of preparing comparable labor force data by Lowell D. Ashby; three projects by Daniel O. Price, including a methodological analysis of Census tract data and social structure; a study of research methods in mass communication by Roy E. Carter, Jr.; research in interdisciplinary theory in the behavioral sciences, by John Gillin; two projects on methodology in culture and personality by John J. Honigmann; a graduate seminar in methodology in political science directed by Alexander Heard; two projects by George E. Nicholson related to fractional replications by factoral experiments; and an investigation of the properties of demand equations by Ralph W. Pfouts.

In the late 1950s, Lowell D. Ashby began research in a field that in the 1970s came to be called "social indicators" by the Social Science Research Council. As early as 1957, Ashby and W. Allen Spivey prepared a monograph dealing with social and economic indices, "Linear Differential Equations and Applications to Economic Theory," which was published in mimeograph form by the Institute, and four years later Ashby was using these concepts in his analysis of the North Carolina economy with special reference to the structure of employment.[88] It was not until 1970, when Angell Beza included a study of social indicators in North Carolina in his section of Southeastern Regional Survey III, that an Institute project dealt specifically with social indicators.[89] Only one article published by an Institute research affiliate has included the term "social indicators" in its title, and that was "Measurement Tests for Evaluation of Social Indicators," in *Socio-Economic Planning Sciences*. It was written in 1972 by Emil Malizia of the Department of City and Regional Planning.

In the 1960s methodological research continued, and projects in sociology included "A Theory of Value," by William R. Catton, Jr.; "Examination of the Possible Application of Electronic Computers in Social Science Research," by Daniel O. Price; and "An Inventory of Research in Marriage and Family Behavior," by Reuben Hill, a field that was further explored by Charles E. Bowerman and his associates in their study of parent and peer orientation of adolescents.[90] Ashby and Pfouts continued their research in economics and each occasionally published as many as two or three articles within a year. George Nicholson in the Institute of Statistics continued to turn out such articles as "Estimation of Parameters from Incomplete Multivariate Samples." In anthropology John Honigmann experimented with sampling reliability. John Gillin, in addition to dealing with theories of folk culture in his southern communities studies, began work in sociocultural therapy, and John Gulick was at work on cultural research in the Middle East as well as continuing his Cherokee studies.

In the spring of 1960 the Institute began a new policy of publishing an unnumbered series of paperbound monographs and working papers of primary interest to social scientists, only to find that some of the publications also had a wider appeal. Within the year, the Institute had issued twelve publications, three in medical sociology, four in urban studies, three in political behavior, one on social desegregation, and one in anthropology.[91]

Six years later, in 1966, the Institute announced the launching of a new series dealing specifically with methodology. Richard L. Simpson, acting director of the Institute, had appointed a committee composed of Hubert M. Blalock, Jr., in sociology, William Keech in political science, and George C. Hemmens in city and regional planning to screen manuscripts for inclusion in the series.[92] During the year two monographs were issued, *A Natural Order of Cultural Adoption and Loss in Trinidad*, by Frank T. Cloak, Jr.; and *Principal Components and Curvature in Occupational Stratification*, by Alden D. Miller. In the 1970s the Institute also published two monographs on political behavior: *The Application of Psychophysical Scaling Techniques to Measurement of Political Variables*, by Allen Mayhew Shinn, Jr., published in 1970; and one by George B. Rabinowitz, *Spatial Models of Electoral Choice: An Empirical Analysis* in 1973. In 1970 and 1971 two monographs on causal theory appeared, one by Michael T. Hannan, *Problems of Aggregation and Disaggregation in Sociological Research*, an elaboration of Blalock's causal-models approach to "change of unit" problems, the other by H. T. Reynolds, *Making Causal Inferences with Ordinal Data*. Although Bruce Eckland in sociology had an early interest in the relation of genetic factors to human behavior and had published several articles in the field, he did not specifically stress the methodological aspects of genetic studies. In 1972 an exploratory monograph on the feasibility of phylogenetic inferences from a classificatory analysis within a genetic unit of societies/languages was prepared by Philip J. Epling from the School of Public Health with the assistance of Jerome Kirk and published by the Institute as *The Dispersal of the Polynesian Peoples: Explorations in the Phylogenetic Inference from the Analysis of Taxonomy*.

Most of the methodological studies in the Institute were published as articles in professional journals, primarily because of the rising costs of book publication. Several books by Institute staff, however, did appear. In 1960, for example, Ralph W. Pfouts edited *Techniques of Urban Economic Analysis*, to which he contributed two chapters, and the next year he edited a volume in honor of Harold Hotelling, who had organized the Department of Statistics, *Essays in Economics and Econometrics*.

In sociology Hubert M. Blalock, Jr., not only produced articles in professional journals on causal inferences and alternative models to status interaction, but also in 1964 a book, *Causal Inferences in Nonexperimental Research*. Two years later, he edited with his wife, Anne B. Blalock, *Methodology in Social Research*. In 1969 he produced *Theory Construction: From Verbal to Mathematical Formulations*, and in 1970 *An Introduction to Social Research*. His last book as a member of the Institute staff before he moved to the University of Washington was one he edited, *Causal Methods in the Social Sciences*, which was published in 1971. David R. Heise replaced Blalock in the field of quantitative sociology. He compiled *Personality and Socialization* in 1972 and the following year his *Personality: Biosocial Bases* was published.

Other sociologists during this period had also been contributing to the development of theory and methodology in their respective fields. In the area of stratification, Gerhard E. Lenski, who came to the University in 1963 and served a term as chairman of the Department of Sociology, published in 1966 *Power and Privilege: A Theory of Stratification*. He continued his research in technology and social organization and in 1970 published *Human Societies*. The second edition of this volume, which Lenski revised in collaboration with his wife, Jean, appeared in 1974. He has pioneered research in societal-evolutionary theory.

Two sociologists in the field of demography were added to the department in 1966—Amos H. Hawley and N. Krishnan Namboodiri. Hawley came to Chapel Hill from the University of Michigan, where he had achieved a distinguished career. Namboodiri was educated at the University of Kerala, India, and took his doctorate in sociology at the University of Michigan. One of Hawley's major research interests was the demography of East Asia. In 1966 he delivered an address on world population growth at the Second National Population Seminar in Bangkok, Thailand, and published several articles on the program of family planning in Thailand. After coming to Chapel Hill he collaborated with Edgar W. Butler on research in the urbanization of society and prepared the section on human ecology for the *International Encyclopedia of the Social Sciences*. In 1973–74 he was demographic adviser to the government of Malaysia. Namboodiri's research in demography was largely in the area of quantitative analysis. In 1968 the Government of India Press published his *Changing Population of Kerala* as one of its Census of India Monographs. His expertise in quantitative analysis was revealed in his "On a Biregional Extension of the Weak Ergodic Theorem," a chapter he contributed to *Essays in Demography*, edited by Ashish Bose, which was published in London. Namboodiri became chairman of the Department of Sociology in 1976.

Senior Institute staff members from the Department of Psychology, among them Grant Dahlstrom, Harold G. McCurdy, Harriet L. Rheingold, John Schopler, John W. Thibaut, and George S. Welsh, also had been publishing books and articles in professional journals that were concerned with improvements in theory and methodology. In 1967 Chester A. Insko published *Theories of Attitude Change*, and in 1971, in collaboration with D. W. Schoeninger, *Introductory Statistics for the Behavioral Sciences*, which had an accompanying workbook. The L. L. Thurstone Psychometric Laboratory, operating independently of the Institute for Research in Social Science, continued to turn out articles on methodology and theory in the *L. L. Thurstone Psychometric Lab Report*.

During the thirty years between the time Blackwell came to the Institute as director and the close of the Institute's first half century of research, development in theoretical and methodological concepts produced by the staff burgeoned. Blackwell's first impulse as director was to bring the staff into closer contact with the thinking of young scholars elsewhere who were beginning to open up new vistas of thought and to employ mathematical models more extensively in shaping methodology. He wanted to bring some of these young researchers into the Institute, and in this he largely succeeded. The Institute directors who followed Blackwell—Price, Prothro, and Munger—continued to stress the development of quantitative analyses in the behavioral sciences: in organization and small group research, in political behavior, in medical sociology and community health, in urban and regional studies, in demography, in the study of world areas, in research on marriage and the family, in social change, in stratification, in studies of personality, child psychology, and infant behavior, in economics, and in mass communication. The research accomplished in these and related fields stimulated similar work elsewhere and brought recognition to the Institute and to the University not only in the southern region but throughout the nation and around the world.

An Overview

This venture in the social history of an institution has attempted to trace the development of the Institute for Research in Social Science at the University of North Carolina through its first fifty years. Those fifty years have been momentous ones in terms of the rapid social changes that have taken place in the South and in the nation. The Institute was founded in 1924 by Howard W. Odum, a unique figure in the annals of American social science. Odum had come to Chapel Hill from Georgia in 1920 to found the Department of Sociology and the School of Public Welfare. He was committed to the idea that "cooperative research in the social sciences" could point the way to the solution of the economic, social, cultural, and racial problems that had long held the South in bondage. He guided the Institute through its formative years and through the Great Depression, and he lived to see the acceptance of many of his ideas concerning the reconstruction of the life of the region. His efforts brought the Institute and some of its constituent social science departments into the upper ranks of American universities. No person in this century has excelled Odum in vision, dedication, persistence, and practical results in the advancement of social science research.

In 1924 the University of North Carolina was still a small instisition, with fewer than 2,500 students and a faculty of 150. Chapel Hill was still "the village" that it was often called, and it lacked many of the amenities of "civilized" living. The state was relatively poor, and its financial support of the University was at best only modest. Worst of all, the prevailing mood of the people of the state was one of provincialism and conservatism. There was a strong distrust of some of the social sciences, particularly of sociology, which was not infrequently confused with socialism. Odum was often put on the defensive in those early years by ministers, editors, and even by his own colleagues, who contended that sociology, *Social Forces*, and the Institute were threatening the religious and social structure of the state. Powerful leaders in industry tried, with some success, to block the Institute's studies of industrial and labor relations. Yet somehow the Institute lived through those turbulent years and finally reached the point where it could take for granted the priceless condition known as academic freedom.

The Institute was the first of several similar research organizations that were started with assistance from philanthropic foundations in the mid-1920s. Its structure was simple: professors in the social science departments conducted researches with the help of research assistants, who were usually advanced graduate students pursuing their doctorates. The unique feature here was that it was not the professor but the research assistant who was subsidized directly for his research. The professor could expect to be relieved of a portion of his teaching load in order to pursue his research, and he could count on clerical assistance, field expenses, and other necessities from the Institute, but he did not "profit" from his status as a member of the Institute staff. The research assistant, however, received one of the most attractive stipends then available in any university, $1,500 a year, for being assigned to a particular professor in his field of interest and for doing research that he would likely be doing anyway for his doctorate. The amount of supervision exercised by the professor and the degree of collaboration between prosessor and assistant varied greatly, but on the whole the student enjoyed considerable freedom. The Institute's foundation benefactors questioned this arrangement and pressed Odum to explain the difference between the research assistants and ordinary graduate fellows. Odum was hard put to explain the difference, but the fact was that he had hit upon a very fruitful device, for aside from the work of Odum himself, it was the work of the young assistants that helped to establish the reputation of the Institute in its formative years. The basic role of the assistants continued with little change until recent years. Today, however, the research assistant tends more and more to be an inconspicuous employee attached to a project organized by a professor affiliated with the Institute rather than a visible member of the staff of the Institute proper. For whatever reasons and with whatever consequences, the assistant's role has undergone a drastic change.

Senior or professorial membership on the Institute staff grew from half a dozen faculty members drawn from social science and related departments in 1924 to 150 drawn from 21 departments, bureaus, and other units of the University in 1974. The early staff members had a presumption of tenure in the Institute, with a tendency to hang on after their research productivity had declined, until the 1940s when a new director, Gordon Blackwell, introduced such ideas as annual review, staff rotation, and temporary affiliation. Today affiliation with the Institute is a simple matter, easy to obtain and easy to terminate. There is no presumption of permanent tenure, and while there are some members who have been on the roster for years because of their productivity, the majority have relatively short terms, according to the duration of their particular projects. In earlier years the Institute's funds, drawn from foundation grants and other sources, were the sole support for the researches of its senior staff members. Today many staff members find their own funds and then turn to the Institute for technical assistance in processing their data by computer.

In the 1940s and 1950s the entire senior and junior staff could sit down for lunch together in Room 407 in Alumni Building and listen to their colleagues report on their researches or hear a talk by a distinguished visitor. Staff luncheons and special seminars were considered valuable devices for communication and for building esprit de corps. Today such an assembly of staff members and assistants anywhere on the campus would be considered virtually impossible—and perhaps irrelevant.

The Institute has been fortunate in the quality of its administrative personnel. Its directors—Howard W. Odum, Gordon W. Blackwell, Daniel O. Price, James W. Prothro, and the incumbent Frank J. Munger—have all been men of vision, integrity, and intellectual vigor. Each man has left his distinctive mark on the Institute. Odum founded it, steered it through its infancy and adolescence, personally rescued it from financial insolvency, and imprinted it with his own dynamism and breadth of interests. Blackwell enlarged the staff, brought in new blood, presided over the era of large-scale contract research for the federal government, and strengthened the commitment to interdisciplinary research. Price built the Statistical Laboratory into a vital factor in the Institute's operations and overcame the financial crisis that accompanied the termination of contract research. Prothro broadened the staff membership, greatly enlarged the University's financial support, and brought the Institute's data bank and computer facilities to a new high level. Munger, who took over in the Institute's fiftieth year, has continued to emphasize the Institute's technical capabilities in serving the research interests of its affiliates.

The administrative structure of the Institute has changed over the years as the needs of the Institute and the University have evolved. The original eight-person Board of Governors was enlarged to twenty-five members in 1934, with representation from the Raleigh and Greensboro branches of the new Consolidated University system. This large board had certain dysfunctional aspects, and the Executive Committee, a smaller body, was created in 1948 to assist in the management of the Institute. The structure was changed again in 1961 when the Board of Governors was converted into the Administrative Board, a panel of twelve that was to meet once or twice a year. The Administrative Board was to be supported by the new Advisory Committee, a smaller working committee that was intended to meet more frequently, but the Advisory Committee apparently had difficulty in finding a useful function, and after a few years it was abandoned. Thus the Institute had come full circle back to the original pattern of a single small governing body. Until 1961 the president (or later the chancellor) of the University was ex-officio chairman of the Board of Governors and presided over its meetings. Since that time the director has served as chairman and presiding officer. In the process of streamlining the administration of the Institute, the role of the director in decision-making has been enhanced, while the direct participation by University officialdom has been diminished.

Finances have been a perennial problem for the Institute. In the early years foundation grants were the only source of support, and annual budgets were typically in the range of $40,000 to $50,000. The Institute was in danger of extinction on several occasions. In the postwar era a surge of federal contract projects brought a certain amount of affluence, and annual budgets rose to the range of $400,000 to $500,000, with the attendant risks involved in becoming heavily committed to research for the defense establishment. Gradually state funds for the Institute increased, and some of the newer foundations, such as the Ford Foundation and the National Science Foundation, made generous grants. The Institute completed its first fifty years in good financial condition. In its fiftieth year, in fact, it finally achieved what all of its directors had hoped for: adequate state funds for its regular operating budget.

The business of the Institute is research, of course, and in this it has been eminently successful. The preceding chapters have detailed the research undertakings of the Institute in numerous areas. In the beginning there was a rather heavy concentration on the folk culture of the Negro people and on problems of black-white relations. About forty per cent of the publications by staff members during the Institute's first five years lay in this area of race and folk studies. These studies drew national attention to the Institute and helped to secure its perpetuation through the renewal of foundation grants. In later years, race studies comprised a smaller proportion of the research effort as the total program became more and more diversified, but they have remained an important interest of the Institute, as shown by its rather extensive studies and publications concerning desegregation in higher education, public school desegregation, public school closings and other efforts to evade desegregation, the aspirations of Negro mothers for their children, the Negro adolescent, the black voter, leadership, and many other areas.

During the Institute's second decade, its main focus was on regionalism. During this period fully a third of the publications were devoted to the development of the concept of regionalism, the delineation of the South and its subregions, the analysis of particular problems of the South, the relation of regionalism to social planning, and the application of the idea of regionalism on a national scale.

The South, of course, has always been a special concern of the Institute. Indeed, it was Odum's love affair with his native region and his conviction that research could point the way to social progress that led to the creation of the Institute in the first place. Both before and after the special flowering of the theory of regionalism, the Institute staff made studies of a great variety of problems that were close at hand in the state or region. In the earlier period, there were studies of textile villages, labor relations, occupations, income and wages, county government, taxation policies, farm tenancy, and migration. In later years the Institute's abiding concern for the region is shown in its studies of political behavior, history, demography, and other aspects of southern society. Closely related to these studies, and sometimes overlapping with areas such as race or region, is a long line of studies of "social problems," that is, studies concerned with such topics as child welfare, infant and child development, personality, marriage and the family, the changing role of women, delinquency and crime, housing, recreation, community organization, and public welfare administration.

Following the Behavioral Science Survey of 1953–54, the Institute reoriented its program to some extent to emphasize the behavioral science approach rather than the descriptive approach to the study of human behavior. Among the most fruitful efforts of behavioral science research were the studies conducted by interdisciplinary teams in the areas of urban and regional studies, political behavior, social aspects of health and the health professions, complex organization, and small group behavior. In addition, anthropologists and sociologists have looked at culture and culture change in Africa, Malaysia, Southern Asia, the Middle East, the Arctic, and Latin America, as well as in the United States itself; political scientists and others have observed political behavior in Latin America, Europe, and elsewhere; while other teams or individuals have worked in educational sociology, mass communications, public opinion, social attitudes, child development, and community health. Alongside all of these projects, members of the Institute staff have made notable contributions to theory and methodology in social science research and to the development of the Institute's capabilities in the planning of research and the electronic storage and retrieval of data. The Institute's data processing facilities and services have helped to put the University among the best equipped institutions in the nation.

Thus, while there has always been emphasis on the study of the southern region, the interests of the Institute have come to transcend the regional and ''social problems'' approaches and have become more and more universalistic in both the spatial and logical senses of the word. And today, with staff affiliates drawn from many different departments and units of the University regardless of their traditional labels, the diversity of research interests is greater than it has been at any other time in the Institute's career.

In conclusion something should be said by way of evaluating the achievements of the Institute for Research in Social Science. Has it been an asset to the University? Has it done anything for the state, the region, and the nation? Has it succeeded in its original objectives?

To begin with, it is quite obvious that the Institute has been an asset to the University. Within a few years of its founding, its publications and the growing reputations of those who were connected with it gave evidence that something new and vital was stirring in the social sciences at Chapel Hill. Graduate students in the social sciences from all over the nation began to see the University as a desirable place to study. Many talented young scholars came to the University because they were able to obtain appointments as research assistants in the Institute. Furthermore, some of the early research assistants received faculty appointments after completing their doctorates and continued their careers with the Institute, thus having a role in the staff expansion in the social sciences that took place at the University in the late 1920s.

Still further, once the Institute was firmly established it became a positive factor in the recruitment of professional staff in the social sciences. The prospect of being a research professor or research associate in the Institute, with time allotted for research and with facilitating services available, was an attraction that enabled the University to employ a number of excellent scholars whose services it might otherwise not have obtained. In addition, the fact that the Institute has brought to the University grants of about $10 million is a matter of no small magnitude in the financial life of the University and its community.

Almost from its beginning, the Institute sought to serve the State of North Carolina in practical ways. Early projects like Odum's work with the North Carolina Prison Commission, Steiner and Brown's study of the chain gang, and Wager's surveys of county government, helped to establish the Institute's reliability in the eyes of state officials. In later years the state continued to profit in innumerable ways from the researches of the Institute and the personal participation of Institute staff members in advisory roles. Odum himself maintained a close personal relationship with most of the governors of the state, beginning with Governor O. Max Gardner, and over the years he counseled them on many of the social issues that confronted the state. He was responsibile for the appointment of the State Planning Board, and he was an important catalyst in the formation of the Research Triangle, an institution that has already paid handsome dividends to the State of North Carolina.

Another significant contribution of the Institute has been its catalyzing effect on the development of the social sciences, especially in the South, where there was a paucity of good social science departments and very little research being done in the 1920s. The Institute's publications were, of course, a stimulus to research and teaching, but much more important was the role of the Institute's alumni, especially the research assistants who had earned their doctorates at Chapel Hill. As social science departments were gradually established or enlarged in southern colleges and universities, it was often these young scholars who staffed them. This was particularly true in sociology. Indeed, for many years these scholars played a dominant role in sociology departments in the South and in the Southern Sociological Society. Thus the ideas and techniques they had acquired at Chapel Hill became a part of that growing ferment which helped to change the face of the South. It should be added, of course, that many of the Institute's alumni over the years have made their academic careers outside the South. Dozens of them have attained distinction as professors in leading educational institutions in the nation.

Not all of the alumni have been teachers or researchers, for they represent a wide variety of occupational interests—administration, social work, medicine, the law, religion, business, journalism, and civil service. A few examples drawn from the Institute's first quarter-century will serve to illustrate the point. John Roy Steelman, who made an early study of mob action in the South (1928), became commissioner of the United States Conciliation Service, a trusted adviser to President Harry S. Truman, director of the Office of War Mobilization and Reconversion, and chairman of the National Security Resources Board. Arthur Raper, who wrote *The Tragedy of Lynching* and *Preface to Peasantry* while he was working for the Commission on Interracial Cooperation, went to the United States Department of Agriculture, where he had a distinguished career in the area of community development both at home and abroad. John E. Ivey, Jr., became executive director of the Southern Regional Education Board, then executive vice president of New York University, dean of the College of Education at Michigan State University, and president of Midwest Programs in Airborne Instruction. George L. Simpson worked with Governor Luther H. Hodges and William C. Friday to lay the groundwork for the Research Triangle Park, served as assistant to James Webb, director of the National Aeronautics and Space Administration, and then became chancellor of the Georgia State University System. A complete listing of alumni and their achievements would go a long way toward validating the statement that no academic unit in any southern university has helped to launch more people in distinguished careers of public service than the Institute for Research in Social Science at the University of North Carolina.

Considering the Institute's researches and publications, the public service aspect of the work of its senior staff, and the far-flung influence of its alumni, it seems clear that the Institute has been not only an observer and critic of the South and its ailments but a seminal force that has helped change the psyche of the southern people and bring the South to the point that it is no longer the nation's "No. 1 problem" but the nation's most promising region. The idea of regionalism, which Odum had to defend against those who could see nothing in it but a sophisticated form of sectionalism, has become so taken for granted that regional and subregional organizations for dealing with all sorts of interests and problems now exist in every part of the nation. The researches and practical work in city and regional planning that developed under the wing of the Institute have helped to make the whole notion of planning acceptable and have provided staff for the planning departments of dozens of rapidly growing urban areas in the South and elsewhere. The researches and demonstration projects conducted by Institute staff members in public health and the medical profession have introduced new ideas and practices into the whole problem of health and the delivery of medical care. In a score of other areas one could marshal considerable evidence of the effect of the Institute on the course of social change in the South. Even in the area of race relations—that sensitive area in which Institute researches used to provoke scurrilous attacks—the almost miraculous changes that have taken place since World War II might in some measure be attributed to the leavening effect of the work that was done at Chapel Hill. Even those who believe that in such an area as race relations it is impossible to demonstrate a causal relation between ideas and social changes would at least have to concede that in this field some of the Institute's studies were prophetic.

When the Institute was founded in 1924 social science research was in its infancy. For those who came to join Odum's new enterprise, there was an aura of excitement and pioneering that later generations could not share. The glamour has faded, and research has become very much taken for granted. The pioneers of 1924 have left the stage, and in the meantime many generations of scholars have come and gone. But each decade brings new challenges and new opportunities, and the need for pioneering never ceases. Individuals come and go, but the Institute lives on, a dynamic and vital force in the intellectual life of the region and the nation. Perhaps Odum's vision of what research "in service to society" could do to change society has been rewarded to a greater extent than even he could have foreseen.

Notes

Chapter 1

1. Guy B. Johnson, in Howard W. Odum, *Folk, Region, and Society*, p. 5.
2. Howard W. Odum to Harry W. Chase, May 3, 1920, Howard W. Odum Papers.
3. "A School of Public Welfare at the University of North Carolina," a memorandum by Eugene C. Branson, December 1919, p. 1, Eugene Cunningham Branson Papers. This was Branson's reconstruction of his 1916 memorandum that had been lost.
4. Ibid.
5. Eugene C. Branson to Odum, December 5, 1919, Branson Papers.
6. Odum to Branson, December 3, 1919, Odum Papers.
7. Branson to John Sprunt Hill, September 9, 1919, Branson Papers.
8. Branson to Hill, December 12, 1919, Branson Papers.
9. Branson to Horace H. Williams, December 12, 1919, Branson Papers.
10. Quoted in Louis R. Wilson, *The University of North Carolina, 1900–1930*, pp. 446–47.
11. *The University of North Carolina Record, The Graduate School, 1921–22*, no. 192, pp. 85–87; The School of Public Welfare, Announcement 1920–21, *The University of North Carolina Record*, nos. 177–78, pp. 12–19.
12. Odum to Clifford Lyons, June 16, 1952, Odum Papers.
13. Harry W. Chase, "To the Members of the Executive Committee of the Board of Trustees of the University of North Carolina," May 12, 1924. Throughout this letter Chase mistakenly referred to the Laura Spelman Rockefeller organization as "Institute" rather than "Memorial."
14. Harry W. Chase, Memorandum to Beardsley Ruml, May 12, 1924, University Papers.
15. Beardsley Ruml to Harry W. Chase, June 16, 1924, University Papers.
16. Chase, "To Members of the Executive Committee," July 8, 1924, University Papers.
17. "First Meeting for Preliminary Organization," Minutes, Board of Governors, June 30, 1924.
18. Odum to Guy B. Johnson, April 7, June 18, 1924, Guy B. Johnson Papers. See also Odum to Johnson, April 28, May 9, June 5, August 8, 1924; Johnson to Odum, May 12, June 14, June 26, 1924.
19. Minutes, Board of Governors, July 25, August 22, October 8, 1924.
20. Howard W. Odum, "University Research and Training in the Social Sciences," p. 519.

Chapter 2

1. Quoted in Guion Griffis Johnson, *Ante-Bellum North Carolina*, p. 22.
2. Ibid., p. 829.
3. Ibid., pp. 31–36.
4. Bureau of the Census, *Fourteenth Census of the United States*, vol. 6, pt. 2, *Agriculture* (Washington: Government Printing Office, 1922); C. Horace Hamilton, *North Carolina Population Trends*, 1: 33; 3: 92–111.
5. Hamilton, *North Carolina Population Trends*, 3: 142.
6. Ibid., 3: 187.
7. For general economic and political trends in North Carolina, see also Robert D. W. Connor, *North Carolina: Rebuilding an Ancient Commonwealth, 1584–1925* (Chicago: American Historical Society, 1929), 2: 573–631, and Hugh T. Lefler and Albert R. Newsome, *North Carolina: The History of a Southern State*, rev. ed. (Chapel Hill, 1963).
8. Louis R. Wilson, *The University of North Carolina, 1900–1930*, pp. 179–291.
9. This was said in the literal sense, for in those days there were indeed railroad tracks in the village and even on the campus. The line from University Junction to Carrboro, which had been built in 1882, was extended to the campus in 1921 to facilitate the delivery of coal to the power plant and of heavy construction materials for several new buildings that were erected in the postwar period. The line crossed Pittsboro Street at grade level just north of the present site of the Nash and Miller buildings, crossed South Columbia Street on a narrow wooden trestle, continued to the power plant, which then lay north of the present site of Venable Hall, then crossed the South Mall and continued eastward in the Saunders Hall area. The railroad was useful in the building of Steele, Saunders, Murphey, and Manning, as well as the four dormitories that lie south of the Arboretum and west of Raleigh Street. It was nearly ten years before the tracks were removed from the central campus area (see ibid., pp. 369, 375–78).
10. In the 1920s women were still rather rare in the student body. In 1921 only 47 were enrolled. In 1923 the number had grown to 89. Spencer Hall, the first dormitory for women, was completed in 1925, after prolonged controversy. The *Tar Heel* issued an "extra" on March 14, 1923, with a large headline that asked "Shall Co-Eds Have Dormitory Built Here?" and an intemperate editorial headed "Women Students Not Wanted Here." The results of a student referendum were cited: of 1,100 students who voted, 937, or 85 percent, disapproved of the presence of women on the campus (see ibid., pp. 379–81).
11. Memorandum in Guy B. Johnson Papers, July 1924.
12. Wilson, *University of North Carolina*, pp. 512–14.
13. Ibid., pp. 515–23.
14. "Personal Recollections," Guion Griffis Johnson Papers.
15. Howard W. Odum, "Memorandum for the Board of Governors, Institute for Research in Social Science," April 24, 1927.
16. The foregoing account is based on personal recollections and on letters and memoranda in the Guy B. Johnson Papers. For Hughes's poem "Christ in Alabama" and his article "Southern Gentlemen, White Prostitutes, Mill-Owners, and Negroes," see *Contempo*, December 1, 1931, p. 1. For press reaction, see such newspapers as

the *Charlotte Observer*, the *Greensboro Daily News*, and the *Raleigh News and Observer* from November 20, 1931 through March 1932.

17. *Journal of Social Forces* 1 (November 1922): 56.

18. Howard W. Odum, "Effective Democracy," p. 180.

19. Fred C. Hobson, Jr., *Serpent in Eden*, p. 90.

20. H. L. Mencken, "The South Rebels Again," a syndicated column, *Chicago Tribune*, December 7, 1924. Mencken had earlier called the *Journal* "the most interesting and important journal, and by long odds, that the South has ever seen" (*Baltimore Evening Sun*, October 20, 1924).

21. As a result of Clark's editorial in the *Southern Textile Bulletin*, December 20, 1923, John J. Parker of Charlotte, a trustee of the University and judge of the U.S. Fourth Circuit Court, wrote to President Chase to inquire about Clark's charges. Chase stoutly defended the *Journal* (Chase to Parker, University Papers). For a fuller account of this incident, see Wayne Douglas Brazil, "Howard W. Odum, The Building Years, 1884–1930," pp. 411–15.

22. *Raleigh News and Observer*, March 4, 1925.

23. Eugene C. Branson to Harry W. Chase, November 17, 1921, University Papers. This ominous attitude was not confined to North Carolina. It probably existed in many states throughout the nation.

24. For a detailed discussion of this controversy, see Brazil, "Howard W. Odum, " pp. 421–46. See also Willard B. Gatewood, Jr., "Embattled Scholar," pp. 379–92.

25. *Raleigh News and Observer*, February 21, 1925.

26. "Personal Recollections," Guy B. Johnson Papers.

27. Howard W. Odum to Frank H. Hankins, March 13, 1925; Odum to Harry Elmer Barnes, March 7, 1925, Odum Papers. Hankins had been one of Odum's professors when Odum was a student at Clark University. At the time of the controversy Barnes and Hankins were no longer editors of the book review section of the *Journal*.

28. Odum to Governor Angus W. McLean, March 6, 1925; Odum to Walter Murphy, March 7, 1925; Odum to L. R. Varser, March 6, 1925, Odum Papers.

29. This fact helped to dampen the anger of the attackers during the turmoil over Bernard's and Barnes's essays. The Baptist Pastors' Conference of Gaston County had asked the governor in March 1925 to investigate the financing of the *Journal* and to cut off any public funds.

30. Wilson, *University of North Carolina*, pp. 467–68.

31. Ibid., pp. 212, 213, 216–17. Publication of the *News Letter* began in 1914 under Branson's supervision. After his retirement in 1932, his successor, Samuel Huntington Hobbs, Jr., assumed responsibility, and after Hobbs's retirement the Institute continued its publication. As Wilson points out, the *News Letter* was not without its critics. A member of the Faculty Advisory Committee brought a copy of the first issue to a meeting of the committee in the office of the president of the University and handed "the nasty sheet" to the president, declaring it to be a disgrace to the University (ibid., p. 216).

32. Minutes, Board of Governors, May 20, 1925.

33. *Raleigh News and Observer*, April 14, 1925.

34. *Southern Textile Bulletin*, December 20, 1923.

35. *Preface to Peasantry*, 1936; *Sharecroppers All* (with Ira De A. Reid), 1941; *Tenants of the Almighty*, 1943; *Rural Life in the United States* (with Carl C. Taylor and

others), 1949; *Regional Patterns of Rural Life* (with Carl C. Taylor), 1949.

36. Eugene C. Branson, "Improved County Government in North Carolina," September 15, 1924, Branson Papers.

37. "Work of the Institute for Research in Social Science, 1925–1926," p. 2, Louis R. Wilson Papers.

38. Chase to Beardsley Ruml, attached to Minutes, Board of Governors, February 7, 1927.

39. Minutes, Board of Governors, March 30, 1927, p. 1.

40. Odum, "Memorandum, April 24, 1927," pp. 1–2.

41. Ibid., p. 1.

42. *Raleigh News and Observer*, June 17, June 18, 1927.

43. Odum to Will W. Alexander, June 18, 1927; Odum to Ruml, June 20, 1927; Thomas Jesse Jones to Odum, June 28, 1927 (two letters under this date), Odum Papers.

44. "Personal Recollections," Guion Griffis Johnson Papers.

45. Jones to John R. Mott (copy marked "confidential"), Odum Papers.

46. Odum to Alexander, June 22, 1927, Odum Papers.

47. Odum to Ruml, June 20, 1927, Odum Papers.

48. Odum to Alexander, June 22, 1927, Odum Papers.

49. Jones to Odum, June 28, 1927, Odum Papers.

50. Minutes, Board of Governors, July 11, 1927, p. 2.

51. Thomas J. Woofter, Jr., *Black Yeomanry*; Guion Griffis Johnson, *A Social History of the Sea Islands*; Guy B. Johnson, *Folk Culture on St. Helena Island*; Clyde V. Kiser, *Sea Island to City*. The study helped to stimulate a movement that culminated in the organization of the National Archives. In searching for data in government files in Washington, a research associate was compelled to lose time by going through endless stacks of dusty files in the departments of War, the Navy, the Treasury, and the Court of Claims. She asked an official in the Treasury Department why the federal government had not set up a national archives center similar to the one that her former professor R. D. W. Connor had helped to establish for the state of North Carolina. "We will support any effort to do this," he replied, and suggested that it would be a good time to start while David H. Blair of North Carolina, Commissioner of Internal Revenue, was in office. Blair had signed the letter of intent giving the researcher permission to view the Treasury files. She returned to Chapel Hill and related the experience to Connor, who became interested in the project at once. In 1934, he became the first archivist of the United States. ("Personal Recollections," Guion Griffis Johnson Papers.)

52. Minutes, Board of Governors, May 23, 1926.

53. "Ten Years' Progress in the Social Sciences at the University of North Carolina."

54. "Memorandum on the Institute for Research in Social Science, University of North Carolina, for the Report of the Lake George Conference," p. 9.

55. Ibid., p. 10. For additional summaries prepared by Odum of the work of the Institute in the first decade, see "Institute for Research in Social Science, Report of the Director," and "Studies and Materials, Institute for Research in Social Science, University of North Carolina, 1924–1932."

Chapter 3

1. Minutes, Board of Governors, January 22, 1934.

2. Minutes, Advisory Board, June 14, 1945.

3. Minutes, Board of Governors, June 1, 1948.

4. Ibid.

5. Minutes, Board of Governors, December 9, 1952.

6. Minutes, Board of Governors, May 7, 1953.

7. Minutes, Board of Governors, December 9, 1952, May 27, 1953; Minutes, Executive Committee, February 3, April 10, 1953.

8. "Annual Report," 1960–61, pp. 22–23.

9. Minutes, Board of Governors, October 5, 1961.

10. Wayne Brazil, writing of the early years of the Institute, says that "absenteeism from Board meetings was rampant." He cites the following evidence: "Of the eight original members of the Board, three were regularly absent from its meetings. Edwin Greenlaw, the Dean of the Graduate School, missed eight of the first ten meetings. D. D. Carroll missed seven of the first eleven sessions, and Branson missed five of the first twelve." He is quite right about Greenlaw, who was put on the Board because of his position but who, as a specialist in English literature, had virtually no interest in social science. However, Brazil does not consider that the board agreed in the beginning that when a member could not be present he could designate a stand-in from his department. Carroll was on leave of absence during most of 1924–25, and his place was filled by W. E. Atkins for four consecutive meetings. Branson's alternate was S. H. Hobbs, who sat in for him at three of the first twelve meetings. When attendance is tabulated on this basis, the record shows that Carroll's seat was vacant at two of the first eleven meetings and that Branson's seat was vacant at two of the first twelve sessions. The ratio of actual attendance to maximum possible attendance was 74 percent, and if Greenlaw's near-zero mark were simply written off the record, the ratio would reach 82 percent. (Wayne Douglas Brazil, "Howard W. Odum, the Building Years, 1884–1920," p. 510.)

11. Minutes, Board of Governors, May 22, 1927.

12. Minutes, Board of Governors, January 16, 1944.

13. Minutes, Board of Governors, May 27, 1953.

14. "Annual Report," 1950–51.

15. "Annual Report," 1956–57, pp. 37–38.

16. Minutes, Executive Committee, November 16, 1957, appended rough draft of Price's memorandum, "Long Range Plans for the Institute for Research in Social Science"; Minutes, Board of Governors, November 21, 1957, and appended revised draft of the memorandum.

17. "Annual Report," 1960–61, pp. 1–2, 22–23.

18. "Annual Report," 1965–66, p. 3.

19. "Annual Report," 1960–61.

20. Ibid.

21. "Annual Report," 1965–66.

22. Memorandum, Richard L. Simpson to Administrative Board, October 18, 1966. Attached to Minutes, Administrative Board, November 22, 1966.

23. James W. Prothro, "Report of Ad Hoc Committee to Study the Functions of the Institute for Research in Social Science."

24. "Recommendations to Vice-Chancellor Palmatier by the Administrative Board of the Institute for Research in Social Science."

25. "Annual Report," 1967–68, p. 7.

26. Minutes, Administrative Board, February 23, 1970.

27. Minutes, Administrative Board, March 12, 1971.

28. "Annual Report," 1968–69, 1972–73.

29. Minutes, Administrative Board, March 2, 1971.

30. A copy of this three-page statement, headed "Institute for Research in Social Science," is appended to Minutes, Administrative Board, February 26, 1969.

31. "Annual Report," 1972–73, pp. 3–8.

32. Ibid., p. 11.

33. "Annual Report," 1973–74.

34. Minutes, Executive Committee, September 24, 1957.

35. "Annual Report," 1958–59, pp. 3–4.

36. "Annual Report," 1960–61, pp. 1–4.

37. Minutes, Board of Governors, June 30, 1924.

38. Minutes, Board of Governors, May 23, 1926.

39. A copy of Odum's draft of the proposed letter from Chase to Ruml is appended to Minutes, Board of Governors, February 7, 1927.

40. Minutes, Board of Governors, May 19, 1955.

41. "Annual Report," 1956–57, p. 2.

42. J. Carlyle Sitterson to Gordon Blackwell, October 24, 1955, appended to Minutes, Executive Committee, November 1, 1955.

43. "Annual Report," 1962–63, pp. 2–3.

44. Ibid., pp. 5–6.

45. Odum Papers.

46. Odum Papers. G. A. Duncan, of Dublin, held an International Fellowship and had been steered to Chapel Hill by Beardsley Ruml. Odum had given him the status of a research assistant.

47. Minutes, Board of Governors, February 7, 1927.

48. Odum's six-page statement, headed "Memorandum for the Board of Governors, Institute for Research in Social Science, April 24, 1927," is appended to Minutes, Board of Governors, April 24, 1927.

49. Minutes, Board of Governors, May 22, 1927.

50. Howard W. Odum, "Statement of the Director of the Institute, Board Meeting of February 23, 1928, Carolina Inn."

51. J. G. de Roulhac Hamilton to President Harry W. Chase, December 9, 1926, University Papers. Hamilton felt that historical research simply did not lend itself to this kind of collaboration. However, he did praise the Institute for other kinds of service that it had given him, and he reiterated to Chase his "fundamental suggestion for strengthening the work of the Institute . . . namely: to establish here a great collection of Southern material." The Institute, through assistance with clerical work and travel, as well as a grant of $2,000 in 1929, greatly facilitated Hamilton's work, which eventually resulted in the excellent Southern Historical Collection at the University.

52. The preceding discussion of trends in the number and status of the research assistants is based on information contained in the annual reports of the director of the Institute for the years mentioned.

53. Minutes, Board of Governors, June 30, 1924.

54. Minutes, Board of Governors, December 2, 1925.

55. Minutes, Board of Governors, April 13, 1927.

56. Minutes, Board of Governors, October 31, 1928.

57. Minutes, Board of Governors, November 3, 1929, and appended agenda prepared by Odum.

58. Memorandum, Howard W. Odum to William T. Couch, October 28, 1929, filed with Minutes, Board of Governors, November 3, 1929.

59. The figures on publications in the first decade were tabulated from the list of publications in Howard W. Odum and Katharine Jocher, eds., *In Search of the Regional Balance of America*, pp. 67 ff. The publications for the fifth decade were tabulated from lists of publications contained in the annual reports of the director of the Institute.

Chapter 4

1. Harry W. Chase, "To the Members of the Executive Committee of the Board of Trustees of the University of North Carolina," May 12, 1924; Beardsley Ruml to Harry W. Chase, June 16, 1924, University Papers.

2. "Proposed Agenda for Institute Board Meeting, Wednesday Evening, December second [1925]," p. 1, appended to the minutes of the meeting.

3. Agenda for the board meeting of May 23, 1926, appended to the minutes of the meeting.

4. Agenda for board meeting of September 29, 1926. Apparently this meeting was not held, as there are no minutes of such a meeting, and the proposal was not approved for submission to the Laura Spelman Rockefeller Memorial until February, 1927.

5. Minutes, Board of Governors, February 7, 1927, and Howard W. Odum, draft of the "Proposed Letter from President to tbe Memorial," appended to the minutes.

6. Minutes, Board of Governors, March 30, 1927.

7. Minutes, Board of Governors, April 13, 1927, and Howard W. Odum, "Memorandum for the Board of Governors, April 13, 1927," p. 4, appended to the minutes.

8. Minutes, Board of Governors, July 11, 1927, February 23, April 18, July 3, October 31, 1928, and appended memoranda and budget materials.

9. George E. Vincent to Chase, January 16, 1929, appended to Minutes, Board of Governors, April 18, 1928.

10. Chase to Howard W. Odum, August 29, 1929, Odum Papers.

11. Odum to Chase, September 4, 1929, Odum Papers.

12. Odum to Sydnor Walker, November 11, 1929, and "Endorsement" dated November 16, 1929, Odum Papers.

13. Odum to Chase, June 4, 1930, Odum Papers.

14. Howard W. Odum, "Ten Years' Progress in the Social Sciences at the University of North Carolina."

15. Minutes, Board of Governors, December 10, 1930.

16. Odum to Will W. Alexander, December 8, 1930, Odum Papers.

17. Howard W. Odum, "Suggested Cooperative Plan for the University of North Carolina, 1930–1940."

18. Odum to Louis R. Wilson, September 11, 1930, Odum Papers.

19. Odum to President Frank P. Graham, September 24, 1931, Odum Papers.

20. "Annual Report," 1930–31.

21. Minutes, Board of Governors, January 30, 1932.

22. Odum to Graham, February 16, 1932, Odum Papers.

23. Odum to Graham, February 17, 1932, Odum Papers.

24. Walker to Odum, April 14, 1932, Odum Papers.

25. Minutes, Board of Governors, January 20, 1932.

26. Odum to Benjamin B. Kendrick, July 3, 1933, Odum Papers.

27. Howard W. Odum, "Basic Memorandum for a Five-Year Terminating Grant from the Rockefeller Foundation Beginning July 1, 1935."

28. Howard W. Odum, "Supplementary Program of Regional Development and Education, Institute for Research in Social Science, University of North Carolina."

29. Graham to Albert R. Mann, Vice-President, General Education Board, March 10, 1938, Odum Papers.

30. Minutes, Board of Governors, May 30, 1938.

31. Laura Spelman Rockefeller Memorial Fund, *Report, 1926*, p. 9.

32. Walker to Odum, January 8, 1935, Odum Papers.

33. Minutes, Board of Governors, May 31, 1938, and appended notes.

34. Walter A. Jessup, Carnegie Corporation, to Odum, March 6, 1942, Odum Papers.

35. Odum to Robert B. House, June 12, 1943, Odum Papers.

36. Minutes, Board of Governors, September 22, 1943.

37. "Annual Report," 1944–45, pp. 21–22.

38. "Annual Report," 1950–51, pp. 6–7.

39. Minutes, Board of Governors, May 15, 1951.

40. "Annual Report," 1953–54, p. 35.

41. "Annual Report," 1954–55, pp. 26–27.

42. Minutes, Board of Governors, December 10, 1951.

43. Minutes, Board of Governors, June 1, 1948.

44. "Annual Report," 1948–49, p. 12.

45. "Annual Report, 1954–55, pp. 22–23, and 1957–58, p. 32.

46. Minutes, Executive Committee, November 19, 1951.

47. Minutes, Board of Governors, December 10, 1951.

48. Minutes, Executive Committee, January 31, February 18, 1952, and letter of Executive Committee to House, February 20, 1952, appended to the minutes.

49. Minutes, Board of Governors, May 18, 1954, and "Annual Report," 1954–55, p. 28.

50. Minutes, Executive Committee, March 9, 1960.

51. Minutes, Administrative Board, January 12, 1965.

52. Minutes, Administrative Board, March 12, 1971.

53. See the financial sections of the various annual reports for the years cited.

54. Minutes, Administrative Board, February 26, 1969.

55. Minutes, Administrative Board, February 23, 1970.

56. "Annual Report," 1973–74, p. 3.

Chapter 5

1. "The Religious Folk-Songs of the Southern Negroes," p. 265.

2. "Folk and Regional Conflict as a Field of Sociological Study," *Publications of the American Sociological Society* 25 (May 1931): n. 23; reprinted in Howard W. Odum, *Folk, Region, and Society*, pp. 239–55.

3. "Folk Sociology as a Subject Field for the Historical Study of Total Human Society and the Empirical Study of Group Behavior," p. 233; reprinted in Odum, *Folk, Region, and Society*, pp. 293–354.

4. "Racial Integration in Southern Higher Education," p. 312.

5. "A Sociologist Looks at Racial Desegregation in the South," p. 10.

6. "The Course of Race Conflict and Racial Movements in the South," in *Race Relations*, eds. J. Masuoka and P. Valien, p. 110.

7. At the meeting of the University Board of Trustees in February 1947, when President Graham presented a list of professors returning from leave, Trustee John Clark moved that Johnson's name be stricken from the list. He cited an address, "Christianity and Race Relations," which he had heard Johnson deliver in a Greensboro church a few days earlier, as evidence of Johnson's unfitness to hold a professorship. Some interesting fireworks ensued, but Clark's resolution could muster only 4 of the 100 votes on the board. For newspaper accounts of this episode, see such newspapers as the *Raleigh News and Observer*, the *Greensboro Daily News*, the *Charlotte Observer*, and the *Atlanta Constitution* for February 12, 1947.

8. Howard W. Odum, "An Approach to Diagnosis and Direction of the Problem of Negro Segregation in the Public Schools of the South," p. 37.

9. Guy B. Johnson, "Personality in a White-Negro-Indian Community," pp. 516–24. The paper was prepared for presentation to the annual meeting of the American Sociological Society in 1938. It contained a brief passage on the probable mixed ancestry of some of the Indians. Being aware of the Indians' sensitivity on the matter of Negro ancestry, Johnson wished to withhold the paper from publication until the research was completed. The program chairman overlooked his instructions and turned the paper over to the editor of the *American Sociological Review*. Johnson learned this too late to halt its publication. In September 1940 Guy and Guion Johnson visited the Indian college at Pembroke to see a pageant portraying the history of the Robeson County Indians. During intermission while Guy Johnson was taking a stroll behind the stands, he was accosted by two robust young men who nudged him into the shadows under the stands and demanded to know if he was "the man who wrote that article about us." Johnson stalled as best he could, asking them what article they were talking about, what journal they had seen it in, and so forth. He mentioned another

journal, the *American Journal of Sociology*, and they said they were quite sure that they had seen the article recently there. Johnson was then able to say quite truthfully, "I give you my word of honor that I have not had a paper published in that journal in the last two years." They let him go, but he did not feel secure until he and Mrs. Johnson were well on the road to Chapel Hill.

10. John P. Gillin and Emmett J. Murphy, "Notes on Southern Culture Patterns," pp. 422, 432.

11. "Annual Report," 1955–56, pp. 22–23.

12. For five years the Department of Sociology and Anthropology operated a summer fieldwork training course under a National Institute of Mental Health grant, which sent students to northern Canada, Mexico, and the Caribbean for field experience.

Chapter 6

1. Carl Sauer to Howard W. Odum, October 4, 1934, Odum Papers.

2. Ibid.

3. Howard W. Odum and Katharine Jocher, eds., *In Search of the Regional Balance of America*, p. iii.

4. Richard Hofstadter, *Social Darwinism in American Thought*, pp. 5–9.

5. Wayne Douglas Brazil, "Howard W. Odum, the Building Years, 1884–1930," chaps. 1–2.

6. Howard W. Odum, "Folk Sociology as a Subject Field for the Historical Study of Total Human Society and the Empirical Study of Group Behavior," pp. 193–223; reprinted in Howard W. Odum, *Folk, Region, and Society*, pp. 293–354.

7. Hofstadter, *Social Darwinism in American Thought*, chap. 7.

8. See Odum's editorial notes, *Journal of Social Forces* 2 (January 1924): 282–86; also quoted in Odum, *Folk, Region, and Society*, pp. 355, 359.

9. Odum, *Folk, Region, and Society*, pp. 272–73; reproduced from Howard W. Odum, *Understanding Society*, chap. 20.

10. Odum and Jocher, eds., *In Search of the Regional Balance of America*, p. 3.

11. R. Jackson Wilson, *In Quest of Community*, pp. 119–20.

12. Odum and Jocher, eds., *In Search of the Regional Balance of America*, p. 8.

13. John Donald Wade, "A Vast Repository of Information on the South," *Knoxville Journal*, November 2, 1930, quoted in Brazil, "Howard W. Odum," p. 600.

14. Howard W. Odum and Katharine Jocher, *An Introduction to Social Research*, pp. vii–viii.

15. Odum to Edmund E. Day, May 23, 1930, Odum Papers.

16. Odum to Sydnor Walker, May 30, 1933, Odum Papers.

17. John W. Powell, "Physiographic Processes," in National Geographic Society, *The Physiography of the United States*, 1: 1–32.

18. Fulmer Mood, "The Origin, Evolution, and Application of the Sectional Concept, 1759–1900," p. 92.

19. Ibid., p. 7. See also Vernon Carstensen, "The Development and Application of Regional-Sectional Concepts, 1900–1950," pp. 99–118.

20. Odum, *Folk, Region, and Society*, pp. 179–80.

21. Odum and Jocher, eds., *In Search of the Regional Balance of America*, p. 5.

22. Odum, *Folk, Region, and Society*, pp. ix, 219–21.

23. Odum and Jocher, eds., *In Search of the Regional Balance of America*, p. 6.

24. Ibid., p. 8.

25. Ibid., pp. 8–9.

26. Ibid., p. 9.

27. Ibid.

28. Odum lists the members of the Southern Regional Committee as Benjamin B. Kendrick, North Carolina College for Women, chairman; Nathaniel B. Bond, University of Mississippi; Wilson Gee, University of Virginia; Joseph Peterson, George Peabody College; George W. Stocking, University of Texas; and Raymond D. Thomas, Oklahoma Agricultural and Mechanical College, in Minutes, Board of Governors, January 20, 1932, p. 2. The history of the Social Science Research Council makes no reference to the work of the Southern Regional Committee, but does list it as a council committee (Elbridge Sibley, *Social Science Research Council*, p. 130).

29. Minutes, Board of Governors, January 20, 1932, p. 1.

30. Ibid., p. 3. At the meeting on January 20, 1932, the Board did approve Odum's proposal for the reorganization of the Institute into a regional body "as a basis for study and planning," but no study committee was appointed and no further action was taken at subsequent meetings of the Board.

31. Howard W. Odum, "Memorandum to the Board of Governors of the Institute for Research in Social Science," May 30, 1932. For a lengthy discussion of alternative proposals, see Minutes, Board of Governors, May 15, 1934.

32. The only tangible result of Odum's proposal seems to have been a plan for cooperation with Duke University. Odum was a member of the committee that drafted *A Plan of Cooperation: Duke University, The University of North Carolina*. For further discussion of Odum's later proposals, see chapters 7 and 9.

33. Howard W. Odum, "University of North Carolina Institute for Research in Social Science," pp. 6–7.

34. Howard W. Odum, *Southern Regions of the United States*, pp. x–xi.

35. *Washington Post and Times Herald*, November 14, 1954.

36. Ibid.

37. Odum, *Southern Regions*, p. 1.

38. Ibid., p. 3.

39. Ibid., pp. 2–3.

40. Ibid., p. 603.

41. Harvey Lebrun, "A Near Encyclopedia of Social Planning," pp. 278–85.

42. Harvey A. Kantor, "Howard W. Odum," p. 284.

43. Odum to George Fort Milton, February 8, 1934, Odum Papers.

44. Twelve Southerners, *I'll Take My Stand*, p. ix. The twelve were John Crowe Ransom, Donald Davidson, Frank L. Owsley, John Gould Fletcher, Lyle H. Lanier, Allan Tate, Herman Clarence Nixon, Andrew Nelson Lytle, Robert Penn Warren, John Donald Wade, Henry Blue Kline, and Stark Young.

45. Ibid., pp. xiv, xix. See also Donald Davidson to John Donald Wade, March 3, 1934, Odum Papers.

46. Fred C. Hobson, Jr., *Serpent in Eden*, pp. 215, 170n; Donald Davidson, "Howard Odum and the Sociological Proteus," p. 388.

47. Louis Wirth, "The Limitations of Regionalism," pp. 392–93. Wirth's criticism was given in 1949 after the appearance of Odum's second major work on regionalism. Odum was the closing speaker at the conference in which Wirth delivered his criticism. Harvey A. Kantor is of the opinion that "Odum approached his topic with all the heady enthusiasm of a young student taken by a strong idea" and "deftly rebutted" Louis Wirth (Kantor, "Howard W. Odum," p. 289). Odum replied to Wirth in "The American Blend: Regional Diversity and National Unity," *Saturday Review of Literature*, August 6, 1949, pp. 92, 96, 169–72.

48. Eugene P. Odum, "The Emergence of Ecology as a New Integrative Discipline," p. 1291.

49. Kantor, "Howard W. Odum," p. 285.

50. Howard W. Odum and Harry Estill Moore, *American Regionalism*, p. 18. For a summary of other definitions of regionalism, see ibid., p. 276.

51. Ibid., chap. 25.

52. Ibid., pp. 435–36.

53. Ibid., p. 437.

54. Howard W. Odum, "The Promise of Regionalism," pp. 413–16.

55. For a brief evaluation of Odum's concepts that are applicable to present-day problems, see Kantor, "Howard W. Odum," pp. 290–92.

56. George Brown Tindall, *The Emergence of the New South*, p. 606; George Brown Tindall, "The Significance of Howard W. Odum to Southern History," p. 300.

57. Odum to Walker, May 2, 1933, Odum Papers.

58. By 1947 opposition to state planning as a concept had become so outspoken that the General Assembly failed to renew appropriations for the State Planning Board. The next year the State Planning Committee, of which Odum was made a member, was set up to prepare a proposal for the 1949 General Assembly urging renewal of the appropriation. The General Assembly took no action in 1949, claiming that the proposal of the State Planning Committee had arrived too late for consideration. A smaller committee to consider reactivation or replacement of the State Planning Board met in 1950, but because of strong opposition to state planning it let the matter rest. Philip P. Green, Jr., professor in the Institute of Government at the University of North Carolina at Chapel Hill, outlined in a telephone interview with Guion Johnson, August 15, 1977, the varying approaches to state planning taken by North Carolina governors since 1949.

59. *Durham Morning Herald*, July 5, 1975. For regional planning groups elsewhere, see John C. Bollens and Henry J. Schmandt, *The Metropolis and Its People, Politics and Economic Life*.

60. Odum and Jocher, eds., *In Search of the Regional Balance of America*, p. 51.

61. Rupert B. Vance with Nadia Danilevsky, *All These People*, pp. vii, viii.

62. Odum to Walter A. Jessup, March 6, 1942, Odum Papers.

63. Jackson Davis to Frank P. Graham, December 18, 1941, Odum Papers.

64. Odum and Jocher, eds., *In Search of the Regional Balance of America*, p. 43.

65. Odum to Robert B. House, June 12, 1943, Odum Papers.

66. Odum to Harry W. Chase, March 23, 1943, Odum Papers.

67. Kantor, "Howard W. Odum," p. 290.

Chapter 7

1. Howard W. Odum, "Folk Sociology as a Subject Field for the Historical Study of Total Human Society and the Empirical Study of Group Behavior," p. 194.

2. H. L. Mencken, "The Sahara of the Bozart," in *Prejudices: Second Series*, pp. 136, 137. Mencken's essay was first published in the *New York Evening Mail*, November 13, 1917.

3. Clarence Heer, *Income and Wages in the South*, p. 66.

4. Ibid., p. 68.

5. Howard W. Odum and Katharine Jocher, eds., *In Search of the Regional Balance of America*, p. 83.

6. Ibid.

7. Ibid., pp. 83–85.

8. Rupert B. Vance, *Human Geography of the South*, p. 467.

9. Benjamin B. Kendrick, "The Colonial Status of the South," p. 19.

10. Vance, *Human Geography*, p. 468.

11. Walter Prescott Webb, *Divided We Stand*, pp. 94–95.

12. William T. Couch, ed., *Culture in the South*, p. 103. This book was not a product of Institute planning although several Institute staff members contributed essays. In fact, its publication disturbed Odum because he felt that it might endanger the Institute's research on regionalism then under way.

13. Among the publications of Rupert Vance were *The South's Place in the Nation*; "Planning the Southern Economy," *Southwest Review* (1935); "The Changing Economy of the Southeast," *Occupations* (1936); and "The Regional Distribution of Economic Opportunity," in *Problems of a Changing Population*, published by the National Resources Committee in 1938. Among articles by Howard W. Odum were "Promise and Prospect of the South," *Proceedings of the Southern Political Science Association* (1936); "Cotton and Diversification," *Proceedings of the Southern Social Science Research Conference*, New Orleans (1935); "The South Is an Area of Scarcity instead of a Land of Abundance," *The South Today*, a series of syndicated news articles (1936); and "What is the Answer?" *Carolina Magazine* (1939).

14. Walter R. McDonald, *The Southern Governor's Conference*.

15. Quoted in George Brown Tindall, *The Emergence of the New South, 1913–1945*, p. 593.

16. Tindall gives an account of developments during this period in ibid., pp. 592–606.

17. For a list of these articles, see Odum and Jocher, eds., *In Search of the Regional Balance of America*, pp. 76–81.

18. Thomas A. Krueger, *And Promises To Keep*.

19. Wilson Gee to Howard W. Odum, October 11, 1938, Odum Papers; Odum to Will W. Alexander, November 30, 1938, Odum Papers.

20. Odum to Prentiss M. Terry, August 15, 1938, Odum Papers.

21. The completed monographs were C. F. Korstian and Lee M. James, *Forestry in The South*; Harriet L. Herring, *Southern Resources for Industrial Development*; and Edith Webb Williams, *Research in Southern Regional Development*, all published by Dietz Press, Richmond, 1948. In 1949 Walter P. Taylor's *Land Wildlife Resources of the South* was also published by Dietz Press. See Gordon W. Blackwell, "Report of the Director for 1945," pp. 14–15; Minutes, Board of Governors, June 1, 1948, p. 2.

22. "Annual Report," 1953–54, p. 7.

23. Interview with Gordon W. Blackwell, September 18, 1975.

24. At this time Price was supervising research on subregional migration in the Tennessee Valley by John K. Folger under a grant from the Tennessee Valley Authority. Folger and John Rowan published an article on the findings in *Social Forces* (December 1953). Price was also directing the doctoral dissertation of Sara E. Smith, "The Intermetropolitan Migrant in the Southeast, 1935–1940."

25. Interview with Blackwell, September 18, 1975.

26. "The Formulation and Administration of Regional Development Programs," October 21, 1952, p. 9, a research proposal attached to Minutes, Executive Committee, February 3, 1953.

27. For a discussion of the Urban Studies Program, see chapter 10.

28. "Annual Report," 1960–61, p. 5.

29. "Recommendations to Vice-Chancellor Palmatier by the Administrative Board of the Institute for Research in Social Science," p. 5.

30. James W. Prothro, "Report of the Ad Hoc Committee to Study the Functions of the Institute for Research in Social Science," p. 6.

31. "Annual Report," 1968–69, p. 4.

32. "Annual Report," 1971–72, p. 7.

33. Ibid., p. 30.

34. Minutes, Board of Governors, June 30, 1924, p. 2; July 25, 1924, p. 1; August 22, 1924, pp. 1, 2.

35. *Southern Textile Bulletin*, December 20, 1923, p. 22.

36. Odum to A. M. Trawick, March 17, 1924, Odum Papers.

37. Howard W. Odum, "Memorandum for Institute Meeting, December 17, 1924," pp. 2–3.

38. Minutes, Board of Governors, December 17, 1924, p. 1.

39. Walter J. Matherly, C. T. Murchison, D. D. Carroll, and Harriet L. Herring, "Memorandum Concerning the Proposed Investigation of the Economic and Social Aspects of the Southern Textile Industry by the Institute for Research in Social Science at the University of North Carolina," attached to letter from D. D. Carroll to President Harry W. Chase, January 19, 1926, University Papers.

40. "The Pinehurst Meeting," *Southern Textile Bulletin*, December 3, 1925, p. 26.

41. For a summary of the controversy, see memorandum in University Papers, folder for February 17–18, 1926, unsigned and undated.

42. Willard B. Gatewood, Jr., "Embattled Scholar," p. 379.

43. Harriet L. Herring, *Welfare Work in Mill Villages*, p. 99.

44. Carl Emmett Rankin, *The University of North Carolina and the Problems of the Cotton Mill Employee*, p. 104.

45. Minutes, Executive Committee, January 31, 1952, p. 3. Blackwell's memorandum to Logan Wilson of January 21, 1952, is attached to the minutes.

46. University of North Carolina, "The University of North Carolina Survey of Behavioral Science, 1953–1954," p. 561.

47. Interview with Blackwell, September 18, 1975.

48. "Annual Report," 1968–69, pp. 20–21.

49. Ibid., p. 27.

50. Glen Gilman, *Human Relations in the Industrial Southeast*, p. xi.

51. Jennings J. Rhyne, *Some Southern Cotton Mill Workers and Their Villages*, p. vi.

52. Rankin, *The University of North Carolina and the Problems of the Cotton Mill Employee*, 105–6; Tindall, *Emergence of the New South*, pp. 76–78; Wayne Douglas Brazil, "Howard W. Odum, the Building Years, 1884–1930," pp. 472–74. See also Broadus Mitchell and George S. Mitchell, *The Industrial Revolution in the South*; Thomas Tippett, *When Southern Labor Stirs*.

53. Rhyne, *Some Southern Cotton Mill Workers*, pp. 203, 211, 213.

54. Ibid., pp. 205–6.

55. Frank Tannenbaum, *Darker Phases of the South*, pp. 55–70.

56. Mitchell and Mitchell, *Industrial Revolution in the South*, pp. 264–66.

57. Eugene C. Branson and J. A. Dickey, "How Farm Tenants Live in Mid-State Carolina," *North Carolina Club Yearbook, 1921–22*, p. 69.

58. Brazil summarizes this episode in "Howard W. Odum," pp. 534–44.

59. Odum to Worth M. Tippy, telegram, August 10, 1926; Odum to Tippy, September 20, 1926, Odum Papers. For the correspondence between Odum and Paul Blanshard, see letters dated April 18, 22, 25, 1927, Odum Papers.

60. Paul Blanshard, "Servants of the Spindle," *New Republic*, September 21, 1927, pp. 114–16; September 28, 1927, pp. 143–45.

61. *Greensboro Daily News*, December 11, 1927.

62. Chase to Haywood Parker, March 8, 1928, University Papers.

63. "Blanshard and His Buddies," *Southern Textile Bulletin*, January 19, 1928, p. 18.

64. "The Greensboro Conference," *Southern Textile Bulletin*, December 15, 1927, p. 22; "Our Greatest Menace," ibid., January 5, 1928, pp. 22, 27; "Blanshard and His Buddies," ibid., January 19, 1928, pp. 18, 22; "Organizing," ibid., February 2, 1928, p. 20; "Blanshard and Mitchell," ibid., May 23, 1929, p. 20. Thomas Holland was a research assistant in the Institute. His project began in 1926.

65. "Our Greatest Menace," ibid., January 5, 1928, p. 22.

66. Ibid.

67. Chase to Parker, March 8, 1928, University Papers.

68. Chase to Odum, Carroll, and Frank P. Graham, March 6, 1928, University Papers.

69. Chase to Parker, March 8, 1928, University Papers.

70. *Raleigh News and Observer*, July 15, 1928; July 20, 1928. See also Chase to J. W. Crabtree, secretary of the National Education Association, July 16, 1928, University Papers. A report, "Present Research Personnel of the Institute for Research in Social Science," February 23, 1928, contains the following statement: "T. J. Woofter, Jr., [is] also editing for publication the Eutsler, Holland, Newcomb studies." These studies, however, do not appear in Odum and Jocher, eds., *In Search of the Regional Balance of America*, as having been published, with the exception of one by

Roland Eutsler, "Agricultural Credit and the Negro Farmer." Eutsler was not involved in the Greensboro conference. For further information on Newcomb's study, see Chase to James A. Gray of Reynolds Tobacco Co., May 3, 1927, University Papers.

71. "Guardians of the South," *Textile Bulletin*, May 15, 1944, pp. 38–39.

72. "Annual Report," 1955–56, pp. 17, 38, 41.

73. The Textile Workers Union of America is still trying to organize the mills that have not yet unionized in North Carolina, despite setbacks in Cannon Mills in Kannapolis and in the Stevens mills at Roanoke Rapids. See David R. Nelsen, "Textile Union Organizers Say Efforts Bearing Fruit," *Durham Morning Herald*, February 22, 1976.

74. Conference program attached to Minutes, Board of Governors, April 8, 1940.

75. "Annual Report," 1959–60, pp. 1–2.

76. "Annual Report," 1969–70, p. 36.

77. John C. McKinney and Edgar T. Thompson, eds., *The South in Continuity and Change*, p. 198.

78. Ibid., p. 223.

79. Rupert B. Vance, *Human Factors in Cotton Culture*, p. 297.

80. Ibid., p. 307.

81. Ibid., p. 318.

82. Arthur F. Raper, *Preface to Peasantry*, p. 406.

83. Ibid.

84. Arthur F. Raper and Ira De A. Reid, *Sharecroppers All*, p. v.

85. Ibid., p. vii.

86. Ibid., p. 255.

87. Ibid.

88. "Annual Report," 1953–54, p. 9; 1954–55, p. 11.

89. Howard W. Odum, "Studies and Materials, Institute for Research in Social Science, University of North Carolina, 1924–1932," pp. 4, 5.

90. "Report of Research Carried On by Research Associates, 1928–1929 and Suggested Plans for the Coming Year," p. 2.

91. "Annual Report," 1934, p. 2.

92. Odum and Jocher, eds., *In Search of the Regional Balance of America*, pp. 74–75.

93. "Annual Report," 1953–54, p. 37.

94. "Annual Report," 1968–69, p. 4.

Chapter 8

1. In an editorial in the *Journal of Social Forces* 2 (September 1924): 730–35, Odum pleaded for "a more articulate South" and stressed "the prevailing ignorance in high places." He wrote, "What we need more than anything else is the ability and willingness to face the truth, through social study and interpretation with the corresponding ability and willingness to make the necessary adjustments."

2. "Howard W. Odum," *Washington Post and Times Herald*, November 14,

1954; "Howard W. Odum, Sociologist, Dies," *New York Times*, November 10, 1954; "Milestones," *Time Magazine*, November 22, 1954.

3. Benjamin Harrison Chaffee [Morris Mitchell], "Mine Own People," p. 497.

4. "Annual Report," 1944–45, pp. 1–3.

5. Roy Melton Brown, *Public Poor Relief in North Carolina*, pp. 118–19. An Institute study in 1941 by Anne Williams Tillinghast, "A Statistical Study of the Social Work Personnel in the North Carolina County Departments of Public Welfare, November, 1941," found a higher level of educated staff than previously but still a scarcity of trained social workers.

6. Ibid., p. 117.

7. Ibid., p. 162.

8. The Durham County home was built in 1924 and did not close until 1969. In 1932 the home had 100 inmates, including 25 in the mental ward and a number of prisoners. See George Lougee, "The County Home: Her Memories Vivid," *Durham Morning Herald*, October 15, 1976.

9. Howard W. Odum and Katharine Jocher, eds., *In Search of the Regional Balance of America*, p. 82.

10. In 1938, Harriet L. Herring and Margaret Clark Neal, with the assistance of WPA workers, had prepared "The North Carolina Conference for Social Service: The Record of Twenty-five Years, 1912–1937," which was not published.

11. Gordon W. Blackwell and Raymond F. Gould, *Future Citizens All*, p. 136.

12. Ibid., p. 133.

13. M. Elaine Burgess and Daniel O. Price, *An American Dependency Challenge*, p. 186.

14. *Social Forces* 21 (October 1942): 120.

15. *Social Forces* 28 (December 1949): 222.

16. *University of North Carolina Record: Research in Progress, January 1954–December 1955*, p. 289.

17. L. A. Williams, "The South as a Field for Sociological Research," *Journal of Social Forces* 1 (January 1923): 112.

18. Ibid., p. 114.

19. L. A. Williams, "The Intellectual Status of Children in Cotton Mill Villages," *Social Forces* 4 (September 1925): 186.

20. "Interviewed," *Southern Textile Bulletin*, December 31, 1925, p. 22.

21. Ibid. See also "Breeding Radicals," ibid.; "He Who Fights," ibid., January 7, 1926, p. 22; "The Voice of an Ally," ibid., January 14, 1926, p. 22.

22. Odum and Jocher, eds., *In Search of the Regional Balance of America*, pp. 81, 82.

23. Spencer B. King, Jr., *Selective Service in North Carolina in World War II*; Minutes, Board of Governors, June 1, 1948, p. 2.

24. The Human Betterment League of North Carolina, *Twenty-five Years of Human Betterment, 1947–1942*. The League's emphasis has consistently been on prevention rather than institutional care. It is an educational rather than a research agency.

25. Minutes, Executive Committee of the Board of Governors, November 2, 1960, p. 2.

26. "Proposed Study of the Child-Care Institution as a Factor in Rehabilitating Family Life," p. 2.

27. The Chapel Hill Workshop is an agency of the School of Social Work that is concerned with work with child care institutions.

28. Martin Gula, review of *Houseparents in Children's Institutions*, by Alton Broten.

29. "Annual Report," 1965–66, 1966–67, 1968–69. Robinson resigned as director of the Frank Porter Graham Child Development Research Center in the spring of 1969.

30. "Annual Report," 1960–61, p. 6.

31. "Applicants for Affiliation," in Minutes, Administrative Board, February 23, 1970.

32. Minutes, Executive Committee, October 24, 1950, p. 2. An interdisciplinary proposal for research to be done on a contract basis for the American Bar Association on "the effects of mass media of communication on crime and delinquency" depended upon a grant from the Association.

33. Francis S. Wilder, "Crime in the Superior Courts of North Carolina," pp. 423–27.

34. Howard W. Odum to L. R. Wilson, January 25, 1927, Odum Papers. See also Wayne Douglas Brazil, "Howard W. Odum, the Building Years, 1884–1930," p. 550.

35. Jesse F. Steiner and Roy M. Brown, *The North Carolina Chain Gang*, p. vii. The book stimulated a study of the chain gang system by women's clubs, many of which later joined in the effort to abolish road work for prisoners that arose in the 1960s as a result of the report of the Spencer Commission on the court system of North Carolina. With the abolition of the county convict camps, the number of prisoners in the state prison system began to accumulate so rapidly that several sessions of the General Assembly were obliged to consider proposals to build high-rise prisons to take care of the influx. In 1975 the General Assembly again approved road work for prisoners on a limited basis.

36. Ibid., p. 5.

37. Ibid.

38. Ibid., p. 7.

39. Ibid., pp. 17–18.

40. Ibid., pp. 15, 18.

41. Quoted in ibid., p. 184.

42. Howard W. Odum, "A Survey of the North Carolina Prison System," 1930.

43. Minutes, Executive Committee, June 27, 1952; Minutes, Board of Governors, December 9, 1952, p. 3; ibid., April 1, 1953.

44. "Annual Report," 1970–71, p. 14.

45. Carl Emmett Rankin, *The University of North Carolina and the Problems of the Cotton Mill Employee*, pp. 175–76.

46. Minutes, Executive Committee, November 19, 1951, p. 2.

47. Reuben Hill, "A Critique of Contemporary Marriage and Family Research," p. 270. Leonard S. Cottrell, Jr., and Nelson Foote completed a review of family research since 1945, and Cottrell published a summary of the findings as "New Directions of Research on the American family" in *Social Casework* 34 (1953): 54–60. In 1955 the University of Chicago Press brought out the study under the title of *Identity and Interpersonal Competence*. After his retirement at Cornell University, Cottrell joined the Department of Sociology at the University of North Carolina at Chapel Hill and affiliated with the Institute for Research in Social Science. As early as

1928, Katharine Jocher had written "Methods of Research in Studying the Family," *Family* 9 (1928): 80–85.

48. Hill, "A Critique of Contemporary Marriage and Family Research," pp. 272, 276.

49. "Annual Report," 1970–71, p. 11.

50. Howard W. Odum, "Memorandum for Institute Meeting, December 17, 1924," p. 4.

51. Minutes, Board of Governors, December 17, 1924, p. 2.

52. Odum and Jocher, eds., *In Search of the Regional Balance of America*, p. 81.

53. Minutes, Board of Governors, January 18, 1926, pp. 1–2.

54. *Social Forces* 3 (May 1925): 612–16.

55. *Family* 9 (1928): 234–36.

56. Mary Phlegar Smith, "Legal and Administrative Restrictions Affecting the Rights of Married Women to Work."

57. Kathryn McHale, review of *The American Woman*, by Ernest R. Groves, pp. 597–98.

58. Julia Cherry Spruill, *Women's Life and Work in the Southern Colonies*, p. 366.

59. Margaret Jarman Hagood, *Mothers of the South*, p. 4.

60. Ibid., p. 244.

61. Ibid., p. 243.

62. *University of North Carolina Record: Research in Progress, October 1945–December 1948*, p. 405.

63. "Annual Report," 1961–62, Appendix A, p. 7; 1965–66, p. 16.

64. "Annual Report," 1954–55, p. 43.

65. Jesse F. Steiner, "Community Organization in Relation to Social Change," p. 102.

66. Ibid., pp. 102–3.

67. During this time Guion Johnson was chairman of the board of the National Publicity Council for Health and Welfare Services (New York), and the board members, who were representatives for national agencies, repeatedly declared, "Our only guidelines in community organization come from Jesse Steiner's publications."

68. "Annual Report," 1944–45, pp. 15–16

69. Ibid., p. 5

70. Ibid., pp. 20–21.

71. *The University of North Carolina Record: Research in Progress, January 1949–December 1949*, p. 241; interview with Gordon W. Blackwell, September 18, 1975.

72. Interview with Blackwell, September 18, 1975.

73. Ibid.

74. Minutes, Board of Governors, November 7, 1944, p. 4. See also Gordon W. Blackwell, "1944 Program of the Institute for Research in Social Science, October 18, 1944," appended to these minutes, p. 13.

75. Howard W. Odum, *Southern Regions of the United States*, p. 193.

76. Minutes, Board of Governors, November 7, 1944, p. 4; "Annual Report," 1944–45, p. 14.

77. Gordon W. Blackwell, "1944 Program of the Institute," p. 13, attached to Minutes, Board of Governors, November 7, 1944.

78. The Urban Studies program is discussed in chap. 10.

79. Minutes, Board of Governors, November 7, 1944, pp. 4–7.

80. Blackwell, "1944 Program of the Institute," pp. 2–3.

81. Blackwell also cited *Social Forces* as a medium of communication in the professional field, the *News Letter* as a means of reaching people throughout the state, and the contemplated publications of the North Carolina Council for Social Studies in cooperation with the Extension Division and the Institute as a source of information for social studies teachers in the schools.

82. Harvard, Massachusetts Institute of Technology, Columbia, Cornell, Illinois, and the University of Washington. See Minutes, Board of Governors, November 7, 1944, p. 5.

83. Minutes, Board of Governors, November 7, 1944, pp. 6–7.

84. Ibid., p. 7; "Annual Report," 1944–45, pp. 16–17.

85. Blackwell, "1944 Program of the Institute," p. 7.

86. Thirteen monographs were proposed for this study, including Howard W. Odum, "Southern Offering," a descriptive summary of resources and the results of their waste in the South; Rupert B. Vance, "The Southern People and Resource Development"; Edith Webb Williams, "Research and Southern Regional Development"; Paul W. Wager, "Government's Role in Southern Resource Development"; S. H. Hobbs, Jr., "Water Power Resources in the South"; Harriet L. Herring, "Industrial Opportunities for Southern Resource Development"; and Rupert B. Vance, "Agricultural Opportunities for Southern Resource Development." See "Annual Report," 1944–45, pp. 14–15.

87. Blackwell, "Progress Report, November 1944 to June 1945," p. 4, appended to Minutes, Board of Governors, June 14, 1945.

88. Ibid., p. 19.

89. Ibid., p. 5; "Annual Report," 1948–49, pp. 14–15.

90. "Annual Report," 1944–45, p. 17.

91. Minutes, Advisory Board, December 9, 1947, pp. 3–4.

92. "Annual Report," 1948–49, p. 6.

93. Interview with Blackwell, September 18, 1975.

94. Minutes, Board of Governors, June 1, 1948, p. 5.

95. "Annual Report," 1948–49, pp. 15–16.

96. Minutes, Executive Committee, September 28, 1953, p. 3.

97. Ibid., October 15, 1948, p. 3.

Chapter 9

1. University of North Carolina, "The University of North Carolina Survey of Behavioral Science, 1953–54," p. 509.

2. Ibid., pp. 34, 557–58.

3. Interview with Gordon W. Blackwell, September 18, 1975.

4. Ibid.

5. "Annual Report," 1948–49, pp. 16–17.

6. Minutes, Executive Committee, November 14, 1949, p. 4.

7. Minutes, Executive Committee, October 24, 1950, pp. 2, 4. The Minutes, Board of Governors, December 5, 1950, p. 4, explain that the grant "is not to be allocated to specific projects but . . . is for training students and staff, for planning research, for temporary staff appointments, for working out methods of carrying out research, and similar purposes."

8. In addition to Daniel O. Price and James D. Thompson, members of the core committee were Harold A. Bierck (Department of History); Frederic N. Cleaveland (Political Science); Norman E. Eliason (English); John J. Honigmann (Anthropology); James C. Ingram (Economics); and John W. Thibaut (Psychology). The self-study culminated in a 604-page mimeographed report.

9. University of North Carolina, "Survey of Behavioral Science," p. 26.

10. Ibid.

11. Ibid., p. 141.

12. Ibid., pp. 143–46.

13. Ibid., p. 135.

14. Ibid., p. 134 n. 1.

15. Ibid., pp. 110–11.

16. "Annual Report," 1954–55, p. 3. The junior staff consisted of twenty-seven members from eight departments.

17. Ibid., pp. 4, 5.

18. Ibid., pp. 5–13. See also Gordon W. Blackwell, "Multidisciplinary Team Research," pp. 367–74.

19. "Annual Report," 1954–55, p. 13.

20. "Annual Report," 1955–56, pp. 4–13.

21. Minutes, Executive Committee, February 15, 1950, p. 5. Each annual report summarized the work of the Statistical Laboratory.

22. "Annual Report," 1955–56, p. 4.

23. "Annual Report," 1957–58, p. 20.

24. Howard W. Odum to Robert M. Hutchins, February 14, 1952; February 22, 1952, Odum Papers.

25. Louis R. Wilson, *The Research Triangle of North Carolina*, p. 4.

26. Ibid., pp. 15–18.

27. Ibid., p. 18. For Governor Hodges's account of the founding of the Research Triangle Park and the creation of the Research Triangle Institute, see Luther H. Hodges, *Businessman in the State House*, pp. 203–23. For details concerning the important role of Romeo H. Guest, president of Romeo H. Guest Associates of Greensboro, see William B. Hamilton, "The Research Triangle of North Carolina," pp. 254–78. Hamilton states that "Odum becomes germane" to the establishment only in so far as Simpson, "who worked with Odum," became director of the Research Triangle Committee. Hamilton, however, did not have access to the Odum papers or to the Minutes of the Board of Governors of the Institute for Research in Social Science.

28. "Annual Report," 1965–66, p. 13.

29. James W. Prothro, "Report of the Ad Hoc Committee to Study the Functions of the Institute for Research in Social Science," p. 2. The committee members were James W. Prothro, chairman; John C. Cassel; F. Stuart Chapin, Jr.; Arnold S. Nash; and Richard L. Simpson.

30. Ibid., p. 6.

31. Ibid., pp. 3–5.

32. "Annual Report," 1967–68, p. 11.

33. The University of North Carolina, "A Proposal to the National Science Foundation for Support to Achieve an Academic Center of Excellence in Science at the University of North Carolina at Chapel Hill."

34. Minutes, Executive Committee, November 14, 1949, p. 4; Minutes, Board of Governors, December 9, 1949, p. 3.

35. University of North Carolina, "Survey of Behavioral Science," p. 435. The members of the Organization Research Group as first set up were Nicholas J. Demerath, Frederic N. Cleaveland, John W. Thibaut, Frederick L. Bates, James D. Thompson, Wallace Lambert, James Weiner, and George Tracy.

36. Ibid., p. 49.

37. Ibid., p. 416.

38. Ibid.

39. Ibid., p. 417.

40. Minutes, Board of Governors, December 5, 1950, p. 2. "Annual Report, 1950–51," p. 7, listed the amount of the first Air Force grant as $70,000 for one year, "to be extended," and the purpose of the grant to be for a study of daytime and nighttime distribution of population in selected industrial cities and for a study of foreign planning.

41. Gordon W. Blackwell, "Factors in Multidisciplinary Team Research," in University of North Carolina, "Survey of Behavioral Science," p. 580.

42. University of North Carolina, "Survey of Behavioral Science," p. 428.

43. Among these reports were: Frederick L. Bates, "Status and Priority as Tests of Democratic Society: An Operational Analysis," *Social Forces* 31 (October 1952): 34–38; Frederic N. Cleaveland, "Administrative Decentralization in the U.S. Bureau of Reclamation," *Public Administration Review* 13 (Winter 1959): 17–29; Nicholas J. Demerath, "Initiating and Maintaining Research Relations in a Military Organization," *Journal of Social Issues* 8, no. 3 (1952): 11–23; Wallace E. Lambert with Harold G. McCurdy, "The Efficiency of Small Human Groups in Solution of Problems Requiring Genuine Cooperation," *Journal of Personality* 20 (1952): 478–94; Herbert W. Eber and Harold G. McCurdy, "Democratic Versus Authoritarian: A Further Investigation of Group Problem Solving," *Journal of Personality* 22 (1953): 238–69; John W. Thibaut and Harold H. Kelley, "Experimental Studies of Group Problem Solving and Process," in *Handbook of Social Psychology*, ed. Gardner Lindzey (1954); and James D. Thompson with Nicholas J. Demerath, "Some Experience with the Group Interview," *Social Forces* 31 (December 1952): 148–54. These articles are among the twenty-two listed by the "Small Groups and Complex Organizations Report" in University of North Carolina, "Survey of Behavioral Science," pp. 438–39, as being most helpful in the development of theory.

44. "Annual Report," 1957–58, pp. 30–31.

45. "Annual Report," 1959–60, pp. 3–5.

46. "Annual Report," 1960–61, pp. 5–6, 15–17.

47. "Annual Report," 1971–72, p. 34.

48. Institute for Research in Social Science, "Publications by the Senior Research Faculty, 1973–74," p. 18.

49. Interview with Blackwell, September 18, 1975.

50. University of North Carolina, "Survey of Behavioral Science," p. 48.

51. Ibid.

52. Arthur F. Bentley, *The Process of Government*, quoted with approval in University of North Carolina, "Survey of Behavioral Science," p. 321.

53. University of North Carolina, "Survey of Behavioral Science," p. 322; Elbridge Sibley, *Social Science Research Council*, pp. 44–45.

54. Oliver Garceau, "Research in the Political Process," pp. 69–85.

55. "Annual Report," 1955–56, p. 4.

56. University of North Carolina, "Survey of Behavioral Science," pp. 335–46.

57. Ibid., p. 337.

58. Ibid., p. 340.

59. Ibid., p. 341.

60. Ibid., pp. 341–42.

61. Ibid., p. 342.

62. Ibid., pp. 353–55.

63. Alexander Heard served as Ford Research Professor of Government at Harvard University in 1957 and did not assume his responsibilities as dean of the Graduate School until January 1958.

64. Floyd Hunter completed research on national power leaders before he left the Institute, and the manuscript was published in 1959 as *Top Leadership, U.S.A.*.

65. Heard obtained financing from the Stern Family Fund for his study of money in politics. The National Science Foundation made a grant for a series of monographs on state government, the Social Science Research Council made a grant for a study of politics in Latin America by Federico Gil, and the Falk Foundation made a grant for expansion of the program of the Political Behavior Committee. See "Annual Report," 1956–57, pp. 4–10 and 1957–58, p. 9. For an account of the grant from the Maurice and Laura Falk Foundation for the program of the Political Behavior Committee, see University of North Carolina, "Proposal for a Center of Excellence in Science," 6: 16.

66. See "Annual Report," 1957–58, pp. 7–11.

67. Prothro, "Report of the Ad Hoc Committee," pp. 1–2.

68. A brief statement of the establishment of the graduate degree program in public administration in September 1966 appears in University of North Carolina, "Proposal for a Center of Excellence in Science," 6: 22.

69. Minutes, Board of Governors, July 11, 1927, p. 2.

70. Howard W. Odum, "Suggested Cooperative Plan for the University of North Carolina, 1930–1940'"; Odum to President Frank P. Graham, February 16, 1932, Odum Papers. See also Odum to Graham, February 17, 1932, Odum Papers.

71. *A Program of Cooperation*, p. 13.

72. *The University of North Carolina Record: Research in Progress, October, 1934–October, 1935*, p. 72, contained a report from the School of Public Administration but *Research in Progress* for the following year had no mention of the school.

73. Institute for Research in Social Science, "Applications for Membership, 1973–1974," p. 4, attached to Minutes, Administrative Board, May 3, 1973.

74. Howard W. Odum, "Memorandum of Procedures at North Carolina with Special Reference to President Graham's Nullifying Activities," p. 1.

75. Gordon W. Blackwell, "1944 Program of the Institute," pp. 6, 10, 15.

76. "Annual Report," 1944–45, p. 8.

77. *University of North Carolina Record, Research in Progress, October 1945–December 1948*, no. 464, p. 325.

78. "Annual Report," 1948–49, p. 9.

79. Gordon W. Blackwell to Chancellor Robert B. House, October 1946, Chancellor's Papers.

80. Frederic N. Cleaveland left the University of North Carolina in 1971 to become Provost of Duke University.

81. Prothro, "Report of the Ad Hoc Committee," p. 6.

82. The thirteen states were Alabama, California, Florida, Illinois, Louisiana, Massachusetts, Minnesota, New York, North Carolina, Ohio, Pennsylvania, South Dakota, and Texas.

83. "Annual Report," 1967–68, p. 10.

84. "Annual Report," 1971–72, p. 9.

85. "Annual Report," 1972–73, p. 9. Institute for Research in Social Science, "Publications by the Senior Research Faculty, 1973–74," p. 14, lists the following publication for the project: James W. Prothro with David M. Kovenock and associates, *Explaining the Vote*. In 1974 two additional volumes were published by the Institute, *Political Attitudes in the Nation and the States*, by Merle Black, David M. Kovenock, and William C. Reynolds, and *Electoral Choice in America*, by Gerald C. Wright, Jr. A volume by Mark Schneider, *Ethnicity and Politics: A Comparative State Analysis*, is forthcoming as is *Guide to the Comparative State Elections Project Survey Data*, by Elizabeth M. Fischer and David M. Kovenock.

86. "Annual Report," 1966–67, p. 9.

87. "Annual Report," 1967–68, p. 9.

88. "Annual Report," 1968–69, p. 8.

89. "Annual Report," 1969–70, pp. 5–6.

90. "Annual Report," 1970–71, p. 6.

91. The number of interviews actually obtained was 1,130, each approximately ninety minutes in length.

92. "Annual Report," 1970–71, p. 6.

93. For a summary of the report on Southeastern Regional Survey III, see "Annual Report," 1971–72, pp. 7–8.

94. Odum and Jocher, eds., *In Search of the Regional Balance of America*, pp. 47–48.

95. The Chapel Hill division of the Institute of Statistics was authorized in 1945 when the Board of Trustees of the University of North Carolina approved reorganization of the Department of Experimental Statistics at State College (now University) in Raleigh and the creation of the Institute of Statistics with faculty at both Raleigh and Chapel Hill. Professor Gertrude M. Cox had organized the State College Department of Experimental Statistics in November 1940 and the department was officially authorized with Professor Cox as chairman the following January. On July 1,

1946, the Department of Mathematical Statistics was authorized at Chapel Hill with Professor Harold Hotelling as chairman. The University of North Carolina received a grant from the General Education Board for this purpose and brought Professor Hotelling from Columbia University to set up the new department at Chapel Hill and to serve as director of the recently authorized section of the Institute of Statistics at Chapel Hill. Professor Cox remained as director of the Institute in the Consolidated University System and Professor Hotelling served as associate director. Both professors served at intervals on the governing board of the Institute for Research in Social Science. See *The Institute of Statistics, the Consolidated University of North Carolina. A Record of Research: I, July 1, 1948 to June 30*, 1951 (n.p., n.d.).

96. "Annual Report," 1950–51, pp. 3–4.

97. "Annual Report," 1956–57, pp. 25–26.

98. "Annual Report," 1957–58, pp. 30, 32.

99. "Annual Report," 1955–56, pp. 19–21.

100. "Annual Report," 1958–59, p. 2.

101. Ibid., p. 3.

102. Minutes, Advisory Committee, September 13, 1962, p. 3.

103. Prothro, "Report of the Ad Hoc Committee," p. 4.

104. "Annual Report," 1967–68, p. 8.

105. For a short period between 1969 and 1971, the Social Science Statistical Laboratory was called the Division of Data Analysis.

106. "Annual Report," 1971–72, p. 5.

107. "Annual Report," 1969–70, p. 6. The Louis D. Harris Political Data Center was a collection of all the opinion surveys conducted by Louis Harris and Associates. The center also housed the data from the Inter-University Consortium for Political Research, of which the Department of Political Science was a charter member and James W. Prothro its first chairman. Through the Consortium and the department the Institute acquired the original data from every major presidential election survey and from five additional surveys.

108. "Annual Report," 1971–72, p. 7.

109. "Annual Report," 1972–73, p. 6.

Chapter 10

1. Institute for Research in Social Science, "1957–58 Annual Report of the Urban Studies Research Program," p. 1.

2. "Annual Report," 1950–51, p. 7.

3. Minutes, Executive Committee, November 14, 1949, p. 2.

4. "Annual Report," 1955–56, pp. 10–12.

5. Institute for Research in Social Science, "Annual Report of the Urban Studies Research Program," 1957–58, pp. 1–2.

6. Ibid., p. 10.

7. Institute for Research in Social Science, "Annual Report of the Urban Studies Research Program," 1960–61, pp. 11, 15–22; 1961–62, pp. 5–7.

8. Institute for Research in Social Science, Center for Urban and Regional Studies, "A Ten-Year Interdisciplinary Effort in Urban Studies," p. 2.

9. Institute for Research in Social Science, "Annual Report of the Urban Studies Research Program," 1961–62, p. 1; F. Stuart Chapin, Jr., memorandum to Guion Griffis Johnson, September 23, 1976, Guion Griffis Johnson Papers.

10. Institute for Research in Social Science, "Annual Report of the Urban Studies Research Program," 1960–61, pp. 13–14. Minutes, Executive Committee, October 28, 1959, p. 2.

11. Those who contributed to the volume in addition to F. Stuart Chapin, Jr., were Ralph W. Pfouts, Robert L. Bunting, Lowell D. Ashby, William N. Parker, David G. Davies, Benjamin Walker, Robert T. Daland, John A. Parker, E. William Noland, Bradbury Seasholes, Frederic N. Cleaveland, John Gulick, Charles E. Bowerman, Kurt W. Back, Robert L. Wilson, Richard L. Simpson, and Shirley F. Weiss.

12. Hope Tisdale Eldridge, review of *Urban Growth Dynamics in a Regional Cluster of Cities*, ed. F. Stuart Chapin, Jr., and Shirley F. Weiss, pp. 255–56.

13. "Annual Report," 1960–61, p. 7.

14. Institute for Research in Social Science, Center for Urban and Regional Studies, "Research in Progress," August 1968, p. 2.

15. Ibid., p. 6; Chapin, memorandum to Guion Johnson.

16. Center for Urban and Regional Studies, "Research in Progress," August 1969, p. 3.

17. Center for Urban and Regional Studies, "Research in Progress," August 1968, p. 6.

18. Center for Urban and Regional Studies, "Research in Progress," August 1969, pp. 4–6.

19. *New Communities U.S.A.* was written by Raymond J. Burby III and Shirley F. Weiss with the research assistance of Thomas G. Donnelly, Edward J. Kaiser, and Robert B. Zehner. The volume also included the findings of David F. Lewis, Norman H. Loewanthal, Mary Ellen McCalla, Barbara G. Rogers, and Helene Smookler.

20. Mitchell Simon, "UNC Team Studies Communities," *Chapel Hill Newspaper*, March 16, 1976.

21. Center for Urban and Regional Studies, "Research in Progress," August 1969, p. 6.

22. Ibid.

23. Center for Urban and Regional Studies, "Annual Report," 1969–70, p. 2.

24. "Annual Report," 1973–74, p. 5.

25. Center for Urban and Regional Studies, "Annual Report," for 1969–70, p. 2.

26. Howard W. Odum, "Editorial Notes," p. 475.

27. For example, Guion Griffis Johnson's *Ante-Bellum North Carolina* contained a chapter "Sanitation and Health," and Julia Cherry Spruill's *Woman's Life and Work in the Southern Colonies* included a chapter on the health hazards to women in their childbearing role. In 1932 Emily White Stevens produced a monograph, *The Diet Pattern of the South*, as a study in regional sociology and in the next year followed up with an article on the subject in the *New Republic*, October 25, 1933, pp. 297–99. Odum's regional studies stressed the importance of good health as a means of pulling the southern people "up from the bottom," and Vance's *All These People* contained three chapters (chapters 22–24) on the health and vitality of the people.

28. Cecil G. Sheps and John J. Wright, "Reports of the North Carolina Syphilis Studies," *Journal of Veneral Disease Information* 30 (1949): 35–53, 187–94, 211–17.

29. Gordon W. Blackwell, "Behavioral Science and Health," pp. 211–15.

30. "Annual Report," 1953–54, p. 11.

31. Floyd Hunter, Ruth Connor Schaffer, and Cecil G. Sheps, *Community Organization*, pp. vii–xii.

32. "Annual Report," 1953–54, pp. 11–12. The Senior staff members listed for this project in Minutes, Executive Committee, September 28, 1953, p. 1, were Harvey L. Smith, director; Frank M. LeBar; Harley Shands; Kerr L. White; and George C. Ham.

33. Among the behavioral scientists listed in addition to Harvey Smith in University of North Carolina, "The University of North Carolina Survey of Behavioral Science, 1953–54," as doing research in some phase of the social aspects of health were Loren McKinney in historical studies of medicine in the Middle Ages, John Gillin and John Honigmann in the culture of individual communities and the impact of culture on personality, Harriet L. Herring in textile communities, Paul Wager in local government, Nicholas Demerath in studies of complex organizations, John Thibaut in the study of small group behavior, Gordon Blackwell in community organization, Rupert Vance in demography, Reuben Hill in family organization and value systems, S. H. Hobbs, Jr., and George L. Simpson in the economic and social aspects of life in North Carolina, Harold Meyer in recreation in a hospital setting, and Rashi Fein in the economics of illness and medical care.

34. University of North Carolina, "Survey of Behavioral Science," pp. 160–67.

35. Ibid., p. 169.

36. Ibid., pp. 170–72.

37. Ibid., pp. 159–70.

38. Interview with Gordon W. Blackwell, September 18, 1975. See also Minutes, Executive Committee, November 2, 1960, pp. 3–4.

39. "Annual Report," 1955–56, p. 9.

40. "Annual Report," 1957–58, pp. 14–15; 1960–61, p. 10.

41. James W. Prothro, "Report of the Ad Hoc Committee to Study the Function of the Institute for Research in Social Science," p. 2.

42. In 1954 the University of North Carolina Press published Cecil G. Sheps and Eugene Taylor's *Needed Research in Health and Medical Care*. In 1956 the Institute published as one of its monographs *Patterns of Psychiatric Nursing*, by Harry W. Martin and Ida Harper; also in 1956 George C. Ham, a psychiatrist associated with the Institute's health research program, contributed a chapter, "Management of the Multiple Complainer," to *Management of Emotional Problems in Medical Practice*, edited by Samuel Leibman, and wrote three other professional articles as well. Among other publications coming from the Program on the Social Science Aspects of Health were two chapters by Harvey L. Smith in collaboration with others in *The Patient and the Mental Hospital* (1957), edited by M. Greenblatt, D. Levinson, and R. Williams. In 1961 the Institute published Smith's brief report *Society and Health in a Mountain Community*, and his *Experience With a Patient Planning Organization*, which he produced with Robert G. Brown and James E. Somers. In 1963 his *Adaptation* appeared as an outgrowth of his early efforts to set up a sociological frame of reference

for obtaining clinical data, and it included interview guides for taking life histories. Among others in the field who produced monographs or professional articles were Jean H. Thrasher, Harley Shands, Kerr L. White, and Eugene A. Hargrove.

43. University of North Carolina, "Survey of Behavioral Science," p. 182.

44. "Annual Report," 1973–74, pp. 17–18.

45. "New IRSS Publications."

46. "Annual Report," 1973–74, pp. 10, 11, 14–15, 17–18, 19.

47. "Annual Report," 1944–45, p. 5.

48. Johnson's first trip in 1959–60 was made possible by a Kenan Leave of Absence from the University of North Carolina, a visiting professorship from Rhodes University, Grahamstown, South Africa, and traveling fellowships from the United States–South Africa Leader Exchange Program and the Ford Foundation. His trip in 1961 was a study tour under the auspices of the Phelps-Stokes Fund.

49. "Annual Report," 1955–56, p. 2.

50. University of North Carolina, "Survey of Behavioral Science," pp. 123–24.

51. Ibid., pp. 124–25.

52. "Annual Report," 1957–58, p. 25.

53. Ibid., p. 35.

54. "Annual Report," 1958–59, pp. 16–17.

55. William R. Keech, whose primary interest was political behavior, collaborated with Joel Schwartz on an article, "Group Influence and the Policy Process in the Soviet Union," for the *American Political Science Review* 62 (September 1968), and in 1970 they jointly contributed a chapter "Public Influence and Educational Policy" to *The Behavioral Revolution and Communist Studies*, edited by Roger Kanet. "The Elusive New Soviet Man" by Schwartz appeared in *Problems of Communism* (September–October 1973). During the academic year 1972–73 Steven Rosefielde in economics was doing research with the 1966 Soviet input-output tables, and by the following year he had produced five publications, including *Soviet International Trade in Hacksher-Ohlin Perspective: An Input-Output Study* (Lexington, Mass.: Lexington Books, 1973). At this time he was also doing research on structural aspects of comparative economic systems.

56. "Annual Report," 1958–59, p. iii.

57. Minutes, Advisory Committee, February 9, 1962, p. 2; March 16, p. 1.

58. Minutes, Administrative Board, February 27, 1968, p. 1. In 1966 the University of North Carolina, "A Proposal to the National Science Foundation for Support to Achieve an Academic Center of Excellence in Science at the University of North Carolina at Chapel Hill under the Science Development Plan for Colleges and Universities," stated that the Institute of Latin American Studies "enjoys well-established relationships with the Latin American Faculty of Social Science (FLACSO) in Santiago, Chile" (6: 21).

59. In 1972 Robert T. Daland contributed a chapter, "The Paradox of Planning," to *Contemporary Brazil: Issues in Economic and Political Development*, edited by H. Jon Rosenbaum and William G. Tyler. He also published an article on Brazilian bureaucrats in the *Journal of Comparative Administration* 6 (August 1972): 167–203. The next year his "Research Needs for the 1970s in Latin American Development Administration" appeared as a chapter in *Latin American Development Administration*, edited by Jerry L. Weaver. In 1974 James W. Prothro with the assistance of P. E.

Chaparro completed research growing out of Prothro's one-year residence in Chile, which was published as "Public Opinion and the Movement of the Chilean Government to the Left, 1952–1972" in the *Journal of Politics* 36 (February 1974). Enrique A. Baloyra, whose interest was in Venezuelan elections, had published "Comparing Political Regimes" in *International Interactions* 1 (1974): 55–57.

60. Edward E. Azar's *Probe for Peace* was published in 1973, and in the same year he served as editor of *Review of Peace Science* as well as *International Interactions: A Transnational Multidisciplinary Journal*. In 1974 the University of North Carolina Press published Jurg Steiner's *Amicable Agreement versus Majority Rule*, and he contributed to professional journals three articles dealing with hostilities among subcultures and norms of political decisionmaking. Alan J. Stern's "The Italian Communist Party in the Red Belt: Patterns at the Grassroots" was published in *Problems of Communism* 23 (March-April 1974): 42–54. In 1973, James W. White contributed a chapter, "The Meiji Restoration," to *Crisis, Choice, and Change*, edited by Gabriel Almond and Scott Flanagan, and he wrote an article, "Tradition and Politics in Studies of Contemporary Japan," for *World Politics* 26 (April 1974): 400–427.

61. Susan E. Clarke, "Memorandum on Comparative Urban Studies Program," March 25, 1977.

62. Interview with Blackwell, September 18, 1975.

63. "Education in the Secondary Schools of the South," *The Southern Association Quarterly* 4 (August 1940): 523–29, reprinted in Howard W. Odum, *Folk, Region, and Society*, pp. 436, 437.

64. Odum, *Folk, Region, and Society*, p. 357.

65. Ibid.

66. Interview with Blackwell, September 18, 1975.

67. For a more detailed account of the effort at research interpretation see chapter 8. See also University of North Carolina, "Survey of Behavioral Science," p. 101.

68. Among the articles on childhood and infant education published by Earl S. Schaefer during 1972–73 were "The Family and the Educational Process," in *Families of the Future*, edited by the College of Home Economics, Iowa State University; "Does Education Really Pay Off?" in *PTA Magazine*; and "Parents as Educators: Evidence from Cross-Sectional, Longitudinal, and Intervention Research," in *Influences on Human Development*, edited by Urie Bronfenbrenner.

69. University of North Carolina, "Survey of Behavioral Science," pp. 53–54.

70. *The Report of the Governor's Commission on the Status of Women*, p. 56.

71. University of North Carolina, "Survey of Behavioral Science," p. 99.

72. "Annual Report, 1973–74," p. 12.

73. Minutes, Board of Governors, May 27, 1953, attachment.

74. University of North Carolina, "Survey of Behavioral Science," p. 102.

75. Ibid., p. 123.

76. For the report on research proposed on mass communication see ibid., pp. 283–301.

77. "Annual Report," 1954–55, pp. 8, 45.

78. For example, John B. Adams, "Communication Research Centers: A New Concept," *Zeszyty Prasoznawcze* (Krakow) 24 (Summer 1966); "Mass Media and National Development," *Bulletin de l'Association Internationale des Etudes*

et Recherches sur l'Information 7/8 (March 1968): 52–57; "Badania nad Rozpowszechnianiem wiadomosci w USA" [Communications Research in the USA], *Zeszyty Prasoznawcze* (Krakow) 35 (Summer 1968): 117–21.

79. John B. Adams, ed., "Articles on Mass Communication in U.S. and Foreign Journals," *Journalism Quarterly* 41 (Autumn 1964); "A Qualitative Analysis of Domestic and Foreign News and the APTA Wire," *Gazette* 10 (Winter 1965): 285–95. In 1962 Adams edited "A Select Bibliography from Foreign Journals" for *Journalism Quarterly* 39 (Summer–Autumn 1962): 403–7, 550–52.

80. Interview with Blackwell, September 18, 1975.

81. Guion Griffis Johnson, "Reflections on Research and Writing in Social History," Guion Griffis Johnson Papers.

82. University of North Carolina, "Survey of Behavioral Science," p. 46.

83. Ibid., p. 47. The Human Relations in Industry Group was not affiliated with the Institute.

84. "Annual Report," 1970–71, pp. 3–5.

85. Minutes, Administrative Board, February 23, 1970, p. 2.

86. Elbridge Sibley, *Social Science Research Council*, pp. 24, 25.

87. Among these were Emmett Earl Baughman, "A Comparative Analysis of Rorschach Forms with Altered Stimulus Characteristics," *Journal of Projective Techniques* 18 (June 1954): 151–64; Nicholas J. Demerath, John W. Thibaut et al., "Narrowing the Gap Between Field Studies and Laboratory Experiments in Social Psychology," Social Science Research Council, *Items* 8 (December 1954): 37–42; Gordon W. Blackwell, "A Theoretical Framework for Sociological Research in Community Organization," *Social Forces* 33 (October 1954): 57–64; F. Stuart Chapin, Jr., "Employment Forecasts for City Planning," *Journal of the American Institute of Planners* 20 (Spring 1954): 60–73; Frederic N. Cleaveland, "Political Behavior," mimeographed, Institute for Research in Social Science, 1954; and John Gillin, "Methods of Approach to the Study of Human Behavior," in *Aspects of Culture and Personality*, edited by Francis L. K. Hsu.

88. In 1955–56 Ashby was developing techniques for identifying social indicators. His research project in the Institute was "Development of a Method for Preparation on Comparable Bases of Monthly National, Regional, and State Labor Force Data." See "Annual Report," 1955–56, p. 15.

89. "Annual Report," 1970–71, p. 6.

90. University of North Carolina, "Proposal for a Center for Excellence," 6: 2, 7–10, 16–18; 5: 5–6.

91. These studies are still relevant more than fifteen years after publication. Among them are John J. Honigmann's *Three Pakistan Villages*; John Gulick's *Cherokees at the Crossroads*; Harvey L. Smith's *Society and Health in a Mountain Community* and *Experience with a Patient Planning Organization: An Interim Analysis*, written with Robert G. Brown and James E. Somers. See "Annual Report," 1960–61, pp. 23–24.

92. "Annual Report," 1966–67, p. 7.

Bibliography

Manuscript Sources

Institute for Research in Social Science, Official Records

Except where otherwise noted, the following official records are deposited at the
Institute for Research in Social Science, University of North Carolina at Chapel Hill.

"Annual Report of the Director," 1924–25 to 1975–76.
Blackwell, Gordon W. "1944 Program of the Institute for Research in Social Science,
     October 18, 1944." Attached to Minutes, Board of Governors, November 7,
     1944.
————. "Progress Papers, November 1944 to June 1945." Attached to Minutes,
     Board of Governors, June 14, 1944.
Chase, Harry W. "To the Members of the Executive Committee of the Board of
     Trustees of the University of North Carolina," May 12, 1924. University
     Papers.
————. "To Members of the Executive Committee of the University of North
     Carolina," July 8, 1924. University Papers.
Clarke, Susan E. "Memorandum on Comparative Studies Program," March 25, 1977.
     Prepared for the authors. Guion Griffis Johnson Papers.
Institute for Research in Social Science. "Annual Report of the Urban Studies
     Research Program," 1957–58 to 1961–62.
————. "Publications by the Senior Research Faculty, 1973–74."
Institute for Research in Social Science, Center for Urban and Regional Studies.
     "Research in Progress," 1963–69.
————. "A Ten-Year Interdisciplinary Effort in Urban Studies," 1963.
Institute on Southern Regional Development and the Social Sciences. "Report of the
     Committee on Regional Development in Agricultural Economics and Rural
     Sociology." Appended to agenda for meeting of Board of Governors, Institute
     for Research in Social Science, January 22, 1937.
Matherly, Walter J.; Murchinson, C. T.; Carroll D. D.; and Herring, Harriet L.
     "Memorandum Concerning the Proposed Investigation of the Economic and
     Social Aspects of the Southern Textile Industry by the Institute for Research in
     Social Science at the University of North Carolina." Attached to letter from D.
     D. Carroll to President Harry W. Chase, January 19, 1926. University Papers.
Minutes, Advisory Board, December 9, 1947.
Minutes of the Administrative Board, 1961–75.
Minutes of the Advisory Committee, 1961–62.
Minutes of the Board of Governors, 1924–61.

Minutes of the Executive Committee of the Board of Governors, 1948–61. (The minutes of meetings held between June 4, 1945, and December 9, 1947, are missing.)

"New IRSS Publications," [1975].

Odum, Howard W. "Basic Memorandum for a Five-Year Terminating Grant from the Rockefeller Foundation Beginning July 1, 1935," March 20, 1935. Appended to Minutes, Board of Governors, March 27, 1935.

———. "Institute for Research in Social Science, Report of the Director," November 10, 1932.

———. "Memorandum for Institute Meeting, December 17, 1924." Attached to Minutes, Board of Governors, December 17, 1924.

———. "Memorandum for the Board of Governors, Institute for Research in Social Science, April 24, 1927." Appended to Minutes, Board of Governors, April 24, 1927.

———. "Memorandum of Procedures at North Carolina with Special Reference to President Graham's Nullifying Activities," October 21, 1940.

———. "Memorandum on the Institute for Research in Social Science, University of North Carolina, for the Report of the Lake George Conference," November 13, 1934.

———. "Memorandum to the Board of Governors of the Institute for Research in Social Science," May 30, 1932.

———. "Statement of the Director of the Institute, Board Meeting of February 23, 1928, Carolina Inn."

———. "Studies and Materials, Institute for Research in Social Science, University of North Carolina, 1924–1932," January 1, 1933.

———. "Suggested Cooperative Plan for the University of North Carolina, 1930–1940," undated.

———. "Supplementary Program of Regional Development and Education, Institute for Research in Social Science, University of North Carolina," March 7, 1938.

———. "A Survey of the North Carolina Prison System." Survey undertaken for the Governor's Prison Commission. Mimeographed, 1930.

———. "Ten Years' Progress in the Social Sciences at the University of North Carolina," December 1, 1930. Appended to Minutes, Board of Governors, December 10, 1930.

———. "University of North Carolina Institute for Research in Social Science." Memorandum to Wilson Gee, University of Virginia, August 31, 1933.

"Present Research Personnel of the Institute for Research in Social Science." Attached to Minutes, Board of Governors, February 23, 1928.

Price, Daniel O. "Long Range Plans for the Institute for Research in Social Science," November 13, 1957. Appended to Minutes, Board of Governors, November 21, 1957.

"Proposed Study of the Child-Care Institution as a Factor in Rehabilitating Family Life." Attached to Minutes, Board of Governors, November 2, 1960.

Prothro, James W. "Institute for Research in Social Science." Appended to Minutes, Administrative Board, February 26, 1969.

———. "Report of the Ad Hoc Committee to Study the Functions of the Institute for Research in Social Science," October 18, 1966. Appended to Minutes, Administrative Board, November 22, 1966.

"Recommendations to Vice-Chancellor Palmatier by the Administrative Board of the Institute for Research in Social Science," December 6, 1966. Attached to Minutes, Administrative Board, November 22, 1966.

"Report of Research Carried On by Research Associates, 1928–1929, and Suggested Plans for the Coming Year." Attached to Minutes, Board of Governors, April 18, 1929.

University Records

The University of North Carolina. "A Proposal to the National Science Foundation for Support to Achieve an Academic Center of Excellence in Science at the University of North Carolina at Chapel Hill under the Science Development Plan for Colleges and Universities," July 30, 1966.

The University of North Carolina. "The University of North Carolina Survey of Behavioral Science, 1953–54," 1954.

University Papers. In the Southern Historical Collection, Louis Round Wilson Library, University of North Carolina at Chapel Hill:

Annual Report series of the President of the University.

Chancellor's Papers, section on the Institute for Research in Social Science, 1947–54.

Institute for Research in Social Science Papers, 1924–52.

President's Papers: Harry Woodburn Chase, 1919–30; Frank Porter Graham, 1930–49.

Personal Papers

Except where otherwise noted, the following personal papers are deposited in the Southern Historical Collection, Louis Round Wilson Library, University of North Carolina at Chapel Hill.

The Eugene Cunningham Branson Papers.

The Guion Griffis Johnson Papers. In private possession, Chapel Hill.

The Guy Benton Johnson Papers.

The Howard Washington Odum Papers. (A) In the Southern Historical Collection.

    (B) In possession of Mary Frances Odum Schinhan, Chapel Hill.

The Rupert Bayless Vance Papers.

The Louis Round Wilson Papers.

Interviews and Conversations

Blackwell, Gordon W. Recorded interview, Greenville, S.C., September 18, 1975. Typescript deposited with Institute for Research in Social Science.

Jocher, Katharine. Interviews and conversations on numerous occasions, Chapel Hill, 1974–77.

Price, Daniel O. Interview, Austin, Tex., May 20, 1977.

Other interviews and conversations on various dates at Chapel Hill with the following:

E. Earl Baughman, Mrs. John S. Bennett, Treva Williams Bevacqua, Angell Beza, F. Stuart Chapin, Jr., Leonard S. Cottrell, Jr., Arthur Fink, Elizabeth Fink, William C. Friday, Robert E. Gallman, Philip P. Green, Jr., John Gulick, C. Horace Hamilton, Clarence Heer, John J. Honigmann, Alan Keith-Lucas, Clyde V. Kiser, Gerhard E. Lenski, Emil E. Malizia, Frank J. Munger, Howard Thomas Odum, John A. Parker, James L. Peacock, James W. Prothro, John Shelton Reed, Jr., Mary Frances Odum Schinhan, Cecil G. Sheps, Richard L. Simpson, Harvey L. Smith, John W. Thibaut, Rupert B. Vance, and Paul W. Wager.

Published Records

Center for Urban and Regional Studies. "Annual Report," 1969–74.
Institute for Research in Social Science. *Research Previews*. Issued 58 times, 1953–76. Incorporated in *University of North Carolina News Letter* in November 1976.
The University of North Carolina Record: Research in Progress, 1924–76.
The University of North Carolina Record: The General Catalog, 1920–76.
The University of North Carolina Record: The Graduate School, 1924–76.

Newspapers and Periodicals

The Chapel Hill Newspaper. 1972–76.
The Chapel Hill Weekly, 1924–72.
Contempo. Chapel Hill, 1931–33.
The Daily Tar Heel. University of North Carolina at Chapel Hill, student newspaper, 1923–76.
The Durham Morning Herald. 1924–76.
The Greensboro Daily News. 1924–76.
The Raleigh News and Observer. 1924–76.
The North Carolina Club Yearbook. Chapel Hill: University of North Carolina Press, 1915–16 to 1931–32.
The Review of Regional Studies. Blacksburg, Virginia: The Southeastern Regional Science Association and Virginia Polytechnic Institute, 1971; Birmingham: School of Business Administration, University of Alabama in Birmingham, 1974.
Social Forces. 1922–76. (The first three volumes were titled *The Journal of Social Forces*.)
The Southern Textile Bulletin. 1923–76. (After March 1933, *The Textile Bulletin*.)
The University of North Carolina News Letter. 1914–76.

Books, Articles, Pamphlets, and Dissertations

This section of the bibliography includes selected major publications of Institute staff members and affiliates, certain works that influenced Howard W. Odum and other social scientists during the early years of the twentieth century, and other works relevant to the history of the Institute. Articles in periodicals and unpublished studies that are mentioned in the text merely to illustrate the variety and scope of the Institute's work are, with a few exceptions, not listed here. Typescripts of the unpublished studies are in the custody of the Institute, and in many cases they are also available as theses or dissertations in the Louis Round Wilson Library of the University of North Carolina at Chapel Hill.

Allen, R. H., et al. *Part-Time Farming in the Southeast*. Works Progress Administration, Research Monograph 9. Washington, D.C.: Government Printing Office, 1937.

Almond, Gabriel; Flannagan, Scott; and Mundt, Robert J., eds. *Crisis, Choice, Change: Historical Studies of Political Development*. Boston: Little, Brown, 1973.

Appelbaum, Mark I., and Thompson, Vaida D. *Population Policy Acceptance: Psychological Determinants*. Chapel Hill: Carolina Population Center, University of North Carolina, 1974.

Ashby, Lowell DeWitt. *Growth Patterns in Employment by County, 1940–1950 and 1950–1960*. United States Department of Commerce, Office of Business Economics, Regional Economics Division. 8 vols. Washington, D.C.: Government Printing Office, 1965–66.

———. "Linear Difference Equations and Applications to Economic Theory." Chapel Hill: School of Business Administration, University of North Carolina, 1957. Mimeographed.

———. *The North Carolina Economy: Its Regional and National Setting, with Particular Reference to the Structure of Employment*. Chapel Hill: School of Business Administration, University of North Carolina, 1961.

Ashby, Lowell DeWitt, and Spivey, W. Allen. "Per Capita Income Payments to Individuals, Their Nature and Reliability." A Report to Governor Luther H. Hodges. Chapel Hill: Department of Economics, University of North Carolina, May 1955. Mimeographed.

Azar, Edward E. *Probe for Peace: Small State Hostilities*. Minneapolis: Burgess Publishing, 1973.

Bailey, Thomas Pearce, Jr. *Race Orthodoxy in the South, and Other Aspects of the Negro Question*. New York: Neale Publishing, 1914.

Baughman, Emmett Earl. *Black Americans: A Psychological Analysis*. New York: Academic Press, 1971.

Baughman, Emmett Earl, and Dahlstrom, W. Grant. *Negro and White Children: A Psychological Study in the Rural South*. New York: Academic Press, 1968.

Becker, Howard, and Hill, Reuben, eds. *Family, Marriage and Parenthood*. 2nd ed. Boston: D. C. Heath, 1955.

Beecher, John. "The Sharecroppers' Union in Alabama." *Social Forces* 13 (October 1934): 124–32.

Berelson, Bernard, et al., eds. *Family Planning and Population Programs: A Review of World Developments*. Chicago: University of Chicago Press, 1966.

Beyle, Thad L., and Lathrop, George T., eds. *Politics and Planning: Uneasy Partnership*. New York: Odyssey Press, 1971.

Beyle, Thad L., and Williams, J. Oliver, eds. *The American Governor in Behavioral Perspective*. New York: Harper & Row, 1972.

Black, Merle; Kovenock, David M.; and Reynolds, William C. *Political Attitudes in the Nation and the States*. Chapel Hill: Institute for Research in Social Science, 1974.

Blackwell, Gordon W. "Behavioral Science and Health." *Social Forces* 32 (October 1953): 211–15.

————. "Multidisciplinary Team Research." *Social Forces* 33 (May 1955): 367–74.

Blackwell, Gordon W., and Bachrach, Arthur J., eds. "Human Problems in the Changing South." *Journal of Social Issues* 10 (1954): 1–48.

Blackwell, Gordon W.; Brooks, Lee M.; and Hobbs, S. H., Jr. *Church and Community in the South*. Richmond, Va.: John Knox Press, 1949.

Blackwell, Gordon W., and Gould, Raymond F. *Future Citizens All*. Chicago: American Public Welfare Association, 1952.

Blalock, Hubert M., Jr. *Causal Inferences in Nonexperimental Research*. Chapel Hill: University of North Carolina Press, 1964.

————. *An Introduction to Social Research*. Englewood Cliffs, N.J.: Prentice Hall, 1970.

————. *Theory Construction: From Verbal to Mathematical Formulations*. Englewood Cliffs, N.J.: Prentice-Hall, 1969.

————. *Toward a Theory of Minority-Group Relations*. New York: John Wiley & Sons, 1967.

————, ed. *Causal Models in the Social Sciences*. Chicago: Aldine, 1971.

Blalock, Hubert M., Jr., and Blalock, Anne B., eds. *Methodology in Social Research*. New York: McGraw-Hill, 1968.

Blanshard, Paul. "Servants of the Spindle." *New Republic*, September 21, 1927, pp. 114–16; September 28, 1927, pp. 143–45.

Bollens, John C., and Schmandt, Henry J. *The Metropolis: Its People, Politics and Economic Life*. New York: Harper & Row, 1965.

Bowerman, Charles E.; Campbell, Ernest Q.; and Cramer, M. Richard. *Social Factors in Educational Achievement and Aspirations among Negro Adolescents*. Monograph Series. Chapel Hill: Institute for Research in Social Science, 1966.

Bowerman, Charles E.; Pope, Halliwell; and Irish, Donald. *Unwed Motherhood: Personal and Social Consequences*. Monograph Series. Chapel Hill: Institute for Research in Social Science, 1966.

Branson, Eugene C., and Dickey, J. A. "How Farm Tenants Live in Mid-State Carolina." In *North Carolina Club Yearbook, 1921–22*. Chapel Hill: University of North Carolina Press, 1922.

Brazil, Wayne Douglas. "Howard W. Odum, the Building Years, 1884–1930." Ph.D. dissertation, Harvard University, 1975.

Brearley, H. C. "Homicide in South Carolina: A Regional Study." *Social Forces* 8 (December 1929): 218–21.

_____. *Homicide in the United States*. Chapel Hill: University of North Carolina Press, 1932.

Bronfenbrenner, Urie, ed. *Influences on Human Development*. Hinsdale, Ill.: Dryden Press, 1972.

Brooks, Lee M., et al. *Manual for Southern Regions of the United States*. Chapel Hill: University of North Carolina Press, 1937.

Broten, Alton. *Houseparents in Children's Institutions: A Discussion Guide*. Chapel Hill: University of North Carolina Press, 1962.

Brown, Cecil K. *The State Highway System of North Carolina*. Chapel Hill: University of North Carolina Press, 1931.

Brown, Roy Melton. *Public Poor Relief in North Carolina*. Chapel Hill: University of North Carolina Press, 1928.

Burby, Raymond J., III, and Weiss, Shirley F. *New Communities U.S.A.* Lexington, Mass.: Lexington Books, 1976.

Burgess, M. Elaine. *Negro Leadership in a Southern City*. Chapel Hill: University of North Carolina Press, 1962.

Burgess, M. Elaine, and Price, Daniel O. *An American Dependency Challenge*. Chicago: American Public Welfare Association, 1963.

Butler, Edgar W. *An Empirical Examination of the Relationship of Vertical Occupational Mobility and Horizontal Residential Mobility*. Los Angeles: Population Research Laboratory, Department of Sociology, University of Southern California, 1965.

Butler, Edgar W., et al. *Moving Behavior and Residential Choice: A National Survey*. Washington, D.C.: Highway Research Board, National Research Council, 1969.

Calhoon, Richard P.; Noland, E. William; and Whitehill, A. M., Jr. *Cases on Human Relations in Management*. New York: McGraw-Hill, 1958.

Campbell, Ernest Q.; Bowerman, Charles E.; and Price, Daniel O. *When a City Closes Its Schools*. Monograph Series. Chapel Hill: Institute for Research in Social Science, 1960.

Campbell, Ernest Q., and Pettigrew, Thomas F. *Christians in Racial Crisis: A Study of Little Rock's Ministry*. Washington, D.C.: Public Affairs Press, 1959.

Carstensen, Vernon. "The Development and Application of Regional-Sectional Concepts, 1900–1950." In *Regionalism in America*, edited by Merrill Jensen. Madison: University of Wisconsin Press, 1952.

Chadbourn, James H. *Lynching and the Law*. Chapel Hill: University of North Carolina Press, 1933.

Chaffee, Benjamin Harrison [Morris Mitchell]. "Mine Own People." *Atlantic Monthly* 136 (October 1925): 496–502.

Chapin, F. Stuart, Jr. *Human Activity Patterns in the City: What People Do in Time and in Space*. New York: John Wiley & Sons, 1974.

_____. *Urban Land Use Planning*. New York: Harper & Brothers, 1957.

Chapin, F. Stuart, Jr.; Denton, Alfred M.; Gould, John C.; and Wirth, Theodore W. "In the Shadow of a Defense Plant: A Study of Urbanization in Rural South Carolina, a Final Report of the Savannah River Urbanization Study." Chapel Hill: Institute for Research in Social Science, 1954. Mimeographed.

Chapin, F. Stuart, Jr., and Weiss, Shirley F., eds. *Urban Growth Dynamics in a Regional Cluster of Cities*. New York: John Wiley & Sons, 1962.

Chapin, F. Stuart, Jr., and Zehner, Robert B. *Across the City Line: A White Community in Transition*. Lexington, Mass.: D.C. Heath, 1974.

Clark, David. "Blanshard and His Buddies." *Southern Textile Bulletin*, January 19, 1928, pp. 18, 22.

────. "Blanshard and Mitchell." *Southern Textile Bulletin*, May 23, 1929, p. 20.

────. "The Greensboro Conference." *Southern Textile Bulletin*, December 15, 1927, p. 22.

────. "Organizing." *Southern Textile Bulletin*, February 2, 1928, p. 20.

────. "Our Greatest Menace." *Southern Textile Bulletin*, January 5, 1928, pp. 22, 27.

────. "The Pinehurst Meeting." *Southern Textile Bulletin*, December 23, 1925, p. 26.

Cleaveland, Frederic N. *Science and State Government: A Study of the Scientific Activities of State Government Agencies in Six States*. Chapel Hill: University of North Carolina Press, 1959.

Cleaveland, Frederic N., et al. *Congress and Urban Problems: A Casebook on the Legislative Process*. Washington, D.C.: Brookings Institution, 1969.

Cloak, F. T., Jr. *A Natural Order of Cultural Adoption and Loss in Trinidad*. Working Papers in Methodology Series. Chapel Hill: Institute for Research in Social Science, 1967.

Couch, William T., ed. *Culture in the South*. Chapel Hill: University of North Carolina Press, 1934.

Cramer, M. Richard. "School Desegregation and New Industry: The Southern Community Leaders' Viewpoint." *Social Forces* 41 (May 1963): 384–89.

Crane, Julia G. *Educated to Emigrate*. Assen, Netherlands: Royal Van Gorcum, 1971.

Dahlstrom, W. Grant; Welsh, George S.; and Dahlstrom, Leona E. *An MMPI Handbook: A Guide to Its Uses in Clinical Practice and Research*. Rev. ed. Minneapolis: University of Minnesota Press, 1960.

Davidson, Donald. *The Attack on Leviathan: Regionalism and Nationalism in the United States*. Chapel Hill: University of North Carolina Press, 1938.

────. "Howard Odum and the Sociological Proteus." *American Review* 8 (February 1937): 385–417.

Davidson, Elizabeth H. *Child Labor Legislation in the Southern Textile States*. Chapel Hill: University of North Carolina Press, 1939.

Douty, H. M. "Labor Unrest in North Carolina, 1932." *Social Forces* 11 (May 1933): 579–88.

Eckland, Bruce K., and Alexander, Karl. *Effects of Education on the Social Mobility of High School Sophomores Fifteen Years Later*. Final Report, Project No. 10202. Washington, D.C.: National Institute of Education, 1973.

Eckland, Bruce K.; Alexander, Karl; Cain, Pamela; and Gibson, David. *Wives and Workers: Labor Supply and Socioeconomic Attainments*. Final Report, Contract No. 1–HD52836. Washington, D.C.: National Institute of Child Health and Human Development, 1978.

Elder, Glen H., Jr. *Adolescent Achievement and Mobility Aspirations*. Chapel Hill: Institute for Research in Social Science, 1962.

_____. *Adolescent Socialization and Personality Development*. Chicago: Rand McNally, 1968.

_____. *Children of the Great Depression: Social Change in Life Experience*. Chicago: University of Chicago Press, 1974.

_____, ed. *Linking Social Structure and Personality*. Beverly Hills: Sage, 1973.

Elridge, Hope Tisdale. Review of *Urban Growth Dynamics in a Regional Cluster of Cities*, edited by F. Stuart Chapin, Jr., and Shirley F. Weiss. *Social Forces* 42 (December 1963): 255–56.

Erasmus, Charles J. *Man Takes Control: Cultural Development and American Aid*. Minneapolis: University of Minnesota Press, 1961.

Etzioni, Amitai, ed. *The Semi-Professions and Their Organization*. New York: Free Press, 1969.

Eutsler, Roland B. "Agricultural Credit and the Negro Farmer." *Social Forces* 8 (June 1930): 565–73.

Fesler, James W. *Area and Administration*. Tuscaloosa: University of Alabama Press, 1948.

Fink, Arthur E., et al. *The Field of Social Work*. 6th ed. New York: Holt, Rinehart & Winston, 1974.

Foote, Nelson N., and Cottrell, Leonard S., Jr. *Identity and Interpersonal Competence: A New Direction in Family Research*. Chicago: University of Chicago Press, 1955.

Fosdick, Raymond B. *A Philosophy for a Foundation, on the Fiftieth Anniversary of the Rockefeller Foundation, 1913–1963*. New York: Rockefeller Foundation, 1963.

_____. *The Story of the Rockefeller Foundation*. New York: Harper & Row, 1952.

Garceau, Oliver. "Research in the Political Process." *American Political Science Review* 45 (March 1951): 69–85.

Garfinkel, Harold. "Inter-Racial and Intra-Racial Homicide in Ten Counties in North Carolina, 1930–1940." Master's thesis, Department of Sociology, University of North Carolina, 1942.

_____. "Research Note on Inter- and Intra-Racial Homicides." *Social Forces* 27 (May 1949): 369–81.

Gaston, Paul M. *The New South Creed: A Study in Southern Mythmaking*. New York: Alfred A. Knopf, 1970.

Gatewood, Willard B., Jr. "Embattled Scholar: Howard W. Odum and the Fundamentalists, 1925–1927," *Journal of Southern History* 31 (November 1965): 379–92.

_____. *Preachers, Pedagogues, and Politicians: The Evolution Controversy in North Carolina, 1920–1927*. Chapel Hill: University of North Carolina Press, 1966.

Gee, Wilson. *Social Science Research Organization in American Universities and Colleges*. New York: Appleton-Century, 1934.

Giddings, Franklin Henry. *The Principles of Sociology: An Analysis of the Phenomena of Association and of Social Organization*. New York: Macmillan, 1899.

Gil, Federico G. *The Political System of Chile*. Boston: Houghton Mifflin, 1966.

_____. *United States–Latin American Relations*. New York: Harcourt Brace Jovanovich, 1971.

Gillin, John P. *The Culture of Security in San Carlos: A Study of a Guatemalan*

Community of Indians and Ladinos. New Orleans: Middle American Research Institute, Tulane University, 1951.

————. *A Peruvian Coastal Community*. Washington, D.C.: Government Printing Office, 1947.

————. *The Ways of Men*. New York: Appleton-Century, 1948.

Gillin, John P., and Murphy, Emmett J. "Notes on Southern Culture Patterns." *Social Forces* 29 (May 1951): 422–32.

Gilman, Glen. *Human Relations in the Industrial Southeast: A Study of the Textile Industry*. Chapel Hill: University of North Carolina Press, 1956.

Goslin, David A., ed. *Handbook of Socialization Theory and Research*. Chicago: Rand McNally, 1969.

Green, Fletcher M. *Constitutional Development in the South Atlantic States, 1776–1860*. Chapel Hill: University of North Carolina Press, 1930.

————. "Duff Green, Industrial Promoter." *Journal of Southern History* 2 (February 1936): 29–42.

————. "Duff Green, Militant Journalist of the Old School." *American Historical Review* 52 (January 1947): 247–64.

————, ed. *Essays in Southern History Presented to Joseph Gregoire de Roulhac Hamilton by His Former Students at the University of North Carolina*. Chapel Hill: University of North Carolina Press, 1949.

Greenblatt, Milton; Levinson, Daniel J.; and Williams, Richard H., eds. *The Patient in the Mental Hospital*. Glencoe, Ill.: Free Press, 1957.

Groves, Ernest R. *The American Family*. Philadelphia: J. B. Lippincott, 1934.

————. *The American Woman: The Feminine Side of a Masculine Civilization*. New York: Greenberg, 1937.

————. *Conserving Marriage and the Family: A Realistic Discussion of the Divorce Problem*. New York: Macmillan, 1944.

————. *Marriage*. New York: Henry Holt, 1933.

Groves, Ernest R., et al. *Sex Fulfillment in Marriage*. New York: Emerson Books, 1942.

Gula, Martin. Review of *Houseparents in Children's Institutions*, by Alton Broten. *Social Forces* 41 (May 1963): 430.

Gulick, John. *Cherokees at the Crossroads*. Monograph Series. Chapel Hill: Institute for Research in Social Science, 1960. Rev. ed., 1973.

————. *The Middle East: An Anthropological Perspective*. Pacific Palisades, Cal.: Goodyear Publishing, 1976.

————. *Social Structure and Culture Change in a Lebanese Village*. New York: Wenner-Gren Foundation, 1955.

————. *Tripoli: A Modern Arab City*. Cambridge: Harvard University Press, 1967.

Hagood, Margaret Jarman. *Mothers of the South: Portraiture of the White Tenant Farm Woman*. Chapel Hill: University of North Carolina Press, 1939.

————. *Statistics for Sociologists*. New York: Reynal and Hitchcock, 1941.

Hagood, Margaret Jarman, and Price, Daniel O. *Statistics for Sociologists*. Rev. ed. New York: Henry Holt, 1952.

Hall, G. Stanley. *Adolescence, Its Psychology and Its Relation to Physiology, Anthropology, Sociology, Sex, Crime, Religion and Education*. 2 vols. New York: Appleton, 1904.

Hamilton, C. Horace. *North Carolina Population Trends: A Demographic Source-book*. 3 vols. Chapel Hill: Carolina Population Center, 1974.

Hamilton, William B. "The Research Triangle of North Carolina: A Study in Leadership for the Common Weal." *South Atlantic Quarterly* 65 (Spring 1966): 254–78.

Hannan, Michael T. *Problems of Aggregation and Disaggregation in Sociological Research*. Chapel Hill: Institute for Research in Social Science, 1970.

Hawley, Amos H. "Human Ecology." In *International Encyclopedia of the Social Sciences*. New York: Macmillan, 1968.

———, ed. *Roderick Duncan Mckenzie on Human Ecology: Selected Writings*. Chicago: University of Chicago Press, 1968.

Hawley, Amos H., and Prachuabmoh, Visid. "Family Growth and Family Planning: Responses to a Family Planning Action Program in a Rural District of Thailand." *Demography* 3 (1966): 319–31.

Heard, Alexander. *The Costs of Democracy*. Chapel Hill: University of North Carolina Press, 1960.

———. *The Costs of Democracy: Financing American Political Campaigns*. Garden City: N.Y.: Doubleday, 1962.

Heard, Alexander, and Strong, Donald S. *Southern Primaries and Elections, 1920–1949*. University: University of Alabama Press, 1950.

Heath, Milton S. *Constructive Liberalism: The Role of the State in Economic Development in Georgia to 1860*. Cambridge: Harvard University Press, 1954.

Heer, Clarence. *Income and Wages in the South*. Chapel Hill: University of North Carolina Press, 1930.

———, [Director of Research]. *Report of the Tax Commission to Governor O. Max Gardner*. Raleigh: Edwards and Broughton, 1932.

Heise, David R. *Personality: Biosocial Bases*. Chicago: Rand McNally, 1973.

———, ed. *Personality and Socialization*. Chicago: Rand McNally, 1972.

Heller, Alfred, ed. *The California Tomorrow Plan*. Los Altos, Cal.: William Kaufmann, 1972.

Hemmens, George C. "Analysis and Simulation of Urban Activity Patterns." *Journal of Socio-Economic Planning Sciences* 4 (Spring 1970): 53–66.

———, ed. *Urban Development Models*. Washington, D.C.: Highway Research Board, National Academy of Sciences, 1968.

Herring, Harriet L. *Passing of the Mill Village: Revolution in a Southern Institution*. Chapel Hill: University of North Carolina Press, 1949.

———. *Southern Industry and Regional Development*. Foreword by Howard W. Odum. Chapel Hill: University of North Carolina Press, 1940.

———. *Welfare Work in Mill Villages: The Story of Extra-Mill Activities in North Carolina*. Chapel Hill: University of North Carolina Press, 1929.

———. "Working Mothers and Their Children." *Family* 9 (1928): 234–36.

Herring, Harriet L., and Neal, Margaret Clark. "The North Carolina Conference for Social Service: The Record of Twenty-Five Years, 1912–1937." Mimeographed, 1938.

Herring, Harriet L., et al. *Part-Time Farming in the Southeast*. Works Progress Administration, Research Monograph 9. Washington: Government Printing Office, 1937.

Hill, Reuben. "A Critique of Contemporary Marriage and Family Research." *Social Forces* 33 (March 1955): 268–77.

———. *Families under Stress: Adjustment to the Crises of War Separation and Reunion*. New York: Harper and Brothers, 1949.

Hill, Reuben; Stycos, Mayone; and Back, Kurt W. *The Family and Population Control*. Chapel Hill: University of North Carolina Press, 1959.

Hinkle, Roscoe, C., Jr., and Hinkle, Gisela J. *The Development of Modern Sociology: Its Nature and Growth in the United States*. New York: Random House, 1954.

Hobbs, Samuel Huntington, Jr. *North Carolina: An Economic and Social Profile*. Chapel Hill: University of North Carolina Press, 1958.

Hobson, Fred C., Jr. *Serpent in Eden: H. L. Mencken and the South*. Chapel Hill: University of North Carolina Press, 1974.

Hodges, Luther H. *Businessman in the Statehouse: Six Years as Governor of North Carolina*. Chapel Hill: University of North Carolina Press, 1962.

Hofstadter, Richard. *Social Darwinism in American Thought*. Rev. Ed. Boston: Beacon Press, 1955.

Honigmann, John J. *Three Pakistan Villages*. Monograph Series. Chapel Hill: Institute for Research in Social Science, 1958.

———. *The World of Man*. New York: Harper and Brothers, 1959.

Honigmann, John J., and Honigmann, Irma. *Arctic Townsmen*. Ottawa: Canadian Research Center for Anthropology, Saint Paul University, 1970.

———. *Eskimo Townsmen*. Ottawa: Canadian Research Center for Anthropology, University of Ottawa, 1965.

Howell, Joseph T. *Hard Living on Clay Street*. Garden City, N.Y.: Doubleday, Anchor Press, 1973.

Hsu, Francis L. K., ed. *Aspects of Culture and Personality: A Symposium*. New York: Abelard-Schuman, 1954.

Hudson, Charles. *The Catawba Nation*. Athens: University of Georgia Press, 1970.

Hufschmidt, Maynard M., ed. *Regional Planning: Challenge and Prospects*. New York: Praeger, 1969.

Human Betterment League of North Carolina. *Twenty-five Years of Human Betterment, 1947–1972*. Winston-Salem: Human Betterment League of North Carolina, 1972.

Hunter, Floyd. *Community Power Structure: A Study of Decision Makers*. Chapel Hill: University of North Carolina Press, 1953.

———. *Top Leadership, U.S.A.* Chapel Hill: University of North Carolina Press, 1959.

Hunter, Floyd; Schaffer, Ruth Connor; and Sheps, Cecil G. *Community Organization: Action and Interaction*. Chapel Hill: University of North Carolina Press, 1956.

Ingram, James C. *International Economic Problems*. New York: John Wiley & Sons, 1966.

Insko, Chester A. *Theories of Attitude Change*. New York: Appleton-Century-Crofts, 1967.

Insko, Chester A., and Schoeninger, D. W. *Workbook to Accompany Introductory Statistics for the Behavioral Sciences*. Boston: Allyn & Sons, 1971.

Insko, Chester, and Schopler, John. *Experimental Social Psychology: Text with Illustrative Readings*. New York: Academic Press, 1972.

Irish, Marian D., and Prothro, James W. *The Politics of American Democracy*. 5th ed.

Englewood Cliffs, N.J.: Prentice-Hall, 1971.

Ivey, John E., Jr.; Demerath, Nicholas J.; and Breland, Woodrow. *Building Atlanta's Future*. Chapel Hill: University of North Carolina Press, 1948.

Jenkins, William S. *Pro-Slavery Thought in the Old South*. Chapel Hill: University of North Carolina Press, 1935.

Jensen, Merrill, ed. *Regionalism in America*. Foreword by Felix Frankfurter. Madison: University of Wisconsin Press, 1952.

Jocher, Katharine. "The Institute for Research in Social Science." *University of North Carolina Extension Bulletin* 26 (July 1946): 111–19.

_____. "Methods of Research in Studying the Family." *Family* 9 (1928): 80–85.

Johnson, Gerald W. *The Wasted Land*. Chapel Hill: University of North Carolina Press, 1937.

Johnson, Guion Griffis. *Ante-Bellum North Carolina: A Social History*. Chapel Hill: University of North Carolina Press, 1937.

_____. "Feminism and the Economic Independence of Women." *Social Forces* 3 (May 1925): 612–16.

_____. *A Social History of the Sea Islands of South Carolina and Georgia with Special Reference to St. Helena Island, South Carolina*. Chapel Hill: University of North Carolina Press, 1930.

Johnson, Guy B., "The Course of Race Conflict and Racial Movements in the South." In *Race Relations: Problems and Theory*, edited by J. Masuoka and P. Valien. Chapel Hill: University of North Carolina Press, 1961.

_____. *Folk Culture on St. Helena Island*. Chapel Hill: University of North Carolina Press, 1930.

_____. *John Henry: Tracking Down a Negro Legend*. Chapel Hill: University of North Carolina Press, 1929.

_____. "The Negro and Crime." *Annals of the American Academy of Political and Social Science* 217 (September 1941): 93–104.

_____. "Negro Racial Movements and Leadership in the United States." *American Journal of Sociology* 43 (July 1937): 57–71.

_____. "The Negro Spiritual: A Problem in Anthropology." *American Anthropologist* 33 (April-June 1931): 157–71.

_____. "Personality in a White-Negro-Indian Community." *American Sociological Review* 4 (August 1939): 516–24.

_____. "Racial Integration in Southern Higher Education," *Social Forces* 34 (May 1956): 309–12.

_____. "A Sociologist Looks at Racial Desegregation in the South." *Social Forces* 33 (October 1954): 1–10.

_____. "A Study of the Musical Talent of the American Negro." Ph.D. dissertation, Department of Sociology, University of North Carolina, 1927.

Joint Committee on Intellectual Cooperation. *A Program of Cooperation: Duke University, the University of North Carolina*. Durham and Chapel Hill: n.p., 1935.

Jorrin, Miquel, and Martz, John D. *Latin American Political Thought and Ideology*. Chapel Hill: University of North Carolina Press, 1970.

Kanet, Roger E., ed. *The Behavioral Revolution and Communist Studies: Applications of Behaviorally-Oriented Political Research on the Soviet Union and Eastern Europe*. New York: Free Press, 1971.

Kantor, Harvey A. "Howard W. Odum: The Implications of Folk, Planning, and
    Regionalism." *American Journal of Sociology* 79 (September 1973): 278–95.
Kantor, Mildred B., ed. *Mobility and Mental Health*. Springfield, Ill.: Charles C.
    Thomas, 1965.
Kaplan, Berton H. *Blue Ridge: An Appalachian Community in Transition*. Morgan-
    town: Office of Research and Development, Appalachian Center, West Virginia
    University, 1971.
Kaplan, Berton H., and Cassel, John C. *Family and Health: An Epidemiological
    Approach*. Chapel Hill: Institute for Research in Social Science, 1975.
Kaufman, Harold F.; Morland, J. Kenneth; and Fockler, Hert H., eds. *Group Identity
    in the South: Dialogue between the Technological and the Humanistic*. State
    College: Mississippi State University, 1975.
Keech, William R. *The Impact of Negro Voting: The Role of the Vote in the Quest for
    Equality*. Chicago: Rand McNally, 1968.
Keith-Lucas, Alan. *The Church Children's Home in a Changing World*. Chapel Hill:
    University of North Carolina Press, 1962.
Kendrick, Benjamin B. "The Colonial Status of the South." *Journal of Southern
    History* 8 (February 1942): 3–22.
————, and Arnett, A. M. *The South Looks at Its Past*. Chapel Hill: University of
    North Carolina Press, 1935.
Kettell, Thomas Prentice. *Southern Wealth and Northern Profits*. Introduction,
    Bibliography, and Index by Fletcher M. Green. Tuscaloosa: University of
    Alabama Press, 1966.
Key, V. O., Jr., with the assistance of Heard, Alexander, *Southern Politics in State and
    Nation*. New York: Alfred A. Knopf, 1949.
King, Spencer B., Jr. *Selective Service in North Carolina in World War II*. Chapel Hill:
    University of North Carolina Press, 1949.
Kirk, Jerome, and Epling, Philip J. *The Dispersal of the Polynesian Peoples:
    Explorations in Phylogenetic Inference from the Analysis of Taxonomy*. Chapel
    Hill: Institute for Research in Social Science, 1972.
Kiser, Clyde V. *The Milbank Memorial Fund: Its Leaders and Its Work, 1905–1974*.
    New York: Milbank Memorial Fund, 1975.
————. *Sea Island to City: A Study of St. Helena Islanders in Harlem and Other
    Urban Centers*. New York: Columbia University Press, 1932.
Kline, Gerald F., and Tichenor, Philip, eds. *Current Perspectives in Mass Communi-
    cations Research*. Beverly Hills: Sage, 1972.
Kovenock, David M., with Prothro, James W., et. al. *Explaining the Vote: Presidential
    Choices in the Nation and States, 1968*. Parts 1 and 2. Chapel Hill: Institute for
    Research in Social Science, 1973.
Kreuger, Thomas A. *And Promises to Keep: The Southern Conference for Human
    Welfare, 1938–1948*. Nashville: Vanderbilt University Press, 1967.
Kutkus, Grace. "Triangle J. Chairman Sees Plenty of Work for Group." *Durham
    Morning Herald*, July 5, 1975.
Landsberger, Henry A., ed. *The Church and Social Change in Latin America*. Notre
    Dame: University of Notre Dame Press, 1971.
————. *Comparative Perspectives on Formal Organizations*. Boston: Little, Brown,
    1970.

_____. *Latin American Peasant Movements*. Ithaca: Cornell University Press, 1969.

_____. *Rural Protest: Peasant Movements and Social Change*. New York: Barnes and Noble, 1973.

Laura Spelman Rockefeller Memorial Fund. *Report, 1926*. New York: Laura Spelman Rockefeller Memorial Fund, 1927.

Layton, Bruce David. "Attributions of Interpersonal Influence." Ph.D. dissertation, Department of Psychology, University of North Carolina, 1973.

Lebrun, Harvey. "A Near Encyclopedia of Social Planning." *Social Forces* 16 (December 1937): 277–85.

Lefler, Hugh T., and Wager, Paul W. *Orange County, 1752–1952*. Chapel Hill: Orange Print Shop, 1953.

Lehnen, Robert G. *American Institutions, Political Opinion, and Public Policy*. Hinsdale, Ill.: Dryden Press, 1976.

Leibman, Samuel, ed. *Management of Emotional Problems in Medical Practice*. Philadelphia: Lippincott, 1956.

Lenski, Gerhard E. *Human Societies*. New York: McGraw-Hill, 1970. Revised edition with Jean Lenski. New York: McGraw-Hill, 1974.

_____. *Power and Privilege: A Theory of Social Stratification*. New York: McGraw-Hill, 1966.

Lewis, Hylan. *Blackways of Kent*. Chapel Hill: University of North Carolina Press, 1955.

Lewis, Michael, and Rosenblum, Leonard, eds. *Friendship and Peer Relations*. New York: Wiley, 1975.

Lindzey, Gardner, ed. *Handbook of Social Psychology*. Cambridge, Mass.: Addison-Wesley, 1954.

Lumpkin, Katherine DuPre, and Douglas, Dorothy Wolff. *Child Workers in America*. New York: R. M. McBride, 1937.

McCleery, Richard H. "Power, Communications, and the Social Order: A Study of Prison Government." Ph.D. dissertation, Department of Political Science, University of North Carolina, 1956.

McCurdy, Harold G. *The Personality of Shakespeare: A Venture in Psychological Method*. New Haven: Yale University Press, 1953.

_____. *The Personal World: An Introduction to the Study of Personality*. New York: Harcourt, Brace & World, 1961.

McDonald, Walter R. *The Southern Governors' Conference: A Brief History*. [Raleigh: North Carolina Department of Conservation and Development, 1959].

McHale, Kathryn. Review of *The American Woman: The Feminine Side of a Masculine Civilization*, by Ernest R. Groves. *Social Forces* 16 (May 1938): 597.

McKinney, John C., and Thompson, Edgar T., eds. *The South in Continuity and Change*. Durham: Duke University Press, 1965.

MacRae, Duncan, Jr. *The Social Function of Social Science*. New Haven: Yale University Press, 1976.

Mangum, Charles S., Jr. *The Legal Status of the Negro*. Chapel Hill: University of North Carolina Press, 1940.

_____. *The Legal Status of the Tenant Farmer in the Southeast*. Chapel Hill:

University of North Carolina Press, 1952.

Martz, John D. *Ecuador: Conflicting Political Culture and the Quest for Modernity*. Boston: Allyn & Bacon, 1972.

Masuoka, Jitsuichi, and Valien, Preston, eds. *Race Relations: Problems and Theory*. Chapel Hill: University of North Carolina Press, 1961.

Matherly, Walter J. *Business Education in the Changing South*. Chapel Hill: University of North Carolina Press, 1939.

Matthews, Donald R. *U.S. Senators and Their World*. Chapel Hill: University of North Carolina Press, 1960.

————, ed. *North Carolina Votes: General Election Returns by County for President of the United States, 1868–1960; Governor of North Carolina, 1868–1960; United States Senator for North Carolina, 1914–1960*. Chapel Hill: University of North Carolina Press, 1962.

Matthews, Donald, and Prothro, James W. *Negroes and the New Southern Politics*. New York: Harcourt, Brace & World, 1966.

Mayer, Robert R. "Community Leadership for School Desegregation." *Urban Education* 3 (1971): 129–41.

————. *Social Planning and Social Change*. Englewood Cliffs, N.J.: Prentice-Hall, 1972.

Mell, Mildred Rutherford. "A Definitive Study of the Poor Whites of the South." Ph.D. dissertation, Department of Sociology, University of North Carolina, 1938.

Mencken, H. L. *Prejudices: Second Series*. New York: Alfred A. Knopf, 1920.

Metfessel, Milton. *Phonophotography in Folk Music: American Negro Songs in New Notation*. Chapel Hill: University of North Carolina Press, 1928.

Meyer, Harold D., and Brightbill, Charles K. *Community Recreation: A Guide to Its Organization and Administration*. Boston: D. C. Heath, 1948.

————. *Recreation Administration: A Guide to Its Practices*. Englewood Cliffs, N.J.: Prentice-Hall, 1956.

Milbank Memorial Fund. *Selected Studies of Migration since World War II*. New York: Milbank Memorial Fund, 1959.

Miller, Alden D. *Principal Components and Curvature in Occupational Stratification*. Chapel Hill: Institute for Research in Social Science, 1967.

Mitchell, Broadus, and Mitchell, George S. *The Industrial Revolution in the South*. Baltimore: Johns Hopkins Press, 1930.

Mitchell, George S. *Textile Unionism and the South*. Chapel Hill: University of North Carolina Press, 1931.

Mood, Fulmer. "The Origin, Evolution, and Application of the Sectional Concept." In *Regionalism in America*, edited by Merrill Jensen. Madison: University of Wisconsin Press, 1952.

Moore, Harry Estill. *What is Regionalism?* Southern Policy Papers, no. 10. Chapel Hill: University of North Carolina Press, 1937.

Morland, J. Kenneth. *Millways of Kent*. Chapel Hill: University of North Carolina Press, 1958.

Morrison, Joseph L. "Mencken and Odum: The Dutch Uncle and the South." *Virginia Quarterly Review* 42 (Autumn 1966): 601–15.

Murchison, Claudius T. *King Cotton Is Sick*. Chapel Hill: University of North Carolina Press, 1930.

Namboodiri, N. Krishnan. *Applied Multivariate Analysis and Experimental Design*. New York: McGraw Hill, 1975.

_____. *Changing Population of Kerala*. A Census of India Monograph. Coimbatore: Government of India Press, 1968.

_____. "On the Dependence of Age Structure on a Sequence of Mortality and Fertility Schedules: An Exposition of a Cyclical Model of Population Change." *Demography* 6 (August 1969): 287–99.

National Emergency Council. *Report on Economic Conditions of the South*. Washington, D.C.: Government Printing Office, 1938.

Nelson, David S. "Textile Union Organizers Say Efforts Bearing Fruit." *Durham Morning Herald*, February 22, 1976.

Noland, E. William. "Industry Comes of Age in the South." *Social Forces* 32 (October 1953): 28–35.

Noland, E. William, and Bakke, E. Wight. *Workers Wanted: A Study of Employers' Hiring Policies, Preferences and Practices in New Haven and Charlotte*. New York: Harper and Brothers, 1949.

North, Walter M. "Change and Transition in the Southeastern United States: Patterns of Development in a Half Century of Accelerating Change." Ph.D. dissertation, Department of Sociology and Anthropology, University of North Carolina, 1952.

Odum, Eugene P. "The Emergence of Ecology as a New Integrative Discipline." *Science* 195 (March 25, 1977): 1289–93.

Odum, Eugene P., and Odum, Howard T. *Fundamentals of Ecology*. Philadelphia: Saunders, 1953.

Odum, Howard W. *An American Epoch: Southern Portraiture in the National Picture*. New York: Henry Holt, 1930.

_____. "An Approach to Diagnosis and Direction of Negro Segregation in the Public Schools of the South." *Journal of Public Law* 3 (1954): 8–37.

_____. "The Assumptions of Regional Balance." *World Economics* 3 (October–December 1945): 57–66.

_____. *Cold Blue Moon: Black Ulysses Afar Off*. Indianapolis: Bobbs-Merrill, 1931.

_____. "Editorial Notes." *Journal of Social Forces* 1 (May 1923): 471–76.

_____. "Effective Democracy." *Journal of Social Forces* 1 (January 1923): 178–83.

_____. "Folk and Regional Conflict as a Field of Sociological Study." *Publications of the American Sociological Society* 25 (May 1931): 1–17.

_____. *Folk, Region, and Society: Selected Papers of Howard W. Odum*. Edited by Katharine Jocher, Guy B. Johnson, George S. Simpson, Jr., and Rupert B. Vance. Chapel Hill: University of North Carolina Press, 1964.

_____. "Folk Sociology as a Subject Field for the Historical Study of Total Human Society and the Empirical Study of Group Behavior." *Social Forces* 31 (March 1953): 192–223.

_____. "The Promise of Regionalism." In *Regionalism in America*, edited by Merrill Jensen. Madison: University of Wisconsin Press, 1952.

_____. *Race and Rumors of Race: Challenge to American Crisis*. Chapel Hill:

University of North Carolina Press, 1943.

———. *Rainbow Round My Shoulder: The Blue Trail of Black Ulysses*. Indianapolis: Bobbs-Merrill, 1928.

———. *The Regional Approach to National Social Planning: With Special Reference to a More Abundant South and Its Continuing Reintegration in the National Economy*. Chapel Hill: University of North Carolina Press, 1935; New York: The Foreign Policy Association, 1935.

———. "The Religious Folk-Songs of the Southern Negroes," *American Journal of Religious Psychology and Education* 3 (July 1909): 265–365.

———. *Southern Regions of the United States*. Chapel Hill: University of North Carolina Press, 1936.

———. *Understanding Society: The Principles of Dynamic Sociology*. New York: Macmillan Co., 1947.

———. "University Research and Training in the Social Sciences." *Journal of Social Forces* 3 (March 1925): 518–24.

———. *The Way of the South: Toward the Regional Balance of America*. New York: Macmillan Co., 1947.

———. *Wings on My Feet: Black Ulysses at the Wars*. Indianapolis: Bobbs-Merrill, 1929.

———, ed. *Public Welfare in the United States*. Annals of the American Academy of Political and Social Science 105, no. 194 (1923).

Odum, Howard W., and Jocher, Katharine. *An Introduction to Social Research*. New York: Henry Holt, 1929.

———, eds. *In Search of the Regional Balance of America*. Chapel Hill: University of North Carolina Press, 1945.

Odum, Howard W., and Johnson, Guy B. *The Negro and His Songs*. Chapel Hill: University of North Carolina Press, 1925.

———. *Negro Workaday Songs*. Chapel Hill: University of North Carolina Press, 1926.

Odum, Howard W., and Moore, Harry Estill. *American Regionalism: A Cultural-Historical Approach to National Integration*. New York: Henry Holt, 1938.

Odum, Howard W., and Willard, D. W. *Systems of Public Welfare*. Chapel Hill: University of North Carolina Press, 1925.

Oxley, Lawrence A. *Capital Punishment in North Carolina*. Raleigh: State Board of Charities and Public Welfare, 1929.

Parker, Coralie. *The History of Taxation in North Carolina during the Colonial Period, 1663–1776*. New York: Columbia University Press, 1928.

Parker, Francis H. "Genesis of the Department of City and Regional Planning at Chapel Hill." Chapel Hill, April 12, 1974. Mimeographed.

Parker, John A. *Industrial Planning in the USSR*. Chapel Hill: Institute for Research in Social Science, 1954.

Parker, John A., et al. *Analysis of Production Processes in the Soviet Heavy Machinery-Building Industry: Interim Report, Phase I*. Chapel Hill: Institute for Research in Social Science, 1957.

Parkins, Maurice F. *City Planning in Soviet Russia*. Chicago: University of Chicago Press, 1953.

Paydarfar, Ali A. *Social Change in a Southern Province of Iran*. Chapel Hill: Institute for Research in Social Science, 1974.

Peacock, James L. *Indonesia: An Anthropological Perspective*. Pacific Palisades, Cal.: Goodyear, 1973.

Peacock, James L., and Kirsch, A. Thomas. *The Human Direction: An Evolutionary Approach to Social and Cultural Anthropology*. 2nd ed. New York: Appleton-Century-Crofts, 1973.

Pfouts, Ralph W., ed. *Essays in Economics and Econometrics: A Volume in Honor of Harold Hotelling*. Chapel Hill: University of North Carolina, 1960.

————. *The Techniques of Urban Economic Analysis*. West Trenton, N.J.: Chandler-Davis, 1960.

Pierson, William Whatley, Jr., ed. *Studies in Hispanic-American History*. James Sprunt Studies in History and Political Science, vol. 19, no. 2. Chapel Hill: University of North Carolina Press, 1927.

Pounds, Norman J. G., and Parker, William Nelson. *Coal and Steel in Western Europe*. Bloomington: Indiana University Press, 1957.

Powell, John W. "Physiographic Processes." In *The Physiography of the United States*, by the National Geographic Society, vol. 1. New York: American Book Co., 1895.

President's Research Committee on Social Trends. *Recent Social Trends in the United States*. 2 vols. New York: McGraw-Hill, 1933.

Price, Daniel O. "Distance and Direction as Vectors of Internal Migration, 1935 to 1940." *Social Forces* 27 (October 1948): 48–53.

————. "Estimates of Net Migration in the United States, 1870–1940." *American Sociological Review* 18 (February 1953): 35–39.

————. "Factor Analysis in the Study of Metropolitan Centers." *Social Forces* 20 (May 1942): 449–55.

————. "Some Socioeconomic Factors in Internal Migration." *Social Forces* 29 (May 1951): 409–15.

————. "University Research." In *Research and the Future of the South*. Report of the Eighth Annual Legislative Work Conference of the Southern Regional Education Board. Atlanta: Southern Regional Education Board, 1959.

Rabinowitz, George B. *Spatial Models of Electoral Choice: An Empirical Analysis*. Chapel Hill: Institute for Research in Social Science, 1973.

Rankin, Carl Emmett. *The University of North Carolina and the Problems of the Cotton Mill Employee*. New York: Columbia University, 1936.

Raper, Arthur F. *Preface to Peasantry: A Tale of Two Black Belt Counties*. Chapel Hill: University of North Carolina Press, 1936.

————. *The Tragedy of Lynching*. Chapel Hill: University of North Carolina Press, 1933.

————. "Two Black Belt Counties: Changes in Rural Life since the Advent of the Boll Weevil in Greene and Macon Counties, Georgia." Ph.D. dissertation, Department of Sociology, University of North Carolina, 1931.

Raper, Arthur F., and Reid, Ira De A. *Sharecroppers All*. Chapel Hill: University of North Carolina Press, 1941.

Reed, John Shelton, Jr. *The Enduring South: Subcultural Persistence in Mass Society*.

Lexington, Mass.: Lexington Books, 1972. Paperback edition, Chapel Hill: University of North Carolina Press, 1974.

Reisman, Stephen R., and Schopler, John., "An Analysis of the Attribution Process and an Application to Determinants of Responsibility." *Journal of Personality and Social Psychology* 25 (March 1973), 361–68.

The Report of the Governor's Commission on the Status of Women: The Many Lives of North Carolina Women. Raleigh: n.p., 1964.

Reynolds, Henry Titchner. *Making Causal Inferences with Ordinal Data*. Chapel Hill: Institute for Research in Social Science, 1971.

Rheingold, Harriet L. "To Rear a Child." *American Psychologist* 28 (January 1973): 42–46.

Rheingold, Harriet L., and Eckerman, Carol O. "The Infant's Free Entry into a New Environment." *Journal of Experimental Child Psychology* 8 (December 1969): 271–83.

Rhyne, Jennings, J. *Some Southern Cotton Mill Workers and Their Villages*. Chapel Hill: University of North Carolina Press, 1930.

Richardson, Richard J., et al. *Delay in the Superior Courts of North Carolina: An Assessment of Its Causes*. Raleigh: Administration Office of the Courts, 1973.

————. *Public Attitudes toward the Criminal Justice System and Criminal Victimization in North Carolina*. Raleigh: Governor's Committee on Law and Order, 1971.

Robinson, Halbert B., and Robinson, Nancy M. *The Mentally Retarded Child: A Psychological Approach*. New York: McGraw-Hill, 1965.

Rosenau, James N., ed. *Linkage Politics: Essays on the Convergence of National and International Systems*. New York: Free Press, 1969.

Rosenbaum, H. Jon, and Tyler, William G., eds. *Contemporary Brazil: Issues in Economic and Political Development*. New York: Praeger, 1972.

Rubin, Morton. *Plantation County*. Chapel Hill: University of North Carolina Press, 1951.

Rupen, Robert A. *Mongols of the Twentieth Century*. Bloomington: Indiana University Press, 1964.

Sanders, Wiley B. *Juvenile Offenders for a Thousand Years: Selected Readings from Anglo-Saxon Times to 1900*. Chapel Hill: University of North Carolina Press, 1970.

————. *Negro Child Welfare in North Carolina*. Chapel Hill: University of North Carolina Press, 1933.

Sanders, Wiley B., and Ezell, Curtis W. *Juvenile Court Cases in North Carolina, 1929–1934*. Raleigh: State Board of Charities and Welfare, 1937.

Schaefer, Earl S. "Factors that Impede the Process of Socialization." In *The Mentally Retarded in Society: A Social Perspective*, edited by Michael J. Begab and Stephen A. Richardson. Baltimore: University Park Press, 1975.

Schiffman, Ruth Y. "Occupations in the United States and the South, 1910–1930." Ph.D. dissertation, Department of Sociology, University of North Carolina, Chapel Hill, 1936.

Schoeninger, Douglas W., and Insko, Chester A. *Introductory Statistics for the Behavioral Sciences*. Boston: Allyn & Bacon, 1971.

Schopler, John, and Layton, Bruce David. *Attributions and Interpersonal Power and Influence*. Morristown, N.J.: General Learning Press, 1972.

Scott, Andrew McKay. *Competition in American Politics: An Economic Model*. New York: Holt, Rinehart & Winston, 1970.

————. *The Functioning of the International Political System*. New York: Macmillan, 1967.

————. *Political Thought in America*. New York: Holt, Rinehart & Winston, 1959.

Scott, Andrew McKay, and Wallace, Earle. *Politics, U.S.A.: Cases on the American Democratic Process*. New York: Macmillan, 1961.

Scott, Andrew McKay, et al. *Insurgency*. Chapel Hill: University of North Carolina Press, 1970.

Scott, Joan Wallace. *The Glassworkers of Carmaux: French Craftsmen and Political Action in a Nineteenth Century City*. Cambridge: Harvard University Press, 1974.

Sheps, Cecil G., and Taylor, Eugene E. *Needed Research in Health and Medical Care*. Chapel Hill: University of North Carolina Press, 1954.

Shinn, Allen Mayhew, Jr. *The Application of Psychological Scaling Techniques to Measurement of Political Variables*. Chapel Hill: Institute for Research in Social Science, 1970.

Shivers, Lyda Gordon. "The Social Welfare Movement in the South: A Study in Regional Culture and Social Organization." Ph.D. dissertation, Department of Sociology, University of North Carolina, 1935.

Sibley, Elbridge. *Social Science Research Council: The First Fifty Years*. New York: Social Science Research Council, 1974.

Simon, Mitchell. "UNC Team Studies Communities." *Chapel Hill Newspaper*, March 16, 1976.

Simpson, George L., Jr. *The Cokers of South Carolina: A Social Biography of a Family*. Chapel Hill: University of North Carolina Press, 1956.

Simpson, Richard L. "The School Teachers: Social Values, Community Role, and Professional Self-Image." Chapel Hill: Institute for Research in Social Science, 1969. Mimeographed.

Simpson, Richard L., and Simpson, Ida Harper, eds. *Social Organization and Behavior: A Reader in General Sociology*. New York: John Wiley & Sons, 1964.

Simpson, Richard L., et al. *Occupational Choice and Mobility in the Urbanizing Piedmont of North Carolina*. Chapel Hill: Institute for Research in Social Science, 1960. Mimeographed.

Smelser, Neil J., and Lipset, Seymour M., eds. *Social Structure and Mobility in Economic Development*. Chicago: Aldine, 1966.

Smith, Harvey L. *Adaptation: Clinical and Social*. Chapel Hill: Institute for Research in Social Science, 1963.

————. *Society and Health in a Mountain Community*. Chapel Hill: Institute for Research in Social Science, 1961.

Smith, Mary Phlegar. "Legal and Administrative Restrictions Affecting the Rights of Married Women to Work." *Annals of the American Academy of Political and Social Science* 143 (1929): 255–64.

Spencer, Herbert. *Principles of Sociology*. 5 vols. New York: Appleton, 1880–96.
Spruill, Julia Cherry. *Women's Life and Work in the Southern Colonies*. Chapel Hill: University of North Carolina Press, 1938.
Steiner, Jesse F. "Community Organization in Relation to Social Change." *Journal of Social Forces* 1 (January 1923): 102–8.
——, ed. *The American Community in Action*. New York: Henry Holt, 1928.
Steiner, Jesse F., and Brown, Roy M. *The North Carolina Chain Gang: A Study of County Convict Road Work*. Chapel Hill: University of North Carolina Press, 1927.
Steiner, Jürg. *Amicable Agreement versus Majority Rule: Conflict Resolution in Switzerland*. Chapel Hill: University of North Carolina Press, 1974.
Stevenson, Harold W.; Hess, Eckhard H.; and Rheingold, Harriet L., eds. *Early Behavior: Comparative and Developmental Approaches*. New York: John Wiley & Sons, 1967.
Stone, Olive M. "Agrarian Conflict in Alabama: Sections, Races, and Classes in a Rural State from 1800 to 1938." Ph.D. dissertation, Department of Sociology, University of North Carolina, 1939.
Summer, William Graham. *Folkways, A Study of the Sociological Importance of Usages, Manners, Customs, Mores, and Morals*. Boston: Ginn, 1907.
Tannenbaum, Frank. *Darker Phases of the South*. New York: G. P. Putnam, 1924.
Taylor, George R., and Ellsworth, Lucius F., eds. *Approaches to American Economic History*. Charlottesville: University of Virginia Press, 1971.
Thibaut, John W., and Kelley, Harold H. *The Social Psychology of Groups*. New York: John Wiley & Sons, 1959.
Thibaut, John W., and Walker, William Laurens. *Procedural Justice: A Psychological Analysis*. Hillsdale, N.J.: Laurence Erlbaum Associates, 1975.
Thompson, Edgar T., ed. *Perspectives on the South: Agenda for Research*. Durham: Duke University Press, 1967.
——, ed. *Race Relations and the Race Problem: Definition and Analysis*. Durham: Duke University Press, 1939.
Tindall, George Brown. *The Emergence of the New South, 1913–1945*. Baton Rouge: Louisiana State University Press, 1967.
——. "The Significance of Howard W. Odum to Southern History: A Preliminary Estimate." *Journal of Southern History* 24 (August 1958): 285–307.
——. *South Carolina Negroes, 1877–1900*. Baton Rouge: Louisiana State University Press, 1966.
Tindall, George Brown, et al. "The Status and Future of Regionalism—A Symposium." *Journal of Southern History* 26 (February 1960): 22–56.
Tippet, Thomas. *When Southern Labor Stirs*. New York: J. Cape & H. Smith, 1931.
Tulchin, Joseph S., ed. *Problems in Latin American History*. New York: Harper & Row, 1973.
Twelve Southerners. *I'll Take My Stand: The South and the Agrarian Tradition*. New York: Harper and Brothers, 1930.
Udry, J. Richard. *The Social Context of Marriage*. 3rd ed. Philadelphia: J. B. Lippincott, 1974.
The University of North Carolina, Institute of Statistics. "A Record of Research, I: July 1, 1948 to June 30, 1951." N.p., n.d.

Vance, Rupert B. "The Development and Status of American Demography." In *The Study of Population: An Inventory and Appraisal*, edited by Philip M. Hauser and Otis Dudley Duncan. Chicago: University of Chicago Press, 1959.

_____. "Howard W. Odum." In *International Encyclopedia of the Social Sciences*. New York: Macmillan, 1968.

_____. *How the Other Half Is Housed: A Pictorial Record of Sub-Minimum Farm Housing in the South*. Southern Policy Papers, no. 4. Chapel Hill: University of North Carolina Press, 1936.

_____. *Human Factors in Cotton Culture*. Chapel Hill: University of North Carolina Press, 1929.

_____. *Human Geography of the South: A Study in Regional Resources and Human Adequacy*. Chapel Hill: University of North Carolina Press, 1932.

_____. "Population Density in Virginia: Migration and Urbanization." In *Exploring Virginia's Human Resources*. Charlottesville: University of Virginia Press, 1965.

_____. *Regional Reconstruction: A Way Out for the South*. Chapel Hill: University of North Carolina Press, 1935; New York: The Foreign Policy Association, 1935.

_____. "Regional Science." In *International Encyclopedia of the Social Sciences*. New York: Macmillan, 1968.

_____. *The South's Place in the Nation*. Public Affairs Pamphlets, no. 6. New York: Public Affairs Committee, 1936.

Vance, Rupert B., and Blackwell, Gordon W. *New Farm Homes for Old: Rural Public Housing in the South*. Tuscaloosa: University of Alabama Press, 1946.

Vance, Rupert B., with Danilevsky, Nadia. *All These People: The Nation's Human Resources in the South*. Chapel Hill: University of North Carolina Press, 1945.

Vance, Rupert B.; Demerath, Nicholas J.; Smith, Sara; and Fink, Elizabeth M. *The Urban South*. Chapel Hill: University of North Carolina Press, 1954.

Vance, Rupert B.; Ivey, John E., Jr.; and Bond, Marjorie N. *Exploring the South*. Chapel Hill: University of North Carolina Press, 1949.

Vinter, Robert D., ed. *Readings in Group Work Practice*. Ann Arbor, Mich.: Campus Publishers, 1967.

Wager, Paul W. *County Government in North Carolina*. Chapel Hill: University of North Carolina Press, 1928.

_____, ed. *County Government across the Nation*. Chapel Hill: University of North Carolina Press, 1950.

Walker, Sydnor H. *Social Work and the Training of Social Workers*. Chapel Hill: University of North Carolina Press, 1928.

Ward, Lester Frank. *Applied Sociology, A Treatise on the Conscious Improvement of Society by Society*. Boston: Ginn, 1906.

Weaver, Jerry L., ed. *Latin American Development Administration: Accomplishments of the 1960s, Research Priorities for the 1970s*. Austin, Tex.: Institute of Latin American Studies, 1973.

_____. *Latin American Development: A Selected Bibliography, 1950–1967*. Santa Barbara, Cal.: ABC-Clio, 1969.

Webb, Walter Prescott. *Divided We Stand: The Crisis of a Frontierless Democracy*. New York: Farrar & Rinehart, 1937. 2nd ed. Austin, Tex.: Acorn Press, 1942. Rev. and abridged ed., Manchaca, Tex.: Chaparral Press, 1947.

Westling, Mark, ed. *Ecology and the Economy, a Concept for Balancing Long-Range Goals: The Pacific Northwest Example*. Vancouver, Wash.: Pacific Northwest River Basins Commission, 1973.

Wilder, Francis S. "Crime in the Superior Courts of North Carolina." *Social Forces* 5 (March 1927): 423–27.

Williams, Edith Webb. *Research in Southern Regional Development*. Richmond, Va.: Dietz Press, 1948.

Williamson, Joel, ed. *The Origins of Segregation: A Compilation*. Boston: D. C. Heath, 1968.

Wilson, Everett K., ed. *Social Forces 1922–1972: Cumulative Index, Volumes 1–50*. Chapel Hill: University of North Carolina Press, 1974.

Wilson, Louis R. *The Research Triangle of North Carolina: A Notable Achievement in University, Governmental, and Industrial Cooperative Development*. Chapel Hill: Colonial Press, 1967.

————. *The University of North Carolina, 1900–1930*. Chapel Hill: University of North Carolina Press, 1957.

Wilson, R. Jackson. *In Quest of Community: Social Philosophy in the United States, 1860–1920*. New York: John Wiley & Sons, 1968.

Wirth, Louis. "The Limitations of Regionalism." In *Regionalism in America*, edited by Merrill Jensen. Madison: University of Wisconsin Press, 1952.

Woofter, Thomas J., Jr. *Black Yeomanry: Life on St. Helena Island*. New York: Henry Holt, 1930.

————. *The Plight of Cigarette Tobacco*. Chapel Hill: University of North Carolina Press, 1931.

————. *Race and Ethnic Groups in American Life*. New York: McGraw-Hill, 1933.

————. *Southern Population and Social Planning*. Southern Policy Papers, no. 1. Chapel Hill: University of North Carolina Press, 1936.

Wright, Gerald C., Jr. *Electoral Choice in America: Image, Party, and Incumbency in State and National Elections*. Chapel Hill: Institute for Research in Social Science, 1974.

Index